AMONGST FARM HORSES

THE HORSELADS OF EAST YORKSHIRE

AMONGST FARM HORSES

THE HORSELADS OF EAST YORKSHIRE

Stephen Caunce

ALAN SUTTON

First published in the United Kingdom in 1991 by
Alan Sutton Publishing Ltd · Phoenix Mill · Far Thrupp · Stroud · Gloucestershire

First published in the United States of America in 1992 by
Alan Sutton Publishing Inc. · Wolfeboro Falls · NH 03896–0848

British Library Cataloguing in Publication Data

Caunce, Stephen
    Amongst Farm Horses. The horselads of East Yorkshire
    1. Yorkshire (England). Agriculture. Personnel, history
    I. Title
    305.563094283

ISBN 0 86299 875 1

Library of Congress Cataloging in Publication Data applied for

Typesetting and origination by
Alan Sutton Publishing Limited.
Printed in Great Britain by
WBC Print Ltd., Bridgend.

Contents

Acknowledgements   vii

The Main Contributors   ix

Abbreviations   xii

Chapter One	Introduction	1
Chapter Two	The Farmworkers of the East Riding	16
Chapter Three	The Yearly Bond	30
Chapter Four	The Horselads	45
Chapter Five	The Hiring Fairs	54
Chapter Six	The Fairs as a Labour Market	66
Chapter Seven	The Hierarchy	74
Chapter Eight	Learning the Job	86
Chapter Nine	Horse Feeding	96
Chapter Ten	Handling the Horses	108
Chapter Eleven	The Foreman and the Horses	123
Chapter Twelve	Food	137
Chapter Thirteen	In the Farmhouses	148
Chapter Fourteen	Leisure	158
Chapter Fifteen	Holidays	172
Chapter Sixteen	The Development of the East Riding Farm Servant System	188
Chapter Seventeen	The End of the Yearly Bond in the East Riding	206
Chapter Eighteen	Conclusion	220

Glossary   226

Select Bibliography   233

Index   241

The author gratefully acknowledges a financial contribution towards the publication of this volume received from The Twenty-Seven Foundation.

Acknowledgements

This book is a shortened and slightly amended version of my doctoral thesis for Leeds University which I began in 1972. It took many more years to complete than I ever anticipated and I owe thanks not only to those who assisted with the original research, but also to those who have provided the support and encouragement needed to bring it to a conclusion. Tony Green and John Chartres were my supervisors at Leeds University and I owe the latter special thanks for the work he put in after 1987 when I revived it after a long period out of contact with the university. My first wife, Gloden, contributed historical knowledge and helped with a variety of problems, but her long illness and subsequent death tragically prevented her from seeing the outcome. My second wife, Jean, provided the support necessary to give the writing up the attention it needed after such a long delay and was remarkably tolerant of the seemingly endless process of reworking old research that had to be undertaken to bring it up to date. Anne Ezikwa typed it with great accuracy when it was finally ready, which was a mammoth task. I also should thank all the staff of the libraries in and around the East Riding for their help, together with all those others who gave assistance on matters of detail.

The basis of the study, however, was the oral testimony I collected between 1972 and 1975. The main contributors are listed below, with brief biographical details to help readers put their words, quoted throughout the book, in context, but in addition I must record my gratitude to Mr Easterby, Mr Hobson, Mr Holland, Mrs Jarvis, Mrs Lawler, Mrs Martin, Mr Moore, Mr Morton, Mrs Parker, Mr Pearson, Mrs Rispin, Mr Sissons, Mrs Tate, Mr Townsend, and Mr Windass, who also provided information. All those who responded to my appeals for information and talked, sometimes for hours, of their memories have left behind something permanent, though most of them are sadly now dead. I hope that this, constructed to a large extent from their words, is a fair and appropriate tribute to them all and to a way of life that has now vanished.

Most of the photographs are copied from originals loaned to me in the course of recording the tapes. The first, and largest, collection mostly shows Manor Farm, Thixendale but also includes numbers 14, 18, 20, 21, and 25. This belonged to Mr Walker and I owe him thanks not only for the actual photographs but also for providing a stimulus that brought out most of the rest. The same collection, which presumably returned to Thixendale on his death, was seen there quite independently by Dr Colin Hayfield, who published them locally as part of the work of the Wharram project. I am grateful for his co-operation in making them available now to a national audience for the first time and for much extra information which he unearthed for the captions. He also allowed me to use numbers 12, 18, and 31 from others he collected for *Thixendale Remembered* and 13 and 62 from the later *Birdsall Remembered*, which together form a comprehensive pictorial record of life years ago on the high Wolds.

Numbers 22, 24, and 52 came from Mr Rispin; 35, 43, 44, 45, 46, and 47 from Mr Playforth; and 1, 23, 26, 48, 53, 56, 59, and 60 from Mr Masterman. Brian Haigh kindly copied number 38 from George Walker's *Costumes of Yorkshire* (1814). Several others come from a variety of collections, and I must thank them as follows for allowing me to reproduce them: 54 appeared in *Birdsall Remembered* but it is the property of Lord Middleton. Nos. 2, 15, 16, 34, 37, 39, and 61 were collected by Mr D.A. Waddingham of Beverley. No. 32 is a photograph collected by Margaret Bateson as part of her B.A. dissertation, 'The Dialect of Rillington', for the School of English of the University of Leeds. No. 7 is from *Victorian and Edwardian Yorkshire From Old Photographs* by A.B. Craven, published in 1971 by Batsford. No. 58 was provided by Humberside County Council Leisure Services and 63 by the North Yorkshire County Library.

The Main Contributors

Edward Appleyard, born 1923, was first hired at the age of twelve by Easterby's near Tadcaster, a farm that specialised in breeding heavy horses, where he remained until 1944. He became a horsedealer and farmer, but gave up dealing in 1957. Two untaped interviews.

Robert Ashby, born 1897 in Beverley, started work at the age of thirteen and was employed mostly on Wold farms around Market Weighton and Driffield. He also worked in Holderness at Aike and went to the West Riding for several years. After returning from service in the First World War, he settled in Huddersfield and worked as a horseman there until mechanisation forced a change and he became a lorry driver. Letter and untaped interview.

George William Baines, born 1908 in Howden, was the son of a farm foreman and one of four children. He started work in 1922 and worked in the Vale of York on both sides of the county border. Before his marriage in 1935 he was a waggoner and a single farm foreman. He then rented a farm at Crofton near Wakefield, but was eventually forced to give it up. Died 7 November 1973. Tapes 4/1, 4/2, 8/2 and 9/1 (with untaped addendum).

John Brambles, born 1914, was the son of a farm foreman in Burton Fleming, where he spent all his life except for a short period during the Second World War when he travelled widely as a tractor driver for the Agricultural Executive. Hired out first in 1928, he spent fourteen years living-in and working amongst horses becoming a waggoner at the age of nineteen. Tapes 17/2 and 18/1 (with untaped addendum).

Mr I. Carter, born in Birdsall 1901, started work at the age of fourteen on the Birdsall Estate of Lord Middleton. He became a waggoner in 1921 and a single foreman shortly after. He was able to remain horseman after he married due to the fact that he was an estate worker. On retirement he had completed fifty years service on the estate. Now dead. Tape 12/2.

J. Clarence Fisher was born in 1907 in Garton near Hull. He started work at the age of twelve helping a carrier for one year, and went on to be a nominal waggoner in his second year of farm service. He took a farm in Garton with his brother in 1935 and used some horsepower up to the early 1950s. He sold his last horse in 1968. Tapes 6/1 (end) and 6/2.

Mr T. Friend, born 1904, spent most of his time as a farm servant in the area to the north of York but he also worked in the East Riding. From the age of twelve he worked with horses, until their replacement by tractors in 1948. He lived in until 1946. Tape 16/1 and 16/2.

Mr A.L. Harper, born 1900, started work at the age of thirteen as a house-servant at Scagglethorpe for two years and then spent a further two years amongst horses before setting out on a life as a shepherd, which took him to retirement. Apart from army service he worked exclusively on the Wolds east of Driffield. Tapes 16/2 (end) and 17/1.

Edward Jarvis, born at Mount Ferrant Farm, Wharram in 1892, was the son of a small farmer. Leaving school at the age of twelve, he worked at home for two years, then was sent out for hire. He stayed mostly nearby on the northern Wolds, and ran away when he experimented by going to the Hunmanby area. Spent most of his life as a forester on the Birdsall estate and eventually took over Mount Ferrant. Now dead. Tapes 11/2, 12/1, 13/1 and 13/2.

William Johnson was born in 1893 at Hutton Cranswick. One of ten children, his father was a small holder and general carrier who turned his hand to coal delivery, milk delivery, haulage, or whatever came to hand. Mr Johnson started work in 1906, at the age of thirteen, as a farm servant and had become a waggoner by the time he joined the army in 1915. He worked mostly on the Wolds around Driffield. He married during the war and became first a labourer, then a hind, and finally a farmer at Fridaythorpe in 1931. He died in 1976. Tapes 5/1, 5/2, 9/2, 10/1, interview 3 untaped, 15/1, 15/2 (with untaped addendum), 23/1, 23/2, 25/1, 28/2 and 29/1.

David Lawler, was born *c.* 1900 and started work at the age of fourteen. He spent his time as a farm servant in the York and Market Weighton areas until 1925, by which time he had become a waggoner. He married in 1933. Tapes 16/1 (end) and 16/2.

Harold Masterman, one of seven children, was born in 1896 at Stoney Creek on the Humber, though when he was nine the family moved to nearby Thorngumbald. His father was a farm foreman and stallion leader. He began work in 1909, at the age of thirteen, and worked as a servant in the Hedon area of south Holderness, apart from one year spent on the Wolds, before joining the army in 1914. He married after the war and took a job as a farm labourer in Thorngumbald, eventually becoming a farm foreman (but not a hind) there. In the 1930s he left farming, because of the low wages, to work in factories in Hull. Died in 1980. Tapes 10/2, 11/1 (with untaped addendum), 20/1, 20/2 and 21/1.

Jonathan Milner was born in 1898 in Duggleby, but grew up in North Grimston. He was one of the ten children of a butcher. He began work at the age of twelve, spending all his time as a farm servant on the Wolds south of Malton and rising to be a waggoner. He was in the army for one year in 1918 and married in 1925. After the First World War he worked as a quarryman at North Grimston and Burdale, where he was blinded in an accident in 1937. He lived for most of his married life at Wharram. Tape 24/1.

Bernard Playforth was born in 1913 in Beverley and grew up in Burn, near Selby. He was one of three children and his father was a timber labourer. All his time as a hired lad was spent in or close to Kilham. After marrying in 1938 he took a labourer's job there and was still employed on a farm in the village when he died in 1979. Tapes 18/1 (end), 18/2, 19/1, 19/2, 22/1, 22/2, 24/2, 25/2, 27/2 and 28/1.

Mr A.M. Pridmore was born in 1888 at Barmby on the Marsh near Selby. His father operated the railway swing bridge at Drax on the old Hull and Barnsley Railway, now abandoned. He began work in 1902 in the Howden area, where he mostly remained while a horselad, though he spent one year in South Milford. At the age of eighteen he was old enough to join the railway as an engine cleaner, which was his real ambition, though this meant leaving the county. Tapes 3/1 (end), 3/2, 7/2 (end) and 8/1.

Thomas Rispin was born in Kilham in 1897 and spent all his life there apart from one year at Hunmanby as a hired lad. He was one of eleven children; his father had a smallholding and ran a coal business. He started work, at the age of thirteen, in 1910 and became a waggonner by 1918. He married in 1923 after twelve years in service and later became a hind until the 1930s. Both he and his wife are now dead. Tapes 18/1 (end), 18/2, 22/2, 24/2 (with untaped addendum), 27/2 and 28/1.

Harold Tate was born in Kilham in 1905 and spent all his life there apart from a few years as a hired lad. He started work at the age of thirteen and became a waggoner. Brandesburton Moor was the furthest from home he ventured. He is now dead. Tapes 19/1, 19/2, 22/2, 25/2 and 28/1 (end).

Mr S. Walker was born in 1903 in Thixendale. He started work at the age of twelve, spending most of his time locally as a hired lad. He spent one year as a shepherd lad and rose to be a waggoner before marrying in 1923. Because he worked for Sykes of Sledmere he was able to keep working as a horseman on their estate after his marriage. Tapes 7/1 and 7/2.

Abbreviations

Agricultural Labourers	*Report by Mr Wilson Fox on the Wages and Earnings of Agricultural Labourers in the United Kingdom* (P.P. 1900, LXXXII).
Ag. Stats.	*Agricultural Statistics*, published annually up to and including 1918 by the Board of Agriculture and Fisheries; afterwards by the Ministery of Agriculture and Fisheries; and from 1952 by the Ministery of Agriculture, Fisheries and Food. Up to and including 1920, the horse population of the East Riding is given in table 3, thereafter in table 2.
Annals of Brid.	Annals of Bridlington, collection of newspaper clippings compiled by Taylor and Matthewman, Bridlington Public Library.
Bev. Guar.	*Beverley Guardian.*
Brid. Chron.	*Bridlington Chronicle.*
Brid. F.P.	*Bridlington Free Press.*
Brid. Gaz.	*Bridlington Gazette.*
Earnings and Hours	*Report on the Earnings and Hours of Labour of Workpeople in the United Kingdom – V, Agriculture in 1907* (P.P. 1910 LXXXIV).
E.M. News	*Eastern Morning News.*
H.D. Mail	*Hull Daily Mail.*
H. News	*Hull News.*
Kelly's	*Kelly's Directory of the North and East Ridings of Yorkshire, 1909* (1909).
Mal. Gaz.	*Malton Gazette.*
Mal. Mess.	*Malton Messenger.*
PRO	Public Record Office.
Second Report	*Second Report on the Wages, Earnings and Conditions of Employment of Agricultural Labourers in the United Kingdom* (P.P. 1905, XCVII).
Wages and Conditions I and II	*Report on the Wages and Conditions of Employment in Agriculture* (P.P. 1919, IX): I, *General Report.* II, *Reports of Investigators.*
Yorks. Her.	*Yorkshire Herald.*

Chapter One

Introduction

The nineteenth century was a time of great change in farming, when horse-powered machinery gradually but inexorably took over the field work and large farms became much more like industrial businesses. In adopting a new technology and a greater market orientation, most farming counties also suffered traumatic social change, however much the Edwardian era may seem to us like the last remnant of a timeless tradition. The East Riding of Yorkshire seems to have escaped the worst effects of this process, while still modernizing its farming methods to the full. It was the smallest of the three ridings into which the county of Yorkshire was divided until 1974 and, perhaps surprisingly to outsiders, it was and remains almost wholly given over to high-quality arable farming. Yorkshire is a huge county, big enough to contain nearly every type of landscape that can be found anywhere in England. If large parts of it are moors and rugged upland country, virtually all the south-eastern corner is under the plough and the East Riding remains one of the most completely rural areas in England.

The West Riding was one of the pioneering areas of the Industrial Revolution, and its proximity is perhaps the most obvious explanation of the East Riding's stability in the nineteenth century. The woollen trade, on which industrialisation was based, had looked to the East Riding for its raw material for centuries, and now the swelling populations of the mill towns provided an ever-growing market for the county's grain, vegetables, and meat as well. Industry was not a threat to farms in East Yorkshire but a stimulus and a bringer of prosperity. Wages for farm labourers were higher than in any other arable county during the nineteenth century, though we must remember that this does not mean that they were well paid. They were prosperous only in comparison with their counterparts further south, not town workers or their own employers.

From the middle of the century onwards, commentators realised that a gulf had opened in farm wages. In those counties where there was competition for labour wages were far higher than in those where labour was plentiful and no alternative employment existed. On the whole, arable counties were usually low-wage counties because they rarely felt the effects of industrial competition, while northern pastoral counties had a relative shortage of labour. Some observers felt there were was a direct connection between arable farming and low wages, which was certainly not true, but it is a fact that the East Riding and, to a much lesser extent, the northern part of Lincolnshire and parts of Nottinghamshire,[1] formed a unique area where the arable and high-wage zones overlapped as shown on map 1a. Pockets of arable

1

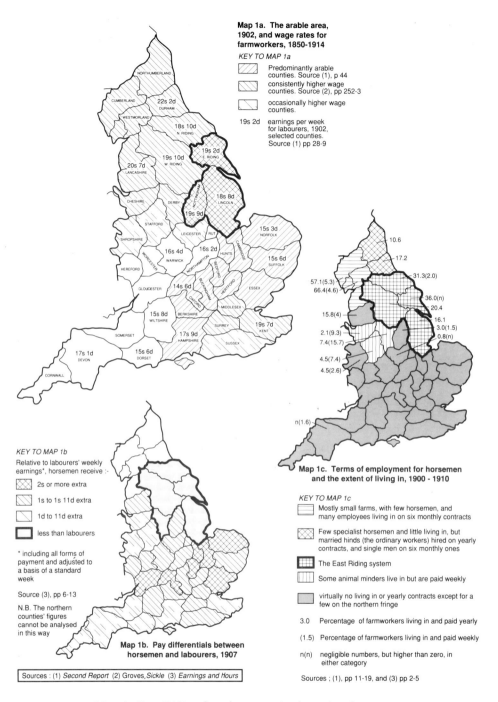

Map 1a. The arable area, 1902, and wage rates for farmworkers, 1850-1914

KEY TO MAP 1a

Predominantly arable counties. Source (1), p 44

consistently higher wage counties. Source (2), pp 252-3

occasionally higher wage counties.

19s 2d earnings per week for labourers, 1902, selected counties. Source (1) pp 28-9

KEY TO MAP 1b

Relative to labourers' weekly earnings*, horsemen receive :-

2s or more extra

1s to 1s 11d extra

1d to 11d extra

less than labourers

* including all forms of payment and adjusted to a basis of a standard week

Source (3), pp 6-13

N.B. The northern counties' figures cannot be analysed in this way

Map 1b. Pay differentials between horsemen and labourers, 1907

Sources : (1) *Second Report* (2) Groves, *Sickle* (3) *Earnings and Hours*

Map 1c. Terms of employment for horsemen and the extent of living in, 1900 - 1910

KEY TO MAP 1c

Mostly small farms, with few horsemen, and many employees living in on six monthly contracts

Few specialist horsemen and little living in, but married hinds (the ordinary workers) hired on yearly contracts, and single men on six monthly ones

The East Riding system

Some animal minders live in but are paid weekly

virtually no living in or yearly contracts except for a few on the northern fringe

3.0 Percentage of farmworkers living in and paid yearly

(1.5) Percentage of farmworkers living in and paid weekly

n(n) negligible numbers, but higher than zero, in either category

Sources ; (1), pp 11-19, and (3) pp 2-5

Map 1. East Riding farm horsemen in the national context

prosperity did exist elsewhere, but there was nothing on a comparable scale. This limited prosperity was enough to cushion the impact of change on traditional culture in the county. It gave its people the resilience to preserve a way of running farms into the twentieth century, that disappeared a hundred years before in most other places. This interlocked with and coloured village society on a multitude of levels, not just economic, but it was most visible in the way of horses were worked and cared for.

Horses now seem the epitome of unmechanized farming, but they had increased dramatically in numbers during the nineteenth century precisely because farming was starting to mechanize and they were the best source of power available then. The customs and traditional practices that surrounded their care grew up as the best solutions to real problems that existed in a practical world. The continuity of tradition evident in the East Riding is not a sign of an isolated, backward region, but of one still coping with the pressures of change on its own terms. In studying it, we gain insight into the way that farms were run in earlier times, into the rural society of those times, and into other counties which had been similar a century before but which had then followed a different track, obscuring their earlier form. We also see custom and tradition as living forces, not as curiosities or fossils.

Rural societies are often seen as static but they do evolve, sometimes at a rapid rate. Their customs are most easily studied where they have survived more or less unchanged after their function has vanished, for then they draw attention as anachronisms. It is, however, rare that more than the outward form will survive in such a case, precisely because they no longer fit the times. We can see the dance steps of a morris troupe in an increasing number of places today, or less frequently we can see a performance of a mummers' play, but without extensive research we cannot discover the reason villagers once included the dance or play in their lives as a vital, living part of their culture. Such things must have a reason for surviving, or for being revived, but it is not the same reason as when they were not identified as 'folk' survivals.[2] Living customs are the machinery of society, shaping the peoples' lives to a tacitly agreed and functional pattern.

As society changes, so must custom: square pegs must become round if the holes they fitted into lose their sharp edges. By doing so they retain a continuity of function that survival by ossification would destroy. Neither remains the original: the square peg looks the same, but it lacks a purpose and loses meaning, while the rounded one retains a connected function but loses its appearance in greater or lesser degree. Functional customs in our own society tend to be taken for granted and hence overlooked, yet they are the ones with a future, and the ones that contribute most to understanding cultural change. Thus, Elizabeth Gutch set out to compile a conventional folk lore book on the East Riding around the turn of the century, and in the preface she remarks on the difficulty she had in finding material of the right type,[3] that is, the quaint and anachronistic. Until the 1920s the East Riding's relative prosperity made it one of the most self-confident rural areas of England and its cultural pattern was more evolutionary than preservationist. By looking at the way such a society worked, earlier cultural patterns can be observed in action in a modified form, which will often explain the function of customs and institutions preserved only in outward form in a more ossified society, and we gain perspective from two incomplete but complementary viewpoints. A more rounded view of the past societies should be possible, just as we now understand biological evolution better because we use the behaviour of living, related species to explain features preserved in fossils from bygone eras.

Even in this century, the overwhelming majority of East Riding children were hired out as servants who lived on their employer's premises once they left school. For boys, this meant becoming farm servants, most of whom worked among the horses. They left their parents' homes and moved into farmhouses instead, often spending the next decade or more in self-contained groups of youngsters who largely ran their own lives. They received board and lodging as part of their wages and they had very little time for anything other than work. Naturally, this was no life for a married man and so there was a clear division in society between the single servants and the married labourers, who lived in cottages in villages. They did not regard this as strange or in any way worthy of comment because it affected everyone below the upper classes in a county community that was still very self contained. This is exactly the way that most teenagers had been employed in England as a whole in the eighteenth century, even if the actual work they did was different, and the memories of those who began their working life in this way are a unique record of a system usually assumed to be dead beyond recall. This book is an attempt to pull some of those memories together and to explain the way this system worked.

The inter-war depression forms a crucial watershed in the life of the East Riding. It was not a total break, but it unleashed a process that overwhelmed the traditional way of life as the years went by. The East Riding of 1950 was manifestly a different place from that of 1914, even apart from purely technological change. The period before the First World War was remembered, predictably, as a time of stability with no hint of how close total change was, yet this is not the conventional Edwardian 'golden age'. Work was hard and long and farmworkers recalled their own desires for the changes that were to come later. The sense of stability derived more from the lack of any visible prospect of change. Horse farming had mechanized as far as it could with the limited power available to it, and socially there was no reason to expect any upheaval in the county. Workers were non-unionized and relatively acquiescent in things as they were. Those who disliked farming or horses, or who resented their lack of opportunities, were not trapped, for the nearby industrial towns of the West Riding offered the chance of a new life for those daring or discontented enough to take it.

The isolation of the county and its total dependence on farming were two crucial factors in explaining the persistence of this old way of life while all around it was changing. It is not on the road to anywhere but itself, for main trunk roads and railways going north up the eastern side of England strike inland to avoid the vast estuary of the Humber, two miles wide near its mouth. They then go up the Vale of York, bypassing the East Riding completely to keep clear of the North York Moors and the Hambleton Hills. There is no need here for any extensive survey of the county's land and farming as good books on the subject already exist,[4] but it is essential to have some idea of the background against which the county's farmworkers lived out their lives.

Map 2. The East Riding and its vicinity, c. 1914

It was the smallest of the three ridings into which the ancient county of Yorkshire was divided until 1974, but with slightly more than three-quarters of a million acres it was as big as many independent counties and from 1888 it had its own county council. Hull, or more correctly, Kingston-upon-Hull, is the county's one city and it is, of course, a major seaport, but its users mostly pass quickly along the county's southern edge, seeing little of it, having no reason to halt on the way. On the east coast, Bridlington and, to a lesser extent, Filey, Hornsea, and Withernsea are seaside holiday resorts and they account for the majority of visitors to the area. The central feature of the East Riding is the Wolds, a range of chalk hills running north from the Humber, and getting higher and wider as they go. They frequently reach 500 feet in height, and some exceed 750. Between Driffield and Malton they swing round towards the coast, narrowing down and descending as they approach Bridlington.

They enclose the valley of the river Hull and the substantial, undulating plain of Holderness between themselves and the North Sea, while on the western side is the Vale of York.

The Vale is a large zone that includes sections of all three ridings and it has a definite sub-culture of its own. Boundaries are, after all, only lines on the map however loyal to their own county people may be. The rivers Ouse and Derwent form a significant barrier between the people of the East Riding and their neighbours of the North and West Ridings, but in terms of styles of farming and many other economic aspects of life they unite the valleys they flow through as much as they divide them. The section of the Vale of York that was cut into the East Riding by the Ouse therefore sometimes did things in ways that differed significantly from the rest of the riding, but it always remained self-consciously part of it despite this. There are times, however, when it is useful to think in terms of a greater East Riding that includes parts of all the neighbouring counties, even though they were self-consciously separate for most things, for the distinctive way of life that was so strong in the county did not stop dead at the boundaries. It ran on, even across the Humber in north Lincolnshire, gradually fading out as other influences overwhelmed it.

The 1911 census found 432,759 people living in the East Riding. Only 94,784 lived on the 711,000 acres classed as rural – just over 20 per cent of the people on 95 per cent of the land area. Hull accounted for another 277,991, with a further 9,967 in its suburbs of Hessle and Cottingham. The remaining 50,017 lived in the market towns and more especially the coastal resorts. Far more than in any other northern county, the thinly spread rural population was almost all directly or indirectly reliant on agriculture.[5] Figure 1a shows that, excluding scholars, the retired, and the unoccupied, nearly 60 per cent of all males in the rural East Riding worked on farms in 1911, whether as farmers, their relatives, or employees. Hardly any other occupations existed on any scale, and they mostly served agriculture or those engaged in it. Even the inclusion of the market towns, as in figure 1b, changes matters very little except by increasing the proportion of service workers. Furthermore, figure 1c shows that youths had even less choice of occupation than males had as a whole, for 76 per cent of fifteen- to sixteen-year-olds worked on farms.

In 1793 Isaac Leatham knew of only one 'manufactory' in the whole county outside Hull,[6] and the 1831 census report remarked that 'the East Riding would be entirely agricultural did not the town of Kingston-upon-Hull (with its suburb Sculcoates) contain the manufactures indispensable to an active Sea-port'.[7] The lack of raw materials and water power, together with the sparseness of the population, encouraged from the start a division of labour with the industrializing West Riding rather than direct competition. Two centuries ago, Isaac Leatham said that coal and lime were exchanged for food, resulting in 'so happy a combination . . . as each county is adapted to supply the wants of the other [and] . . . the most convenient channel of communication is afforded by the adjoining rivers'.[8] Nothing since has led to any real change and the East Riding today is still almost completely lacking in manufacturing industry, being described in 1970, for instance, as 'an almost rural backwater'.[9] Even the spread of the Yorkshire coalfield across the Ouse, with pits sunk between Selby and York, has made little impact.

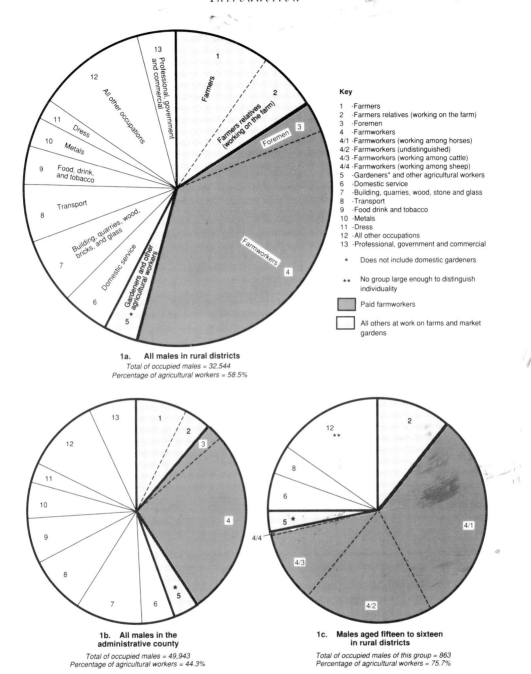

1a.   All males in rural districts
Total of occupied males = 32,544
Percentage of agricultural workers = 58.5%

Key

1 -Farmers
2 -Farmers relatives (working on the farm)
3 -Foremen
4 -Farmworkers
4/1 -Farmworkers (working among horses)
4/2 -Farmworkers (undistinguished)
4/3 -Farmworkers (working among cattle)
4/4 -Farmworkers (working among sheep)
5 -Gardeners* and other agricultural workers
6 -Domestic service
7 -Building, quarries, wood, stone and glass
8 -Transport
9 -Food drink and tobacco
10 -Metals
11 -Dress
12 -All other occupations
13 -Professional, government and commercial

*   Does not include domestic gardeners

**   No group large enough to distinguish
        individuality

        Paid farmworkers

        All others at work on farms and market
        gardens

**1b.   All males in the
        administrative county**

Total of occupied males = 49,943
Percentage of agricultural workers = 44.3%

**1c.   Males aged fifteen to sixteen
        in rural districts**

Total of occupied males of this group = 863
Percentage of agricultural workers = 75.7%

Source : *Census, 1911*, X, pt. II (P.P.1913-14, LXXIX, Cmd 7019), pp. 638-40 and 644-6

Fig. 1. The occupations of males at work in the East Riding, 1911

The towns of the county did not grow at anything like the rate of their West Riding equivalents, as Table 1 shows. Beverley was in a class of its own as the centre of the county's administration and its immense and glorious Minster symbolizes its position as the capital of the rural East Riding. With its churches and courts it had, of course, a high proportion of professional occupations, but for ordinary people agriculture was the dominant occupation even here. Mr Ashby, a native, certainly saw no alternative to farmwork when he left school, and he was in no way exceptional. Great Driffield, Selby, Malton, and Bridlington were the other major market centres, even though neither Selby nor Malton was in the East Riding. Selby lay entirely in the West Riding and served a large section of the Vale of York on both banks of the river Ouse, and while Malton had a twin town, Norton, across the Derwent in the East Riding, this was largely a suburb. Bridlington, York, and Hull also acted as market towns for the areas near them, though that was not their primary role. York, like Malton and Selby, was outside the county, and like Beverley it was an ecclesiastical and administrative centre. It also had industry,

Table 1. *Populations of the market towns serving the East Riding, together with the coastal resorts and other urban areas within the administrative county, April 2nd, 1911.*

Town	Population, 1911
Bridlington (m)	14,334
Beverley (m)	13,654
Selby (m) †	9,048
Malton (m)††	4,822
Norton	3,990 } 8,812
Driffield (m)	5,676
Hessle	5,319
Cottingham	4,648
Filey	3,228
Hornsea	3,024
Pocklington (m)	2,556
Withernsea	2,278
Market Weighton (with Arras) (m)*	1,770
Hedon (m)	1,171
Patrington (m)*	1,147

KEY   (m)   –   market town
           †   –   located in the West Riding
           ††   –   located in the North Riding
           *   –   not classed as an urban district

Source: *Census, 1911, I* (PP 1912–13, CXI, Cmd 6258) pp. 356–62.

notably connected with the railways, and it consumed a good deal of agricultural produce.

Hull was larger and therefore consumed more and offered more employment, but it was founded as a port and its eyes have always been out to sea rather than gazing back over the land. In the early years of this century, men were employed to crew both merchant ships and trawlers, and to load and unload them in the docks. Others worked on the railways and waterways, moving the cargoes in and out, while still others found jobs in factories processing the fish, oil-seed, and grain that came in through the docks. After Liverpool and London, though a good way after, Hull was consistently the third largest port in the country, but it differed from them, as the *Victoria County History* noted, in having 'no large body of consumers near at hand so there was comparatively little scope for skilled handicrafts'. As a result, 'its industrial development in the nineteenth century was . . . closely linked to its overseas trade, and basically this has remained so to the present day: heavy industry is virtually absent'. Moreover, 'a . . . characteristic of industry in Hull was the high proportion of jobs which were either seasonal or casual, or unusually uncertain in their prospects'.[10] It was not equipped to offer the high wages or secure employment that would have proved a magnet for discontented farmworkers, especially as the towns and cities of the West Riding were near at hand.

Besides the larger centres there was a group of lesser towns, some in decline and some growing. Hedon and Patrington had both been eclipsed by Hull, Hornsea by Beverley, and Howden by Selby and Goole. Market Weighton and Pocklington, though small, were well-served by canals and railways, and were still improving their standing in the early years of this century, though in the long run further concentration and the diminishing of their rail links prevented them rivalling the larger centres. Withernsea and Filey developed solely as holiday resorts, and Hornsea failed as a market even as it succeeded, in a modest fashion, in attracting tourists. We are therefore concerned largely with a population living in villages and on isolated farmsteads.

The three rural zones of the Wolds, Holderness, and the Vale were a definite reality for these people and they were reluctant to move from one to another. Each was physically different and they were therefore farmed in different ways that suited their particular soil types. The Wolds, being made of chalk, suffered a chronic shortage of water, while the Vale of York and Holderness both had an excess. The Wolds are mostly covered by a thin, light loam liberally sprinkled with flints which is in places only two or three inches deep. The slopes can be steep enough to make fieldwork difficult, or even impossible. In the Vale the predominant soil is light and sandy, though to the south there is heavier warp land. Where the underlying drainage allows the soil to dry out thoroughly, there are problems caused by its tendency to blow away in the wind and large areas are naturally covered by heath. Holderness soil is mostly clay, making it hard to drain and hard to work, but soil conditions here are the most variable and patchy.

As long as the land was farmed and managed in a manner sympathetic to the problems, there were very few parts of the county where good crops could not be grown in the early twentieth century. Farmers found, however, that in its natural state large areas had to be either left alone or used very lightly, and in Holderness the

9

heavy soil's need for extensive fallows severely curtailed production. On the Wolds, between the middle ages and the nineteenth century a large proportion of the land was used only as a sheepwalk or rabbit warren. Defoe commented that 'the middle of this Riding or Division of Yorkshire is very thin of Towns [i.e. villages] and consequently of People, being overspread with Woulds . . . on which they feed great Numbers of Sheep, and breed also a great many Black Cattle and Horses'.[11] To ensure their water supply, the villages are located along the foot of the slopes or in the lower valleys. The nearby land could be ploughed as common fields, which often ran up onto the Wolds, but the rest had been left for centuries as pasture, except for an occasional catch crop. The sheep which grazed the pasture were well suited to the conditions and its fertility was built up and maintained by this system of management. Outside the villages there was only a very occasional farmhouse before 1750 and a large part of the Wolds' 300,000 acres was covered by fine but fragile grass cover.[12]

In the Vale of York the large areas of boggy wilderness were then similarly unsettled but were of far less use. They occurred in pockets rather than in one consolidated mass and could be very sizeable – Spalding Moor covered 7,000 of the 11,500 acres of its township before the eighteenth century.[13] With the adjacent Bishopsoil and Wallingfen commons, this constituted a huge area of land that could be used only as rough pasture. The many villages were located on sites chosen to make the most of the good land, giving the appearance of a random scatter that covered most of the landscape. Holderness villages were laid out less randomly, but there was no one determining factor as on the Wolds. In the Hull valley they stood back from the flood plain, leaving an empty zone down its length, while over the marshy areas beyond they were located on hillocks of clay or gravel to get the driest possible situation. Historically, cattle raising was more important than on the Wolds or in the Vale because the arable potential of much of the soil could not be unlocked without extensive drainage. Paradoxically, Holderness had the smallest amount of land that was beyond active cultivation, yet it was least able to make efficient use of the remainder.[14]

The East Riding is the only northern county with no intractable moorland. Enclosure had proceeded alongside improvement in the eighteenth and nineteenth centuries as better techniques and greater demand allowed even the more difficult land to be brought under the plough. By the twentieth century, nearly every corner of the county was farmed except for the steepest wold slopes and a few small patches of the Vale that remained boggy common or rough heath. Holderness still used more fallows than average and it still maintained some permanent pasture for its stock, but less than 0.6 per cent of the county's land was listed in the 1873 New Domesday survey as commons or waste.[15] Moreover, good arable land had even been reclaimed from the Humber, particularly at Broomfleet and Sunk Island. Where tracts of land were enclosed they were let as isolated farms, sometimes with a few labourers' cottages nearby, and no new villages were created. The extra demand for labour to work the new farms, which were mostly large ones, ensured that existing villages did not decay but became in many cases, especially on the Wolds, dormitory settlements for distant farmsteads.

The Wolds adopted strict rotations, usually based closely on the classic four-course, for with its thin soil it was imperative that fertility should be maintained. Young, in the 1760s, saw only one example, at Risby, but by 1848 Legard reported that such rotations were universal.[16] Sheep still had a vital part to play though they were now fed on clover and turnips rather than roaming freely. The soil proved capable of sustaining high yields of first rate corn, especially barley. Bullocks were bought in and over-wintered in the fold yard to turn the straw into manure, then sold again. Apart from impossible slopes, a few acres of grass for the horses was the only part of the farms not under the plough. Holderness was also corn country, but its rotations were more complex and were often devised to suit the particular conditions of each area. Fallows were needed even in this century and crops such as beans were extensively grown as part of the rotations. Cattle rearing was an important enterprise in its own right because of the quantity of both permanent and rotational grass, and sheep were widely kept. In the Vale the most distinctive crops were root vegetables.

The Wolds were covered with large new farms during enclosure, many of them long distances from the nearest settlement, but even here some small and medium farmsteads did survive, usually in the village centres.[17] In Holderness no such sizeable tracts, except Sunk Island, were divided up, and family farms remained common in the Vale of York where few employed more than two or three hands. On the whole, however, the county was characterized by large holdings. In 1919, 37 per cent of farms were above 300 acres, compared to a national average of 26 per cent and one of the highest proportions of any arable county.[18] In Holderness farms of 300 to 800 acres were usual, while those on the Wolds commonly contained between 500 and 1,000 acres, and Caird recorded that in the mid-nineteenth century, the farmers there were 'probably the wealthiest men of their class in the country'. Such men were gentlemen farmers, but they were also nearly all tenants.[19] In 1873 twelve families, each with more than 10,000 acres, together owned 30 per cent of the rural East Riding.[20] Until the break-up of the large estates in the depression between the First and Second World Wars, there was very little scope for owner-occupation.

There was also very little scope for the aspiring farmer among the ranks of the farmworkers. East Riding farms were, for the time, highly mechanized. The capital required for setting up as a farmer was beyond the means of most working men.[21] In times of depression there were more opportunities, but only because circumstances had made tenancies difficult to let, and so failure was likely. For the vast majority of boys in the East Riding, their future clearly lay in working for others until they retired or died. Those who saw this as a dead end were usually faced with moving to Hull or, more probably, the West Riding.

The backbone of all the farms was the horse. There were 40,704 of them on farms in the East Riding in 1913.[22] Some jobs, such as hoeing and hedge laying, were still done by hand, but farmers used machinery wherever they could. While steam engines were used on all farms for threshing at least, and on the larger ones for many more tasks such as chopping roots, they were hardly used in fieldwork at all. Farmworkers customarily assessed farms not by their acreage but by horse numbers, which in some respects reflected the farm's status better than its size. A farm with rough land that could not be ploughed used fewer horses than one with every acre under cultivation, though the comparison was only valid within a district. As acreages increased, moreover, farms usually could make better use of their horses, which reduced the number required per hundred acres. This also varied according to the amount of land to be fallowed or held as pasture.

Mr Fisher of Garton estimated that, in his experience, five horses per hundred acres was common, while Mr Milner put it as low as two on the high Wolds farms. Four was commonly given as a reasonable average. Many farms had extra horses besides those they actually needed, because it was common practice to breed from mares. A few farms regarded breeding as an enterprise like any other, undertaken with a view to selling as many horses as possible at high prices. Most farmers, however, undertook breeding to supply their own needs and looked on the proceeds of any sale of surplus foals as a welcome bonus. They had no county-wide preference for any particular breed, but they took any amount of trouble to ensure that the horses they kept were as good as they could be.

Farm servants were still hired throughout the north of England, but outside the greater East Riding, northern farms were either dominated by pasture, leading to low labour requirements and hence few servants, or their servants were hired by a different system that involved married as well as single men. Interest in farm servants in the early modern history of England has been growing in recent years, and it centres on the special niche that was created for adolescents and young adults, exactly the type still hired in the county. By examining the reasons for their survival in the East Riding we can learn a lot about their disappearance from the rest of the arable zone in the early nineteenth century.

Was this just a different way of paying for labour, or was it something more? The written evidence suggests the latter, but does not allow a close examination for servants created, and figured in very few written records, and very few of them give us any sense of what the system offered to those involved in it to persuade them to take up such a distinctive lifestyle. Now, if we are prepared to accept the results, we can get round some of these difficulties directly by talking to men who were farm servants. Because so many men who were part of the system were still alive, the East Riding offered unique possibilities to a historian and during 1973 and 1974 I tape-recorded conversations describing a way of life that seemed to have very little to do with the present century. At the end I had about thirty six hours of recordings, which after a great deal of effort turned into hundreds of pages of transcripts. These then had to be collated to form a coherent account.

The views on which this book are based are those of farmworkers on their own lives. They are personal reminiscences and to get a rounded view we must always be aware that one man's meat is another man's poison, but there were enough people involved to allow personal dislikes to be disentangled from those of the whole group. Even though only one person's testimony is often all that is quoted, there are usually several others available saying much the same thing and though the impression may be created of individual testimony, the direction of the book was fixed by the evidence as a whole. Oral history, the recovery of historical data through the collection of reminiscences, is no longer a new phenomenon and it does not require justification: the book itself must provide that and the reader must be the judge of its effectiveness. A few points should be made, however, on the way the tapes were turned into written history.

Quotes have only been edited where it was necessary to preserve the continuity of the central theme, and this is marked. Sometimes they read a little awkwardly, but this is because they are transcriptions of unrehearsed speech. Many, probably the majority, of the sections edited out were false starts verbally cancelled out by the speakers themselves, rather than lengthy arguments discarded by me as unwanted during writing. The rhythms are those of speech, and punctuation is obviously arbitrary, but it is placed to maintain the natural flow as much as possible. The only element occasionally removed without note is 'you know' and then only when it occurs so frequently as to be disruptive. To mark this editing would be just as disruptive and would mislead because nothing of substance has gone. It also seemed pointless to indulge in bizarre spellings of ordinary words pronounced with a Yorkshire accent, and which were used in an ordinary manner, when normal spelling is not itself phonetic. Dialect is rendered as clearly as possible to preserve authenticity, and a glossary of words or usages likely to confuse is provided. Similarly, where the pronunciation of a normal word varies markedly from the conventional spelling I have used a simple phonetic spelling to preserve the sense of Yorkshire speech. Thus, 'fellow' is frequently used, and is invariably said and written as 'feller'.

Where possible, oral evidence has been added to and checked against the usual historical sources. On the whole, however, apart from certain limited aspects, these rarely offered a great deal. Newspapers, for instance, might be expected to cover village festivities, but they seem to have had no interest in them if they were run by and for the poor. Reports of wage rates and court cases were useful, but a history dependent on newspapers alone would hardly mention farmworkers. Equally, it was surprising that contemporary local historians and commentators rarely judged farming to be a subject of interest to their readers, but this was so. Even more rarely did they include a study of the farmworkers. They presumably saw them as so omnipresent and unchanging as to need no attention. This is matched, perhaps, by the rarity of references to farmers in the tapes. The poor seem to have lived in their own world, and therefore until very recently most writers apart from folklorists looked through farmworkers rather than at them.

Reservations must be expressed about the quality of what record there is. Just like oral history, much writing is the unfettered expression of personal opinion, but the fact that it is in print, and that it survives, gives it a respectability that it may not deserve. H. Rider Haggard, for instance, produced an interesting survey of farming that included detail on the East Riding in 1902, but it was based solely on discussions with farmers of at least a thousand acres. This is oral history from the top down.[23] Such works may not be deliberately misleading, but their authors frequently had little real understanding of farmworkers' lives and most written records were inevitably produced directly or indirectly by the top social strata of the countryside. The Rev M.C.F. Morris of Nunburnholme and Mary Simpson, daughter of the vicar of Carnaby both wrote extensively on the life of the East Riding poor, and Morris even published the results of some early oral history as *The British Workman Past and Present* in 1928. He had spent hours talking to William Blades, of Nafferton, who was born in 1839, about his life on farms, and yet the sections giving Blades' experiences are quite overshadowed by the author's lengthy comments, which are nothing more than his own personal opinions.

Mary Simpson devoted herself for many years to what can only be described as missionary work among East Riding teenagers. Most days she spent hours teaching and counselling both individuals and groups. She even read to lads as they ploughed, walking up and down beside them in the fields to make contact with those who would not or could not attend her evening classes. She was an ardent letter writer, both to friends and to those she had taught, and collections of these letters were published, giving a fascinating insight into village life in the second half of the nineteenth century. What they also show, however, was that she completely discounted her success in secular education, notably in her efforts to spread literacy among farmworkers, because all her students, seemingly without exception, remained true to their origins and became Methodists rather than Anglicans. The nature of her comments on moral issues, particularly, shows what caution is needed with such sources for she was never capable of a sympathetic understanding of village life as she found it. She unequivocally wished to enforce the acceptance of an Anglican concept of the desirable ordering of society, whether villagers agreed with her or not, and her writings show clearly that they did not.[24]

By combining written and oral sources it is possible to consider why certain customs survived when others did not and, more importantly, how this relates to the evolution of the culture of farmworkers of the East Riding, in a functional sense. The written sources provide material that could be obtained in no other way, so to recognize their limitations is not to reject them. In particular, they allow the story to be taken back through the nineteenth century and beyond. We must use all the information available in the most appropriate manner and because change was going on continuously, especially after the First World War, it is hard to provide accurate descriptions of the basic system unless we choose a baseline to work around. The years up to and including 1914 are the most suitable because then there was still a single system, with a few geographical variants of only slight importance, which had been in existence for some time, whereas later there was a progressive disintegration. Later developments, and earlier history, are always dated, whereas any undated description can be assumed to be of this period.

Notes to Chapter One

1. See J. Obelkevitch, *Religion and Rural Society: South Lindsey 1825–75* (1976), especially chap. 2 which shows that this area had strong affinities with the East Riding, but that the relatively greater prosperity of the latter was creating a divergence between the two areas.

2. T. Hardy, *Return of the Native* (1878, Macmillan, 1974), p. 141, has a good description of the differing motivations of traditional participants and revivalists in folk activities.

3. *Examples of Printed Folk-lore Concerning the East Riding of Yorkshire* (1911), County Folklore Series, vol. 6.

4. See A. Harris, *The Rural Landscape of the East Riding of Yorkshire, 1700–1850* (1961), K.J.

Allison, *The East Riding of Yorkshire Landscape* (1976), and B. Dyson (ed.), *A Guide to Local Studies in East Yorkshire* (1985).

5. *General Report*, pp. 8–9 and 26.
6. I. Leatham, *A General View of the Agriculture of the East Riding of Yorkshire* (1794), p. 59.
7. *Census, 1831, Enumeration Abstract*, II (P.P. 1833, XXXVII), pp. 750–1.
8. Leatham, *General View*, p. 12.
9. P. Lewis and P.N. Jones, *The Humberside Region* (1970), p. 11, and see also chaps 4 and 5, especially figs. 11 and 12.
10. K.J. Allison (ed.), *The Victoria County History of the County of York, East Riding*, (1969) I, pp. 258, 1, and 219.
11. D. Defoe, *A Tour Through the Whole Island of Great Britain* (1738, Davies, 1927), p. 643.
12. M.B. Gleave, 'Dispersed and Nucleated Settlement on the Yorkshire Wolds, 1770–1850', *Institute of British Geographers Transactions and Papers*, 30 (1962), 105–6.
13. D. Neave, *Notes on the History of the Church and Parish of Holme-on-Spalding Moor, Yorkshire*, (n.p. 1970), p. 1.
14. See W.H. Long, 'Regional Farming in Seventeenth-Century Yorkshire', *Agricultural History Review*, 8, (1960), 103–14; and I. McConville, 'Some Aspects of the Human Geography of the East Riding', *Hull University Institute of Education Studies in Education*, 1, no. 5 (June 1951), 36.
15. *Return of Owners of Land*, II, East Riding Section (P.P. 1874, LXXII), pp. 571–600, quoted in J.T. Ward, *East Yorkshire Landed Estates in the Nineteenth Century* (York, 1967), p. 3. See also *General Report*, p. 19, which shows that the East Riding had less than half the average national proportion of woodland, a very low figure for an arable county.
16. A. Young, *A Six Month's Tour Through the North of England* (1770), I, p. 165, and G. Legard, 'On the Farming of the East Riding of Yorkshire', *Transactions of the Yorkshire Agricultural Society*, 11 (1848), 104–5.
17. M.B. Gleave, 'Settlement', 110.
18. *General Report*, p. 5.
19. J. Caird, *English Agriculture in 1850–51* (1852), p. 310, and see W. Holtby, *South Riding* (1936), for a detailed portrait of this type of wealthy tenant farmer in her character Carne. Her own father was a man of this type.
20. Quoted in Ward, *Landed Estates*, p. 5. A full list of the largest hundred landowners, who all had more than 970 acres with only one exception, is given, p. 72.
21. Haggard, *Rural England*, p. 370, estimated the capitalization needed for a large Wolds farm in 1901 at £8 per acre.
22. In 1913 there were 40,704 horses on farms in the East Riding, Agricultural Statistics, 1913, (1914), p. 47.
23. *Rural England* (1902), see pp. 363–4.
24. Mary Simpson published various tracts and pamphlets, but the most interesting of her writings are the collections of her letters edited by the Rev F.D. Legard. These appeared as *Ploughing and Sowing: or, Annals of an Evening School in a Yorkshire Village, and the Work that Grew out of it* (1861), and *Gleanings: Being a Sequel to 'Ploughing and Sowing'* (1876). For the other titles, see the bibliography. C.B. Freeman, *Mary Simpson of Boynton Vicarage: Teacher of Ploughboys and Critic of Methodism*, East Yorkshire Local History Series no. 28 (York, 1971) is a brief biography.

Chapter Two

The Farmworkers of the East Riding

Farm work is one of the most varied jobs in existence and every farm, however large or small, has to cope with both a daily routine and a yearly round that require a wide range of skills, especially when everything depends on horses. During some seasons the work was overwhelming, while at others it was desultory. How these peaks and troughs were catered for, and how normal routines were matched to the labour available varied from area to area and it would be a serious mistake to assume that one farmworker was very much like another. In the East Riding the servants and labourers formed very separate groups before the Second World War, with different terms of employment and different jobs. Since the farm servants were all single men, youths, and boys living in on the farm and getting their keep as part of their wages, they were conveniently available on the farm at all hours, and it was natural for them to look after the livestock. For most of them this meant horses, as Mr Johnson said:

> There was what they called the horselads and labourers. Well, the labourers hadn't much to do with the horses unless, just odd times; if, say, they had a [horselad] poorly or anything of that, then they would say to a labourer, 'Well, you drive [his horses]', you see, but [a labourer] went home, you see. He started at, oh, it would be seven then [after the First World War], seven in t'morning till five at night, but he didn't feed or do them horses, somebody else had to, but they would ask him just to go with them. A labourer did, you know, he did hedging, helped in t'sheepfold or – see, there's the shepherd, beastman, but they often wanted help, you know, and labourers, you know, they got their orders every morning: 'Well, they want some help in t'sheepfold', or 'you help the beastman', or otherwise they'd send them to hedge [and, off the Wolds, to ditch] . . . But that was the labourers' job. And the lads, what they called the hired lads, you see, they drove the horses and fed them and harnessed them and all such as that.

With the married men mostly living in cottages in the villages, it was sensible to use them on the jobs, and there were plenty of them, that did not involve animals. This sharp division between horselads and labourers owed little or nothing to relative skill or other agricultural considerations. Most labourers had been horselads and they were certainly not helpers to the horselads as a bricklayer's labourer is to the bricklayer. In 1919, for instance, an official investigator commented that, 'in the East Riding the ordinary labourer is a highly-skilled man, who can do any work on a farm. . . . The term "ordinary labourer" is, perhaps not quite applicable to this class of man. He comes really in the class of "First-class Agricultural Labourer. . . ." The East Riding man is considered to compare favourably with any farm worker'.[1] As long as there was work for the horses, the horselads and the labourers worked separately with little contact. Work rarely ran out, especially where there were fallows, which always needed ploughing, but at such times the lads often joined the labourers in their tasks. Harvest was the main time when the whole farm labour force, with exception of possibly the stockmen, acted together on one job. At this time of year the labourers almost lived like the lads, as Mr Rispin and Mr Playforth explained:

> Mr R: First year I was off [1910], I remember well, like, wages was sixteen shillings for a labourer, . . . and then when they come in at harvest they gave them a pound and their grub, do you see. They all come into house, same as we did, like, in harvest.
> Mr P: They got their . . . food, like.
> Mr R: They didn't meat at home, like, and they used to come and meat with us; well they got a pound and their food.
> Mr P: They were only four bob a week better off. For all them extra hours.
> Mr R: Aye, that's right.
> Mr P: And they used to come on the Sunday for their dinner [as well].

Labourers and horselads were hired in fairly equal numbers. The farmer decided upon the exact proportions of each by balancing cost, experience, ability, strength, and convenience to get the right blend. Lads were always available for work while labourers went back to the village at the end of their day. Young lads could be hired very cheaply, but they lacked strength and experience. A top horselad's wages, including his keep, were comparable to a labourer's, and while an old labourer might not have the strength and speed of a young man, his experience and skill could more than make up for it. Each farmer balanced these factors in his own fashion.[2]

There were a handful of married horsemen, as Mr Pridmore confirmed:

> Sometimes the farmers used to keep these men on that got married and use 'em as horsemen, you see, and they didn't have anybody hired in the house in their place. So these men used to take over the pair of horses, you see, but perhaps the other lad that was there used to have to feed 'em before this man got there and . . . he took them when he came.

No matter how good a horseman a married man was, there was always difficulty in fitting him into the system. Some were paid overtime for the time spent amongst the horses. Mr Carter worked on Lord Middleton's estate at Birdsall in the 1920s and he told me, 'We got a shilling for every time we went. We got a shilling for going out – morning, and a shilling for dinner time and a shilling for night time'. Only a senior horseman whose abilities were prized was worth so much trouble. Married horsemen were most common on the home farms of large estates, partly because tied cottages were more likely to be available on these farms. In addition, it was the large landowners who were least likely to accept that local customs were the natural guide to farming methods, and it was them who formed the backbone of the agricultural societies. To someone interested in 'scientific' farming, a change in farm organization away from the traditional ways of the East Riding would seem far less of an upheaval than to the average farmer.[3]

The special characteristics that this induced in the East Riding's labour force is reflected to some degree in the 1911 census, as shown in figure 2. Unfortunately, farmworkers were classified on the assumption that there were three relatively small, skilled elite groups (the horsemen, shepherds, and cowmen) and a large residual group of unskilled labourers. The East Riding figures were forced into this mould despite its unsuitability, and so were distorted badly.[4] 3,954 people were listed as horsemen and 6,499 as not distinguished, the nearest thing to a labourer category. The total of labourers is higher than that of horselads because of the catch-all nature of the category. Some young East Riding farm servants only worked with horses part of the time, and were not therefore classed as horsemen. There was also, as we shall see later in the chapter, a substantial group of casual labourers without regular jobs who would also appear as not distinguished. This means that the data presented in figure 2 must be used with caution, and not only in respect of the East Riding, for the distinction between horsemen and labourers was even less clear in Cumberland and Northumberland. However, the tendency of the imprecision is to mask rather than exaggerate differences between counties, so any differences that do appear are real.

By the age of seventeen, most lads working with horses would have been returned as horsemen, so the figures for the age groups above seventeen give a truer picture than those below. The East Riding had many fewer seventeen- to twenty-year-old labourers than any other county, and though the contrast was not so great, it also had least twenty to twenty-five year olds. Above the age of twenty-five the position reversed, which is what would be expected since this was the closest approximation to the average age of marriage the figures allow, being grouped into five- and ten-year totals.[5] The East Riding had most twenty-five- to thirty-five-year-old labourers.

The figures on horsemen are more reliable, though the number of young lads is understated, as we have seen, and they prove how youthful the horsemen of the East Riding were compared with those of other counties. The contrast is particularly great for the under-twenties and the figures again lessen rather than increase differences. Even Cumberland, with the most similar social system, is markedly different in this respect, although the vast majority of its horsemen were under thirty-five years old. In Northumberland living in was not as common as in the East Riding and Devon was one of the last southern counties in which the system persisted, taking a form similar to that in Northumberland, and their age distributions closely resemble each other. East Suffolk shows the greatest contrast to the East Riding, despite being the only other predominantly arable county shown. In 1911 the

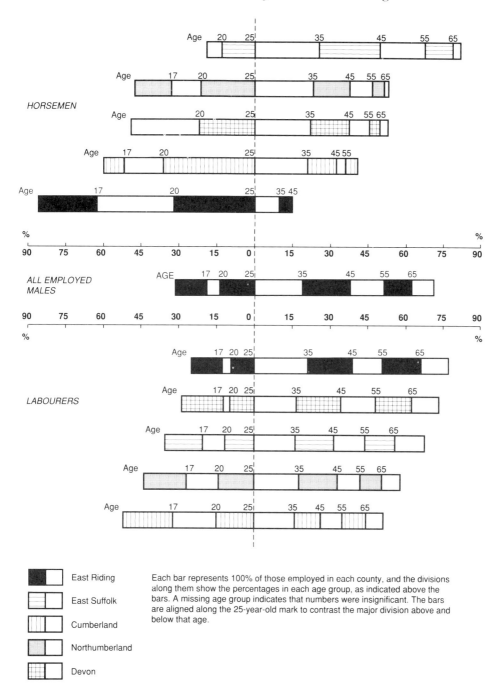

Source : *Census, 1911*, X, pt. II (P.P.1913-14, LXXIX, Cmd 7019), pp. 75, 99, 450, 546, and 645.

Fig. 2. The age distribution of horsemen and labourers on farms in selected counties of England, 1907

average age of a horseman in the East Riding was seventeen, in Northumberland and Devon, eighteen, in Cumberland nineteen, but in East Suffolk it ranged from twenty-five to thirty-four. Moreover, the East Riding and East Suffolk have the age distributions which are most heavily weighted on one side or the other of twenty-five. The East Riding had only 15 per cent of its horsemen above that age, while East Suffolk had only 19 per cent below it. A division into horsemen and under-horsemen would make the contrast even sharper, but the census information will not permit such sophistication.

Map 1b summarizes a Board of Trade report on agricultural earnings in 1907 which showed that in all but five of the English counties where the comparison could be made, the ordinary labourer received less for his week's work than the horseman did. The five exceptions were the Yorkshire ridings, Lincolnshire, and Derbyshire, putting the East Riding at the centre of a clear regional grouping that was unique in paying labourers more than horsemen. North Lincolnshire, in particular, had many similarities to the East Riding, and Derbyshire had close links with the southern West Riding. Small numbers of farm servants lived in in Derbyshire as in Yorkshire, though this was not really typical of the county's agriculture taken as a whole. It was predominantly pastoral, but the pasture farms were mostly small, often part-time, with no wage-earning agricultural labourers to include in the figures. This is also true, though to a lesser extent, of the West Riding, where the small farmers of the Pennines are overborne by the large arable holdings in the east. It is clear that the East Riding was the core of the arable farm-servant system, and that it differed most from those counties further south where the actual farming was most similar to this greater East Riding.

In many places, the extra pay a horseman received did not make up for the extra work required of him, so his hourly rate of pay actually dropped. However, the higher total wage and the responsibility of his position marked him out as a senior man, as shown by George Ewart Evans in his accounts of the Suffolk village of Blaxhall.[6] Since the horselads of the East Riding were, on average, approximately half the age of the Suffolk horsemen it is hardly surprising that their position on the farm should be very different. The horseman was the aristocrat of the Suffolk farm workers, a senior man whose skill was born of experience and who attained his position only after many years of working towards it. This was justified by the amount of care and attention horses need to keep them in good shape.

The East Riding, however, entrusted the care of its horses to boys and youths and once they had developed skills through practical experience among horses for eight to ten years, they married and became labourers. On the surface, either the Suffolk horsemen were making a fairly simple job look difficult, or the East Riding was content to have its horses managed incompetently and to squander its skilled labour. In fact, in the East Riding the care of the horses was divided. Most of the really skilled work, such as rearing and breaking foals, was usually done by the foreman, or the farmer, or else by a labourer who was good with horses. The older lads kept an eye on the younger ones and while the foreman, under ordinary circumstances, never fed a workhorse, he was always there if one fell sick or became unmanageable and he was a crucial figure in the farm organization.

Someone who subsists off fifty acres is as much a farmer as someone living the life of a gentleman off a thousand and even in the East Riding many had no choice but to work as hard as any labourer, but once a farmer owned or rented about two hundred acres of arable land (a very rough generalization), he usually employed a hind, or foreman. Between them the farmer and the foreman always decided the general lines along which the farm was to be run, the cropping figures for the year and the work to be done each day, and usually the farmer dealt with the men almost entirely through the foreman, as Mr Baines confirmed, 'Round East Riding then, they were pretty well-to-do, t'bosses, and you hardly saw your bosses: very rare. Your foreman was your main man'.[7] Mr Brambles, recalling the hard times of the inter-war depression, observed that farmers could be bad employers, and that small farmers were usually harder taskmasters than large ones,

> but when you came to look back you realize that the foreman was worse than t'farmer. I suppose he had to try to keep his job, by getting as much out of you as ever he could; although I was never with any bad foreman: you know, you heard other lads talking.

Frequently the foreman was much more than an overseer of the labour force: he had to be 'a good, managing man', as it was put at Thirsk hirings.[8] Mr Johnson recalled:

> One place I was at, the farmer lived . . . at Speeton which was about [twelve miles] off and he only really came once a month. Well I'd to use my own judgement. And then as regards cropping, you know, before we wanted to sow crops, like we'd maybe have a bit of a talk, like, 'should we sow this, should ——?' But the next place, the last place I was at, I generally used to ask him well before crop-sowing time, 'Well then, what are you going to sow? Tell me what you're going to sow.'
> 'We're going to sow this,' and 'We're going to sow that,' he used to tell me, like and that was all there was about it. The farmer, generally, told the foreman what he was going to sow: here and there, in this field and that field, and then it was left to tht foreman to do, see, like working and that: what . . . he said was it, you see, after that.

It was unusual for a farmer to surrender his control over cropping to a foreman, although, as Mr Johnson went on to say, 'A lot of 'em, if they'd a good foreman, like they would ask his advice, you see, "What do you think?".' An absentee farmer inevitably left most of the day-to-day business of the farm to the foreman. One Kilham farmer, for instance, took a second place at Rotsea, twelve miles away. Anyone in this position could only live on one farm and the other they merely visited as and when they could. Another cause of absenteeism was a reluctance to face the isolation of living some distance from the nearest village, let alone the market town with its social life. Another Kilham farmer lived at Bridlington, while still another, of a different generation, lived in Driffield. These owners might still take an active interest in the day-to-day running of the farm, but some did not bother. Odd situations could result: Mr Friend was once hired as head horseman on a three-hundred-acre farm in the North Riding Vale of York, and he recalled, 'That spot I was on at Huby, boss never bothered me. I run that spot. I were only nineteen. Ten men under me.' The farmer often had to allow his foreman to take over some of the financial side of such a farm, with a periodic settling up of accounts. Mr Johnson said:

> We used to put it down in a book – well, I used to pay the men – whoever we had labouring, and when you were a farm lad, you know, you generally took a bit to your place as pocket-money. Then when you got that spent you used to go to the master and say, 'Well, can I have a sub?' Used to call it a sub, you know, and you maybe got five bob, or ten, and you could get a quid when you got to be higher up, like; but a lad – if he got five bob. . . . Well, when we were at Park Farm these lads used to come to me, like, you know, 'Foreman, can I have a sub?' And I paid 'em that, then master paid me. . . . We drew this book up and it was put down, like, whatever payments you'd made. Why, when you were on a farm like that and, you know, your employer lives a long way off, . . . say somebody delivers some stuff to your door and they want paying for it, well you pay 'em, and you put it all down in this book, like, and then at month end or whatever it is, you know, you have a straighten up.

The foreman was usually a *hind*, that is, a married man who boarded the farm servants on behalf of the farmer. His terms of employment differed from everyone else's, as Mr Johnson explained:

> You used to get your wages every week, but it was a month's notice generally, either way. . . . I don't know if it was in the law, really, written down, but t'was understood thing. . . . Last farm I was at, well, I had house rent free and I had a cow for my use, and I had potatoes found, and I'd five bob a week extra – I'd five bob a week more than a labouring man whatever his wages, like; his wages went up, mine did. . . .
>
> He said to me when I first went, 'Well,' he said, 'now I don't want you to be always hard at work,' he said. But where you will work, see – anything wrong on a night, animals or owt like that, well, you maybe have to put two or three hours in doing that, maybe practically all night. Well next day, if you were busy, well you just had to work same as usual, but you waited of a time when you were a bit [slacker], then you could have an hour off somewhere, go somewhere, something like that: it was left up to you.

The house given to a hind was usually no mere cottage, as Mr Johnson also explained:

> He lives in the farm house, if there is a farm house there which – we were farm hinds for about twelve years and I never lived where there was a master house, we always used live in the farmhouse, you see, but a lot of places there was the farmhouse and then the hind house – sometimes it's all one, sometimes it's separate.

East Riding farmers were, on the whole, prosperous and during the course of the nineteenth century, some built themselves new, and better, houses leaving the old one to the hind. This enabled some to have the working farmstead sensibly located in the centre of the holding while they lived on the edge of the farm, closer to civilisation. The amount of physical work a foreman had to do depended upon the other calls on his time, the farmer's attitude and his own temperament. Mr Baines said:

> The foreman used to [join in]. He used to come round, like, and see that everything were all right and that you were all going all right, but he used to do some work as well. You got some o't' farm foremen as used to get jobs as farm foremen as weren't as good as the men on the farm – occasionally. You know, some on 'em were really good old men, and you got some men you were working under, like, as a foreman, they were probably sixty year old, you know, and they were really good hands, they could do anything – could give you a lot of good advice as well.

The foremen all had to pitch in at times of pressure, like harvest, and most would go ploughing, though not all. At other times they might go along on a job mainly to supervise, but each farm was different. The farmers who employed them, as opposed to the small farmers who acted as their own foremen, had a much more consistent attitude. Some did no physical work at all; some devoted their time to visiting markets where they could spend a good deal of pleasurable time transacting their business; some helped at those times when every hand was needed; but none was involved on a regular daily basis. They were owners and employers, not workers, and believed firmly in the old saying that 'It's no good keeping a dog and barking yourself.' The foreman rarely had anything to do with any cattle or sheep on the farm, however. He would be an ex-horseman, not an ex-stockman, and so, as Mr Tate said, 'Quite a lot o't'foremen, you know, wouldn't know nowt about sheep. Only knew about horses.' Mr Brambles added, 'That shepherd had his job routine and the chap amongst bullocks had his job routine, foreman wouldn't bother wi' them a lot. If t'shepherd wanted some help he would go to t'foreman and ask for somebody and, do you see, and he got 'em if they could spare 'em.'

The shepherds and beastmen were normally responsible only to the farmer. In this respect they were on equal terms with the foreman, who was counted as the head-horseman. They might have a lad to help them, known as the shepherd lad and beastman lad respectively, who were always farm servants and would be boarded by the hind with the horselads, but the shepherd and beastman might be either single or married. Mr Harper was a shepherd for six months in 1916 until called up for the First World War. He returned in 1919,

> and I went back to shepherding. . . . and I just did forty-three year – experienced shepherd. All weathers – sunshine, rain, snow, hail, blow.
> *Did you get a cottage then when you were a shepherd?*

Yes – well I was single for – I was about twenty-seven before I got married and my first cottage was at Haisthorpe, in between Brid and Driffield.
You stayed in the farmhouse until you got married?
Yes.

Whereas most horsemen gave up working with horses on marriage, cows and sheep provided jobs for life, and so most shepherd lads and beastman lads went on to train until they became a shepherd or beastman. There were exceptions like Mr Milner:

I did a bit of shepherding, . . . it was just to put my time in . . . . I had six months, maybe a year at Duggleby - hardly a year . . . and then I was shepherd lad at Heslerton Wold when I first went there. And then our waggoner lad [a horselad] left and they wanted me to take his spot, so I did. I did get to clipping stage up there. But, mind you, they were specialists at it, clipping. I couldn't touch them. I did do a bit o' clipping at Harry Beal's. I got so's I could do twenty in t'day.
But you preferred horses?
Oh aye. Oh, I've been a beastman and all. I were beastman at Bella – second year I was there.

Since Wolds farms only kept bullocks in the fold yards over the winter to turn the straw into manure, some economized by using inexperienced young men like Mr Milner as beastmen, or, to be more precise, bullockies. Others gave the task to older bachelors who lacked the strength or the desire to become waggoners or hinds, and wished to opt out of horse keeping.[9] When the cattle had gone, 'Why, he'd work on t'farm wi' the other men in summer, like,' Mr Tate observed, which provided an extra man at harvest. Most farm servants who worked with cattle or sheep were therefore quasi-apprentices. Mr Harper commented, 'We had to be shepherd lads for a couple of years before we durst take a [full] spot.' They usually wished to train to be shepherds or beastmen, for most lads without this commitment regarded the jobs as Mr Masterman did:

I wouldn't have nothing to do with bullocks, cows – oh no. No. Cows was seven days a week, winter and summer . . . , why horses, in summer they're turned out into t'field, Saturday night till Monday morning. Well, you've no need to bother with horses on Sunday, but cows you had. You had to milk them twice a day. I never had anything to do with cows. I never liked cows.

Shepherding was equally unattractive to the average lad, with the long hours at lambing and the need to rescue sheep when the winter weather was at its worst, even though those who worked among the stock were relatively well paid. A single shepherd, for instance, was usually offered £24 to £30 a year at Driffield between 1890 and 1910, whereas a senior horselad was only offered £20 to £25.[10] The exact premium varied with experience and responsibility, but shepherds were usually better paid than everyone except the foreman. Farmers often looked for an older lad,

24

who was likely to be a steadier worker than a young teenager. A lad who did want to work among the stock might have to wait some time for a vacancy to arise because few shepherd lads or beastman lads were required in comparison to the number of horselads. The shepherd became largely independent of the foreman's control by day, but as a living-in farm servant he was still subject to his authority as head of the household.

In addition to these permanent workers, there were a number of casual labourers. During certain seasons arable farmers have always needed more hands than they can justifiably employ for the rest of the year. Mechanization had reduced the disparity to some extent, but as long as horses were used, the harvest in particular required a large augmentation of the regular staff. Some came from local villages, but others were from farther afield. Many casuals were paid by piece work, in contrast to the regular workers, and every village had a few men who relied on such employment. Mr Johnson said:

Say they wanted [to] thrash, you know, it was a big farm as had enough; you see, they wanted so many casuals. . . . Because it took about twelve men to run a threshing set, you see, so there were these casuals. A lot of them, you know, they wouldn't have a regular job if they'd chance o' one, they liked this better, you know. And I mean they would maybe go on – some weeks you know, they maybe had a day or two's threshing during winter, one week, two or three days, maybe a full week, and maybe some days it was bad weather, not a day at all, and they used to, when they had a good do they used to booze, you know, and there was a lot of 'em like that.[11]

Besides those who simply did not like to be working all the time there were some men skilled enough to make a better living working on their own for anyone who needed their services, and they were usually too independent to want to be tied to one master. They had to be able to turn their hand to a different job with each season, but those with the ability could earn far more money than an ordinary labourer. They might save enough to set up as small farmers or else establish a business in the village, probably carrying on with some seasonal work to supplement their income.[12] However, some preferred enjoyment to saving, spending their money as fast as they earned it. Casuals could work when they wished and if they felt like going drinking for a week, there was no-one to stop them.

In their search for work they might travel long distances, which often appealed to the independent-spirited. Mr Jarvis described to me how, before the First World War, he had gone with a gang of such men out of the riding up to the Pateley Bridge area. He was a small farmer's son and that year he had missed being hired as a horselad:

I went with a lot o' chaps, a lot older than myself; they said, 'Are you going to th'ay country?' Well I hadn't a clue where hay country was. I said, 'Good God, where's th'ay country?' I said, 'We have plenty hay at home, where's th'ay?'

'Well, its better paid if you come to th'ay country.'

I said, 'Is that what you say? Well, I'd better come to th'ay country
then. . . .' These fellers went every year from villages round here . . . so
I goes, I was like a pet foal, I followed on. So my dad says, 'Where are you
going?. . . .'

I said, 'These fellers from Leavening says we've got to go to Leeds and then
be engaged.' In Leeds, you know. Briggate . . . , that was the great place
where they used to pick fellers up for th'ay. They said to me, 'Do you know
anything about hay?'

'Well,' I said, 'I've been brought up among hay! All my life, So,' I says, 'I
ought to do. . . .'

'You aren't very old.'

I said, 'No, but,' I says, 'I'm willing to use a scythe,' and, I says, 'I'm
willing to work.' And do you know, at that time o' day we got £5 for a
month, hay making. That's all we could get.

Mrs Jarvis: And that was top pay at that time.

Mr J.: Well, we used to go to make hay, we used to go at two o'clock in a
morning because the grass was [short] and you'd got to mow it when the dew
was on because it was on the hill sides. And you were always like this [one leg
higher than the other].

The other source of local labour was women and children, but this was of
declining importance. Even before the First World War very few women worked
regularly on the land in the East Riding. They helped at the various harvests,
especially the root harvests which were the least mechanized, and at hoeing and
singling the roots, but even this was diminishing. Mr Baines said:

Hoeing times, sometimes in harvest, used to get two or three women helping
you, 'cause women could make a load as well as a man and they could use a
fork as well as a man, or a scythe. You could see 'em wi' t'scythe, you know,
and they'd be sharpening it with scythe stone.

They wouldn't get the same pay rates as men?

Oh no. No. And they used to do as much work as a man, you know.

If a farmer still needed extra labour after he had used all the extra hands available
locally, he turned to itinerants and strangers. Tramps, known as Wold Rangers,
were frequently to be seen and most East Riding farms treated them with humanity
whether they needed their labour or not. Mr Baines recalled that when he was a
foreman:

You'd get tramps come and ask you, ask the boss, like, you know, if they
could find a bit o' work and sleep in t'barn or sleep in t'cowhouse or
anywhere, you know. You used to give 'em a bit of food and then they used
to work on t'land and then he'd buzz off to another farm. . . . A lot of tramps
used to knock about and they used to go into Lincolnshire for the first
harvesting and then they'd come round into [the East Riding] and they'd go
and live in lodging houses then because they were getting so much a day;

twelve shillings a day [in the 1930s] like, you know; or first of all they'd
maybe get six bob a day for threshing, well, you see, they could afford to go
into a lodging house then . . . and gangs of men used to go from them
lodging houses potato picking, and take all t'potato picking on one particular
farm. And same wi' t'sugar beet lifting . . . and turnip pulling and mangel
pulling and – oh, they'd all sorts o' jobs, you know.

At slack times their visits were little more than begging trips, though some had
skills of sorts. Mr Playforth said, 'A sieve-mender come round. Called – they used
to call him 'Sievey' and he used to put bottoms in sieves. . . . I think it was
ash-roots or something he used for the job'. Others brought something to 'sell', like
bootlaces, and these men could not afford to use lodging houses. Mr and Mrs Rispin
often had to deal with them in their time as hinds:

> Mr R: Once when I was at Middledale, when we knocked off at night at eight
> o'clock there was six on 'em sat up [on the wall] that wanted a job. Aye. We
> used to give them a drink o'tea and —
>   Mrs R: A bit o'summat – cheese.
>   Mr R: Let 'em sleep there in t'granary. Always used to lock 'em up,
> though. . . .
>   Mrs R: See that they hadn't any matches.
>   Mr R: Used to get in a bag [corn sack], pull a bag over theirselves and that's
> how they used to sleep. Aye. . . . By gum, there used to be a lot o' them, you
> know.

The Wolds seem to have been an area particularly suited to this style of life,
perhaps because farmers needed help so often, and it had a high population of
localized tramps, particularly before the First World War. Some worked well when
they had a job, while others were less reliable.[13] Mr Rispin said, remembering
harvest, 'They would come and see if they could get a job, like. Well some was all
right and another would only stop a couple o' days while he got a bob or two and
then he was missing.'
   The final class of seasonal workers was much more reliable. These were the
Irishmen, who are affectionately remembered both as hard workers and as people.
In 1904, 16,466 of them came to the mainland in search of wages they could never
earn at home. Connaught was the home of 77 per cent of all Irish migratory
labourers and 70 per cent of the Connaught men came from the single county of
Mayo. Munster and Leinster contributed only a few hundred men each and the
majority of the remainder travelled from Ulster to work in Scotland, whereas the
Connaught men made for England. Their numbers were diminishing before 1914 as
mechanization and the shrinking area under corn lessened the need for them, but for
many of them it was the money earned in two or three months in Britain that paid
the rent on their own farms in Ireland. With the trouble in Ireland during the First
World War, security restrictions were placed on travel to and from Ireland, which
more or less finished the practice for the duration of the war. When it resumed it was
on a reduced scale. The depression that followed brought high unemployment so

very few outsiders were needed, and this put an end to these traditional, massive, temporary migrations.[14]

In the East Riding, Irishmen were mainly taken on for the corn harvest. Mr Fisher said:

> They used to . . . come across in big gangs and sort of split theirselves up. One farmer might want two, another might want four, or half a dozen or such as that, you see. But . . . you couldn't get one. If you had one there had to be another one not far off and they used to lodge together, as you might say.
> *Whereabouts did they live? Did people put them up in their houses?*
> No, they would take 'em into their houses for their food but they had to sleep, say, rough – granaries or anywhere like that, you see.

There were some who came for longer: Mr Masterman worked on one farm where a gang of twenty-six was taken on for muck-spreading and harvest. Some Irishmen were paid by straightforward piece-work, receiving their money as they earned it, while others preferred to contract for a lump sum, a system described by Mr Walker: 'At harvest, . . . they used to have so much for t'month, if they got it in under t'month they'd just get their pay just t'same, do you see. If it went over, well, it was just over bad - they had to just stick it.' As hinds the Rispins looked after Irishmen for several years and they discussed their experiences with Mr Playforth:

> Mr R: We always had four Irishmen for harvest. . . . There would be twelve on us at one table and t'old Irishmen at another, like. Both had same food, like. . . . We had t'same Irishmen every year and they were very nice fellers.
> Mr P: Ands if they had a good spot they used to be enquiring about coming back again next year. . . .
> Mrs R: There was uncles and cousins and – you know, they were all sort of related. They were grand chaps, though . . . Never had no bother with them or owt, like. They weren't men that, you know, went boozing about . . . . They'd get dressed and go down the village.
> Mr R: They paid us for their grub theirselves. . . . Master was supposed to pay for it really but they always used pay me.

Though their naivety made them the butt of many jokes, some planned and some accidental, there was apparently no racial tension. Wages in Ireland were so low that some men never went home, but took to an itinerant life following work around the country, as Mr Johnson explained:

> When we were at Weaverthorpe, we only had one and he came, oh, quite a lot of years, and in winter he never went back to Ireland. A lot of them didn't. . . . They used to catch hay harvest up . . . at Skipton and up round there, and Bolton Abbey and up there, and come round and catch that corn harvest [in the East Riding] and then, you know, they would go on to these navvying jobs, digging – them jobs. A lot of time maybe they were out of work.

The labour force of a large East Riding farm was thus by no means a unified group of regular workmen differentiated by skill and status. On a farm which kept plenty of cattle, sheep, and light horses, the foreman, the beastman, the shepherd, and the groom were all responsible to the farmer for one sector of the farm's operations. To the extent that none of them gave orders to the others, they were equals, but the foreman was certainly the first among them. East Riding farms were arable farms above all else and his department was so large that it was sub-divided between horselads and labourers. Moreover, a hind had responsibility for boarding all the single lads as well, often including some who worked in other departments. The system was a functional one, in that it was designed to get the farm work done, but as it relied on a fundamental division between single and married workers, and as the single workers lived on the farms rather than at home, it was far more than just a way of organizing farmworkers. Many characteristic aspects of East Riding rural society stem from making the youths of the county into a separate group, undertaking distinctive work that gave them a clear group identity.

Notes to Chapter Two

1. *Wages and Conditions*, II, p. 383.
2. *Agricultural Labourers*, p. 51, gives details of one 937 acre farm employing 6 servants to 3 labourers, with other staff. A detailed discussion of the comparative balance in 1851 as shown by the census is given in J. Sheppard, 'The East Yorkshire Agricultural Labour Force in the Mid-Nineteenth Century', *Ag. Hist. Rev.*, 9 (1961), 43–54.
3. See N. Goddard, 'Agricultural Societies' in G.E. Mingay, ed., *The Victorian Countryside* (1981), I, 245–59, especially p. 252. W. Bedell, *An Account of Hornsea in Holderness in the East Riding of Yorkshire* (1848), p. 132 states that at that time none of the farmers in Hornsea parish were members of any society.
4. See, for instance, *Agricultural Labourers*, p. 9.
5. *Census, Yorkshire, 1921*, p. 177 shows that only 18.8% of males married before the age of 25 in the East Riding. By the age of 30, however, over half were married, rising to 82% by the age of 40. Females married younger, but only 2.4% did so before reaching 20. By the age of 25, 31% had married, and 62.5% by the age of 30.
6. G.E. Evans, *The Horse in the Furrow* (1967).
7. See H.L. Day, *Horses on the Farm* (Beverley, 1981), pp. 12–13.
8. *Yorks. Her.*, supplement, 12 Nov. 1910.
9. H. Reffold, *Pie for Breakfast* (Beverley, 1984), p. 23.
10. *Yorks. Post*, 11 Nov. 1890, p. 5; 13 Nov. 1900, p. 8; 12 Nov. 1901, p. 10; 27 Nov. 1906, p. 12; and 29 Nov. 1910, p. 12.
11. See F. Kitchen, *Brother to the Ox* (1942), p. 144–5.
12. William Blades, born 1839, whose biography formed the basis of M.C.F. Morris, *The British Workman Past and Present* (Oxford, 1928), was just such a man.
13. A. Antrim, *The Wold Rangers* (Driffield, 1981), is a discursive but full account of the lifestyle of these tramps, written from personal knowledge and decades of observation. See also Reffold, *Pie for Breakfast*, pp. 39, 60–1 and 100.
14. *Second Report*, pp. 138–9, and *General Report*, p. 382.

Chapter Three

The Yearly Bond

Farm servants were set apart from other workers because they had definite contracts that ran for a specified period of time, normally a year or half a year, according to local custom. They were legally enforceable and neither the farmer nor the servant could terminate them unless they could prove breach of contract. In each area of the country where servants were hired, all contracts expired and were renewed together, only excepting those for small, specialist groups like stewards and shepherds, whose work required distinctive arrangements. The actual term dates varied widely from one place to another[1] but East Riding contracts ran from one Old Martinmas Day (23 November) to the next. Anyone who was hired later than usual was only hired to the next term date, not for a full year. At the term dates the servants and farmers congregated in the market towns for special hiring fairs. Bargains were sealed by the employer giving money to the hireling as a token, called the fastening-penny or fest, though much more than a penny was given. Thereafter both sides were committed. As Mr Johnson said: 'If you left during the year, well it was up to your employer whether he paid you any money or he didn't. And he couldn't get out of it because it was a contract.'

Although servants had more or less disappeared from southern England by 1900, the system remained strong throughout the north, Scotland and Wales, as Map 1c shows. Farm servants in these areas were by no means all the same, but the nature of their contracts was a common factor everywhere. Northumbrian farm servants, for instance, could be married or single, and the single ones were hired by the half year. Few farm servants lived in the farmhouses and an outside observer might see little in common with the East Riding system, but the nature of the bond all farm servants worked under led to many similarities in their lives. Most contracts of employment continued as long as both employer and employee wished them to and either party could end them by giving the agreed notice, which was commonly a day, a week, or a month. No amount of notice could break a farm servant's contract and in fact, the only legal way out of the contract was to enter into another that overrode it – by joining the army and accepting the King's Shilling, the military equivalent of the fastening penny.[2] Moreover, as Mr Johnson said, the law said that a person who was hired had undertaken to complete their contract before any payment was due.

All an East Riding lad was entitled to during his year's service was his board and lodging. On completion of the year, the master became due to pay him the entire sum agreed. If either side tried to withdraw before the year was over, magistrates or judges had special powers to enforce the contract, or to award damages for breach of contract, either in a police court or a county court, depending on the amount of wages involved. The legal process was swift, with low costs, and bore little resemblance to conventional breach of contract cases. Wages could only be claimed before the year was over if a breach of contract by the farmer could be proved, though the farmer could not recover his spending on board and lodging in any circumstances. The formalities were clearly stated in something of a test case heard in 1900 at Scarborough County Court:

> A very important decision to the whole agricultural community was given by his Honour Judge Raikes. . . . as to whether their contracts for a year could be avoided either by the farmer or by the servant on giving a month's notice, or some reasonable notice, . . . in . . . an action brought by Coultas Vasey, of Sawdon, farm servant, against John George Monkman, of Brompton, farmer, to recover a sum of £13 6s 8d, wages from 9th January to 18th August last as wagoner. . . . On the 5th January plaintiff was hired by defendant as a wagoner at the wage of £20 from that time up to Martinmas. Some little differences arose, and about June plaintiff decided to leave and asked for his wages. The master declined to pay and informed him that he must complete his contract up to Martinmas. Ultimately the master did offer, if plaintiff would sacrifice £2 as compensation for harvest, he would let him go and pay his wage [to date]. The plaintiff declined, and finally on the 18th of July gave a written notice that he would leave at the expiration of one month. On the 18th August he did leave, and claimed £13 6s 8d. . . .
>
> Mr Hugh W. Pearson, for the defendant, submitted . . . that to entitle the servant to be paid any wage at all he must complete his contract, and that if before that time he was either dismissed for any valid or proper reason, such as misconduct, or if he broke his contract by leaving he forfeited any wage he might have accrued up to the time of such breach of contract. He quoted cases in support of this, and contended that the rule was founded both in reason and in custom, and was incidental to the special nature of agriculture, which varied at every season of the year, so that in winter a servant might be earning little or nothing and have to be kept, whilst at seed time and harvest his services were not only of great value, but that if he was not then ready to carry out his contract incalculable injury might be done to the farmer.
>
> His Honour, in giving judgement, pointed out . . . that as the servant had not established any justification for his breach of contract it [the contract] was one and indivisible; that no wage was earned until the contract was completed at Martinmas and that therefore he must give a verdict for the defendant, which he did. At the same time His Honour thought the result was unsatisfactory and that these contracts binding a servant to the soil for twelve months were antiquated . . . but so long as masters and servants chose to enter into them they must be bound by them, and therefore the defendant was under no legal liability to pay the plaintiff anything, and he was bound to decide accordingly.[3]

Farmer Monkman had no case to answer in law and this is simply a statement of the standard justification of the indivisibility of a yearly hire. The judge had no option but to concur for Coultas Vasey had made no effort to justify his actions within the terms of the yearly bond. No farm servant in the East Riding was paid by the hour, the week, or the piece. His yearly pay was understood to cover the different workloads of the different seasons and the occasional jobs that needed doing over and above normal work, so the lads received no overtime, no piecework, no extra money in harvest, no extra payments as of right by way of customary tips and, conversely, no less money in winter.

Table 2 illustrates the practical differences that arose between the ways in which horsemen were paid in the East Riding, where they were all servants, and in counties further south. The Suffolk horseman's pay is a real case, though the valuations of the allowances in kind are those of the farmer. It is worth noting that the Suffolk horseman lost pay due to bad weather and that the irregularity of his payments meant that the farmer was usually holding back some of the wages he would have been paid had his earnings been averaged out. Of his cash wages 21 per cent came from special payments. Moreover, the tied cottage and the need to harvest his potatoes and garden produce had the effect of tying him to his employer. For the East Riding waggoner, it was generally accepted that a waggoner's wage was divided equally between cash and his keep. The wage is a typical one taken from newspaper reports in 1900, and the fastening penny is at a level described in the oral evidence.

In return for his pay and his keep, the horselad placed himself at the farmer's disposal, working as required for a whole year, within bounds set by reason and customary practice. He rose at four o'clock in summer and an hour or so later in mid-winter, and he did not finish with the horses until half-past six in summer and eight o'clock in winter. He was available for work whenever an emergency arose or pressing circumstances demanded a change in normal work patterns. This, indeed, is the origin of the term farm servant for it denoted a relationship with an employer which was much closer and more onerous than that of the labourer, resembling a family relationship more than a purely economic one, especially as the traditional yearly bond genuinely made demands on the farmer as well as the servant. The farm servants of the East Riding derived benefits from their contracts that labourers outside the northern counties would not have dreamed of.

The advantage that most struck outside commentators was that if the servant's wage never rose to compensate for long hours or especially hard work, neither did it fall when there was little to do. All through the winter, the southern labourer was in constant danger of being laid off by bad weather or simple lack of work, and of seeing his wages cut, possibly to nothing. Without a reliable income, families inevitably got into debt. The East Riding farmer, on the other hand, had bought in advance a whole year of his farm servants' time. If the work was heavy, the farmer gained, but if it was light he lost and he had to accept it. Legally, this applied only to servants, strictly speaking, but East Riding farmers applied much the same principle to their married employees as well and never laid them off. The complaints of the East Riding labourers were rather that the farmers expected constant work from them. If outside work became impossible, they were given maintenance and indoor

Table 2. Descriptive model: the composition of the earnings of horsemen in Suffolk and the East Riding.

	ITEMS			TOTALS		
	£	s	d	£	s	d
SUFFOLK HORSEMAN, 1903						
Basic wages @ 13s per week	31	4				
Harvest wages	7	17	6			
Michaelmas money		10	6			
Journey money		13	6			
Other cash allowances		5	6			
Total cash payments	40	11		40	11	
Fuel	1	2	6			
Potatoes and potato ground		6				
Food and Drink		7	6			
House and Garden	4					
Total allowances	5	16		5	16	
Total earnings				46	7	
EAST RIDING WAGGONER, 1900						
Yearly wage	25					
Fastening Penny		5				
Total Cash Payments	25	5		25	5	
Board and Lodging	25			25		
Total Earnings				50	5	

Source: Suffolk figures, *Wages and Earnings*, p. 41. The East Riding figures are a typical wage as described in the text. The figures from *Wages and Earnings*, p. 40, are not used as they are based on a weekly wage.

jobs whose only justification seemed to be to keep them occupied. Farm servants' wages were likewise unaffected by minor illness,[4] which most people agreed was rare among farm servants anyway. Mr Masterman recalled:

> They would look after you if you was ill. I had a bad cold first year I was away from home – a bad cold, and foreman's wife sent me to bed after tea and she brought me about a pint and a half of boiled beer. Gor blimey, wasn't it – it was horrible! And scalding hot! 'Here,' she said, 'Get this down you,' and stood there till I did and all. By, didn't I sweat? But, by, wasn't it horrible stuff to drink? Boiled beer. It cured me. I didn't half sweat once I got that down me. Oh, they would look after you if you was ill, but you mustn't swing the lead on 'em. Or else you – one farmer, he had a lad and he stopped in bed one morning, he said he was badly. Well, the farmer went up to see him, he knew he wasn't. It was cold, frosty – he knew he wasn't ill, so he said, 'All right, lad,' he said, 'stop here . . . , I'll bring you some medicine.' He took him a whole packet of epsom salts. He says, 'All right, lad, you'll soon be up.' The poor lad was up and all. He daren't go back to bed! He cured him. He was up at work the next morning.
>
> *It didn't affect your pay if you were ill, did it?*
>
> No. Oh no. Gor blimey, I only had nine quid the first year I was hired. Stopped any o'that, I shouldn't have had much left'.[5]

Yet, unless you were a farm servant, it did not matter how little the wage was and how little would be left: sickness meant the end of wages. If help was given it was as charity. It was only farm servants who could say, as Mr Milner did, 'Your wages never stopped.' Indeed, the northern farm servant generally worried about the difficulty of leaving a job he did not like rather than manifesting the more usual attitude, for a working man, of a fear of being sacked. Mr Fisher commented that even if you did wish to leave, 'You had to do summat daft, or summat like that. As long as you did somewhere near a day's work, as you might say, no, you couldn't get away'. Only one person that I met had succeeded in resigning without losing his pay, and his experience confirms rather than contradicts Mr Fisher. Mr Tate told Mr Playforth, another ex-horselad, and myself how he had been annoyed by the length of time he was expected to spend on his horses on one farm, which culminated in a row with the farmer, whereupon he decided to leave:

> I gets my break'ast and goes round the missus, t'old lady . . . and I says, 'Is master up?'
>
> She says, 'No.'
>
> I says, 'Where is he, . . . where's master?'
>
> 'Oh, he's in bed.'
>
> I says, 'Will you try and knock him up?'
>
> 'What for?'
>
> I says, 'I want my money.'
>
> Well, they wouldn't knock him up for that so I sat up [waiting for] him while eight and he never come, so Frank [the foreman] come and said would I

go to Harpham Gate House with four horses while dinner time. I said, 'Yes.'
Damn, when I come home, he'd gone out at ten to twelve! Then he went to a
funeral . . . and he wasn't in at tea-time so I waited on him. I knew where he
was, like, he was courting [a lady from the village] . . . and I waited and I
waited and he come. I stops him and I asks him for it and he was preaching
away, and I was swearing at him. By God, I thought he was off to hit me
with the stick, though!

And, however, I used to send for him across, two or three times a week, to
stables of a night. He daren't but come 'cause he didn't know whether there
was horse badly, you know . . . and as soon as he got his head through [the
door] I used to say, 'Have you brought my money?'

'If I'd known, I wouldn't ha' blooming well come!'

Mr. P: And you didn't get it?

Mr. T: Didn't get it for a month.

A farmer could not only withhold the wages of a lad who left, but he could sue him
for damages as long as he did so before the contract expired. The amount claimed
was usually a conventional figure and no attempt was made to calculate the real
financial loss to the farmer. Thus, farmer Hood of Ryton sued Matthew Fenwick of
Kingthorpe whom he had hired at Malton, but who had not arrived for work, on
the grounds that 'the ploughing had not got done and the horses were standing idle'.
Hood claimed £3 in compensation and got £2 10s, a high sum in 1910 when the best
men's wages were only £22 per year. A month later another farmer won £2 from
each of two ex-employees, 'defendants having left the horses idle, and having to
give more money for other men'.[6] Mr Jarvis was once threatened with a prosecution
which showed how far 'leaving the horses idle' had become a stock complaint that
often bore no relation to any real harm done to the farmer:

I saw the old boss off to Scarborough and he went to t'market. Thinks I, 'Yes,
you're going to market, going to t'train, and as soon as I see you well away
I'm going for my few things and then I'm going back home. . . . So I went
upstairs and I packed my few things. Off I went. I said to t'porter
at . . . Bridlington station, I said, 'What's the next train back to Malton?' He
said so-and-so . . . , 'Are you going to a job?' Well, I didn't know what to
say. I said 'Aye.' I was telling lies. Thinks I, 'I won't say . . . [that] I'm
leaving this [one].' I said, 'Aye.'

So I went to Malton. I had to walk from Malton, it was four or five miles
home. My dad said, 'What are you home for?' I said, 'Well, I've chucked yon
job, its flooded wi' water! I can't stand yon,' I said, 'you want to be a duck
breeder to be [a farmer there. Water] was all over, right up to back
door. . . .' And of course there was no wellingtons at that time o' day, you
know.

Did the farmer try and get you back?

He tried, aye – and he summonsed me for t'horses standing doing nothing.
Well I wasn't doing nothing with the horses. He says it was a breach of
contract, so my dad says, 'Oh, I'll settle it with him,' he says, 'You didn't

touch the horses, did you?' I said, 'I went to help among the beasts, I had nothing to do with the horses,' I says, 'the horses could stop there for a blue month for anything I cared, I was nothing to do with t'horses. But, anyroad, he was summonsing me for t'horses standing idle.'

If a lad left a job because he was homesick, or disliked his companions, or for any other such reason, he had no defence if the farmer sued him, for the farmer had not broken his side of the bargain. Such cases were nearly always settled out of court. Mr Rispin remembered when his brother George ran away for the second time:

He went to Holtby's of Rudston for waggoner. He stopped there a week, then he cleared off from there, like. Well, he'd worked a week for nowt, however Holtby come over to see him: if he didn't go back he would summons him. But if he would give [Holtby] two pound he would let him off. Our George: 'Oh aye, that's better than paying three' [the damages the court might well award] – he come to our house, like, goes to get his two pound, like, to bring him. 'No', [Mr Holtby] says – he made him walk, he made him take it to Rudston, by – we did laugh. It were a dear joke. Aye, he had to give him two pounds.

Mr Brambles listed some of the many reasons lads felt made it worthwhile to sacrifice the money they had worked for:

You got to places where they had a different routine you couldn't fall in with, you see; you know, you maybe get some places where it didn't matter how wet or rough it was, you had to be outside, and then you got to another place where they let you be under shelter and all such as that, and then you got to a place where there wasn't very much food. And then a place where there weren't any good horses, like: I mean to say, they used to – a farm man, he took a pride in his horses and he liked good horses, and if they gave him some horses that weren't very good horses he'd perhaps run away for that reason. I've even known . . . men leave because t'farmer sold his horses.

Lads usually decided quickly whether they were going to stay and most runaways therefore left shortly after the start of the new year. Farmers generally let them go then, as Mr Baines explained:

Wasn't often as they did [take you to court] because I always said if you run away you were no good to t'boss and you were no good to yourself, were you? If you weren't suited and if the place didn't suit you neither, what the devil's good stopping – you'd be no use to nobody. You'd never be settled.

December was an extremely slack month on farms and a farmer rarely lost by replacing an unhappy lad with someone who fitted in better. Only those farmers who were awkward or who were inclined to stand on principle took runaways to court as a rule: in Mr Tate's words 'only them bad old devils'. George Rispin, forced to walk from Kilham to Rudston with his £2, could count himself unlucky, although in his case the threat of prosecution may have been an attempt to teach him a lesson since farmer Holtby, living near at hand, probably knew he had run away before.

A farmer with a vacancy to fill had his choice of those who had missed the hirings altogether, gone unhired, or were runaways. In some parts of the country special runaway hiring fairs were held three or four weeks after the main fairs for those who wished to change around, but in the East Riding they were long since defunct, if indeed they had ever been widespread. In 1900 only one seems to have been remembered: Hollym Fair, once held at Hedon in December.[7] The regular markets enabled lads to meet farmers perfectly well. However, it must never be forgotten that running away was never legally recognised and it remained a calculated risk for a lad. Boys, in particular, depended very heavily on parental support which was not always forthcoming. Some parents would go in person to see if the complaints about the offending farm were justified. Others went further: Mr. Brambles, for instance, told me, 'I had a week at one place . . . I packed up and got away one night, didn't say anything, but however, my father – he was a farm foreman, he says, 'Oh, go back,' he says, 'go back and do t'job properly, tell 'em you aren't stopping.'

Mr Ashby's father was a widower who returned to farm service himself when his son was first hired, giving up the family home. The lad's experience in his fourth year shows how vulnerable those were without parents to turn to. Mr Ashby had been hired onto a very bad farm, and when two other lads decided to leave he was quick to join them. They bundled up their possessions and set off for their homes in Walkington, but the only place Mr Ashby could think of where he could go was Beverley, where he and his father had lived. Next day he went for his box of clothes to a pub ostler in Hull, with whom he had left it till the farmer could collect it. When he got there, he learned the farm foreman had already been and had instructed the ostler to hold onto the box while he went in search of the other lads. Mr Ashby managed to retrieve his clothes but, very frightened by the pursuit and wishing to avoid the risk of a court appearance and the payment of damages, he decided to make for the West Riding. There he took a variety of jobs in factories as well as on farms before he dared to return, several years later.

Thus, while the first week or two of a hire were generally treated as a probationary period, such tolerance could not be relied upon. In any case, even the most liberal of farmers ended this period of grace after the first weeks, and on the lads' side, their willingness to avoid trouble by cutting their losses evaporated as the wages they could expect from another farmer diminished. Mr Baines confirmed that, 'If you run away after you'd been there eleven month, you wouldn't get the wage. That were true enough.' Only serious disputes or a total breakdown in relations between a farmer and servant would induce a lad to leave late in the year. It was then highly unlikely that he would be content to run away and do nothing to recover his wages. It was also likely that serious disputes arising late in the year would concern older lads whose duties were more clearly defined and who were less willing to be put upon, while they also had more to lose because of their higher wages. Coultas Vasey's case fully demonstrates this. He seriously inconvenienced his employer by leaving in August just as hay-making was running into harvest, when every hand was needed. Moreover, few lads were likely to be available to fill his place and if they were, questions were bound to be asked about why they were. On the other hand, Coultas Vasey had worked two thirds of his contract and he was due £13 6s 8d out of a total wage of £20 if he could prove his case. Neither side was likely to back down.

A judge did have the freedom to ignore claims for damages and act as an arbitrator if he felt it was right. He could enforce a contract, dissolve it completely, or rule against one party and award damages. Where, as in the majority of disputes, the contract was tacitly set aside without going to court this had no legal status, but if neither the farmer nor the servant wished to involve the court there was no-one to worry about the niceties of the law. Usually, therefore, the cases that did go before a magistrate or judge would end with decisions for one side or the other, but even then this might not represent an unreserved judgement in their favour. In November 1910, for instance, James Hall, a young farm servant, sued George Meadley, his employer for £4 6s 4d in wages due to him. Both of them came from Patrington. Hall claimed that

> he was engaged as horse-boy, and on Sunday, 21st of August, the defendant told him to fetch the cows, which he claimed was not his work. He went home on that day and on his return at 8.55 p.m., he found the door locked, and he went back home. He asked for his money up to the date of his departure.
>
> The defendant said that he never engaged the plaintiff as horse-boy, but to do everything except milk. He was disobedient. His honour reserved his decision until the hearing of the next case, which was a counter-claim in which Mr Meadley summonsed Hall for £5 5s 8d for loss of time through horses standing idle and leaving without notice. . . .
>
> The result was a verdict against the boy Hall, with costs on the claim, on the grounds of disobedience, while on the counter claim the verdict was in favour of Hall, with costs.[8]

The judge had clearly decided that both were to blame, at least in part, but it is worth noting that while the verdict was scrupulously neutral, its effects were not. Hall was attempting to recover his entire cash income since the previous November, while the farmer sought a sum that must have been relatively trifling to him. Since he kept Hall's wages he nearly covered his claim whereas Hall not only recovered none of his earnings, but he had to pay his costs. Moreover, it is hard to believe that the absence of one boy caused a loss worth a quarter as much again as his wages.

This helps to explain the reluctance of lads to take farmers to court, or to be taken themselves. They also faced the fact that judges and magistrates came overwhelmingly from the same ranks of society as the landlord and the farmer, if indeed they were not landlords and farmers themselves. Doubtless, few of them would side unquestioningly with any farmer against any servant, but most shared so many assumptions with the farmers that they were bound to feel a sympathy for his case that they could not feel for the servant. As most servants also entered unfamiliar territory once they went to court, and were lacking in any experience to guide them in how to put their case to the best effect, they preferred to handle their difficulties by either enduring them or running away.

It was particularly hard for a lad to prove his case because the agreement under dispute was both unwritten and founded in custom rather than legalities.[9] Lads and farmers trusted each other to honour the bargain and, as far as money went, masters always seem to have paid the agreed wage at the end of the year. Honesty aside, they had to hire new lads in the future and they could not risk gaining a reputation as a swindler. It may seem from the cases quoted in this chapter that many contracts ended with a quarrel but this was definitely not so. They are quoted because it was only when the contract failed that its true nature could be seen, for otherwise it functioned so smoothly that no traces were left behind. This can be compared to the tests to destruction run by scientists to ascertain the strength of materials which inevitably result in the failure of whatever is being tested. What is important is not the failure itself, but the information gained thereby that could not otherwise be gathered.

As the dispute between Hall and Meadley showed, differences could arise over the nature of duties that had been agreed and, without witnesses, such differences could not be objectively resolved. Even worse was the question of whether farmers had broken their contract by giving particular orders, or by the standard of board and lodging they supplied, or were alleged to have supplied. At Hedon, town officials must have preferred a written bargain for there was a long tradition there of attempts to persuade farmers to register their hirings at the town hall. Examples have been found dating back to 1663. In the early nineteenth century the following notice appeared for many years:

Forms of Agreement.
    For making valid hirings between Masters and Servants. May be signed and properly attested at the Town Clerk's Office in the Market Place.
    13th November, 1839.   By Order of the Mayor
                                                                              James Iveson
                                                                              Town Clerk.[10]

It is not known whether the practice outlived James Iveson or whether many people followed it, but it was legally superfluous and as it was, in practice, an inconvenience, there is no reason to suppose it was particularly attractive. Certainly it did not survive into the present century. Generally, the giving and taking of the fastening penny was accepted as sufficient security.

As a result when a dispute did come to court, the judge had no written documents to aid him in deciding who was in the wrong. He simply had to decide for himself if an order, which a farmer might deny giving, was reasonable or unreasonable, or if a lad's conduct was justified by the farmer's treatment of him. Moreover, the only help he could get in forming an opinion was to consult local witnesses about prevailing custom, and they were by no means certain to speak with one voice. The yearly bond did not really belong in the courts and it is unfortunate that only when cases were brought there was it defined with any precision. Of all the people I talked to, not one had ever been involved in a court case or told me of a relative or close friend who had. On the other hand, they all knew that hirings could end with summonses and that the legal framework of the yearly bond was not a dead letter.

It is also significant that the yearly bond was not couched in immutable terms but was open to change as long as it was generally agreed. The details were left to custom and if custom changed, so did the standards of conduct that were regarded as acceptable. The bond therefore kept in step with the times and never became anachronistic. This was why the terms of hirings varied so much in different parts of the country. If either farmers or farmworkers, as a group, had wished to withdraw from yearly hiring or to change its terms unilaterally, the courts' role would have been very different, and the trust which allowed everyone to rely on oral contracts would have vanished. In the south-west of England, where the farmers had an overwhelming advantage, such servants as were still hired signed closely defined written agreements that removed all protection from them and subordinated them entirely to the farmers. Courts were not neutral even in the East Riding, but they were not the policemen of an unwanted servitude. They enabled the farmworker to strike a better bargain than he could have without customary and institutional support for the view that he had rights.

The difference this made to the independence and self-respect of the northern farmworker as compared to his southern counterpart is clear in their different attitudes to leaving jobs. Many contemporary writers pointed out a seemingly paradoxical difference:

> The northern long-term men change their situations more frequently than those in the south; and it is certainly a fact that many southern labourers, although subject to a week's notice, remain in the service of the same farmer for the best part and sometimes for the whole of their lives.[11]

The southern labourer was tied to his job too loosely for his liking and clung to it like a limpet, while the northern farm servant who could only change once a year often made use of every such opportunity, as Mr Pridmore confirmed, 'Sometimes they'd ask you to stay on for another year, d'you see, if you would, but I didn't believe in staying two years at one place. I liked a change and I got from one place to another. . . . I changed every year in my farming days.'[12] Others were not quite so determinedly mobile,[13] but it was generally agreed that it was most exceptional to stay at one place longer than three years, no matter how good it was. An ambitious lad could justify the process as Mr Rispin and Mr Playforth did:

> Mr R: Always had chance to stop, Bernard, but my idea was you seed other people's way o' going on – different – didn't you?
> Mr P: Well, if you wanted a foreman's job then you wanted to know different ways of doing different things, didn't you?

However, while this was true enough, most lads just liked to move around, making use of the freest period of their lives. Some moved long distances each time and never stayed anywhere near home, while others changed jobs frequently but stayed on local farms. There was no need to go very far afield, hiring fairs made it easy to change jobs as farmers and farm servants from large areas congregated in the market towns to fill all the vacancies. If a lad wanted a move he did not have to visit distant villages, trudging from farm to farm looking for a job that might not exist. Each fair served a distinct district and as most lads only went to one or two local fairs they were not hired outside the districts they came from unless they wanted to be.

The conventional picture in literature of the rural labourer in the nineteenth century is that of Hodge, immovably fixed in a village where his family has lived for generations, to whom the county town was a distant place rarely, if ever, visited. The truth was not so simple anywhere,[14] but in the East Riding it was much more complex. Farm servants took as their home territory a substantial area such as the north Wolds or south Holderness, and they were completely at home anywhere within it. Beyond, in contrast, lay districts they usually knew little of and cared equally little for. Movement between the Wolds and the lowlands, with their different ways, was particularly restricted. As a young lad Mr Masterman moved from Thorngumbald, near Hedon, to Cottam on the high Wolds, and he recalled:

The reason I got there was that the man where my father worked, at Camerton Hall, bought Cottam. Well I went with him . . . and I didn't like it. I didn't like that land at all. Because on those hills it's flint a lot of it, you know, and . . . I'd been used to ploughing six inches deep here and you could plough here and all your furrow turned over in one piece. You could very nearly get hold of one end and drag it out of the field if you'd been strong enough. But on the Wolds you could only plough about two inches. And when you'd finished it didn't look as if you'd been ploughing. . . . And they all used to follow one another there. They used to call it *fox hunting*. There was ten, twelve of us – twelve ploughing, all in front of one another. Well down here, we all had a plot to ourselves. You didn't follow one another. And you knew which part of the field each man had ploughed and if it wasn't ploughed, well, the farmer knew who'd done it. If it wasn't ploughed very well. But on the Wolds nobody knew who'd done what.
Did many people go from one area to the other or did they all tend to stick where they were?
. . . Oh no. No. It wasn't oft, wasn't oft you found a man off the Wolds come down here. No. Not come down onto strong land.

The feeling was fully reciprocated. Mr Jarvis, who grew up on the Wolds, near Birdsall, took a job on the low lying lands between Bridlingon and Filey, and disliked it so much that he ran away, as we have already seen. His impressions of the place were unreservedly gloomy: '"The blinking place is flooded wi' water!" . . . I said, "he wants . . . ducks to pull his ploughs out there, not horses!"' A lad who grew up on the boundary between two farming areas might be more adaptable, but such lads were exceptions. When Mr Rispin and Mr Playforth talked of seeing different ways, they were talking entirely within the context of Wolds farming. Homesickness

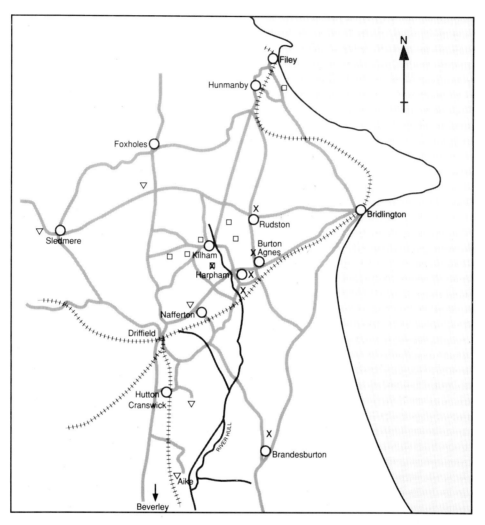

Scale - 1 : 250,000 (4 miles to 1 inch)

Key

The symbols represent farms where Messrs Johnson, Rispin, and Tate were hired

▽   Mr Johnson was born in Hutton Cranswick and was hired first in 1906. He completed eight yearly contracts and was in his ninth when he left farming to join up in 1916

□   Mr Rispin was born in Kilham and he was first hired in 1910, continuing in service until he married in 1923.

X   Mr Tate was born in Kilham and he was first hired in 1918. Only seven years of his career are known.

〰   Selected roads

╫╫╫╫   Railways

Map 3. The mobility of East Riding farm servants

42

serious enough to lead to running away was far more likely if a lad strayed outside the area he was used to, with its familiar farming, landmarks and people.

When Mr Easterby was a young man he knew a lad who grew up near Beverley and who never seemed to be able to settle. One year he got himself hired onto a farm at Fimber, on the Wolds. On the first day he was there they rose in the dark, it being December, and dawn only arrived when they were in the fields. He was unhappy as they set out and as they began ploughing he thought of home and of its greatest landmark, Beverley Minster. As the light grew he wondered if he would be able to see the Minster's twin towers, but it was much too far away. At dinner time he hardly ate and by bedtime he felt quite ill, so that night he walked all the way back to Beverley, a distance of some fifteen or sixteen miles.

Map 3 shows the careers of three farm servants, of whom Mr Johnson was the most adventurous. He was hired for his first year at Cranswick Common Farm only a mile or so from Hutton Cranswick, his home, but once he left there he was never hired anywhere near home again. In due course he became a hind on the Wolds, first at Langtoft, then at Weaverthorpe, and he finally took a farm of his own at Fridaythorpe. Mr Rispin and Mr Tate were more fond of their native patch, Kilham. Mr Rispin spent one year at Hunmanby, which he did not enjoy, and apart from that worked entirely in Kilham. Yet for all that he moved around a lot, by choice, and worked on more farms than Mr Johnson. He became a hind in Kilham. Mr Tate also made one foray away from the Kilham area, in his case to Brandesburton Moor. The rest of his time was spent in the four neighbouring parishes of Kilham, Harpham, Burton Agnes and Rudston. All these hirings came within the Driffield hiring area for although Hunmanby did have a small fair of its own, many of its farmers went to Driffield for lads.

Such willingness to move about and change jobs is conclusive proof that, in the East Riding, the yearly bond preserved the servants' independence rather than reducing it.[15] Lads left jobs freely at the end of a term because they knew that they could find others and that no stigma was attached to changing jobs frequently. It was accepted that lads moved when they wanted a better job, or even when they wanted a change of scene. This is not to say that the yearly bond was the best possible way of organizing employment on all farms, let alone elsewhere. It is simply that in the East Riding of that era it was a traditional system which had evolved with the county's rural society and within which it was still fulfilling a real function. In some other counties it had evolved differently, from a common origin, but with equal success. In others again, it had become an anachronism and died out, or had been abused to bind the servant with its repressive elements while removing all its protection. This is a salutory reminder that elements of social structures must be studied in their context if valid conclusions are to be reached.

Notes to Chapter Three

1. T.E. Lones, ed., *British Calendar Customs*, 3 vols (1936–40), cites a wide variety of dates for hiring fairs around the country, such as 5 Jan. at Berwick, II, p. 78; 14 Feb. – Old Candlemas – at Dorchester, II, p. 156; 25 March – Lady Day – at Okehampton, II, pp. 167–8; 14 May at Abergavenny, II, p. 252; 28 Sept. – Michaelmas – at Gloucester, III, pp. 87–9; 12 Oct. at Stratford on Avon, III, pp. 98–9.
2. Harry Reffold recalled that contracts could be varied if an employer changed farms, which would occur normally at Lady Day, the 25th of March. His servants would have the choice of going with him or remaining. *Pie for Breakfast*, p. 40.
3. *Mal. Mess.*, 10 Nov. 1900, p. 3.
4. *Agricultural Labourers*, p. 51.
5. See Reffold, *Pie for Breakfast*, pp. 70–1.
6. *Mal. Mess.*, 24 Feb. 1900, p. 3, and 13 Jan. 1900, p. 3.
7. Fairfax-Blakeborough, *Yorkshire: East Riding* (1951), pp. 51–2.
8. *E. News*, 9 Nov. 1910, p. 6.
9. *General Report*, p. 383.
10. M. Craven, *A New and Complete History of the Borough of Hedon* (Driffield, 1972), p. 190. A modern equivalent was noted in the *Yorks. Her.*, 17 Nov. 1922, p. 8. Farmers were being encouraged then by the National Farmers' Union to use written contracts.
11. F.G. Heath, *British Rural Life and Labour* (1911), p. 13.
12. See Kitchen, *Brother*, pp. 144–5.
13. Two men were hired for their nineteenth consecutive year on one farm in 1910, *H. News*, 3 Dec. 1910, p. 12.
14. B.A. Holderness, 'Personal Mobility in some Rural Parishes of Yorkshire, 1777–1822', *Yorkshire Archaeological Journal* XLII (1967–70) 451–2. See, for instance, Flora Thompson, *Lark Rise to Candleford* (1939, Penguin 1978), pp. 33–4. K.D.M. Snell, *Annals of the Labouring Poor* (1985), pp. 5–9, discusses the whole issue in some detail.
15. R. Church, *History of the British Coal Industry* (1986), III, 218, holds that annual hiring in the early north eastern mining industry also encouraged mobility there.

1   Mr Masterman, whose reminiscences are used throughout this book, in his best clothes. He was then eighteen years old and had been hired on farms in south Holderness since 1909. This photograph was taken in 1914 when he joined the army. The backdrop is, of course, a studio set. Before the First World War, farm servants simply used clean, new work clothes for best since they could not afford others. Note particularly the leggings.

2 Mr S. Adams, as a farm servant at Newport in 1910, proudly showing off one of his horses. The animals were far more than a job to such lads, and photographers found it well worth visiting farms regularly to take such photographs.
All farm lads wore corduroy bell-bottom trousers at this time and the watch and chain, with decorative attachments, would have been one of their first purchases when they had some money to spare.

3 A young lad with his pair geared for ploughing at Manor Farm, Thixendale, on the Wolds. If any one activity predominated in a horselad's life, it was ploughing, especially for the middle ranks who were often called ploughlads. Because the fields were often distant and the implements difficult to move, ploughs, harrows and such like were often left in the field and this lad is ready to go out to start work. In the background can be seen an old labourer.

This photograph is one of a series taken on this farm, probably in the late 1890s, when it was farmed by Messrs Cook and Taylor. It may be that they were the work of the farmer himself, as they were taken over a period of several years.

4 and 5   Two lads at Manor Farm, Thixendale, out in the field with their teams hitched to their ploughs. The photograph clearly shows the distinctive dress of farmworkers before 1914, but also that there was plenty of room for individual variation. Thus, one lad wears a cap while the other has on a *raddy* or *raddy-doo* hat which could be pulled down over the ears in cold weather.

The chalky surface of the unploughed land suggests that this was a spring ploughing, probably following a turnip crop used to feed the sheep in winter. The thin, flinty soil was easy to work and did not retain a clear furrow pattern as heavier soils did. The plough in the second photograph appears to be a J.H.B. design, named after John Harvey Bell of West Lutton. It was a light, single-furrow plough, popular on this sort of wold land. (Taken late 1890s.)

6 The least lad (the youngest boy on the farm) in the stackyard at Manor Farm, Thixendale. His clothes are obviously hand-me-downs which would have to suffice until his wages were paid at the year-end, and perhaps even longer. His horse also has old harness on, and would itself be well past its prime. (Taken late 1890s.)

7 Labourers were sometimes asked to make up the numbers during ploughing, especially if a lad was sick. Unless this man was one of the rare older farm servants, that is the most likely explanation of this photograph from Manor Farm, Thixendale. (Taken late 1890s.)

8   Seven plough teams going out to work near Beverley, with the waggoner in the lead and everyone in their allotted place in the hierarchy. Note that everyone sits sideways, rather than astride, and that they are riding bareback. (Taken c. 1900)

9 Labourers chopping turnips for the sheep at Manor Farm, Thixendale, during the winter months. Turnips were placed in the hopper on top of the machine and cut into slices or fingers before falling into the box at the bottom. The shepherd, right, needed help at such times and then labourers joined in with him, or at other times the beastman. Up to five men might be employed in the sheepfold at peak times, whereas labourers and horselads worked together very infrequently. (Taken late 1890s.)

10 The same shepherd as seen in the previous photograph, but now in a more conventional scene with his dog and his flock of Leicester longwool cross-breed ewes and lambs. (Taken late 1890s.)

11 Frank Harben, the beastman, with a dairy shorthorn bull at Manor Farm, Thixendale. Manor Farm had a permanent herd of about a dozen cows at this time to provide milk, butter and cheese for the household and the lads. For a Wolds farm this was a high number since few cattle were kept other than bullocks bought in over winter to turn the straw into manure. The man in charge was then often called the bullocky, and he might have little to do with cows in the summer. (Taken late 1890s.)

Mr Harben was born in East Anglia in 1862 and moved up to Thixendale as a boy. He died in 1953.

12 The beastman lad who assisted Frank Harben. The bull, kept at a safe distance by the wooden staff, is the same animal as in the previous picture, although several years older. Behind them is the farmhouse of Manor Farm, Thixendale, the setting for many of these photographs. It is a typical post-enclosure, square-built house.

A beastman or bullocky lad would live in with the horse lads and would probably work as one of them when the bullocks were sold off after the winter. (Taken late 1890s.)

Chapter Four

The Horselads

While the labourers handled a wide variety of jobs and were usually regarded as a pool of workers to be organized according to the needs of the day, the horselads, in contrast, were on the farm specifically to feed and care for the horses, and to work them in the fields. Their lives were highly organized around this central task and they became a remarkably self-contained group. The foreman was responsible to the farmer for the horses, but he had plenty of other concerns and to an outsider it might seem that for long periods he had nothing to do with the horses. The senior horselad, the waggoner, supervised the normal work of his fellows, though a keen foreman would keep an active eye on the stables, especially if he mistrusted any of the lads, as Mr Baines recalled:

> You sometimes used to get your boss out on a morning looking at your horses as you all come by, and he'd bray something with his stick, you know – probably rattle it on some railings or beat it on a drum to make 'em jump and if one didn't jump, he wanted to know why. What were t'matter with it? And he'd come and ask t'waggoner, you see, then, 'What's the trouble? Has it eaten all right?'

Even the keen foremen had to keep their distance, however, if the lads were to be given the chance to do their jobs themselves and if the rest of the foreman's duties were to be attended to. Most were content to wait for trouble to arise without going looking for it, and if the farmer or foreman was taking an active part in the daily routine, it was usually a sign that the waggoner was not doing his job to their satisfaction.

In 1900, the horses worked from six till six when light permitted, and feeding began at 4.30–5.00 a.m. in summer to allow them to digest their food properly before work began. In winter the dark mornings delayed the start of work, so feeding commenced later as well, but this was more than compensated for by the need to give an extra feed, known as fothering up, at eight o'clock in the evening. This was never popular with the lads and it was widely abandoned in the inter-war period. In addition to being fed, they had to be groomed and mucked out, for they needed as much attention as other animals on top of the hours spent in the fields.

Even in an age of long working days, this was asking a lot of married men. Each region of the country had, as a result, devised ways of avoiding the need to make demands that would not be sustainable. This might be achieved by having specialist horsekeepers: in North Cumberland, for instance, one or two men looked after all the horses while others worked them. In East Suffolk the horseman had exclusive responsibility for all the horses at night and first thing in a morning, including giving the first feed, while others joined in to work them and feed and groom them in the evening.[1] In the East Riding the fact that the horselads all lived on the farm and had no family responsibilities made this unnecessary. That they were willing to accept the system, and with it a life with very little free time, was due to their youth and their lack of alternatives. It was seen as an inevitable phase in most people's lives, something everyone did for a while before moving on, rather than a personal choice or a lifelong commitment. This ensured that sufficient willing hands were available and the division of responsibility with the foreman meant they did not need to be fully skilled.

During their time as horselads they lived in a highly structured world that encouraged everyone to progress up an organizational ladder common to all farms as they grew up. The head lad was the waggoner (*wag* for short) as we have seen and in the Vale of York everyone's position was defined directly in relation to him: the next lad was the *second waggoner*, then came the *third waggoner* and so on. More commonly they were called the *second lad* and *third lad*, a terminology that can cause confusion when the rest of the county is examined, for there the next lad after the waggoner was the *third lad*, or *thirdy*, followed by *fourther, fiver etc.* They were never called *third* or *fourth waggoner* and there was no *seconder*. The apparent gap was explained by Mr Carter: 'No, there was no second. That waggoner was supposed to be t'second. There was, like, t'foreman, d'you see, and then, they called him "waggoner" . . . , t'second man. And then they went lower down as they went down you see.' This is the convention I have followed, except when talking specifically about the Vale of York.

All these lads looked after the team of horses that they worked, but variations were possible, as Mr Johnson explained,

> You were responsible for four horses generally. They varied. . . . We'll take a farm, say four hundred acres. There was waggoner. He had six horses, but he'd a young lad to help him. . . . Now then, there'd maybe be what they call a third lad that's next to the waggoner, he'll maybe have four horses [or] he might have six horses and a lad, . . . there can be the waggoner with six and a lad, there can be a third lad with four and there can be a fourth lad with four; or there can be a third lad with six and maybe what they call a box lad, just maybe have two. Different farms have different ways, you see.

These assistant lads were named after those they helped: they were the *waggoner lad* (or *wag lad*), *thirdy lad, fourthy lad*, etc. Not every farm employed such lads and many which did only had a wag lad. Below them again came the nondescripts, if any, like the box lad, who looked after spare horses, including the farmer's trap horse.

The number of lads in each section of the hierarchy was determined by the manner in which the horses were cared for and the farmer decided on the arrangements he wanted mainly on two counts. The more lads who had six horses and a young lad under them, the more young lads there would be in his workforce, and the more lads who looked after four on their own, the older the workers would be. However, depending on the operation being performed, the horse team varied from one solitary horse, say in a cart or a *scruffler*, up to six, in heavy harrows, for instance, on strong land. For most of the year the team was either two, three, or four horses and on average soils the basic plough team was two, though three were required in some places. The usual team for heavy work like drag harrows or taking a heavily laden waggon to the station was four. Everyone who was going to have to do the heavy work regularly, the senior lads and especially the waggoner, had to have four horses available for such duties.

Lads were very possessive about their particular horses and it was impossible for a lad to make regular use of one from someone else's team. On the other hand, two-horse work was much more common – the whole winter was spent in ploughing – so if everyone was simply given four horses, two in each set would be idle for that time. By giving the waggoner and some others six and a lad, the ratio of horses to men was cut from four to one, to three to one, and if the waggoner took four horses, his lad was still left with two. Many farms prided themselves on their ability to rest a proportion of their horses all year round and there had to be a certain number of spare horses as well since it was important to run as many ploughs as possible. If the foreman went to plough he would need a pair, usually from the waggoner's stable, and on some farms a labourer was brought in, as Mr Milner confirmed:

Why, yes, there was odd labourers: there was one at Wharram Percy. Make t'nine up. . . . When we had nine ploughs on at Wharram Percy we had [all the horses] out, you see. Of course, there was waggoner lad and thirdy lad, you see he made an extra one, why an extra two in t'stable, and then there was t'groom lad used to go with us and all.

On most farms, however, there were enough men for the ploughing not to involve the labourers at all. Mr Johnson has already stated that in his experience labourers were used only when a lad was ill, and on a large farm even this was insured against by the employment of a *Tommy Owt*. Mr Rispin explained his function:

We'll say a lad was badly what was doing horses, this Tommy Owt, as they called him, would have to step into his place, you see.
Was the Tommy Owt always a single lad?
Yes, that's right. He always *meated in*, do you see. And that's what them farmers had him for, if a lad was poorly, or owt, like. They'd say, 'you can —, you'll have to —'. They was engaged like that. If they had a lad off he had to step in and do his work, do you see.
What did he do when all the lads were all right?
Oh, he had to go to plough or owt, do you see. Sheepfold, owt you like to send him to. Say a labourer was poorly or owt, shepherd was poorly, well, he'd to go to t'sheepfold, like. That's what they called 'em *Tommy Owts* for.

As a servant, a Tommy Owt was a better substitute for a sick horselad than a labourer could be. On smaller farms it might be a labourer who was called Tommy Owt, but such men were not actually employed as stand-ins, as a servant was. They were merely given the title because they did not mind being a general reserve and they were not called on to look after horses, though they might drive them. When the labourers needed a horse in connection with their work, say to cart away the refuse from hedge-cutting, or if the beastman wanted one, they took any one that was available, though sometimes the beastman had his own. To many labourers, the occasional chance to work with a horse again must have been welcome, since most horselads were very fond of their teams and to be severed from them so totally was a wrench.

In most of the riding, a lad in charge of four horses saw to their every need. If he had six and a lad the duties were divided between them, as Mr Tate explained, 'He'd maybe have six horses to feed would this man, and t'lad would have four [of them] to brush, and four to clean out, and four to water.' However, in the Vale of York, Mr Baines said, 'The waggoner on a farm, as a rule, attended to all the horses, he fed them with hay and he didn't clean them out, but he cleaned the horses.' Mr Appleyard confirmed that the same system applied in the Vale in the North Riding, but said that twelve horses were all one man could feed. Thereafter, two men divided the feeding between them. Mr Lawler and Mr Friend elaborated on the system as they knew it:

> Mr L: It depends what you went at. If you went for a fourth lad you had four horses to do, if you went as a waggoner you just had a couple to do.
> Mr F: Different jobs, you see. Head horseman did all t'feeding and second lad gets fodder in and that, muck 'em out in a morning, and then you all had your own horses to brush and that, groom.
> *The waggoner fed them all, did he?*
> Mr F: Yes, aye, he did all t'feeding.
> *Did he just give the corn out to people or did he actually feed them?*
> Mr F: No, he put it in t'horse's manger.

Thus, practices did vary, for this contrasts with the waggoner grooming all the horses further south around Howden and Selby in Mr Baines's account. Under this arrangement, assistant lads were unnecessary, so everyone was allocated a team. It was in the Vale, as well, that the Tommy Owt was most commonly a labourer, and all this may be due to the generally smaller size of farms there. There were certainly more farms without foremen, and the enhanced importance of the waggoner in the Vale explains why the lads' positions were graded relative to him rather than the foreman. Mr Baines described his duties as waggoner on a thousand acre farm there as follows:

> You'd to get all the men up . . . on a morning, out o' bed, all the single men that were living in. You'd to see they were out and in the stable at five. And you had full control over all t'men, after foreman had give you your instructions on a morning. You see, you had to tell men what to do and where

to go. He used to say so-and-so wanted doing and so-and-so wanted doing, and then you used to see that them jobs was done and we had a ruling, when you went out on a morning and you got yoked in your plough you used to plough, unless something went wrong with it or your horses, you used to plough till dinner-time, till the last round and as soon as it was the last round before loosing out for dinner [the waggoner] used to stay at the far end of the field and soon as all the other men and lads saw you stood there they used to stand. . . .

We used to bridle out on a morning, we'll say in t'fields at seven, we used to bridle out on a morning at seven o'clock. When I used to go and touch my bridle and look at my watch all t'others used to do t'same – it was hung on the wall, you know, on a peg, and you used to get your bridle and go and bridle your horse out and I used to send my first – *string horse* . . . , used to come out of the stables first and stand outside and then I used to lead the other one out after it, then tie 'em together. Then I used to jump on their backs and every man was mounted then and used to all go to work, probably eight or nine pair of horses, or ten. . . .

Your seconder next year probably'd go on to a farm and be a waggoner if he were fully experienced on t'job and he could control men. See sometimes you'd twenty-four under you striking turnips out in a field, or mangels. And your waggoner were your first man there again.

Much of that description would apply to any waggoner, but the general impression is of a man who is more of a sub-foreman than a head lad, as he was elsewhere. When Mr Friend was talking of his time running a three hundred acre farm in the Vale at nineteen years old with ten men under him I asked him if he was the waggoner or the foreman and he replied that you could call him either as you wished: what mattered was that he was head horseman.

Elsewhere it mattered a great deal. On the Wolds the foreman usually issued the morning's orders to everyone and allocated the jobs for himself, not doing it through the waggoner. In the fields the waggoner kept order among the lads and ensured that everyone kept working at the tasks they had been set, but when I asked Mr Brambles if the waggoner could give orders to the labourers, he replied:

Oh no, no. They would soon have told you where to get off, I reckon. Foreman was the . . . , do you see, foreman was the man. And on a big farm or an estate they would have what they called a head labourer and he was head of them, but we didn't give any orders – in fact waggoner, if there was a foreman, waggoner hardly gave anybody any orders.

Yet the similarities between the two sets of men were more important by far than the differences. On nearly every farm in the riding the waggoner stood above the others, not just because he was the head lad, but also because he alone was expected to do various jobs that were either heavier or more skilled, or both, than those the rest had to do. Only on the largest farms did the third lad join in some or all of these jobs, and the very fact that he could join in meant that he was really skilled enough to be a waggoner in his own right on a smaller farm. The crucial job was corn carrying, taking it up to the granary on threshing days, and out again to go off the farm. The bags themselves weighed 5½ lbs, and full sacks of oats and barley averaged 16 stones, wheat 18 stones, and peas and beans 19 stones. Mr Carter recalled

> They were great big, strong men, you know. Waggoner-man . . . , he carried corn and next chap carried corn – t'waggoner and t'thirdy . . . and then t'others, some of them was forking off t'stack and some stacking straw and two least lads used to have to carry chaff from t'machine. That was their job. . . . And if they wanted another corn carrier and there wasn't one handy, 'course they had to fetch one from one o' t'other farms, because them two men just got that money for that job, you see. They couldn't put another man in because they wouldn't do it, because they wasn't paying them money to be a corn carrier.

Mr Baines also added that:

> Many a time you used to carry all that up into t'granary . . . and then it used to stop there probably a week until trucks come in at station before you could deliver it back. And then you'd all to carry down. We used to put three ton on a waggon and a pair of horses in a waggon and deliver it to station. It were all humping, you know, all hard work, all rough.

The granary might be sixty or seventy yards from the threshing machine, and was invariably on the first floor up a flight of steps. By contrast the coalman, the most obvious modern carrier of heavy sacks, delivers bags weighing 8 stones – less than half the weight of a wheat sack. There was skill involved as well as strength, but strength was vital and no-one under the age of eighteen could be expected to display it unless he was physically advanced beyond his years.[2] There were waggoners who were younger, but they were usually on small farms which employed only young lads and where, in practice, the farmer did the waggoner's job. In such cases the title was nominal. Fred Kitchen took such a position in the West Riding, where they were more common, before the First World War and later wrote:

> I decided to leave my very good place as horselad for the sake of becoming an inferior waggoner. Both the boss and the missus asked me to stay on and were surprised at my wanting to leave as most lads stayed with them until they grew too big to be lads any longer. . . .
>   Now, though I fancied myself a waggoner, I could neither 'stack, thack nor carry barley' – the qualifications always asked of a waggoner at the 'hirings' – but I had got the notion it was more creditable to be top boy in a second class than bottom boy in a first class, so when it came to corn sowing a man in the village was set on to do it.[3]

Of thirteen people who became waggoners, one was fourteen when he got the job, one was fifteen, one was seventeen, three were eighteen, two were nineteen, two were twenty and three were twenty-one. Of the last five, one considered himself be over the average age and one under. The fourteen and fifteen year olds were certainly not capable of a full waggoner's duties, and one of them was appointed during the dire labour shortage of the First World War. The wide range of ages confirms that what mattered most was a lad's build and ability, not his age. Mr Appleyard said that he became a waggoner 'when I was old enough,' which sums it up. Moreover, some were held back, like Mr Milner, by spending time among the sheep or cows while others were acquiring the necessary skills among the horses.

As Fred Kitchen remarked, besides carrying corn, a real waggoner had to be able to *stack* and *thack*, that is, make corn and hay stacks and then thatch them, and as Mr Baines said, he had to be able to control men, for if he could not keep them ploughing steadily all day long, his employer would regard him as a dead loss. Because he was the head horselad, he had the best horses and was expected to have the most skill, so he was responsible for all the more difficult jobs that the horses had to do. Accordingly, when they went to plough it was usually the waggoner who cut the first furrows that everyone else used as a guideline, unless the foreman wished to do the job himself. When drag harrows had to be used it was almost always the waggoner who used them because they were so heavy that they were potential horse killers.

Whenever a delivery had to be made off the farm or something had to be collected the waggoner always went. If only one waggon was needed he went alone. If more were needed he was accompanied, but he went as a matter of course, as his title suggests. Mr Fisher said, 'If, say we'd had a threshing day, had a good lot of corn, we'd maybe take that to the station and there would be perhaps three of you, but Hull [from Aldborough], that was just the waggoner's job. . . . [It] averaged about once a month. Maybe go twice in a week sometimes.' The same principle applied to any horse job: if only one team was needed, the waggoner had first refusal. In essence the position of the waggoner was one of an adult among youths and that of a man who was often, moreover, interested in getting on. Mr Rispin remembered:

'Course, you see in harvest, like, t'waggoner, he always had to stack on with t'foreman, like, him and foreman, they were making one apiece. You always had to stack, had t'waggoner on them big places, like. Well, I could do all them jobs, like. Where a lot of chaps my age, they'd never got no further than just following horses, they'd never stacked: why, they'd no interest in it, you know.

It would be wrong to draw a simple contrast between the skilled waggoner and the unskilled lads, for the variety of skills needed to see to horses and work them is considerable. The waggoner had to be an all-round man whereas, unless the third lad was a near-waggoner of the type already mentioned, the rest had not and they were differentiated primarily by age. An able lad or one bigger than his contemporaries could well advance beyond the position his years would suggest, while a weak or incompetent lad would drop as far behind. On some farms, for instance, Cowlam (the largest farm in the county at 1,200 acres), the hierarchy reached down to an *eighther* and there were assistant lads as well. The fourther who fed six horses with a lad to help him was likely to be older than the fourther who fed only four. However many horses they fed they all worked at the same jobs at the same pace in the fields. They could not be asked to carry corn and would not be asked to take on a difficult job while the waggoner led the rest in an easier one, though a thirdy seeking to become a waggoner would be on the look-out for any chance to learn and practice new skills. Where assistant lads were employed they were also expected to do exactly the same work in the fields as the others, despite their subordinate position in the stables.

Finally, we come to those single lads who had less precise jobs. The Tommy Owt could be the same age and receive the same wages as any lad up to the thirdy. There were also box lads who were given charge of spare horses, usually young ones, but where a horse was reserved for the exclusive use of the beastman, that would be given to the box lad to look after. If there was a pair left after everyone had taken four or six horses, a box lad would be engaged to tend them. Mr Fisher began as a box lad: 'I wasn't [a full horselad] when I first started. I had five colts to feed, morning and night. And then go with horses if they wanted me, at spare times.' He was most likely to be needed for ploughing, and when he went he also had to do as much as the others.

There were also grooms and groom lads. If the farmer kept bloodstock they had as little to do with the foreman as the shepherd and beastman had. Mr and Mrs Rispin remembered when they were hinds:

> Mrs R: And then you'd got two grooms. . . . One was a youngster.
> Mr R: Oh aye, we kept a lot of hunting horses. 'Course I had nowt to do with them.

On such a farm the groom might well be married and living in a cottage, but the groom lad was invariably a farm servant and went with the other lads to work as required. On most farms there was no bloodstock, but before the arrival of motor cars all farms kept trap horses and it was only after the Second World War that cars replaced the last of them. Then, Mr Johnson said, if there was no box lad, 'They used to have what they called a groom lad. Now that groom lad he had a – he had a lot of jobs. He could be a "back-door lad", he could get sticks into t'house, coals, and feed hens and look after t'pony, generally a young lad.' Whoever occupied the lowest position in the hierarchy, was also known as the 'least lad'. Mr Pridmore began in such a job with three horses:

> We had our own horses, you see – well really, what I had, being t'lad (I was the lad of the four), I used to look after the horse, the hackney horse the farmer used to use for his trap, I had that, and one of the other horses I had was a light legged 'un as well, which his wife used to drive in the trap when she wanted to go anywhere, so I had to have another one like, a spare horse then.

Giving clear definitions for every job title used on every farm is impossible, given the variation in duties that arose from the particular circumstances of individual farms. Foremen could be virtually farm managers or they could be superior workmen. An active foreman often reduced the status of the waggoner while a small farmer who did the heavy work himself had no need of a real waggoner at all. On the other hand, some waggoners had a lot of supervisory responsibility and on large farms the 'thirdy' functioned as a deputy waggoner. These were, however, only variations on a very consistent theme, and the ordinary ploughlad's duties were consistent from farm to farm. They had to feed, groom, and work the horses in the fields, handling the routine work rather than the exceptional jobs. Even here, however, the customs of the Vale of York introduce some variety. The lowest jobs were, as we have just seen, dictated really by the residual amount of work to be accomplished and whether extra hands in the stable were more useful than a general servant who would also help out in the fields when needed.

It is when they are taken as a group, which is the way they saw themselves and the way their society saw them, that the variations can be seen in their true perspective, for the group was a homogeneous one with a strong sense of identity. The constant exchange of lads brought about by yearly hiring helped to keep the underlying unity more important than any superficial tendency to specialization and then fragmentation. Lads moved often and if newcomers had to spend time learning the ropes on every new place, an awful lot of time would be wasted at the farmers' expense. Indeed, many farmers lost a majority of their servants every Martinmas, so it was to everyone's advantage that servants should be at home anywhere and, unless they crossed a regional boundary, they were.

Notes to Chapter Four

1. *Second Report*, pp. 48 and 59.
2. Harry Reffold always refused to carry corn because of the number of men he had seen who were physically deformed as a result of labouring in this way from an early age. Reffold, *Pie for Breakfast*, pp. 39 and 79.
3. Kitchen, *Brother*, pp. 138–44.

Chapter Five

The Hiring Fairs

The key to the success of the farm servant system was the ease with which lads changed jobs, and that was made possible by the hiring fairs. Because the yearly bond was established by act of Parliament, they were known as statute hiring fairs, often shortened to statutes, statties, stattuses, or hirings. They were also known as sittings from the times when the law required the chief constable of every division to sit at every fair to supervise the bargaining. In an age without advertisements, they brought together all the farmers and servants of a district and thereby encouraged the most efficient matching of the requirements of each and the maximum possible choice for both. Since all contracts expired on Old Martinmas Day, November 23rd, it would have been both foolish and wasteful of everyone's time and energy for servants to seek new jobs individually, or farmers new servants. It was a gathering for the sale of labour, just as sellers and buyers of all commodities had gathered together for time out of mind, and it was logical to use the market centres as venues.

Although the fairs were large gatherings, farmers attended them only to hire servants and no other business was done, unless they coincided with a regular market. In 1914 the fairs that served the East Riding were held at York, Selby, Howden, Market Weighton, Pocklington, Malton, Driffield, Beverley, Hull, Hedon, Patrington, Hornsea, Hunmanby, Bridlington, and Scarborough, and the building of the Boothferry Bridge in 1929 added Goole to the list. By 1914, however, Hornsea, Hunmanby, and Patrington were in deep decline, serving very limited groups in their immediate localities. In 1910 'A Line fra Patrington' appeared in the local newspaper in dialect:

> 'We've gitten aboot owered wiv Martemas, which ez bin varra quiet this year. We ad ower festing [hiring] day last Setherday, but neabody cam to toon; lads and lasses awl gan te' ull noo. Bud there war jest a few on 'em cam fer aud acquaintance sake. We'd a few stalls and striking [test-your-strength] machines.'[1]

Hedon was losing trade to Hull to a lesser extent, as was Howden, first to Selby and then to Goole. However, as long as the trade lost by one town went to another, the system as a whole was not harmed. Other fairs were now completely defunct, such as Brandesburton, which had been the principal hiring for north Holderness in the 1840s,[2] but this had not detracted from the general functioning of the system. By bringing more farmers and servants together in fewer centres, indeed, choice was increased and everyone was given the chance to make a better deal. Bicycles, trains and buses helped make the larger fairs more accessible, but everyone remained within walking distance of at least one fair and carrier carts served most, if not all, settlements.

People did like to move about and so even fairs outside the county had some significance. Easingwold, Pickering, Sheriff Hutton, Snaith and Wetherby, for example, all lay within thirteen miles and some more distant fairs seem to have served whole regions rather than a locality. Thirsk was one and Doncaster another, probably the largest. Fred Kitchen used it as a servant in 1910:

> It was the annual hiring or 'stattis' . . . for farm servants from South
> Yorkshire, North Notts, North Lincolnshire, and a small portion of Derby,
> and represented the biggest babel of dialects since the time of Noah. . . . You
> could pick out the Lincolnshire 'fenners' by their fancy for bright blue cords,
> set off with as many pearl buttons as could be conveniently carried on a pair of
> breeches and leggings. They were usually of heavier build than the 'woadies'
> (men from the Yorkshire and Lincolnshire Wolds), being of the broad, chubby
> kind, while the woadies were tall, raw-boned, and straight on the leg. The
> 'Yorkeys', too, often wore carters' smocks, with a whip hanging over their
> necks; so a farmer could guess pretty nearly what district a would-be hireling
> came from.[3]

Using local fairs was, however, the overwhelming rule because a lad was known there, he knew the farmers, and he knew the type of farm on which he would be employed. Even the more adventurous usually did not go too far from home, as Mr Carter, who regularly used Malton, recalled, 'There was a lot moved away. I've known 'em go to Driffield hirings and get engaged out that way. Just moving round a bit, you see.' The majority lived within ten or twelve miles of two or more hirings, and even if they only used one for business it was common practice to visit another for pleasure: to look up friends made on previous farms or relatives from another district, to mingle with the crowds and have a day out.

At nearly all hiring centres there were actually several fairs. Mr Johnson said:

> Hirings day was a fortnight before t'year was up. Now, you were entitled to
> that; to one – but say you went to Driffield hirings, you couldn't go to
> Malton, you couldn't go to Beverley. You just had one – you were entitled to
> that. You didn't ask for that – you went. . . . They called that first hirings.
> Now the second hirings was in the Martinmas week . . . you see, they weren't
> all on one day – say one town had it one day, another town had it another
> day, you see; but Driffield hirings, I think it was on the first Monday in the
> Martinmas week. That was what they called the second hirings. Now, then
> there was what they called Martinmas Thursday – Thursday was the market
> day at Driffield then and they called it Martinmas Thursday. That was the last
> hirings. Now at Beverley, Saturday was the market day and that was
> Martinmas Saturday.

Normally, the first hirings were preliminary sessions held before contracts expired, followed by an intense period of activity in Martinmas week itself. Beyond that it is hard to go on generalizing about the holding of fairs, for each town seems to have had some idiosyncracy, which prevents the drawing up of any rules applicable to all. Most towns had three hirings, as Mr Johnson said, but Hull had only one, Market Weighton had two, and Thirsk had four. Some towns held all their hirings in association with markets: Malton's hirings always fell on a Saturday, unless they were extra ones, privately organized, and Thirsk's were always on Mondays. In other places they held most, but not all, hirings on market day as Mr Johnson has described in Driffield. In all these cases the fairs did not follow dates but were moveable feasts, which sometimes were as complicated to calculate as any religious occasion. Yet Ripon held its main fair on Martinmas Day every year, except when 23 November fell on a Sunday. In some places no pattern at all is discernible: between 1900 and 1922 Howden held fairs on Tuesdays, Thursdays, Fridays, and Saturdays. To complicate matters further, the religious festival of St Martin actually falls on the 11th not the 23rd of November but when the calendar was altered in 1752, leaping forward twelve days to get back in step with the solar year, the East Riding did not adapt itself. Why this should be is unknown[4] – some other areas did make the change, particularly the northern English counties which also used Martinmas as a time for hiring.

In the twentieth century, some employers and landlords made attempts to alter the dates of several fairs, but with no apparent success. In 1901 the *Malton Gazette* advertised a special hiring on Thursday 26 November,[5] with unknown results, but another advertised in 1910 was certainly a failure.[6] Likewise, it was reported from Selby, in 1906, that:

> the first of this season's hirings, arranged by the agent to the Lord of the Manor of Selby (the Earl of Londesborough) took place . . . . There was a poor attendance of servants, while the number of employers of labour present was practically nil. Business seemed to be out of the question, generally speaking, and what little hiring was transacted was done in a semi-private way.[7]

At Sheriff Hutton, in the North Riding, failure was complete:

> After holding the . . . hirings during Martinmas week for the last half-dozen years the result has been such a failure that the Agricultural Club decided to fall back upon the old date. The result on Wednesday [14 November 1900] fully justified the alteration. The farmers turned up in large numbers and hiring was brisk.[8]

Whether or not these hirings fully revived in later years, the immediate result of the Agricultural Club's tampering had been disastrous. There had once been provision for the fair dates to be centrally fixed,[9] but this was now so far in the past that fairs and their particular days were welded together, and most people very sensibly made no attempt to separate them.

If no agreement was reached over wages for another year, or if no offer came by the time of the first hirings, then a lad knew he needed a new job, as Mr Johnson explained, 'They used to ask you about, oh, three weeks before the year was up. They used to come and say, "Now then, are you going to stop again?" . . . If you fancied stopping again then you started bargaining and see what kind of money you were going to have.' At year-end, Mr Baines said, 'As soon as you left your place you had a week's holiday and went to t'hirings, got hired again. . . . Used to be all stood in Selby market, Howden market, Goole market, Hull market – all in big groups – dozens and dozens – hundreds of you anyway.'

Each town had its customary spot where farm servants gathered. At Malton it was the market place itself, but at Howden, Mr Baines said, 'You didn't get hired in the market place, you got hired alongside the big public houses,' and this was just as common. At Bridlington they stood by the Black Lion Hotel in the Old Town and at York, '[It] used to be that little Coppergate, they used to stand up there. Used to be all round t'White Swan – that corner,' said Mr Friend. At Hull, lads gathered by 'King Billy', a statue of William of Orange in Market Place, the Selby hirings took place in Wide Street, and at Scarborough the venue was Newborough Street. At Hedon they spread along Souter Gate, Market Place, and St Augustine Gate. As they stood there, they presented a strange picture to an outsider, as this description of Bridlington in 1895 shows:

> Everyone tried to look smart; it is only right to say that. Many of the girls were neatly dressed, and only their speech betrayed them; but the lads still cling to the past in their sartorial get up, which includes gaudy silk neckties and pearlies. In this matter the [farm servant] of the East Riding is as unique in appearance as the London costermonger, and the Chevalier has not yet appeared who has rightly hit off the typical Yorkshire yokel. If a masher, you will see him in a light salmon-coloured moleskin jacket with black velvet collar, and a pair of smart corduroys, violet coloured, perhaps, and split up at the bottoms, with rows of pearlies on either side. The wagoner has a bit of fancifully twisted cord in his cap, a bright flower (it may be artificial) in his buttonhole, and his jacket is not buttoned – that would not be correct. The proper fastening is two or three inches of brass chain, the better to display a capacious chest. Feathers on some of the bowler hats are suggestive of the fold-yard, while the occasional flashes of bright colour in the feminine head-gear are suggestive of a primitive arcadia rather than the latest Paris fashion.[10]

Although the reference here is to a mixed group of girls and lads, in fact at about this time it was fast becoming the rule that the girls were not hired in the street. I asked Mr Johnson if he had any knowledge of mixed hiring and he replied:

> No, there was a registry for – what they call a register office for them, well that was generally a house in a place – it could be at Driffield, it could be at Malton or Bridlington, and the employers used to go there and leave their requirements and then the girls used to go there and sort 'em out . . . . And – well, all girls didn't go to that; you know, if a farmer knew of a girl that he

thought he would like and knew she was wanting a place he would go to her house where she lived and employ her, you see. No, I never heard of it. This registry office had been on the go a lot of years, so when this did happen – girls and lads all mixed up, getting hired together, I couldn't say. I don't know when.

Only Mr Jarvis, who must have witnessed the very end of it at Malton, remembered mixed hiring. The press contained references to registries in several places, for example, in Malton in 1900 'The Corn Exchange was open for the accommodation of the mistresses and girls, and cheap refreshments and a free entertainment was provided for them,' and in Driffield ten years later 'Female servants and mistresses were accommodated with a comfortable billet in the Temperance Hotel.'[11] This was the result of a campaign begun half a century before by clergymen who believed that allowing both sexes to stand together in a public place had a very bad effect upon morality. Mary Simpson recorded early attempts to break the old pattern after the hirings at Beverley and Bridlington in 1862:

Last year, which was the first year that the experiment was tried at Beverley, it had been a pouring day, and it seemed for some time to hang in the balance whether it would succeed or fail: the girls (doubtless backed by the lads) having long persevered in standing in the streets, till, when quite soaked, they were at last induced to avail themselves of the offered shelter.

This second year there was no doubt from the first; all went, like a flock of sheep, into the large public rooms prepared for them. There were 1300 present at one time, including, of course, the farmer's wives, who were much delighted. Col. L— was watching the proceedings: he takes particular interest in these doings and gives us all the help he can. He said that while in some places where it was being tried the experiment answered well, in others it had failed entirely, he could hardly tell why. When told that it was to be tried at Bridlington, he wrote such directions to the police there as put them quite at our command. . . .

Before the hiring day circulars were sent to all the surrounding clergy, with a request that they would distribute them to the farmers. We ascertained the number of farmers in every parish, and sent one for each farmer; 474 were dispersed in this way. A placard was also put up at every blacksmith's shop. These (both placards and circulars) were all put out in the name of the vicar of Bridlington. . . .

When the day came, it was the loveliest of autumn mornings, a slight frost quite early, and then brilliant sun. I believe I should have been more glad of a rainy day, as making it more probable that the girls would take advantage of the shelter offered them.

Mr M— had enough to do in the streets, with the help of the Scripture Reader, directing the girls the way of the Corn Exchange as they entered the town, a work requiring a good deal of tact and diplomacy. I found the police already at the Corn Exchange, before the appointed hour, a good fire lighted, and all prepared.

The room was soon filled, and the hiring went on briskly. The mistresses were greatly pleased, remarking with surprised satisfaction how much better behaved the girls were than when hired in the streets, where all was confusion and rude joking and jostling among the lads. A table of eatables was kept well supplied, so that none need go out to get food.

The newspapers confirm that their success was by no means immediate or complete, and Mary Simpson records several failures including one experiment at Thirsk that ended in a disturbance.[12] However, by the First World War their aim of segregating the actual hiring had been achieved everywhere. By the same date, another traditional part of hiring was little more than a memory in the county. In many accounts, of hiring fairs across the country, whether literary or factual, great play is made of the symbols used by servants to show their trade.[13] Such tokens were described in the report from Bridlington, but only Mr Lawler and Mr Friend, who used York, recalled them in use in living memory. Mr Friend said:

> If you were a horseman you had a bit of horse-hair in your coat collar, and if you were a shepherd you had a bit o' wool.
> *What did you have if you were a cowman?*
> A bit of hair out o' cow tail.

Others merely knew that this system of identification had existed. Mr Tate, for instance, joked that, 'I don't know what you would be if you were a pig lad. They'd have a sausage.' The tokens themselves were a descendant of the requirement of the Statute of Labourers, enacted five and a half centuries before, that hirelings should stand with their tools in hand to show their trade. No-one gave any reason for the ending of this custom and while it can have made little difference to the horselads, who were in the overwhelming majority, single shepherds and beastmen must have found it harder to get in touch with farmers seeking their skills. Married stockmen were not affected because, like labourers, they could not live as farm servants and so found jobs through advertisements in local newspapers. When these reservations have been made and allowed for, hiring in 1914 still looked much as it always had. As Mr Baines recalled:

> You used to line yourselves up with other lads at side o' t' road and t' farmers were across on t'other side o' t'road and they used to look you over, talk to one another, you know, and, 'Do you know him?' and, 'He looks like a likely lad, y'know,' and they'd say, 'You want to get so-and-so if you're wanting a lad' . . . And, of course, they'd talk among themselves and discuss you among themselves, and they'd say, 'Oh, he'll just do for me. Which is him?' 'There, look.' And they'd come across then . . . . and they'd say, 'Noo, my lad, dost'a want hiring?'

One or two hinds, Mr Rispin among them, had this responsibility delegated to them, but most farmers did their own hiring. It could be a haphazard business unless the farmer saw someone he knew, for there was no system of written references.

The farmer could try to check on certain specific points, as Mr Pridmore recalled, by asking if you wanted hiring and what could you do? 'Can you plough, can you stack, can you thatch, can you do this and can you do the other?' However, he had no way of establishing how accurate the answers were, and unless a lad was totally incompetent, once he was hired the farmer had to put up with any deficiencies that might arise. Frequently, therefore, such exchanges were more banter than anything else, aimed at forming an idea of what type the lad or farmer might be as a preliminary to negotiating over money. Thus, Mr Baines said:

> One chap used to go across and he used to say, 'Can you swing plough, my lad?' . . . and you'd say, 'No, I've never done any swing ploughing.'
> He'd say, 'Can you wheel a big barrowful of manure?'
> You used to say, 'Aye!'
> 'Well tha can learn to swing plough!'

Well known local lads could clearly capitalize on their abilities in this situation where a stranger was bound to be a little suspect. He might look big and strong, but if he could not get on with horses or workmates the job would suffer and he could not be sacked. An employer would naturally tend to prefer someone he knew. Mr Clarvis, who was a farm lad on the Wolds in the 1870s, said:

> I can recall not a few East Riding farmers who had not very good reputations either for the manner they fed or treated their servants, who went to all the sittings, . . . both before and after Martinmas and even then rarely succeeded in engaging their full staff of workmen and therefore had to be content with complete strangers or wasters.[14]

A stranger, unless he really did have something to hide, would almost certainly be hired in a normal year, but it was likely that he would not get as good a job as he would near home. Conversely, someone with a very good reputation rarely went to the hirings at all, other than for a day out. As soon as word got round that he was leaving his present job, farmers would approach him and he soon would be fixed up. If he did decide to make use of the fair he could play off two or three prospective employers and get quite a few pints of beer bought for him before any decision had to be made.

The lads were not the only ones to be discussed, of course. They told each other about their past employers and particularly warned each other off bad meat houses where the food was sparse or bad. Food was of crucial importance to lads and a place that fed well would be popular even though it might be well known for hard work. A lad might even accept slightly less money from a farmer with a good name. News spread quickly, as Mr Playforth said, 'A bad spot, it soon had a bad name, hadn't it? Nobody wanted to go.'[15] In many areas, particularly in Scotland, servants publicly derided bad employers by making up mocking songs about them, which would be loudly sung at the hirings,[16] but there is no evidence of such songs in the East Riding.

Bargaining over actual wages only commenced when both farmer and lad were satisfied with the other's credentials. Lads were not afraid to refuse offers, so it was

Table 3.   *Wage variations in 1890 for waggoners, third lads, and boys, first time out.*

FAIR	DATE	WAGES PER YEAR – £		
		Wags	Thirdies	Boys
Driffield	11 Nov.	17–20	up to 14	10.5
Market Weighton	13 Nov.	17–20	8–10	–
Howden	19 Nov.	15–17	–	6–8
Scarborough	21 Nov.	16–18	–	6–8
York	25 Nov.	14–19	–	3–8
Scarborough	28 Nov.	15–18	–	6

Source: *Yorks. Post*, dates as given, pp. 5, 3, 6, 3, 6, 3 respectively.

no mere formality. Although there was a generally recognised level of wages ruling at any particular fair, it allowed for wide variations (Table 3). Clearly, there was every reason for a lad to bargain as hard as he could before agreeing a figure with a farmer. Once agreement was reached, the farmer handed over the fastening penny, also known as the fest or hiring penny, whereupon they were both bound by the contract. Despite its name the fastening penny was meant to be a substantial sum. As far back as the mid-seventeenth century Henry Best had given, 'to a foreman, five markes per annum, and perhapps 2s. or half a crowne to a godspenny,' as it was then known. He also gave some of his men clothes instead of cash if they preferred it.[17]

By the inter-war years, a waggoner might well get a pound and the smallest lad two shillings or half a crown, though before the inflation of the First World War it was substantially less, along with wages. It was not a fixed proportion of the wage: Mr Harper, for instance, recalled that one year he secured £18 as wages, whereupon,

He says to me, 'Why, what fest does tha want?' – once they'd hired you they'd give you whatever you wanted, like: some on 'em haggle and joggle a bit over t'fastening penny, so I says, 'Well, if I isn't worth five bob,' I says, 'I'm not coming.'
'Well,' he says, 'I'll gi'e you it.'

If the lad was beaten in the main bargaining he might be able to make up for it with the fest. Mr Fisher said, 'After I got to be a waggoner I used to ask for £40 – I would generally get it, by hook or by crook, as you might say. Maybe give you £39 and then t'other pound fest.'[18] Unless they were saving every penny they could, servants regarded the fest as their spending money to have a good time with once they were hired, with youngsters perhaps trying to drown out any fears they might have, as Mr Baines recalled:

He'd . . . give you a fastening penny, probably half a crown or five bob, and they used to think they'd gotten the world, like. . . . You'd also be happy because you'd got a job and you'd be full of woes and wondering whether you were going to a good home: a good place or what-have-you. You know, if you'd a foreman over you that were a bit strict and keen and'd always be shouting and cussing you, like, making you break into a gallop, and if you hadn't a foreman there, like, if you'd got to know all t'details o' t'farm.

Besides giving them a day of comparative wealth, spending the fest symbolized their acceptance of their new contract, for they would thereafter have to use their savings or get another fest to regain their independence. In law, once a lad accepted the fest he was tied to work for the farmer, but as long as he returned the fest it was generally accepted that he could change his mind. Even the farmers who would sue a runaway would take no action in such a case. It was not uncommon for a lad to receive a better offer than one he had already accepted, but it was not something many lads would engineer deliberately. It was definitely not the common practice to take up a poor offer early on for insurance and then go and look for a better one. Similarly it was very unusual for a lad to go about accepting several jobs, and a fest from each farmer, and then to vanish. The public nature of the hirings was a strong guard against such behaviour from anyone disinclined to respect the usual conventions.

With plenty of people who had money to spend, it is no surprise that the hiring fair was more than an occasion for business. Every hiring had a large fun fair attached for this was a golden opportunity to make money when otherwise they would have had been sitting in winter quarters. Everyone who could came to this part of the hirings, regardless of whether they needed a job or not. For the most part the single lads and girls were the only ones with the leisure to attend but, Mr Harper said:

Third hirings, well that was when all t'married men and women used to go to Driffield and Malton. That was a day out for them, do you see? All t'labourers, practically, they used to – the labourers would generally start, and the beastmen, used to get all done up on a morning so they'd nothing to do at night. Then, them that was living round Driffield or Malton, they could just walk, but if you had a train to catch you had to be up early on a morning, you see, to get polished up for t'day, do you see. Well, there was hardly a married man stopped at home – always went to Driffield or Malton. It used to be what they called, 'Gathering Day', did Driffield third hirings.

For people who normally lived in rural isolation even quite a small event could take on large proportions, but hiring fairs should not be underestimated because of this. G.H. Fox remembered the York hirings from his childhood with great delight, even though he was a resident of the city and so less easily impressed:

At one time, this Fair spread up as far as Micklegate, in one direction, and on to Peasholme Green in the other [i.e., right across the walled city]. A menagerie was set up in the yard of 'The White Swan', Pavement. Parliament Street was opened in 1836 and for many years the pleasure Fair was held there until 1924, after which it moved to St. George's Field.

What memories those fairs conjure up! It was a wide and fine street but could barely accommodate the massive fair, with its roundabouts, menagerie, shooting ranges . . . , coconut shies, fortune tellers, marionettes, living wonders of all kinds, moving-pictures, peep-shows, brandy snap and gingerbread stalls and a dozen other attractions.

I experienced it as a child. I will never forget being one of the crowd at night-time when the naphtha flares on the stalls were sending out their flames from their curving pipes and when the varied tunes, blaring from the roundabouts, were vying with each other for supremacy.[19]

Besides those who went to the fair, a town's traders looked forward to hirings day with great relish, and they were joined by a host of itinerant hawkers in offering watches, bicycles, melodeons, mouth-organs, sheet music, clothes – everything that could possibly be sold. This was the only time of year when farm servants had much cash and when the majority could reach the shops in the towns. Effectively a shopkeeper who wanted to get trade from farm servants did it at Martinmas or not at all, so they declared sales and took advertisements in the local papers offering bargains to suit those who lived on farms. Credit was a crucial part of the rural economy of the day and Martinmas was the time when servants settled the accounts they had run up with the tradesmen they had dealt with. It brought a very brief but very welcome surge of cash into the market towns. A watchmaker from York recalled,

My father sold more watches in Martinmas week than in all the rest of the year. It was the ambition of every lad to possess an English lever watch. Sometimes they would pay one half of the price one Martinmas and the other half the next. My father had sold hundreds of watches in Martinmas week. The record of them is written in his books. And there is no mention of a bad debt.[20]

Everyone who spoke to me regarded Martinmas as an enormously enjoyable time, even though it did come in late November when, as Mr Carter remembered, 'It was very often bad weather. Oh yes, you couldn't have picked much worse – you got frost and snow, like, but you wasn't bothered much.'

Money was not essential for enjoyment. Mr Harper recalled how he 'used to walk up and down street, or if you had any relatives, go and see them, or any friends, do you see, you maybe had a friend or two in Driffield – a lot on 'em used to go and see their relatives or owt like that. It used to be a glorious day did Martinmas Thursday.'

There were people who felt that the fairs were no longer what they had been, but this seems to have been merely equating change with decline, at least as long as the farm servant system itself was strong. Thus Mr Clarvis, writing in 1920 as a veteran of the 1870s, said:

Half a century ago around Driffield, all over the Wolds, and in Holderness, Martinmas was Martinmas. Today I cannot find a name suitable; things have so altered and somehow I fail to see much improvement. . . . Martinmas week 1870 and 1920 were as different as the proverbial chalk from cheese.

Yet, for all this, his description of Hedon hirings does not support his case, for it sounds as if the spirit behind it was exactly that behind the fairs of later years:

Those who had got hired prior to the sittings never failed to attend for Hedon fair was one of the great events of the year. I can recall when there was hardly a servant who had not got a place by half-past one in the afternoon and shortly after that the masters and mistresses were seen driving off home, leaving their new men, lads and maidens to enjoy themselves and to spend their fest, or godspenny as some called it. Right merrily did they enjoy themselves too. If they had a mind to dance there was the old-fashioned dance chaimer and fiddle to scrape away hour by hour. I have seen many an old country dance on these occasions – four hands across and down the middle.[21]

The drift from small centres meant larger, more impersonal gatherings which attracted more outsiders to take their share of the money that was on offer, but the fairs as a whole did not diminish in popularity until there were few servants left. In 1901, indeed, Howden fair was so well liked that large numbers turned up 'notwithstanding the terrific hurricane which passed over the district.'[22]

Notes to Chapter Five

1. *H. News*, 3 Dec. 1910, p. 12.
2. Bedell, *Hornsea*, pp. 91–2.
3. Kitchen, *Brother*, pp. 97–8.
4. See K. McCutcheon, *Yorkshire Fairs and Markets to the End of the Eighteenth Century,* Thoresby Society Publications xxxix (1940), pp. 148–9 for a discussion of this issue.
5. *Mal. Gaz.*, 23 Nov. 1901, p. 3.
6. *Yorks. Her.*, 30 Nov. 1910, p. 8.
7. *Yorks. Post*, 24 Nov. 1906, p. 8.
8. *Mal. Mess.*, 17 Nov. 1900, p. 3.
9. McCutcheon, *Yorkshire Fairs*, pp. 156–60, describes the process of control by the chief constable in the East Riding in the seventeenth century. R.W. Malcolmson, *Popular Recreations in English Society 1700–1850* (Cambridge, 1973), p. 23, states control ended in the late 18th century, but in 1850 some was still being exercised; see D. and T. Arthur, 'Available for Hire', *Folk Song Review* (Sept. 1972), 6. See also H.E. Strickland, *A General View of the Agriculture of the East Riding of Yorkshire* (1812), p. 262.
10. *Brid. Gaz.*, 16 Nov. 1895, cutting in Annals of Brid.
11. *Yorks. Post*, 12 Nov. 1900, p. 5; *E. News*, 15 Nov. 1910, p. 6.
12. Simpson, *Gleanings*, pp. 104–6, 123.
13. See, e.g., F. Austin-Hyde, 'Old Time Martinmas Hirings', *York Times* (Autumn 1962), p. 26, and T.E. Kebbel, *The Agricultural Labourer* (1887), p. 91, or T. Hardy, *Far From the Madding Crowd*, (1874, MacMillan, 1974), p. 73.

14. Letter from Mr Clarvis to J. Fairfax-Blakeborough, quoted in his *East Riding*, p. 48.
15. See Reffold, *Pie for Breakfast*, p. 59.
16. D. and T. Arthur, 'Available', 6–8, and see also I. Carter, 'Oral History and Agrarian History – the North East', *Oral History*, vol. 2 no. 1, (1974) 37–9.
17. H. Best, *The Farming and Memorandum Books of Henry Best of Elmswell, 1642,* ed. D. Woodward, British Academy Records of Social and Economic History, New Series, VIII (1984), pp. 138–9.
18. I was told that at York only a halfpenny was given as a token fest by Mr and Mrs Lawler and Mr Friend, whom I interviewed together. I was unable to check it from elsewhere, and I merely record it without comment.
19. *The Dalesman*, (Nov. 1973), 626–7.
20. Quoted in Austin-Hyde, 'Hirings', 26.
21. Mr. Clarvis, in Fairfax-Blakeborough, *East Riding*, pp. 48–9.
22. *Yorks. Post*, 20 Nov. 1901, p. 10.

Chapter Six

The Fairs as a Labour Market

Hiring fairs are probably the only part of a farm servant's way of life that are recorded in print on any scale, or with any degree of accessibility. It is all the more unfortunate, then, that most contemporary written accounts of hiring fairs treated them as no more than a convenient and traditional way of bringing together prospective masters and servants, and a degrading one at that:

> The farmers like the system, of course, because, as they say, 'they get a lot to pick from' and can compare the thews and sinews of a great many candidates for service before engaging one. We do not mean [though others did], that they feel them over as they would a horse, or as their wives would thumb a couple of fowls; but they scan them critically, as the slave merchant would have scanned a negro, and naturally regard them in no other light from that of animals.[1]

Joseph Arch, the great farmworkers' trade union leader, would certainly have agreed with that, and he would have added that the fairs were a means of keeping wages as low as possible. It was his personal experience in the midlands and the south that formed his views, and there were elements even of northern hiring which could seem objectionable. Typical newspaper reports contain no information about the fairs as events and they seem completely at home in the commodity sales and financial section of the newspaper where they are mostly to be found. If the names of commodities were substituted for the various classes of servants whose wages were quoted, they would still read perfectly well. Occasionally there is a short paragraph giving a little more detail, and sometimes they were classed as local news, but the overwhelming impression is that editors viewed them much as they viewed reports of corn sales, horse sales, or iron sales.

Nonetheless, in the north this was not the whole picture. Iron, a cow, or a slave have, after all, no option but to be sold to the highest bidder, but a northern farm servant could and did have a choice. An old story perfectly illustrates this point, concerning a lad approached by a farmer at a hiring, 'Dost' want hiring?' 'Aye, I might,' answered the lad and so they began bargaining. Just as everything seemed settled the farmer asked for a reference. The lad was somewhat nonplussed by this unusual request, but he said he could get one. 'All right,' said the farmer, 'I'll see you here at noon and if the reference is a good one, I'll give you the fest.' They split up and at twelve the farmer was waiting as the lad came up to him. 'Now then,' he said, 'have you got your reference?' 'No,' the lad replied, 'but I've got yours and I'm not coming!'

There was, in the East Riding at least, a balance between the lads on offer and the jobs that needed filling. 'Most of them got hired. It wasn't often that there was any left out. No, they generally got engaged,' said Mr Baines. Servants never refrained from shopping around in the fear that one offer might be all they would get. It is ironic that many middle-class Victorians and Edwardians opposed the fairs, for they were one of the very few places where a workman could genuinely negotiate his own contract directly with an employer without being at a gross disadvantage; a concept dear, in theory, to all the trade union haters of those times. No farmer controlled more than an insignificant percentage of the jobs on offer, so by gathering all the servants and all the farmers together in one place at one time the bargaining power of the two sides was equalized as much as was possible without formal constraints or collective bargaining through representatives. Moreover the majority of the participants either knew each other or had ready access to friends who could supply information. Since no individual at any fair had more than an insignificant percentage of the business transacted under their control, and no particular bargain could set the overall level of wages, this must have been one of the closest approaches in real life to the classical economists' ideal of the perfect market.

The pattern of multiple hirings reinforced the servants' ability to bargain effectively. The first hirings, held a fortnight before the others, were used by both sides to sound out their relative strengths. There was a generally accepted level of wages around which negotiations fluctuated, but wages could rise or fall sharply from one year to the next. Everyone compared the number looking for work against the number of jobs available, and took into account factors such as inflation. They were always conscious of the state farms were in. If the farmers had got behindhand they would be keen to hire, but if everything was going well they might prefer to proceed at a leisurely pace. Thus, at Thirsk in 1906, 'farmers are not quite so ready with their ploughing and sowing as last year, and situations were better to obtain at slightly advanced rates.' First hirings would then see a lot of bargains struck, but otherwise the farmers and the lads withdrew to consider their positions. At Howden in 1900, 'there was not a very large attendance . . . and little hiring was effected. Men held out for big wages and female servants were difficult to engage. It is expected there will be more hiring at the statutes on Thursday next.'[2]

At the end of the first hirings, or even the second, it did not matter that no business had been done. Having judged the kind of bargains they could realistically hope to make, both sides returned to the arena with serious offers and demands. That this affected wage levels is indicated by a long tradition of attempts by a few farmers to abolish first hirings. In 1810 the Holderness Agricultural Society had resolved that:

> by reason of the licentiousness of those servants in husbandry who remain
> unhired after the first statute sittings, that the Secretary do write to the
> Chairman of the East Riding Sessions and to the mayors of Beverley and

Hedon, to request them respectively to direct the High Constables within their respective districts to fix all the statute sessions within one week before Martinmas.[3]

There seems to have been little support for this, but in the mid 1890s a more serious threat emerged. In 1895 it was reported from Bridlington first hirings that:

very little business was done – that the real business . . . will be done after Old Martinmas Day. Tuesday, I suppose, was the day when 'fest' money was paid, that is if a change was contemplated, but I suppose even Hodge has discovered that this is illegal, and the 'fest' or fast money is not binding, in other words, that you cannot make a fresh contract until the old one has expired.[4]

The Statute of Frauds[5] was being used to call into doubt the validity of contracts agreed at first hirings, but the writer's sarcasm was entirely misplaced for it was Hodge's ancient view of the law which was right and the new interpretation which was wrong. In a case of breach of contract heard at Malton:

Mr Hugh W. Pearson, for defendant, submitted that the contract [of the servant he was defending] having been entered into after Martinmas to be fully completed within one year it was a binding contract . . . . His Honour, in giving judgement, pointed out that . . . the Statute of Frauds [therefore] did not apply.[6]

The Statute had been enacted in 1677 to prevent some oral contracts being used to defraud because of their inherent imprecision. It was clearly designed to exclude yearly labour contracts, which were then probably the majority of non-casual hirings, since it was contracts which ran for a year and a day or longer which had to be in writing to be legally valid. Now magistrates were saying that if a man was hired on, say, 11 November, his oral contract could not be enforced because it ran to 23 November following. However, on 11 November he was still working out his old contract and his new one only came into effect when the old one expired on 23 November. At the first hirings a yearly contract was simply agreed in advance.

For some time the effect on hiring before Martinmas was severe. In 1900, at Market Weighton, 'there was little hiring of farm hands, as the farmers' club at their last meeting passed a resolution that there should not be any hiring until after Martinmas Day.' A year later employers were reported to have abandoned Beverley first hirings, while at Howden, 'a fair number of employers of labour were present, but taking them all round there was no active disposition for engagement in view of the recent judicial pronouncement . . . . The main hiring will be next week.'[7]

It may have seemed that the preliminary hirings were doomed to wither away, but the servants were determined not to give up their rights to take days off for the fairs, as in 1922 at Driffield where the farmers stayed away, but 'the farm hands availed themselves of the opportunity for a holiday and found pleasure on the swings, roundabouts and in patronising the many devices for relieving them of their money.'[8] From the tapes it is clear that the new doctrine became accepted, but that everyone had still been involved in hiring before Martinmas. Many farmers were probably as loth to lose the old ways as the lads, and a new equilibrium seems to have been established where farmers accepted that a lad who changed his mind about an agreement could not be sued for breach of contract as long as he showed good faith by returning the fest, or else he could be sued for retaining it.[9] Since the whole system had always rested on trust, this did not involve any real likelihood of mass defaults.

It is ironic that what may have begun as an attempt to restrict the bargaining ability of the lads ended by doing at least as much to increase it, for now it was quite clear that a lad could return a fest with no legal impediment.[10] Moreover, as long as there were two hirings in the Martinmas week, masters would not be able to dictate wages to servants fearful of not being hired at all. It is, indeed, a further irony that in 1641 Henry Best of Elmswell, a large farmer by the standards of his day, should have felt that the more hirings there were, the better: he remarked that the towns lucky enough to be given two hirings by the chief constable 'are the most priviledged; for Masters that wante servants, and servants that wante Masters, have the benefitte of the next sittinge to provide for themselves; whereas those townes that are not called till the latter sittinge have but one day to provide themselves in.'[11]

It is interesting to compare the bargaining power servants had at hirings with that brought by joining a union. Arch's union made no real headway in the East Riding, and modern unions, now all within the Transport and General Workers' Union, had only limited success within one or two regions before the 1930s, so there is little overlap between hirings and effective unions. The hiring fair can usefully be compared to an informal and temporary union directly shaped by the needs of the farm servants. Industrial methods of organization can barely be made to work on farms because men are too scattered, and membership is usually too low and vulnerable for employers to be presented with the sort of solid front needed for results. With the hiring fairs, the farm houses emptied once a year and until the farmer hired his new quota of lads, he could get very little done with his horses – in other words, his position resembled that of someone who had been struck against. There was no need to picket, and such a ritualized strike generated no ill-feeling.[12]

The bargaining was, in its own way, collective. Though the farm lads were scattered over a wide area during the year, for the hirings they were gathered together in one place and faced all their potential employers together. They knew roughly what their friends and neighbours were asking, and getting, and it was hard to play them off against each other. It was accepted that every year lads would try to get better terms than the year before, if only because they were all one year older and more capable, and there was no question of anyone passively accepting a set wage until something caused the employer to order a cut, or forced the employee to confront his boss with a demand for an increase. The hirings had made a ritual of alterations in wages: it caused lads to think actively about the wages they ought to be getting and it caused the masters to accept that they would ask for a rise every year. The ritual nature of the whole proceedings is confirmed by the fact that they took place at Martinmas. Farm activity was at its lowest ebb then, with only the long haul of winter ploughing to be got on with, so a week's enforced idleness was acceptable to the farmers.

The newspapers furnish ample proof that both sides used their industrial power to the full, right across the north. In 1890 at Scarborough, 'a strong demand ruled for labour of all classes, especially adult men and women, and servants held out for top rates.' Ten years later, at York, 'the attendance of servants was smaller than usual. Farm servants of all kinds were asking £2 to £3 more money which farmers are not inclined to give,' while at Malton, 'little hiring was done and both men and women were firm in their demands. It is not anticipated that in this district there will be any deficiency in the labour supply.' The other side of the coin showed at Bridlington in 1904 when 'there was not much business done in the annual hiring of farm servants and those who did change places had to be content to take from 30/– to £2 a year less.'[13]

J. Dunbabin has described how, throughout the nineteenth century in Scotland, Northumberland, and Durham, a series of unions and 'farm servants' protection associations' based around fairs sprang up and died down in these areas,[14] probably because married and single men were both hired at the fairs there. The associations were mostly founded to improve conditions rather than pay, but usually they experienced little success in this and as the day wore on, more and more men settled for higher cash wages. Such unions were based on public meetings rather than in permanent organizations: before a fair a meeting would be called at which ploughmen would attend and speak. During the meeting a consensus emerged of what, if anything, they should demand. Since there were no subscriptions or officials in many cases, and since nowhere did signed up memberships even approach the numbers attending meetings, unions and action meetings were unable to turn apparent strength into institutional power.

Only one issue proved deep-rooted enough not to be bought off and to keep reviving until the point was won. In these areas whole families were often hired by farmers and unless a man had women or children attached to him, to provide extra hands at peak periods, he stood less chance of being hired. Accordingly farmers often made it a condition of hiring that such a servant should himself hire a bondager, that is a woman or girl, whom he would lodge and pay. Unfortunately, the woman had to be paid and boarded all year while the farmer only paid for her services when he needed them, so, quite apart from the difficulties of housing the bondager in a tiny cottage, the servant was usually out of pocket. The system was neither traditional nor popular, and in the 1870s enough unionized pressure was exerted to cause its abandonment in most areas.

Had another union been able to offer expertise and funds to get one of these fair-based agricultural unions onto a solid footing, or had Arch's union been able to learn from the local conditions, rather than simply seeking expansion, it is possible that a new form of unionism more suited to the needs of the industry might have grown up in northern agriculture. On the other hand, the fact that men still did their own bargaining at the fairs and that the fairs were totally independent of any union weakened any long-term claim on men's loyalty that a union could make. Just as today, when the Transport and General Workers' Union, represents most farm-workers on wages boards, whether they are members or not, such a union could only ensure its long term survival by offering fringe benefits and by trying to convince members of abstract advantages of unity.

Public meetings and combinations seem to have been unknown at fairs in the East Riding but, nonetheless, the unions of the northern areas merely exaggerate tendencies that were present in the county. Further north the farmers combined as well as the servants, and there is one known example of this in 1922 when the Selby branch of the National Farmers Union resolved that 'the maximum wage for waggoners over 21 years of age be £35 for the year, this to include the customary hours of haytime and harvest.'[15] However, this was more likely to have been inspired by wartime experience of the Agricultural Wages Boards than by anything else. In the East Riding the strength both sides derived from the fairs was the direct result of their being gathered in one place. People acted as individuals and their strength was primarily defensive, in that either side could resist innovation by the other.

The best evidence of the way in which the hirings could be used to push up wages under the right conditions, and the limitations of the process, is provided by the experience of female servants. Throughout the later nineteenth century fewer and fewer girls were willing to work on farms, prefering to try for places in country houses or towns.[16] Virtually every newspaper report of a hiring which gives girls' wages also comments on the scarcity of girls for hire and their demands for ever higher wages. In 1890, at Scarborough, 'the attendance of female servants was under the average'. In 1901 at Howden, 'young girls, as usual, endeavoured to get very high premiums, the figures being £10 to £12'. There were but few experienced domestics seeking employment. At Hedon in 1900 'female servants were scarce, and demanded an increase on last year's rates, almost all refusing to be hired to milk'.[17] Yet though their wages were always considered high, it was from an employer's viewpoint, and they were not necessarily good wages in any absolute sense. They were still lower than their male contemporaries and there was a very definite limit to what could be obtained, set by employers' notion of the point at which wages became so 'outrageous' that they preferred not to hire at all, but within that limit the girls were able to keep pushing their wages up.

Hirings were like wrestling matches between two very evenly matched opponents who continually tested each other's defences. First one and then the other would score minor victories, but neither was ever seriously in danger of being dominated by the other. Indeed, these two wrestlers had been struggling so long that neither expected to win or lose. Without this balance, which was lacking wherever there was serious unemployment or underemployment, the fairs became one-sided, with farmers arriving simply to pick the men they wanted, state their terms, and leave, rather than to bargain. Then indeed the fairs became degrading, as so many people thought, and they seemed to be an instrument in the labourers' degradation, when in fact they merely made it public.

In the midlands and the south, aspects of hirings that were of little or no significance in the East Riding took on great importance. One instance is the attention paid to the physique of the hirelings. Even in the East Riding the qualities that farmers were seeking in a servant included size and strength, but they looked for a lot more besides. Lads were proud of their physique and the local fashion of fastening a jacket with a piece of chain instead of buttoning it was intended to enhance the size of a lad's chest and hence, by implication, his strength and carrying ability. Most lads did not feel they were being examined like cattle because other factors mattered at least as much: if they had a reputation as a good horseman or a careful, skilled workman, or a good waggoner, the farmer was not concerned with feeling their muscles. It was when jobs were scarce that bonds between masters and men broke down and then servants came to feel that their whole livelihood hinged on the farmers viewing them as stock, or slaves.

Had there been any desire in the lads to get away from hiring in the streets they would have taken to some degree to an alternative offered them in 1910. Labour exchanges were set up all over the country after 1909, and in 1910 in Malton:

> a temporary branch of the Board of Trade Labour Exchange was opened in the Town Hall, but here very little business was done. The labourers had the idea that they had something to pay, but this is quite erroneous, as many a man might be provided with an excellent berth were he not so cautious. Mr. Frank S. Dealve, manager of the York branch of the Labour Exchange was in charge, and . . . he said he found it most difficult to get the farm labourers of Yorkshire to register their names.

Branches were reported to have opened that year, seemingly always from York, at Thirsk, Scarborough, Ripon, Driffield, Malton (twice), Pickering, and Market Weighton. In some cases there was optimism about the future, but nowhere was there actual success. Thus, in Driffield, officials theorized that 'the object of the Exchange was not very well known by the men, or it would have been more generally used.'[18] There is no evidence of the experiment continuing and none of the people who described hirings to me could remember the labour exchanges playing any part in them. The labour exchange was free, it need not have interfered with the yearly hire, and business could still be done centrally, rather than servants having to trail off round distant farms. The servants would, however, have avoided public hiring, and their rejection of the exchanges can only be seen as a vote to maintain the fairs.

This was by no means the first alternative to hiring at a fair that the lads had been offered, though earlier ones were less even-handed. The Revd F.O. Morris, in 1854 suggested that fairs should cease and that thereafter all hiring should be done through a registry. All servants would have to produce written references from farmers as to their moral character, as well as the quality of their work, but farmers would not need any references at all. The whole scheme was to be financed by appropriating the servants' fests, which had the added 'benefit' of stopping servants squandering their money. It is a sign of how far removed men like the Revd Morris were from with their working-class parishioners that he envisaged no objections, and how much we should beware of educated judgements on the fairs.[19]

More seriously, the classified advertisements of local newspapers seemed to offer a practical alternative as most married men used this means to find employment. Only a small percentage of yearly hirings was made in a similar fashion, however, and again we can only judge this as satisfaction with the existing system. It may be objected that one section of the hirelings, the girls, had, in fact, rejected public hiring at the fairs, but here the issue is obscured by many social factors. The evidence of the newspapers and of their wages proves that there was a constant trend for ever more girls to refuse to be hired at all, and those who remained in farm service must have been affected by the same social pressures that produced such a trend. The registries offered the girls a step up towards the respectability associated wth town service, for most town servants were hired through such institutions, and they made farm service a little more acceptable to them. Very few servants, girls or boys, can have thought through what the fairs did for them, but in clinging to them they were wise. While there were aspects of public hiring that would not appeal to people brought up to other ways, what was important was that in the East Riding, both farmers and servants accepted implicitly the limitations placed upon them by the fairs and by the hiring system. It would be very hard to argue that the majority of youngsters from the East Riding lost in any way by continuing to use the fairs.

Notes to Chapter Six

1. Kebbel, *Labourer*, pp. 91–3. See also W. Hasbach, *A History of the English Agricultural Labourer* (1908), p. 84.
2. *Yorks. Post*, 13 Nov. 1906, p. 9, and 26 Nov. 1900, p. 7.
3. The Holderness Agricultural Society, *Extracts from the Minutes of the Holderness Agricultual Society, 1795–1850*, (Hull, 1883), p. 65.
4. *Brid. Gaz.*, 16 Nov. 1895, cutting in Annals of Brid.
5. 29 Car II c.3.
6. *Mal. Mess.*, 10 Nov. 1900, p. 3, and see *Mal. Mess.*, 27 Jan 1900, p. 3, for a contract being ruled invalid.
7. *Bev. Guar.*, 17 Nov. 1900, p. 8; *Yorks. Her.*, 7th Nov. 1901, p. 6; *Yorks. Post*, 20 Nov. 1901, p. 10.
8. *Yorks. Her.*, 18 Nov. 1922, p. 6.
9. *Mal. Mess.*, 27 Jan. 1900, p. 3.
10. See also *General Report*, p. 383.
11. H. Best, *Farming Book*, pp. 140–1.
12. Coal owners in the north east of England in the eighteenth century hired most of their miners on a form of the yearly bond, but staggered the renewal dates precisely to avoid this situation, T.S. Ashton and J. Sykes, *The Coal Industry of the Eighteenth Century* (1929, 2nd ed, 1964), p. 17.
13. *Yorks. Post*, 28 Nov. 1890, p. 3; 24 Nov. 1900, p. 10; 12 Nov. 1900, p. 5; *Brid. Gaz*, 2 Dec. 1904, cutting in Annals of Brid.
14. J.P. Dunbabin, *Rural Discontent in Nineteenth-Century England* (1974), chap. 7.
15. *Yorks. Her.*, 21 Nov. 1922, p. 2.
16. See P. Horn, *The Rise and Fall of the Victorian Servant* (Dublin, 1975) pp. 24–5. See also Heath, *Rural Life*, p. 14–15. Obelkevitch, *Rural Society*, p. 66, notes the same process in Lincolnshire.
17. *Yorks. Post* 21 Nov. 1890, p. 3; 20 Nov. 1901, p. 10, and see also 26 Nov. 1900, p. 7; 9 Nov. 1900, p.8.
18. *Yorks. Her.* 14 Nov. 1910, p. 8; 22 Nov. 1910, p. 8; 25 Nov. 1910, p. 8; 24 Nov. 1910, p. 8; *E. News*, 15 Nov. 1910, p. 6; *Yorks. Her.* 21 Nov. 1910, p. 8; 14 Nov. 1910, p. 8; 29 Nov. 1910, p. 8; *H. News*, 26 Nov. 1910, p. 4; *E. News* 15 Nov. 1910, p. 6.
19. Revd F.O. Morris, *The Present System of Hiring Farm Servants in the East Riding of Yorkshire with Suggestions for its Improvement* (Driffield, 1854).

Chapter Seven

The Hierarchy

Every lad who worked with horses had a clear place in a hierarchy that governed life on every farm. This imposed a rigid and unchangeable way of life during the year, and together with the flexibility between years that the hiring fairs promoted, a highly effective combination for maintaining discipline had been evolved. Conflicts were inevitable within a group of young men and boys who spent their whole time in each others' company and it also served to contain these and move them off the farms. It permeated their lives: 'If there were ten pairs of horses going to work your labourers'd be t'last uns. Your waggoner'd be first. Then your seconder, then your thirder,' said Mr Baines. On the Wolds, the foxhunting style of ploughing provided the longest and most public display of the hierarchy in action. The lads ploughed one behind another in a staggered line, each drawing a new furrow next to his predecessor's rather than working in separate plots, as Mr Carter recalled:

> When they went to plough, waggoner always used to go at first . . . then they all went i' order. He went first, then next man next, all went in their order, like, as they were, you see . . . . There was t'waggoner and then t'third lad and then t'fourth lad and then t'fifth lad, and then waggoner lad followed after and thirdy lad followed after that, then fourthy lad. You see, all t'lads come last. And t'least lad come last. He always come t'last. Last in everything.

Any passer-by could determine at a glance each lad's place in the pecking order during this, the horselads' most basic activity. The same was true, though to a lesser extent, of any job done together. Even when there was no actual line, the portion of a field allotted to each lad was determined by his position in the hierarchy. If several waggons went out, they went in order and even in the stables, the same was true, although it might be partially masked by the need to supervise the youngsters. The waggoner and thirdy, on a big farm, took opposite ends and the rest came in between. The arrangements at Squirrel Hall, when Mr Johnson was waggoner, were typical, though minor variations occurred, and they are shown in figure 3. Even where the younger lads did not feed horses, things were much the same. Ron Creasey worked on a big Holderness farm in the 1940s and he recalled that in their two stables, 'Our horses were in two lots. The waggoner was responsible for feeding eight horses and mucking out two, as were the third and fourth lads. Each of them had two lads to muck out the other six horses.'[1] Thus all the horses fed by one lad stood together, allowing for the division into two stables, and then each lad's

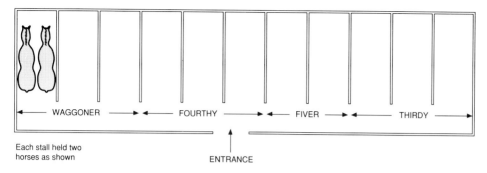

Fig. 3. The stabling arrangements at Squirrel Hall Farm

team stood together within the group, producing an end result like that at Squirrel Hall.

Except where the foreman felt that his greater skill and experience were needed, he left the waggoner in charge of the horses. In the same way, as long as things were not getting out of hand, he also allowed the waggoner to act as head of the hierarchy despite his own nominal right to that position. When he worked with the lads the foreman assumed the leadership, but he had too many duties to participate fully and so he was never truly part of the system. Equally, when labourers or others with no place in the hierarchy joined the lads, they went to the back of the line regardless of age or experience. The hierarchy was only for the horselads and no other group on the farm was similarly organized

Under the yearly bond employers lost the main sanctions on which normal systems of work discipline depended. They had no right to vary wages or to dismiss a hireling without a reason that would satisfy a court. On the other hand, the bond was only for a year and at Martinmas lads were free to move away, while farmers could be rid of any troublesome lad merely by not renewing his contract. There was a tradition of accommodation on both sides that would have been impossible where every problem had to be resolved through positive action, or left to deteriorate. This was why farmers generally tolerated runaways, for they would probably have been so unsettled had they stayed or been forced back, that it was better to let them go. It must also be remembered that farm servants were different from the average workforce in that the majority of them were teenagers, and a good many of them would still be in full time education today.

The very fact that they were working pushed them towards maturity, but there remained a strong tendency for work to shade off into play unless the younger lads were kept to their jobs. The old saying that one boy is worth half a man, but two boys are worth a quarter of a man, and three are worth no man at all, accurately summarizes the dangers of such a concentration of youngsters. In foxhunting, for instance, if the waggoner and the foreman were both present, one of them would sometimes go to the rear of the line: one drawback of the prestigious lead position was that the boys were free to fool about in the rear with no-one to see what they were up to. This was not due to any lack of motivation such as would require strict, even oppressive, discipline to achieve results, for most East Riding lads wanted to do their best at their jobs. Mr Milner said, 'Oh yes. We did. We delighted in it. Seeing who had done jobs good and who had done 'em bad. Why at Heslerton Wold they used to reckon to do everything straight. harrowing, shimming, rolling – all the lot.'

The lads identified with their role on the farm to the extent that those working together commonly called one another by their titles, such as wag, fourthy, sixer, etc., and not by their names. Even in the lower reaches a lad did not feel demeaned by his rank for it was temporary, and a capable lad could not be denied advancement through favouritism because it was so easy to change farms. The multiplicity of positions was neither accidental nor artificial, and they were not arbitrarily allocated to individuals. The descending tiers of rank roughly corresponded to the descending ages of the lads, and these were a good general indication to the farmer of their prowess and usefulness, since a year's growth in his teens made a real difference to a boy. Ranks were not, however, automatically attached to particular ages, for lads of the same age would not have identical capabilities. Moreover, a fourth lad's job on a large farm would probably be filled by an older lad than a theoretically similar position on a smaller place.

The least lad was last in everything: he had the worst horses in the worst harness and he was a prey to all the jokes (many of which are funny only to the perpetrators) that are played on youngsters wherever they are employed, yet if he resented this treatment it was because someone was picking on him. He hated his particular waggoner (or whoever else was to blame), not waggoners as a group. The previous year he had been a schoolboy whereas he was now earning a wage, living away from home and trusted with a plough team. The gulf between him and the boys he had left behind at school was huge and both sides felt it. It was far more important to him than that between him and the waggoner. As he grew older he would inevitably work his way up to the middle ranks, at least, and as long as he had both the desire and the ability, there was nothing to prevent him, in turn, becoming a waggoner.

The waggoner was in authority over the other lads, but he was not separated from them either physically or socially. There was no class basis, for instance, for the subordination of one lad to another. Farmers were not only the boss but, except for the smallest, who employed few men, they clearly came from a different background to their workers. Foremen shared the same original social class as the lads and even had a place in the hierarchy, but even so, their high wages, their power around the farm, and their residence in a good house on the farm gave them an institutionalized authority waggoners lacked. The sheer numbers of waggoners prevented their rank acquiring any exclusivity. Very few farms had more than nine or ten lads, and most had far fewer, yet all but the very tiniest had a waggoner of sorts and there were constant vacancies arising from 'retirements' when they married.

A waggoner saw that the work lads were given was done, but he rarely decided what jobs the lads should do, except in the Vale of York. If he got on well with the others, he would seem like a co-ordinator and pacesetter rather than an overseer. I asked Mr Fisher, a retiring man who seemed unlikely to have made unreasonable demands on his subordinates, if he had had difficulty in getting the others to follow his instructions. He replied, 'Oh no, no! I was maybe lucky, we'll say, but I never had any trouble. I used to say, "Will you do that?" Never had any trouble. Never got any back answers.' Mr Carter echoed this, yet it was not always so easy, as Mr Baines remarked:

> You used to have some rough times – used to have some rough lads to deal with, you know. Lads that were a bit stupid and clumsy and breaking things and that, and o' course your boss couldn't stand owt being broke. And you used to have just a roughish job dealing with 'em. It were nowt to give a lad a smack in t'bog, you know. No.
> *Did they take it or would they fight back?*
> Oh, as a rule – well, just odd uns did, but they knew very well, like, they were beat. You had to be t'boss, you know. You had to be a bit handy yourself. . . . Aye, some chaps were made waggoners that had never been able to cuss at 'em or roust 'em on, 'cause you were rousting 'em every day, all day, like. You know – you saw somebody stop with a pair of horses, 'Hey, come on there! Get going!' Else, if you didn't you were no good to your boss at that time o' day.

One reason for such different experiences is the different sizes of farms. Mr Milner's brother, for instance, became a waggoner on a small farm when aged fifteen and, 'there wasn't much order to be kept where he was, 'cause there was only, like, him and another chap among t'horses.' On the medium sized farms, someone who hired local lads whom he knew and trusted easily established a similar atmosphere of co-operation, and it was on such places that Mr Fisher and Mr Carter worked. If a farmer was not careful, however, he could find that he had hired someone disruptive. This was infrequent, and while they might spoil a year on one farm, the general pattern was one of harmony, with the hierarchy working unobtrusively in most places.

It was on the large farms that such trouble as there was could be found. This is worth examination because it was only when the system was tested severely that its workings became clearly visible. This does not mean that life on large farms was inevitably a battle, but on those where it was most insight can be gained. Some establishments had self-fulfilling reputations for roughness which kept away a lot of lads and attracted others who preferred the more wide-open feeling of life where such a large group inevitably lessened the contact between the lads and their superiors. The remoteness of large farms also kept people away, and the farmers were often prepared to take more chances on strangers to make up the numbers. In any case, having delegated the maintenance of discipline completely, they had the foreman between themselves and the lads, so they stood outside the disputes that arose. They became almost neutral figures.

A major source of problems on large farms was the fact that the ideal hierarchy of descending ages was most at odds with reality here. Older lads tended to predominate and those in the highest reaches might be younger, smaller, or less assertive than someone below them. Mr Johnson recalled one such occasion when he was a hind:

There was some times, you know, where . . . the third lad, he might be a bit bigger than the waggoner, you know, he might be a bit older, even . . . and then he could throw his weight about. . . . I was a foreman on a place and this third lad, he'd been a soldier, been seven years a soldier, and he'd been on a farm before that and he got out of the army and he came back . . . to our place for third lad and t'waggoner was – I think he was frightened of him, and we never got to actual blows but he told me once what he was going to do to me. . . . He went and got drunk and then he went upstairs to bed and made a mess in it. And I said, 'Looks tha, man, if tha ever does that any more,' I said, 'I shall rub thy nose in it!' Well, o' course, then he said what he was going to do at me.

'All right, my lad, come on!'

'Oh,' he said, 'You'll fetch a policeman.'

'No,' I said, 'I promise you I won't fetch a policeman. If you can give me a good hiding, I'll ha' one!'

However he didn't. It got to the employer's ears. He said, 'I'll deal with him.'

I said, 'No, you keep out: this is my trouble,' I said . . . , 'but, I'll tell you one thing: if he doesn't try to show straight from now on till his year's up, he's for the high jump.'

And anyway, well, I had to get at him a lot of times because he was a rough un with his horses. Now when they were in t'stable, t'foreman used to go into t'stable before breakfast and he used to tell all the lads what they were going to do. . . . And this chap he was hammering his horses then. He had four horses, but there was two grand black horses. I broke 'em in myself – they were only about six years old: I broke 'em in myself, these horses. And he was hammering them. I didn't say owt then, and we had our breakfast and then came out again and I said (I was going with 'em that morning), 'We'll go to plough.' I had two young horses. We all got outside, outside o' t'stable, all lined up and he was at these two horses again, and t'waggoner was next to me, and I said, 'Just hold these horses a minute,' and I went, and I said, 'Now then, my lad, you're at them horses again, that's the second time this morning,' I said, 'Pull your horns in!'

'Oh,' he says, 'I'll knock hell out on 'em!'

I said, 'Look, I'll knock hell out o' you! Now,' I says, 'This is enough,' I said . . . (there was a month to his time), 'If I ever see you lift a finger at them horses anymore I'll give you the biggest hiding you've ever had in your life!'

I never saw him touch 'em any more, I was glad to get rid of him. Oh yes, he was older than t'waggoner and t'waggoner couldn't do nowt to him. I said to t'waggoner, I said, 'Look, you, if that chap had done that there in t'bedroom when I was a waggoner,' I said, 'I would have chucked him out o' t'window, then he'd have finished up sleeping in t'fold yard.' You know, he daren't say nowt to him. That was what happened, you see, if he was older than t'waggoner and he thought he knew more but, I mean, . . . none o' t'other lads liked him, but, you know, they were just a bit frightened on him.

13   Grooms, *c.* 1900, at Toft House, Birdsall, the Birdsall Estate stud farm of Lord Middleton until about 1925, when it became a tenant farm. At this time Robert Thornton was employed as stud groom and it is possible that he is the older man shown here on the left of the picture. Young single grooms lived very much as horselads did.

14   The staff of Raisthorpe Manor Farm. Standing second from the left in a felt hat is John Dale, a labourer, and next to him in a dark waistcoat and cap is Smith Palfreyman, who spent winter and spring working in the sheepfold and the rest of the year working as rabbit man. The large man seated on the far left is Robert Wood the shepherd. Third from left, with his hands resting on his knees and wearing a felt hat is William Lacy, the bullocky. There are no young lads, but these large farms did have above average numbers of older servants and some of these must be in the picture. (Taken by Charles Bogg of Malton, *c.* 1897.)

15   The entire male staff of High Gardham Farm, Cherry Burton in 1921. The young man out in front is a Mr Watson who was learning farming from Mr Stickney, the farmer, who is not seen here.

16   The staff of Beswick Rush Farm, Beswick, near the river Hull, *c*. 1930. Also included, besides the labourers, lads, and dog is the female staff of the farmhouse, which is fairly unusual. How many lived in in total is unknown.

17 A proud farmer, Mr R. G. Storey of Manor Farm, Wansford, with a pair of his horses and one of his horselads. Note the immaculate condition of the special show harness worn by the horses. This was more elaborate than anything used in the fields, with plenty of brasses and leather flaps or *housens* fitted to the top of the collars. (Taken 1935 or 1936.)

18   William Hazelwood Sedman at his farm of Martinholme Grange in the 1880s. He remained farmer here until his death in 1921 at the age of 80. His pride and joy was his new bicycle, which was then an expensive possession beyond the reach of ordinary folk. His best clothes show the gulf between these men and their servants.

19   Raisthorpe Manor Farm, *c*. 1900. This fine seventeenth-century farmhouse stands on the site of the former medieval village of Raisthorpe. By the late nineteenth century it was owned by Col. John Burstall and was let firstly to Thomas Bower, then from about 1900 to Joshua Bower, and then to Robert Wood to whom Burstall sold the farm around 1920. Wood sold it in about 1925 to Henry Scales and by 1929 he, in turn, had sold it to Walter Jackson. Very few East Riding farmhouses were of such antiquity, especially on the Wolds where so many were the product of the enclosures around the start of the nineteenth century. (Postcard, R.N. Lister, No. 988, postmarked 1907.)

20   Diamond Cottages, Thixendale, shortly after they were built. These were among the best cottages available to farm labourers in the East Riding in the early twentieth century, and still make attractive houses today. Built by the Sledmere Estate in 1897, they were let at £9 or £10 a year. They had three bedrooms and large gardens. Very few cottages came anywhere near this standard, and many were unfit for human habitation. One of the old chalk cottages that made up Thixendale's earlier housing stock can be seen in No. 36.

21 This was a small farmhouse known as Ash Tree Farm before the enclosure of Thixendale, but like many other village-centre farms of the area, it was later overshadowed by those newly created out on the wold tops. It was divided into two cottages in the nineteenth century and in the late 1890s, when this photograph was taken, the front was occupied by the Boyes family and the rear by the Midgleys. Mr Walker, whose reminiscences contributed to this book, was born here in 1903 by which time it had a smallholding attached. In later years it became a combined post office and shop. To the right, beyond the old school, is another cottage which was occupied by an old shepherd, Jimmy Smith, and his wife Elizabeth.

The women are, left to right, Martha Midgley (née Pudsey), Annie Boyes (née Pudsey), and Katie Pudsey. The children are Alfred Pudsey, Jack Midgley, and possibly Kate Boyes.

Though he admitted that the waggoner was in a nasty spot, Mr Johnson did not hide his scorn for his inability to deal with the third lad himself. The foreman was, in theory, there to back up the waggoner, but if things came to such a pass that the foreman had to intervene, then the waggoner had failed. Except where the foreman was single and so mixed extensively with the lads, taking over a good deal of the waggoner's responsibilities, he left such matters of discipline entirely to the waggoner.

A good waggoner did his job by example. If he had the respect of the other lads the hierarchy became, to an outsider, merely a formality, for the waggoner would rarely need to exert any overt authority. If the lads accepted that he was a good workman and was leading them adequately, they put their effort into emulating, not opposing, him. The system, of course, has strong parallels with those used by many youth organizations and particularly public schools, who also have to contain large numbers of adolescents living in stable groups for long periods. At its worst such a system is simply divisive, setting one section against another and allowing older boys to perpetuate past cruelties inflicted on them by passing them on, in turn, to a new intake of youngsters. In the East Riding it worked well, on the whole, because it was really a system of self-discipline using the lads' natural desire to do their jobs well, and channelling their wish to outdo their companions in the process.

During the long winter days of ploughing from dawn till dusk, tramping up and down a field behind a pair of horses would soon pall without the constant concentration of most farmworkers on drawing a straight furrow and comparing it to a rival's. Lads were bound to lark about now and then, but they usually only needed a shout to get them started again. For the few who did not respond, the waggoners' remedies were crude as Mr Walker recalled:

> I'd soon put 'em back – 'Thoo get back. Thoo doesn't belong here. Get back while your turn!' Aye, you couldn't just – say, like, t'waggoner was getting his horses, like t'lad gets his horses out afore t'waggoner: nowt of that, by t'Lord! He'd soon punch him in the end if he wasn't back. No, you had to take everything in your turns, you know. 'Course you all got used to it, do you see, and you used to do it properly.

On many farms the smaller boys suffered fairly regular chastisement. They were the ones whose attention was most likely to wander and, for the first year or two, their lack of experience often got them into difficulties. Fred Kitchen kept a diary during his first year which contained caricatures of the waggoner and the farmer, and when the waggoner found it, 'I expected some "boot-toe", . . . "boot-toe" being the recognised form of correction for farm lads.'[2] A young boy accepted this as inevitable during his first year or two, but as he grew older and rose through the ranks, the waggoner lost his easy, automatic authority as the age and size gap diminished. Relations ideally moved closer to mutual respect, with lads accepting that the waggoner gave the orders, and him accepting that his authority was limited.

When Mr Johnson was the waggoner at Squirrel Hall, a large Wolds farm, the farmer asked him to stop the lads swearing. The farmer was a keen Methodist and when he passed through the stables to get to his pony in the groom's stable he was offended by the language he heard used:

> He said, 'Well, I want you to put your foot down.' And if you abused a lad in them days, you know, they could have you up, like.
>
> *In court, you mean?*
>
> Aye. And he said, 'If you – I want you to stop them lads and if you have to be rough with 'em and you're summonsed,' he said, 'I'll pay t'fine.'
>
> 'No, no,' I said, . . . 'I don't want to be had up for abusing a lad.' No, I wouldn't go on at that, I wasn't in favour o' that. Now he was all right, he was kept out on it, wa'n't he, like? And I mean I should have gotten into some trouble – and a lot o' my relations, you know, they weren't highly placed and they hadn't a lot o' money, but they would ha' been, I should have gotten some stick if I'd been up at court.

As long as it did not interfere with the work, swearing, or anything else, was almost universally regarded as a lad's own business. Mr Johnson had been willing to fight the disruptive third lad he described earlier, even to threaten to throw him through a window, but this was a different matter entirely. Even the farmer recognised that the lads would resist such orders and that a likely result was Mr Johnson mistreating a lad so badly that he could successfully be sued for assault. What he did not recognise, apparently, was the effect on Mr Johnson's reputation of such a court appearance. A fine had only to be paid, but a bad name took a lot of living down once it was acquired.

A foreman, though he was by no means as vulnerable as the waggoner, could not rely on his position to protect him if he lost the respect of the lads, either. Mr Fisher was once a waggoner under a foreman who continually criticised him, but who was not particularly good at his own job. The situation became so bad that Mr Fisher asked the farmer for permission to leave in mid-year, only to be told that only when the farmer found fault was he to worry. Armed with that, Mr Fisher decided to settle the dispute once and for all:

> He came ploughing at me. I was as tall then as I am now and he was only a little man. I says, 'Two more words and I'll stand you in there' [pointing to a tub of treacle and water kept for the horses]. 'Course I knew I was safe; you see, I knew what the farmer'd say. We got on like a house afire after that.

Sensibly, the foreman accepted, however grudgingly, that he would have to modify his behaviour and where only one person was ignoring the accepted etiquette, most disputes followed this pattern. The offender's consent to having things done correctly being unobtainable by any other means, it was obtained by threats or, if that failed, by force. There was always the possiblity that the offender would prove to be the stronger, but, as we have seen, the hierarchy usually loaded the dice in favour of the waggoner, or, if he failed, the foreman. The number of lads who would actually fight was small, but anyone who went as a waggoner on a large farm had to be prepared. He might well never have much trouble, but if it became clear that he would not, or could not, deal with troublemakers he would lose everyone's respect and find his authority had vanished. Mr Johnson recalled:

> There was one chap [the farmer got in], well, he was a queer lad. He got him during t'year. And I think he was in t'sheepfold, and then he came into t'stable and – I don't know, he was all over t'show, he was one o' them, you know, he didn't know where he wanted to be. However, he came into t'stable. . . . He didn't come from the same village [as me] but I knew him. He hadn't a roof to his mouth. He was a rough – he was same age as me, we were t'same weight and I was a bit hefty in them days. Anyway I had to give him a good plugging at finish 'cause, why, he was going to plug me. I said to him one day – well, he was interfering wi' t'lads, messing about wi' t'lads, instead o' letting them get on with their work; he was taking their attention. I said, 'Look, you let them lads alone: you mind your business and let them alone. . . .' And he came across to me, he was about ten or twelve yards [away] and he came across, he was slinging his fists about. I never knew to this day what he was saying, like; but he was blathering.

He went for Mr Johnson and a rather dirty fight ensued before Mr Johnson finally succeeded in getting the upper hand:

> I dropped right on top of his old bread basket with all the weight I had and he roared out, and anyway, I knelt – it was in a field – I knelt, I kept one knee in his bread basket, t'other on t'floor and I said, 'Now, thoo stop there, I want to talk to thoo.' And I said, 'Now then, is thoo going to get up and fight like a man or is thoo going to be a good lad?'
> 'Oh,' he says, 'I'll be a good lad.'
> 'Aye,' I says, 'thoo'd better!'
> And – he asked for it, like, but I never looked for a fight – but I'd been learned how to take care of myself if I had to.

The lads normally functioned as a group and when a waggoner acted as Mr Johnson did, it was to restore their unity, not to break it. Inevitably, though, there were foremen and waggoners who distrusted mutual respect and consent as a basis for running a farm, and some tried to enforce a more rigid discipline instead. The lads' pride in their jobs soon turned to extreme touchiness in such circumstances and a martinet might well create the very atmosphere of indiscipline he had been seeking to avoid. Similarly, a foreman or waggoner who, through weakness or incompetence, could not gain the respect of the others found himself excluded from the group. A state of guerilla warfare could evolve and the lads only had to cease active co-operation to cause considerable disruption. Mr Milner recalled how a relatively minor incident, which occurred while they were ploughing a fifty acre field of wheat stubble in 1917, rapidly escalated into a concerted humiliation of their foreman. The waggoner had been ploughing the guideline furrows in the next field and he rejoined the main body without waiting for his real position to come round:

It was late on, you know, 'cause snow didn't get away very early and [the foreman] would go with us to plough . . . We were going nicely on across t'field, there was t'foreman, thirdy, me and fiver in the lead and t'waggoner had all t'others behind him. . . . I was sort of hanging back, you know, I was a good *half turn* [the length of the field] behind t'foreman . . . and he shouts across to me, 'Get 'em on, fourth!' And as he passed fiver, he says, 'Heel the blowed sod up!' . . . And I just turned to him and said, 'He bloody well can't!' I set my horses off in a trot, it was where I had to go down into a valley and up a hill, you know. I was going across t'valley, they were trying to follow on, other two, I whipped in at top and I was up to thirdy that was following foreman, right up to top end, to t'other end. And thirdy says to me, 'What the hell is tha on?'

'Well,' I said, 'he wants 'em on. He's told me to get 'em on, told fiver to heel me up.' And fiver was. Us five at one end o' t'field and t'wag [who had not speeded up] was turning t'other end o' t'field with t'other lot behind him. So, when it came to dinner time wag was at far end. We pulled up and lowsed out and, of course, third pulled to one side with his horses to wait for t'waggoner coming up so he could get in his right spot. And the old boss says to him, 'Come on,' he says, 'Leave him . . . if the blowed sod can't keep his spot!' 'Course we telled t'wag when he come into t'stable.

When he went for his corn, for the horses, you know, used to go and have it measured out [by the foreman] and he says to him, 'If I was blowed waggoner, I'd keep my blowed spot!' So, waggoner set about him then. He said, 'How much more ploughing ha'e you done than me, this morning?'

He says, 'I don't know that I've done any.'

[The waggoner] said, 'How much more ploughing have I done than you?'

'Why,' he says, 'I don't know.'

'No,' he says, 'but I do . . . , two headland marks . . . fifty yards long!'

And that finished that, at the time. But after dinner when we'd all got in stable, wag says, 'Now this afternoon keep up, tight up,' he says, 'don't bother about cleaning your ploughs,' and he says, 'Keep tight up!'

But we had plenty o' time when we went back at the afternoon to clean our ploughs [free the share and coulter of weeds and roots]. We kept tight up to t'boss and he had nine ploughs all at him – why eight – he was ninth; and he went down into this dip and he turned round [halfway across the field], you know, and 'course thirdy started to turn round and all. 'Oh,' he says, 'go to t'top, go to t'top.' We did, but we were hard at him by [the time] we got up to t'other end, we gained that half-turn on him. He was going limping over to t'farm to get orders that night, you know, and he said to t'master, he said, 'I'm not going to plough with them lot no more. . . .'

Aye, he copped some stick. We were all in a clique, you know, and if ever . . . they got onto one they got all t'lot there.

Clearly that squabble was caused only in part by the events of that particular day. Mr Milner was at fault in dropping back so badly and it was odd for a waggoner to go into the middle of the line, even to save time and get as much work done as possible, but the foreman was committing an outrageous slight on the waggoner's honour when he refused to wait for him. It was a stupid reaction and he had obviously long since lost the respect of his underlings. He was seen as a bad foreman and no more than an ordinary workman, for when, in the afternoon, the lads were ploughing too fast with the leading edges of their ploughs getting progressively more fouled with rubbish, both of which must have detracted from the quality of their work, he was neither able to keep ahead of them nor to insist on them taking their time to do the job properly. Instead he turned round in mid-field (and how his interrupted furrow could be prevented from spoiling the work is hard to imagine), a response that could only confirm the lads' lack of respect for him.

The foreman's action against the waggoner had resulted in his own exclusion from the hierarchy, not the waggoner's, for all the lads were united in their determination to show how unsuited they thought he was to his job. This was disruptive, but in Scotland such cliques were normal and had been institutionalized as part of the farm servant system. The foreman there acted as a mediator between master and man, ensuring that the men worked, but also ensuring that the farmer provided the food and accommodation he had promised. So that the farmer could not play the men off against him, the foreman could demand that the whole staff leave with him, automatically and without demur, on pain of ostracism or worse, if he felt he had to go, leaving a *clean toon*, or empty farmstead. The farmer accordingly knew that if he offended the foreman he would have to get in an entirely new staff at the next term date.[3]

Such formal organization to resist authority was entirely alien to the East Riding except when it appeared in the face of provocation. The work would be neglected while the lads feuded with either the foreman or the waggoner, so it was worthwhile for a foreman or waggoner to consider carefully before taking any actions that might set them apart from the rest of the hierarchy. Similarly, personal quarrels could seriously interfere with work if two or more lads took to sniping at each other continuously. So far we have been concerned almost entirely with the lads at work, but they also had to eat, sleep, and spend most of their leisure-time together. Their fellow workers were the people the lads would be most intimately involved with for most of a year.

The degree to which the members of a group of farm servants knew each other prior to being hired obviously varied tremendously with the hiring policy of each farmer, but on every farm real friends would be outnumbered by acquaintances, and there would be many places where most or all the lads were strangers to one another. Despite this random selection they had to work as a close-knit group and live in each other's pockets for a year. Tensions and squabbles were inevitable, but the hierarchy was intended to reduce them as far as possible by defining each lad's status so that there was no room for disputes over precedence, who should sit and sleep next to whom, and all the other minutiae of communal life. Mr Brambles told me the length to which this was taken:

When you went for your meals, like, you used to line up for a wash, like, and you went in your order, waggoner first, and everybody went in order. And same when you went to t'table, you all sat down in your order. . . . If you got on a big farm where there was five or six of you and you went for a wash at tea time, or breakfast time, last one was washing in black water very near. Just one bowl of water, do you see.

The one who got the dirty water was, of course, the least lad, who was least able to complain and who could always be brought to book by a bit of boot-toe. In the short term it was unfair, but by the time a lad got to be a waggoner, if he did, he had been in every position and so the balance was righted eventually.

Lads were highly sensitive to any slights that seemed to reduce their status. An irreducible minimum of conflicts was bound to remain, therefore, and these had to be contained since they could not be prevented. Disputes did not really matter as long as they remained at the level of bickering, but lads were by no means unwilling to fight one another: their jobs demanded strength and endurance so they set great store by their physical capabilities. Many were fond of boxing as a pastime and they were, on the whole, prepared to accept a few cuts and bruises. If two lads were arguing seriously neither could be expected to go out of his way to prevent a fight. Fighting was bound to disrupt life on the farm and it was accepted that instead of setting to on the spot, the antagonists would arrange to meet during their own time and settle the quarrel in public. The bigger the potential audience the better, so they would wait until a village fair or, preferably, a hiring day, where settling grievances was a time-honoured occupation of farm servants.

Generally, honour was regarded as satisfied after such a meeting or, at the very least, lads had cleared the air enough to be able to wait for another similar venue for a rematch. As Mr Carter pointed out, the older lads 'used to make a mess o' one another an' all when they did start to fight. Oh, they were great big, strong men,' so in every way one definitive battle was better than a feud. Sometimes a lad with a hot temper or a deeply felt grudge would refuse to follow the usual rules, but this happened infrequently. Mr Milner told me of one lad who conceived a hatred for him, based on an insignificant cause. This is a perfect illustration of the dangers of a running dispute to the smooth functioning of a farm, for it rapidly escalated out of all proportion to the original cause:

I had a fall out wi' a lad over Duggleby. He was shouting about eating date pies. Well, I like date pies, you know. And, we were washing one night, and Mrs Edmundson there were t'hind, and she come out and she asked him what were wrong with date pies and this, you see. Why, straight away he flew at me . . . and said I'd been telling things. She said, 'No, he hasn't. I was stood at that window listening to you.' Well, he came for me, picked sweeping brush up, let go at me with it. I put my right hand up and stopped brush a bit, you see, and at same time I gave him my left and he went in t'other corner o' t'wash-house, down on t'floor, like. And that was that. And he told me he would bring a muck fork to me and stick me with it, after that. Well, me being shepherd lad, I was working in [a room] wi' myself and I hears gate open and I thinks, 'Oh, here he comes.' I thought, 'Well, I'll tackle him outside. I won't be in.'

So I went outside and he was coming through t'gate, but he hadn't his muck fork. 'Oh,' I said, 'I thought tha was bringing t'muck fork.'

He says, 'No, I'm off to see t'gaffer.' So he went up to see t'master. 'Bout me. Just plonking him one. Putting him in his place.

Oh, his father came one Sunday and all, after that. He was going to give me such a good hiding. My dad, he'd been in Grimston pub, . . . I was going to stop at home that Saturday night because it was summer-time, and he said to me, 'Dean't thoo go to Duggleby tonight.'

I said, 'What for?'

He said, 'Why, there's Pudsey come to give thee a good hiding.'

I said, 'Why, right, I'm off!'

So I went to Duggleby and I stopped in that bedroom wi' myself, that night, had my breakfast and my dinner and all. No Pudsey turned up. So I said to t'boss, 'why, he isn't going to come. I'll be off.' He come just after I'd gone. I never had that scrap, though. He had a pal with him. Neither of 'em were much.

This could easily have turned into a full-blooded family feud had Mr Pudsey given Mr Milner the thrashing he intended. It was better all round for lads to put up with each other, and the hierarchy assisted them to do so. It may be significant that Mr Milner was, as he pointed out, a shepherd lad at the time, and so not really part of the horselad's hierarchy even though he boarded with them in the farmhouse.

It cannot be overstated that though this chapter has used memories of disputes to illustrate the nature of the hierarchy, this is not because such disputes were common or normal. It is rather that when the system worked smoothly, it was nearly invisible, except for the influence it had on where the lads slept or stabled their horses. Like the yearly bond itself, only more so, its real nature and the reason for its existence can only be seen when it failed. Particular hierarchies came under strain, and sometimes collapsed, from the unwillingness of certain individuals to participate, but no system is capable of handling every individual. Indeed, its overall success is interesting in showing how far lads' personal lives were entwined with their jobs, for it was a system of social control that could only work as long as they identified with their positions in it.

Notes to Chapter Seven

1. T. Keegan, *The Heavy Horse, its Harness and Harness Decoration* (1973), p. 205.
2. Kitchen, *Brother*, p. 41.
3. Carter, 'Oral History', 40–3.

Chapter Eight

Learning the Job

From the day they went onto farms, boys had a full day's work to do and the waggoner saw that, despite their inexperience and lack of knowledge, it was done. The waggoner could sometimes have a difficult time with his older subordinates, but his advantages of age and size gave him a position of great power over the youngsters, who must often have seemed like pieces of grit in an otherwise well-oiled machine. Integrating these children into the workforce was a problem that has no precise modern counterpart, especially as the transition from the world of school to that of work was so abrupt. An East Riding boy would go off at the start of December with a few clothes in a box to start a whole new life. He visited home when he could, usually once a week at most, but otherwise he was now largely on his own, even though he would have been only thirteen or fourteen years of age.

While the legal basis of the yearly bond was the inclusion of farm servants in an artificially extended family presided over by the farmer or his proxy, there was no requirement on the farmer to stand in for the boy's parents during his time on the farm. On small farms lads may once have been taken into families in much the same way as apprentices were by craftsmen,[1] but even then it would be romantic nonsense to assume that any contractual relationship could force the treatment of a hireling as a son or daughter.[2] Within living memory, the relationship between servant and master was almost entirely economic in the East Riding. The foreman was a paid stand-in for the farmer with no reason at all to extend his duties beyond providing board and lodging. There are times when an analogy with an extended family can cast light on the nature of the yearly bond, particularly as it had once operated, but any general comparisons simply mislead. Some lads certainly found themselves in a family atmosphere on a farm, but more were left entirely to themselves, even though they might visibly be in need of care and attention. Fred Kitchen began work in the West Riding on a small farm where the farmer, a woman, saw to the few living-in workers herself, but his first winter was a nightmare:

> I helped the cowman to feed the stock, staggering along under heavy skeps of meal and turnips. . . . I was too small to keep out of the muck, and waded through slop and cow-muck until I became absolutely lost. My breeches became so caked in pig-swill, calf-porridge, and meal I believe they could have stood up without me inside them. My hands, by the same process, aided by

the raw winds, became so swollen and cracked it was purgatory to wash them. And often I didn't. There was no-one interested in whether I washed them or not, and so I degenerated into a 'reg'lar grub-etten little yarker,' who cried and grinned, trying to force stiff, hard boots over broken chillblains . . . [More] bad weather had made my hands more cracked than ever, while the raw thaw wind turned them blue with cold. My overcoat was tied round with string in place of buttons, an important part of my breeches had worn through with riding on old Short's rough cart saddle, while a trellis-work of binder-twine did service for buckles on my leggings. . . . I had become a little ragamuffin, and knew if I presented myself at home in that state I should cop it. The reason they never knew was because I never went home except on Sunday night, when I was respectable; though I kept my hands out of sight as much as possible and spent a tortuous time trying to get them clean before I went.[3]

Nonetheless, for most lads the freedom of standing on their own two feet was preferable to being carefully looked after if that meant submitting to constant checks on behaviour. If a lad was ill he would be looked after, but no-one attempted to give moral guidance or correct a lad's personal conduct unless they personally felt they ought to, and then such intervention was usually ineffective. Some farmers, for instance, tried to insist on churchgoing,[4] but they were few and far between, and we saw in the last chapter that one farmer tried to get Mr Johnson, his waggoner, to stop his lads swearing – by force, if necessary. A farmer's wife or a hind's wife might mother the lads, as Harry Reffold found, but no-one expected them to[5] and the lads mostly grew up as they pleased once they left home. If their parents had failed to set them on course before, everyone felt it was now too late to correct any straying.

The general philosophy was that a youngster would survive most things and would probably benefit from the experience, however unpleasant, in the long run. This underlay the attitudes to teaching and learning skills, which nearly always came down to throwing the boy in at the deep end and leaving him to extricate himself, ignoring his struggles. Though the wag lad or thirdy lad would probably be learning from the wag and the thirdy respectively, they were employed as assistants and as ploughboys, not as learners: they might even be quite old themselves. Mr Walker commented:

I learnt when I was a kid really. We used to go into t'stables when we were kids at home, do you see, among t'other lads, and that's how we learned.
There were nothing like apprenticeships?
Oh no, no! I could plough when I left school, when I was first hired.[6]

A lad whose father was a farmer, a hind, or one of the few married horsemen would be bound to pick up a lot. Mr Baines, the son of a foreman, said:

Well, nearly every lad in t'East Riding, before he left school had had hold of a plough; if he were interested in farming, and, you know, most on 'em, their brothers or their fathers worked on farms and then they used to spend a lot of time on t'farms, you know. You'd go and, same as my dad, when I was a kid about ten year old, and I used to take his drinkings on a Saturday morning into t'field and if he were harrowing or rolling or ploughing he used to say, 'Now, gerron, my lad, and off tha goes. And thoo can go round while I get my drinkings.' That were his bit o' tea and his summat to eat, and same in t' holiday times; you used to go every morning and take your dad his drinkings. And you learnt by doing little bits here and there. My dad used to say to me when I were at school, he used to say, 'Fetch them beasts up and get 'em in cow house for when I come home out o' t'fields.' I used to get 'em in and I used to be milking, and if I hadn't milked two when he came home he used to be wondering what I'd been doing – give me a rousting, you know. . . . I got nowt for it, like.

It was an advantage if farming was in the family, but it was not essential. Mr Pridmore's father operated the Hull and Barnsley Railway swing bridge over the river Ouse at Drax, so his background was as unsuitable for learning farming as could be found in the villages of the county. His ambition was to be an engine driver, but he had to wait until he was eighteen before he could get a place at a locomotive shed. Even he therefore had to spend some time in farming in the meantime. I asked him if he had had to wait till he left school to start learning about it:

Oh no, no. You see, when you're born in a village, farm lads used to congregate together at night time, you see, well us youngsters used to get about amongst them and used to hear what they were talking about; you see that's how you picked things up. 'Course, I'd known about farming – leading hay and such – right from my schooldays, and of course when you go amongst horses you find out what they feed them on and such as that.

Very few boys were simply passive observers as most had to work outside school hours, again usually on farms. Some helped their fathers as Mr Baines did, and Mr Jarvis similarly had to help with the milking on the family farm. Others took paid jobs and Mr Tate remarked, concerning school:

Half o' your time you weren't there, like. Well, you worked on farms, you know. I worked all holidays. I started when I were about eight, milked so many before school and so many after school and all Saturdays and Sundays, like. And all holidays. And when they were threshing. I'd rather stop and thresh than be at school.[7]

Mr Masterman got a job as groom lad at Camerton Hall, where his father worked, going at six in the morning, taking time off for school, and finishing at eight or nine in the evening - unless the light gave out first. While the school leaving age was fixed at fourteen, anyone who had attended school satisfactorily for five years or could pass an examination of the level of standard IV could leave at thirteen, which the overwhelming majority of working-class children did. Moreover, until the 1920s, those who could pass a physical examination could become half-timers or part-timers in their final year, working half of each day or else combining these permitted absences into one block,[8] as Mr Johnson did:

> I left school when I was thirteen. The summer before that I had three months off. If you passed an examination you could have three months off during the summer: you could help at home or you could go somewhere, you know, to work a bit. I went into a market garden for these three months. Then I went back to school for the winter. And the next spring, I was thirteen years old in January and the spring after that you went to the nearest town and if you passed another examination you could leave school altogether.

By the time a lad was first hired he already knew a great deal about farming; certainly enough to get by on while he gained practical experience, of which some needed a lot. Mr Carter said:

> When you got hired off at November, well, you had to take your luck but it come to you through time. [At ploughing] you made a few what we called *balks*. That was missing a bit, do you see, and you had to turn round, used to make you turn round and put [the plough] in t'furr again and take it out to seal it over. But you got better on that as you went on.

A boy could start at any level at which he could persuade a farmer of his competence. If a farmer would let him look after work horses of his own in his first year, then he could. If he overreached himself, however, he had to take the consequences, usually administered by the waggoner's boot. Mr Tate's first job, for instance, was looking after and working three horses, which meant that he had to know at least the rudiments of correct feeding, grooming and harnessing. Most lads were not so confident of their abilities and Mr Johnson began as a waggoner lad in his own parish. Others began even lower, as a box lad or a groom lad, sometimes with a groom and sometimes on their own. They might start on any size of farm, but Mr Baines voiced the general opinion when he said:

> You generally start off, if you've got a little bit of commonsense and a little bit of luck, you go onto a little farm, where you learn and nearly always the little farms are your best places. . . . You knew you were all right because they'd look after you more, if they just had you there on the farm and you knew you could learn a lot of things where if you went to a big farm you'd have to take your place, probably eighth lad or seventh lad. You were only allowed to do certain jobs.

This does not mean that a boy was spared heavy work: if there were heavy and light jobs and the foreman was sympathetic, the boy would get the light job, but otherwise he had to do his share of the heavy work. What he missed was the work that only required a few teams and so he would learn few skills apart from the basics, like ploughing. On a small farm he would be treated more as an individual and, since there would be only two or three lads at most, he would get to try his hand at most things. Nowhere, however, was there much sympathy for a boy's small size and inexperience. If he could not do the job, most people felt the best way for him to find the pitfalls was by falling into them. Boys were even given unpleasant jobs because they, of all the lads, were least able to complain. Mr Tate told me:

By God, if you were a poor lad, on a farm, leading thorns, we'll say; lad loadening 'em, snowing and blowing. Aye. It was a rum job for a poor lad, you know. Starved to death, you know. I once heard them say, to a lad . . . , he couldn't get down, you know, 'cause it used to be a rum job getting down off a load of thorns, and he once said, 'If tha doesn't get down I'll shove bugger over!' Then, poor lad, he had to get down the best way he could, you know. They hadn't any pity for a poor lad, you know; you'd think they'd never been lads theirselves, wouldn't you? . . . Aye, it were hard work for poor lads sometimes. . . . But, still, like, there was good spots and bad uns.[9]

Mr Masterman described the start of his career like this:

You had to do same as the other lads did. You had to – if you went into field to plough, you ploughed as much as they did.
    What about lifting and that?
    Oh no, that's only job you didn't do, like. But ploughing (. . . say you yoke at this end o' the field, you go – to that end and back, that's one turn. They call it a turn), well, you had to go as many turns as the waggoner did . . . . The waggoner was my boss. I had to go as many turns as he did. If I lost one I had to do that after they'd gone home.
    And they expected that right from the start? They didn't give you time to learn?
    Oh no. And then, leading manure – I had to take as many loads out as what the other lads did. Same in harvest – I'd to fetch as many loads out the fields as the other lads did. Because we used to go in twos. . . . We used to go in pairs. So that there was two stacks going, there was one for each stack. Well I'd to fetch as many loads out o' field as what the other lads did. Some of the lads had double the wage I had, but I still had to – the only thing I didn't do that they did was carry corn from the threshing machine into granary. That's only job I didn't do that they did. I had to do every other job. . . .
    I left school at thirteen and I went to that farm at Keyingham Grange and the next morning – I went one afternoon, they'd told me to go, like – next morning they gave me a pair of horses and a plough and I went with the other lads and I ploughed all day, every day, as long as they did. I know at night I was a right mess. I was all mud, because t'plough knocked me down. When the horses turned in, instead of me knowing what to do with the plough so that the plough swung round, I left t'plough, and the horses going round pulled – the blinking handles caught me at the back of the knees and knocked me down all in the mud and I was all mud. But I soon learnt, I soon learnt how to just lean my plough over so it slided round without knocking me down. I got knocked into a ditch one day with it – caught me behind the knees, I was running too close to the ditch and I went in.

As if his inexperience was not a big enough handicap, the least lad had the oldest and slowest horses while the waggoner, the pacesetter, had the best. A sympathetic supervisor could matter a lot at this time in a boy's life, especially on a big farm where he was easily lost in the crowd, as Mr Rispin recalled:

You got good foremen and bad uns. . . . Say six o' you went to plough, . . . t'foreman, he was a good old – he was a keen horseman but he was good for a little lad, he'd wait till the little lad got, see as he got lowsed out, you know, his strings rolled up and then give him a lift onto t'horse, where you would maybe get another, gets lowsed out and off up t'road and a little lad would maybe be struggling. His horses would maybe set off before he got lowsed out, d'you see. Oh aye. But he was a good old sort was that. Why, I used to do the same, like, when I was foreman. . . .

I went with them one morning and lowsing out at dinner time, t'waggoner set off and left poor little lad, he – his horses set off, well, he hadn't gotten his traces off. But I went to him. He was crying. He wasn't very [old]. Followed 'em in, like, and we got 'em into stable, like, and I said to t'waggoner, 'Don't you come away from that lad no more like that.' I said, 'I'd rather you lowsed out five minutes sooner.' . . . Well, he was only a lad first year off. I said, 'You do t'same. . . .' Oh aye, he never had no more bother, like. Aye, t'poor little lad.

Although there were many advantages to starting on a small farm it would be misleading to say that all lads did so, graduating to larger ones as they became accomplished: all that can be said is that small farms had more than their fair share of youngsters, while the majority of well-paid jobs a lad would look for as he grew older would be found on the large farms. The small farmer could manage the heavy work on his own, while, for the rest, boys were adequate for his needs and only asked for low wages. Once they had mastered the basic skills many were satisfied, for they needed no more to become a third lad, but for anyone ambitious the process of learning never stopped. They had to take every opportunity to gain new skills. Mr Rispin told me, for instance:

Why, I was only a lad, eighteen years old, at Tuft Hill and that's where I started to stack and I stacked right away up to coming on my pension. Every year. Different places, like. Aye. I was only a lad. Eighteen years old when I first started to stack. . . . They put an old man on to show me, do you see, what they called a piker, like, same as these old labourers, you know: they used to show you – they learnt me. I'd two year stacking up there, then I come here for waggoner and there was an old chap there, by Go' he was a good stacker, I got more insight there, like. . . . Every man had a different way of stacking, like, you know. You seed some good stacking and you seed some bad uns.

Everything on a farm was learned by experience with a minimum of theory and teaching. Apprentices today spend large parts of their time in day-release classes at technical college but boys then were felt to have entered the world of adults as soon as they left school. They were not able to take a full part in that world, for the farm servant stage of life can be viewed as an institutionalized adolescence, but they were held to be largely responsible for themselves. The onus was on them to learn, so as to be able to carry out their duties, rather than on anybody else to teach. Lack of knowledge, however understandable, tended to be viewed as a dereliction of duty to be criticised and frequently punished. Particularly before the First World War, Mr Masterman recalled, some waggoners reacted to even a hint of disobedience:

> The waggoners used to use the boot. They did an' all. The lads was well-disciplined – and them boots the waggoner used to wear, you know, they were boots. They weren't like these [modern boots]. They were boots with metal toes and if you got one o' them you knew you'd had – you knew a day or two after. . . . The first waggoner that I was with . . . , he was a feller about six foot three and if you – if he told you to do a thing and you looked as if you didn't want to do it, he'd kick you from one end o' t'stable to the other. So you didn't. You didn't want that twice. But I don't think it did you any harm.

Whether Mr Masterman was as philosophical a day or two after the kicking, when the marks still showed, as he was sixty years on must be open to doubt, but it was a sentiment many lads put into practice when they became waggoners. All too many older lads were willing to equate simple lack of practice, or even ignorance of how to do a job, with disobedience. With the natural inequalities of age reinforced by the hierarchy a young lad was more or less at the mercy of the older lads. Many kicks and clips on the ear, the vast majority of which were not meant maliciously, were given, but very few men wished to hurt those under them. However, a boy could have a very bad year with one who did, and they did exist, as Mr Tate remembered:

> Some on 'em was rough 'uns, you know. Aye. They'd half-kill 'em and nobody would say owt, you know. . . .
> *Nobody would stand up for a little lad?*
> Why no, not that – they might if he had a brother there; like, if his brother was there, big enough to look after him.

Harry Reffold was lamed for weeks by a waggoner's kick, but he was saved from further injury by the thirdy, who was more than a match for the waggoner.[10] Mr Johnson agreed that there were limits to what would be tolerated:

> There was quite a lot on 'em, if they got a bit o'er wild, like, they would strike up, like, and say, 'Now you leave him alone!' I've known that happen quite a lot.
> *So they weren't just at the mercy of people who were twice as old?*
> Oh no, no. No, there was generally somebody who would take their part, like.

Like Mr Tate, Mr Johnson worked on farms on the north Wolds and the difference in their testimony shows how far, in an area like this, different men not only had different experiences, but also coloured them by their own viewpoints. It is difficult to judge the extent of mistreatment boys received and the effect it had on them, given the background of corporal punishment on a scale that would be quite unacceptable today and the difficulties experienced even by contemporaries in deciding when to call a halt. The existence of such mistreatment must be recognised, however, and a boy was particularly vulnerable if he was hired as an assistant to a bully, for he could then be persecuted in the name of discipline, as Mr Tate's brother found out:

> He wasn't very old when he went to a farm at Thornholme . . . and my brother was under [the third lad] – his lad, you see. By, and he did use to kick his backside, did this man. And he said he never seen him since. He said, 'I oft wanted to see him.' Meet him, like, when he was in his twenties. He'd have putten him right.

The safest course was to suffer in silence for cheekiness was not tolerated, and almost any sign of self-assertiveness might be taken as cheekiness. Any argument, however well-founded, was likely to be silenced by a clip round the ear. On the other hand, if physical violence went too far, the perpetrator could be sued for assault. In addition, a waggoner who set too many of his subordinates against him could find them all setting about him at the hirings when he could not revenge himself on them one by one. This was known as smallganging. These were, however, merely guards against really vicious excesses and the lack of any really effective institutional protection for the most vulnerable members of the farm servants' group is probably its greatest weakness. Very little could be done to prevent the unhappiness that minor physical abuse and continuous harassment could cause, as Mr Johnson recalled of his own first year:

> I was waggoner lad and when I went I was only thirteen. The place weren't a bad place, but this waggoner, he was a lad and he was a bit clever. . . . [I] had a watch and we used to carry our watches in t'pocket, watch pocket . . . and used to have a chain and then you had, you know, these bits o' trinkets on end and that. Well, I had a seal, it was shape of a barrel. About like a thimble and it was marked right away round in two different colours and my dad gi'e me it. I went and begged this off my dad, he said, 'No, somebody'll take it off you.' However, at finish he gi'e me this seal, as they called it, and I had it on my watch chain. And this waggoner was asking – kept wanting me to give him this and I wouldn't. Anyway, we used to take our watches out on a night and put 'em out on whatever you had handy, maybe a chair, a row of boxes, old chest: whatever, and then next morning when I got my watch, my watch was broken; glass was broken and my seal was gone, taken off. Anyway I enquired a bit but I had to be very careful what I said, else, you know, I'd 'a' gotten a clout. Anyway, after a bit he pulled his watch out and there was my seal at end of his watch chain.

'Oh,' I said, 'I'd an idea where it had gone.'
'Oh,' he said, 'That isn't yours!'
'It is.'
'Oh no.'
'It is.'
Well, I argued the point with him and I got a clout at finish like, you
know. . . . And he was a bit rough with me. Anyway I said to him one day, I
said, 'All right, now, I will tell you,' I said, 'I shan't be a little lad always.'

Mr Johnson later did see him many times at hiring fairs and he could easily have
taken his revenge as the man was only small, but over the years he lost the desire.

The system put a premium on self-confidence and a lad had to be robust, for
weakness would find little sympathy whether it was genuine or feigned. There is a
direct parallel between the treatment given to boys and to foals. When they talked
about rearing and breaking foals most men made it clear that they saw the most
productive approach as being based firmly on kindness, tempered by a determination to tolerate no nonsense. They beat foals, but only for a reason, and trying to
terrorize a foal into submission was condemned as both cruel and wasted effort.
Boys were credited with more knowledge of what they were doing and accordingly
held more responsible for their acts, but a man who could see the pointlessness of
terrorizing a foal could see that it was stupid and wrong to mistreat a boy without
reason. Most men were rough with boys because they lived in rough times and
because they had come through the same system. Allowances were often made for
their youth, but such allowances soon ceased if a boy came to expect and rely on
them.

No system can protect everyone and plenty of young lads suffer in their first jobs
today, even though the overt physical discipline of East Riding farms would not be
tolerated. Mostly, a boy's new found independence was ample compensation for
any hardships. The least lad's lowly position was offset by his great relief at having
left school. He was trusted with great responsibility in being given even a partial
share in caring for and working horses. The pride thus generated could withstand
many knocks, particularly since a large proportion of the knocks came precisely
because they were held fully responsible for doing a good job. Fred Kitchen said, 'I
must have looked unkempt and forlorn, but I was perfectly happy. I was too busy to
be otherwise, and I always maintain that to be perfectly happy a person should get
busy or interested in something.'[11]

Notes to Chapter Eight

1. See Thompson, *Lark Rise*, p. 396. This concept is extensively discussed in Snell, *Annals*,
   especially chaps 2, 5 and 7.
2. See P. Laslett, *The World We Have Lost: Further Explored* (3rd ed., 1983), chap. 1.
3. Kitchen, *Brother*, pp. 56–7 and 66–7.
4. See Simpson, *Gleanings*, p. 96.
5. See Reffold, *Pie for Breakfast*, p. 59.

6. See also Kitchen, *Brother*, p. 80.

7. See also Day, *Horses*, p. 21, where he recounts that in his experience some boys were fed on the farms they worked on during the holidays, and they would often be hired onto the same farms when they were old enough to leave school.

8. Half-timing is a subject poorly covered by existing scholarship especially as it applied to agriculture. E. and R. Frow, *A Survey of the Half-Time System in Education* (Manchester, 1970), is the best source available and see pp. 23–4 for the legal basis of the system. Half-timing was a relic of early factory legislation intended originally to get children into school but later operating in the opposite direction. The vast majority of the children affected worked in Lancashire and Yorkshire textile mills until the present century. Local bye-laws and the need to adapt it to suit farming, most notably in allowing block absences rather than insisting on half of each working day being spent in school, makes general description impossible. It was formally abolished in 1918 but, with typical vagueness, was still functioning into the 1920s in practice, ibid, p. 81.

9. See also Reffold, *Pie for Breakfast*, pp. 30–4 and 62.

10. Reffold, *Pie for Breakfast*, p. 41.

11. Kitchen, *Brother*, p. 57.

Chapter Nine

Horse Feeding

Each day, before and after the long hours in the field and even on days when no field work was required, a lad had his team of horses to look after. The foundation of good work was good feeding, and the act of feeding itself helped to build up the sense of partnership which was essential if the work was to be done without a struggle. A good co-operative horse team could be left to do a large part of many jobs themselves, allowing the lad to concentrate his attention where it was most needed, but if the partnership went sour life became one long battle. Their horses and the work done with them were the lads' way of showing themselves off to the world and many Sundays were spent comparing them, rather than leaving work behind. They enjoyed competing amongst themselves in this way to see who had the fattest and glossiest horses; but the real competition for a good horselad was with himself, not with others. They continually sought to improve their performance, but it was not a destructive competition between them. If one lad did exceptionally well, he was not an exclusive winner rendering the efforts of the rest worthless. There was always room for good work to win praise.

This chapter is more concerned with the elaboration of a seemingly simple task into a complex social ritual than with the technical details of keeping a horse's strength up, though this is dealt with as far as is necessary. It is not a guide to horse feeding, some of the routine of which has already been touched upon. It is about the interaction between farmers and lads in search of the ideal team, and about the devious ways in which the lads circumvented the obstacles placed in their way by their employers, the law, and circumstances. In practice very few farmers knew exactly what their horses were eating, for the official diet was rarely more than one element, if the largest one, in the total feeding scheme of any lad. Feeding was an activity that took up a significant part of each day, including the dinner hour, as Mr Johnson explained:

> We were supposed to put an hour and a half in at morning, two hours really, before breakfast, an hour at dinner time, apart from your dinner, and two hours at night, but that was when your horses was working real hard. But in winter time, you know, or in rough weather and that, when you weren't out, well they didn't want as much to eat and, you know, they didn't want so much cleaning as that, you see: they didn't get dirty and you didn't put so much time in with them. But if you didn't put an hour in, every meal time, you weren't doing your duty, . . . Sundays or any day.

The chapter is set exclusively in the outbuildings of the farm, and particularly the stable. The horses were usually kept in one stable unless there were too many of them. On the whole, stables were simple utilitarian buildings which varied only slightly from farm to farm. Wherever possible there was only one door, and a gangway running the length of the building, against the outside wall, gave access to the stalls, or stannings, which usually housed two horses each. Since the horses were at work most days, and were rarely in the stable except to eat, rest, and sleep, there was felt to be no need to provide loose boxes or roomy stalls. A double stanning was about 10 feet from one skelbase, or partition, to the next, so the horses could do little more than stand there (hence the name for the stall), or lie down. Not everyone liked this system, as Mr Tate said:

Some places had all single horses, you know. They [single stannings] were, why, they were handiest for some things, like, especially if you had two together and they didn't agree, you know, they would lame one another. . . . Used put a pole between them . . . so they couldn't kick one another. . . . They were tied up for weeks, sometimes . . . in bad weather. . . . Why, I had one at [one] farm there, it had twelve weeks, I think – never had a collar on nor nowt. Tied up all the time.
  Did you exercise it at all?
  No . . . [and] it was no good to the horse: when they had to work it very near killed 'em, you see. Same as you, if you had a month sat in and then had to go outside to work.

In winter the horses slept in the stables and although there was no heating, their bodies kept it pleasantly warm compared to the cold outside. The lads often spent their spare time in the stables because of this. They had half doors and the top half was generally left open, 'unless it was very cold, draughty, or snowing,' said Mr Johnson. There were also ventilation bricks in the walls but these were stuffed with rags if they caused draughts. The windows were glassless hit-and-miss types: they comprised two wooden frames each with alternate slats and gaps, one sliding behind the other. When the slats were aligned the window was open, and when they filled the gaps, it was closed. During cold spells:

It is not unusual to find every vent hole in stables blocked with hay or straw, and the air is so charged with heat and ammonia that it takes your breath away when entering in a morning. . . . Farm horsemen [think] . . . that it not only adds to the comfort of the animals under their charge to *keep t'cawd oot*, but that this also produces a glossy coat.[1]

As the horses got plenty of fresh air while at work, the conditions may not have had the effect the lads thought, but they did no harm.

Each stanning had a manger, or crib, and hay rack, or heck, for each horse. The horse feeder usually had storage bins so that he could bring in several days supply of food at once, rather than fetch and carry every day. In the Vale of York, where the waggoner undertook all the feeding with only the help of the seconder, and then only where there were too many horses for one, much of this fetching and carrying was, of course, done by the other lads. Elsewhere most lads were fully in charge of seeing to their team and did it all personally. It came from nearby outhouses or from the granary in the case of horse-corn, that is, oats. Nearby would be a pond for watering and washing the horses and there was also a saddle room where the harness was cleaned and hung up when not in use.

Oats were the staple diet, either given in their natural state as hard corn, or rolled, roughly milled to crush them without reducing them to flour, which were easier for a horse to digest, particularly if it was old and had bad teeth. Hay was usually provided as a bulky food to give the horses something to chew on and to fill them up. There were areas, particularly on the Wolds, where little or no hay was made, however, and chop was used as a substitute. This was either a straw and hay mixture or straw alone, chopped into short lengths in a chaff cutter. There would be a special chop house where the cutting was done, usually in large enough batches to last a while. Turnips or mangels were given by some farmers as well, whole or cut up as part of the chop.

There were farmers that gave the lads practically nothing but oats to feed to their horses, but this was unwise. Horses become bored with a monotonous diet just as people do, and much of the skill in feeding lay in keeping them interested in what they were eating. Many inexperienced lads, who thought they were doing well by their horses if they continually gave them handfuls of oats, ran into trouble, as Mr Johnson explained:

There's a phrase . . . in the Bible about a stalled ox, well a stalled ox or a stalled cow means it's had that much food its sick o' looking at it, and then it won't eat. Well, that's one thing you had to mind when you were feeding horses: keep 'em well fed but not overdo 'em. Just keep 'em a little bit of appetite on. Because if you got 'em stalled, you wouldn't get 'em to eat, they would maybe come in on a dinner time, they wouldn't eat anything. Well, their flesh goes then.

Many stables had a slurry tub in the corner containing a mixture based on black treacle whose recipe varied according to the generosity of the farmer. One would dilute it with water where another would dissolve cake in it, producing a very rich mixture. The horses loved it, and a small amount of good slurry in the manger would revive a flagging appetite wonderfully. Other things could be added to the food to maintain a horse's appetite, or to improve its appearance. Mr Baines said:

We used to give them linseed cake for their coat: that puts a bloom on them. We used to give them blood salts, or condition salts as they called them then. Rock salt for them to lick in their heck; and we used to feed them well. . . . Every farmer, each individual farm man, and farm waggoner used to like his horses fitter than the next farm and he used to try to keep them that way. And it's good clean feeding that makes a horse fit and bonny, and cleaning, of course: grooming. If you groom 'em well, they've always a good coat and [if] they're fed well as well, they're bound to have. And, we used to do all sorts of

little tricks. We used to use the old jerry – save the contents of the . . .
goesunder, and we used to put it in a bucket and we used to put it on their
food. The stronger it is and the better it is for horses. And it used to make 'em
eat like mad. We used to give 'em mangels, . . . not chopped mangels, whole
mangels.

Farmers generally acknowledged that scope should be given for treating each
horse as an individual, but most of them denied the lads many of the things they
considered vital. Oats and hay or chop were often the only things officially given
out. On only a few farms, like Harrison's of Burton Agnes, were lads allowed
anything they wanted, and the horses worked as hard as they were well fed, Mr Tate
told me:

Them horses ought to have been in a glass case, you know. In winter, you'd
get eight stone [of oats], like, for two days, for four horses, and then at spring
o' year you'd have about seven and two linseed cakes, bucket o' barley, then a
little scuttle of, perhaps, Indian corn. A day. They were well fed, like.

Normally, farmers would not stand the expense of such liberal feeding and the
storehouses were often locked up so that only the beastman or shepherd could get
into them. Cake was intended for the cattle, the roots went to the cattle and sheep,
and meal was for the pigs. Including the extras, Mr Harrison gave his horses more
than normal as well. Standard rations, said Mr Fisher, were 'about a stone a day,
when they were at work, . . . hard corn, and then they used to fill their racks up wi'
hay. But if you got a stone o' corn into 'em, like, they didn't want much hay.' The
lads were usually dissatisfied with such a plain diet and cake was the particular target
of their aspirations. Mr Baines remembered:

Every horse on a night, last thing at night, when you were fothering up (that
were nine o'clock time), as soon as you started . . . to get your linseed cake to
give them a bit each, they used to all start whinnying and jumping about.
They all knew, you know, that it were linseed cake time.

Cake was the first processed and concentrated animal feed and whereas most of
the horses' other food was grown on the farm, it had to be bought in and it was
expensive, so farmers used it sparingly. It came in three varieties: cotton, linseed,
and union, which was a mixture of the others. It was intended for fattening cattle,
putting the maximum weight on in the shortest time, so increasing their sale value
and recovering the cost of the cake. The lads, therefore, took matters into their own
hands and helped themselves whenever they could. They accepted that they were
technically stealing, but, said Mr Johnson:

If somebody had come to you, say, come from somewhere else, you know,
and said, 'Well, can you pinch us four stone o' meal or cake or owt?' I mean,
we wouldn't have done that. But we used to call it pinching. But, I mean, it
never went off the place – the farmers' stock was getting it, we didn't look on

it as stealing, you see. . . . If anybody had, as I say, . . . wanted us to steal something and sell it, oh no, I don't think one in twenty would ha' done that.

Furthermore, it is evident that this pilfering was so widespread and persistent that it could only have gone on with the passive consent of the foreman at least, and very often of the farmer as well. Farmsteads were too small and isolated for such activity to be undetected, especially as their prevalence was common knowledge. When I asked Mr Fisher if everyone took part he replied:

Oh yes. If you thought owt about your horses you did. Aye. This farmer . . . , he said he wouldn't give a toss for one as didn't. . . . I once met him – it was during lambing time and . . . I'd been out somewhere, and I was a bit late, and I thought, 'Well, I'll just fetch these horses a bit o', you know, a bit extra,' and I was just going into cake house . . . and he was coming through at other end, it was a road straight through, you see, and he'd been looking at sheep and we clashed in the middle. . . . All he said was, 'Good night, Clarry.'

The idea that some farmers actually expected lads to steal came up several times. It is certain that few foremen can have seen anything wrong in the lads' behaviour since they themselves had been lads not long before. Mr Johnson explained his attitude as a foreman:

I didn't mind, you know, I didn't keep my eye on 'em that tight, you know, I turned a blind eye – as long as I didn't know, because I was in charge. Now if some of them horses had gone wrong through getting too much wheat or something, and [we'd] gotten a vet and t'vet had said to the employer, . . . 'This horse has had some wheat,' . . . well then, that employer would come to me and say, 'Well, you aren't keeping your eye on them.'

Why then was the pretence maintained that it was stealing? By seeming to deny the lads any cake or meal at all, the farmers succeeded in their real aim, which was to keep down the amounts involved. The lads were so involved in trying to make their horses into objects of general envy that they easily lost sight of the fact that generous feeding was only a short step from overfeeding. Not only was this costly, but Mr Johnson spoke from experience in saying that caution was essential in feeding, even if the horse was not actually harmed:

At Aike everything was open, there was nothing locked up. Never. If we wanted, well, we got it. . . . I was there three years; last year, I was t'waggoner and them horses there, . . . I think it was wi' being so well fed, they'd habit of colic. Gripe, we used to call it: colic, you know, its like human bellyache. But its a serious thing with a horse, they can go on for hours and hours and hours. Well, this horse, it was one I drove to plough. Always looked well, she always carried a lot o' fat, and she was griped one night. . . . Oh, we were hours and hours, me and this farmer, hours and hours and – she was [in the] habit of doing this, and he said, 'Well, I'll sell her.' He'd been going to sell her a few times, but then he, you know, she got better, so he kept her. Anyway, I know I can remember him saying to me, he said, 'Thoo overfeeds this mare!' You know, he just said it like that. 'I don't know,' I said, 'All she gets is a bit o' chaff. . . .' Anyway next day he sold her.

Pilfering had become so much a traditional part of the farm lads' way of life that without it they would have felt lost. Most farmers were probably reluctant to deny them their pleasure and were happy to play their part – if there was no apparent risk involved a lot of the spice would have vanished. Yet there were farms where the horses were very strictly rationed, and where lads often stole simply to make up an inadequate diet. Mr Johnson remembered:

There was only one place I lived at where you were stinted with your horse corn, as they called it. After dinner, every day you took your bag up to the granary and the foreman . . . was there, and he measured it out to you in a bushel scuttle. . . . A bushel of oats is the lightest corn, a bushel of oats is two stone. . . . He filled this bushel scuttle just level, they used to bring a stick over [the top], you know, level – put that into your bag and that was your ration for your horses. Well, when they weren't doing much, you know, in winter time and that, and short days, its all right, but we got to . . . working hard and long hours: it wasn't enough.

These farmers were often genuinely keen to prevent pilfering and lads who were caught might be prosecuted. It is hard to know how many farmers really wanted to stop their lads stealing altogether because many felt honour bound to make a fuss if they caught someone. Otherwise they might as well unlock everything, and while it was safe to let a trusted lad know that you had confidence in his judgement, the same privilege could not be extended to those whose ability was not proven or was not sufficient.

Lads showed great ingenuity in getting what they wanted and then in keeping it hidden until it was needed. Even if the sheds were left unlocked they had to find a time to go in when they would be undisturbed, and they had very little free time in the day. If the sheds were locked there was a variety of ways round the problem. Mr Ashby used to drop a few slabs of cake off on the outskirts of the farm whenever he was sent to fetch a waggon-load from the station. He returned later to pick them up, which itself was no mean feat. Cake today is made up into small nuts and bagged, but in those days it came in very large, unwieldy slabs. Many people preferred carrying the eighteen-stone sacks of wheat, because at least they were flexible and sat upon the shoulders. Carrying slabs of cake secretly round the farmstead took a great deal of doing.

Mr Johnson preferred burglary:

We used to have all sorts of keys. . . . I'd two or three skeleton keys. . . . I could do it now with a mortice lock. If you gave me a key that'll fit in, you know – it's the right thickness – I can file t'guts out till it'll turn that lock. Well – oh, we got that job off. Well now . . . a padlock is a bit different. You can do it with a bit o' bent wire, but a mortice lock, anybody can make – all you do is file what we used to call the guts out and then you've just two prongs left. Yeah. And nine times out of ten, unless its a very complicated lock, it'll turn it. And, oh, we used to make them ourselves, you know, file the insides out. Now these mortice locks, they used to have a staple, you know, in the jamb and in the door. Well if you wanted to be in bad (you couldn't do it that often because you gave the game away), we used to draw the staple, you know, and get in.

Now then, when our horses – we used to look after our horses, why nine lads out of ten did, they'd a pride in their horses – and if, you know, horses was tired of eating oats, well all right, we'll see if we can get a bit o' cake. Oh, maybe take tiles off and get through t'roof – different ways. Watched, you know, when the beastman was feeding his beasts – watch him go in and then watch him go out to wherever his cows are, and you used to nip in and collar something and out again before he came back. But you always had to dodge it.

Mr Milner also used skeleton keys, but Mr Playforth was on one farm where the lads made their own doorway, prising some boards loose with a crowbar. After that they were able to put up and take down the boards at will. Mr Rispin remembered one night when he was a hind: 'I went out one night at Middledale and I says, "I say, do you know, there's a light i' barn?" . . . . And do you know what they'd done? They'd putten our Frank through a little hole to get cake!' Once acquired, things were hidden under the chaff in the chaff house, which the lads were entitled to use, or buried in their corn bins. Mr Baines made hiding places in the hollow, double-boarded partitions between the stalls: 'We used to have loose boards, and we used to have one with a nail at t'top and one with a loose nail at t'bottom and we used get linseed cake and put them in them partitions.'

Lads also helped themselves to wheat and barley. There were many farmers who would tolerate cake stealing but not grain stealing, for wheat and barley are much higher quality grains than oats and must be treated with great caution. To illustrate the point, while a bushel of oats weighed two stones, one of barley weighed three stones, and one of wheat weighed four stones. Mr Johnson said:

> This job I'm going to tell you about, it was a bit dodgy. You used to give them barley and wheat. Now barley isn't – I didn't like barley really, barley is what we used to call heating stuff. It heats the blood and makes 'em itch and scratch, you know. But, a bit's all right, you know, when they're working, but not in wintertime. . . . But wheat – I have given 'em wheat, and you have to be careful . . . because I tell you what happens, you must not give 'em any wheat before they get any water. Because if you, say you feed a horse wheat and then take him to water, well that wheat swells – it swells a lot more 'n oats and then he has colic and, well, it can kill him. But I've given 'em wheat – but I would never advise anybody else to do it, but I used to give 'em it the last thing at night. . . . Before we went to bed we used to go into t'stable and . . . shake their beds up, make their beds up afresh and give them a feed

or two – just depends, you know, what they would eat. And that's the time I used to give 'em wheat. And there was no danger of 'em getting any water before next morning, you see – it would swell gradually. They would work hard on wheat but you had to be very careful, you mustn't give 'em much.

A common way to render the wheat more innocuous was to steep it, as Mr Baines explained:

They used to get basic slag [a fertilizer] in little bags . . . and we used to wash [the bags] in pond or in a tub, a bucket, and then we used to put barley in 'em or wheat in 'em, and we used to have barley in, in preference. We used to put it in the muck hill, where we used to muck the horses out. And we used to leave that for a few days until it just got what we called sprutted, and we used to give each horse a portion every day – every night, at night time, and that makes 'em dance a bit.

An alternative was to use the pond. By soaking the grain, it swelled before it entered the horse, and if it was left in the muck hill they found it even tastier. The main danger in this was that even if the farmer did not see the bags, the pigs might uncover them while rooting for food. Pigs left very little for the horses if they did. Even soaked it was fed cautiously, because it was so much stronger than oats. To say that wheat, or barley, could kill is not an exaggeration, as I was told in confidence:[2]

I lived on a farm . . . , about 1912 I think it would be and I was only a youngster then, and the other man (there was only two of us) – the other lad, well, he was a man twenty-four or -five year old then, and he did all the feeding. Well, he killed one of his horses. . . . He fed it on wheat and bust it. You know, it swelled. Well I didn't know much about it, 'cause I hadn't been at the job long, and I said to the waggoner, I said, 'Don't you think you're giving that horse too much?'
  'Oh, its all right!' But you see, it was dry wheat and . . . when he'd eaten it and it swelled, it swelled up too much. He gave it too much. Killed it. 'Course he had it to pay for. He had to stay there till he worked it out . . . , about two years. Well, a horse then was about, we'll say a good horse was forty pound then, i' them days. . . . Well, say he had twenty-three or -four pound for a year's wage, . . . he'd get a bit of money during the year, but he had to work until he'd paid it off. Or else – why the farmer said he could do that or go to jail. . . . Aye. And that learned me a lesson, though, did that. I never gave horse wheat.

Prosecutions were definitely brought in cases such as this, though usually for breach of contract rather than for the theft itself. The legislation covering the yearly bond made actions quick, easy, and inexpensive, and the farmer did not have to brand a lad who had made a foolish mistake as a criminal. As an instance, in 1899 the following case was heard:

103

At the Pocklington Police Court on Sunday, Robert Fenwick, farmer, Warter, under the Employers and Workmen Act, claimed £5 compensation from his servant Arthur Bugg for seriously damaging one of his horses by wilfully giving it improper food, contrary to the foreman's orders. . . . The horse had inflamation in the feet. Complainant said the horse was worth, perhaps, £20 less than before its illness – Henry Scurr, foreman, said he had frequently found wheat, maize and barley in this horse's crib. He had also seen barley meal. Defendant had been ordered not to use these. There were plenty of oats for the horses. The magistrates allowed £5 compensation, granted the defendant £16 8s wages due, with costs 14s 6d and rescinded the contract.[3]

For all the attendant dangers, feeding wheat or barley would not harm a lad's reputation if he did it correctly, but if anyone was found giving a horse drugs then he could only expect certain dismissal and, probably, prosecution. In 1904 the Bridlington Agricultural Club decided to print 400 quarto cards as notices 'to be . . . posted up on farms warning farm servants' with these words:

The Bridlingon Agricultural Club give notice that proceedings will be taken against any person or persons giving to Horses on these premises any food or drugs not authorised by the occupier of this Farm.

They also decided that, 'if the Committee are of the opinion, after due enquiry, that a prosecution is warranted, the costs of such prosecution shall be borne by the Club.'[4] Mr Johnson remembered working on a farm with similar notices on the partitions between stables and though corn is mentioned with drugs on the notice, it is certain that attitudes were much harder towards drugs. The subject is obscured by secrecy because it was a practice many horselads disliked intensely themselves, so anyone using drugs kept it from the rest of the stable as much as he kept it from the farmer. The intention was to make the horses better eaters and to improve their appearance, and there were some substances that were more acceptable than others. Mr Milner told me that he had used certain powders bought from the chemist, but that he would never use the stronger or more poisonous chemicals like blue stone of vitriol that he knew some other lads were using.[5]

Only one man told me that he had used all the drugs and his reasons for doing so are interesting. He was the lad who had seen a horse killed by wheat, and he reacted by inverting the usual view that drugs were dangerous while wheat and barley were safe if properly handled:

I used to use drugs for 'em. But if a policeman caught you or if t'boss caught you it was a serious job, you know. . . . [There] was fenugreek, aniseed, and butter of antimony and – I think there were about six. Five powders and one liquid. . . . It was worth giving because it cost about ten shillings a year, that's all. . . . If you went to the right chemist . . . , you didn't always sign the [poison] book with everybody. Now they had a chemist here, just down the road here, why his father . . . , I was talking to him one morning and I said, 'Why, are you any relation to the John Smith used to be in Witham, in Hull?'

He said, 'Yes, he's my uncle.' He says, 'I bet you was a horse feeder, then, if you knew him!' By – John, you could get owt you needed. You didn't sign the book with him. . . . Always had good horses though. Always was fat.

. . . Oh, I used give it last thing at night. They – the liquid, you only gave 'em i' winter. You didn't give it 'em when they got out into t'field, at grass – the liquid. The butter of antimony, . . . you used to get wurzels at night, you know. Two or three wurzels. And I used to cut a lump out of one and drop the liquid in, and then just hold it till he got the first bite. When he got the first bite, he got the butter antimony . . . and then before I went out I used to pull a – two or three strands of hair out of the tail and burn it, set fire to it, so's if the boss came in he couldn't smell – he couldn't smell the aniseed, you see.

They used to follow you all over the place. I never used to be frightened of 'em running away and leaving me. . . . I used to fetch all our stuff from the mills in Hull, you know – cake, bran, [meal] for pigs. Used to fetch it from the mill and when I went – 'course you had to leave your horses, sometimes leave your horses in the street and go on, maybe upstairs into an office. . . . And I used to sometimes come down – the horses used to be as far up the stairs as they could get. . . . There was maybe a policeman there. Trying to get them back, 'cause it [the waggon] was stuck across the pavement. . . . People were having to walk round it. I couldn't stop them. I used to get into trouble but I couldn't stop them, . . .

I'd been there when they were born, maybe, broke 'em in, and nobody else had driven 'em . . . When we used to go for a walk [at the farm], well, I mean, we used to go on the road and they used to be following us down the hedge-side in the field.

. . . I went to a farm one year, and the foreman came and told me which horses was mine, and they were like blinking Russian ponies! Why, for hair. They were big Shire horses but for hair – they'd hair that length on them! I thought, 'Oh blimey, they do look right, do them.' Anyway I set about 'em. I soon had that hair off. Drugs, you know, giving 'em drugs at night, it soon took the hair off. They were soon as sleek as [you wanted]. . . . But when you left that farm and somebody else came they went down a lot, but eventually they came back. . . . That was why it was illegal, you know.

But nobody ever found out?

Oh aye, they used to – they didn't like it, but some of the farmers didn't used to bother as long as their horses were getting well looked after. They never used to bother. . . .

How did you learn about drugs and that in the first place?

Well, it wasn't my father! Because [at] Martinmas Week . . . , when we went home; I used to keep my drugs in a Colman's Syrup tin, I used to bury it in the garden because we knew our father, I knew that my father would go turning my belongings over, my old – you know, a big wood trunk, to take our stuff about in. And I knew my father would go rooting about in this box to find if we had any drugs. Well, I used bury it in t'garden. And then when we went back I used go and dig it up. The treacle tin used to keep it dry, you know. 'Cause if my father had found out he might have give me a good thumping.

Oh, it was my eldest brother that gave me the formula. He was nine years older than me. And it was written, it was on the lid o' this trunk, inside, written in ink and I couldn't get it out. And I saw it only a year or so ago, my eldest brother's daughter . . . , she's got her father's box. . . . She said, 'Hey, I've got something to ask you,' she says, 'Come on upstairs.' So I went. I thought 'What's up now, what's she want to know now?' Anyway she opened the lid of this box, it was her father's box, and there was this formula, written in ink.[6]

Farmers realized that chemists provided most lads with their drugs, either knowing full well what they were wanted for, or else having strong suspicions. Accordingly, in 1900 there seems to have been something of a campaign to get government action to control the chemists. The Market Weighton Agricultural Club initiated the action and the Malton Agricultural Club voted to support their efforts to prevent 'the sale of noxious drugs by druggists to farm servants without the written authority of the master.'[7] How much more support the campaign attracted is uncertain, but it is hard to see what the government could have done, given the active collusion of certain chemists. In fact, even when chemists would not co-operate, it was still possible to get drugs by going some way from home. A blacksmith used to keep butter of antimony and spirits of salt, another drug, for use if he drew blood when nailing a shoe onto a horse as they were a safeguard against tetanus. A horselad who could pass himself off as a shoeing smith could therefore get the substances he needed legitimately. Mr Johnson knew a man from his village who called at one shop so often that he became known as 'Smithy' to the chemist.

The lad who used drugs admitted to their long-term effects, which may have been withdrawal symptoms, but someone acting in ignorance could cause much worse results. Mr Playforth and Mr Rispin knew of one farm where a lad drugged a horse until it began having fits, so that it 'was going up t'wall, like, just climbing up t'wall, in the end.' It later died. The withdrawal symptoms were hard on the next lad as well as on the horses, as Mr Johnson testified from personal experience:

After them horses had been done like that and somebody else takes 'em over, they go all haywire, they go all to nothing. I once took some over that a man [had drugged] – well, I reckoned they had because it didn't matter what I did at 'em, you know, they got, they were thin. I was ashamed of 'em, but, you know, you just couldn't get 'em fit, they were missing this stuff. And it took these horses at least six months to get it out of their system.

The respect of other lads depended on having a pair of good fat horses so it is easy to see that lads who did not drug their horses would resent those who did. Whereas feeding stolen cake united all the lads against authority, drugging was a practice that set a lad apart. On the other hand, it cannot be viewed as anything other than the extreme end of the spectrum of determination to get approval through having impressive horses. The use of drugs does not, in itself, show a lack of concern for horses. Every lad tried to find the best combination of feeds and the best tricks to keep his horses' appetites up, and these were trade secrets. They might swap secret for secret but a novice was only given the basic instructions that were common knowledge. More advanced advice would only come from his family or close friends.

There is no evidence that there was ever any organization of those with special skill and knowledge into a society or informal club, as seems to have happened in some other places.[8] The methods and practices of horse feeding in the East Riding were, however, far from a simple matter of organizing the issue of standard rations. They contributed greatly to enriching the life of the farmstead, which could easily have been very barren. The pilfering helped to cement the horselads together by action against those above them, though in a harmless way; but once foodstuffs were obtained, it was each lad for himself. Given the importance of the condition of a lad's horses as an indicator of his ability, and of the respect that was due to him, it is no wonder that so much effort was expended in getting things right. It is also no wonder that the farmers and foremen sought to place a check on overfeeding so that the horses did not become show creatures – wonderful to look at, but of limited use in the fields.

Notes to Chapter Nine

1. Fairfax–Blakeborough, *East Riding*, p. 197.
2. Name withheld from use in text by request.
3. *Bev. Guar.*, 11 Nov. 1899, p. 8.
4. *Brid. Gaz.* 2 Dec. 1904, cutting in Annals of Brid.
5. See also J. Archer, '"A Fiendish Outrage": A Study of Animal Maiming in East Anglia, 1830–70', *Ag. Hist. Rev.*, 33 (1985), 153–4. He argues that a high proportion of supposed animal maiming was in fact the result of the use of drugs and was not deliberate.
6. See footnote 3. The name of the chemist has been changed.
7. *Mal. Mess.* 20 Jan. 1900, p. 3.
8. See T. Davidson, 'The Horseman's Word', *Gwerin*, 1 (1956), 67–74, for a description of the society in Scotland. Evans, *Horse*, pt. IV, describes similar practices in East Anglia but it is not clear if there was ever such a formal system there, and if so, if the two areas were linked together. Although the East Anglians overtly used a system based on magic, in fact Evans felt that its practicality rested on the use of chemicals that were offensive to horses but undetectable by humans.

Chapter Ten

Handling the Horses

A lad who knew how to feed horses well was likely to get a good reputation, but there was plenty of hard work to do to realise the potential good feeding created. He had to improve and maintain their appearance by careful grooming and to handle his horses well at work. Horses were brushed morning and night to keep the coat clean and glossy, and to get rid of loose hair. Mr Appleyard told me that, as far as appearances went, he preferred winter to summer, for then the horses spent their nights in the stable rather than in the field. It meant more work feeding and mucking out, but they were not rolling in grass and mud and spoiling all his hard work with the curry comb and brush. Just as with feeding, there were tricks to grooming also, to make the best impression. Mr Baines said, for instance: 'If we wanted 'em to perform a bit we used to put some . . . turpentine, get it on a cloth, you know, and just used to rub it under their tail and round their tail, and it makes them carry their tail up . . . when they're going out to work.'

The state of the harness was also important as part of the overall turn out, so it had to be kept clean. Besides using saddle-soap to keep it supple, the leather had to be blacked, the brasses polished, and the chain traces periodically scoured with sand. One way of preserving a good set of chain traces, which were prone to rust, was to put them in the bran tub, which sealed them from the air. Harness is essentially practical, not decorative, and it is intended literally to harness the horse's strength to the best effect on any particular job. Different areas reached different solutions to the problem set by the various types of work, and the harness of the south of England was generally much heavier than that of the north, giving the horse extra weight to carry. Of the several possible combinations, plough harness, shown in figure 4, is simplest and it was used whenever possible. Normally, therefore, there were only a few pieces of harness that needed to be regularly cleaned and saddle-soaped; what was not in use could be left hanging in the saddle room for long periods. The youngest lad got the oldest harness, and naturally it was difficult if not impossible to keep it looking good. I asked Mr Tate and Mr Playforth how much time it took up:

> Mr T: Oh, your own time, unless you had it [to do] on a wet day. When it was raining. . . .
> Mr P: No time allowed, was there? . . .
> Mr T: I've spent hours, haven't I? . . . Like if you were off out, we'll say to Driffield or anywhere with 'em, you know, you used to clean 'em all up night afore.

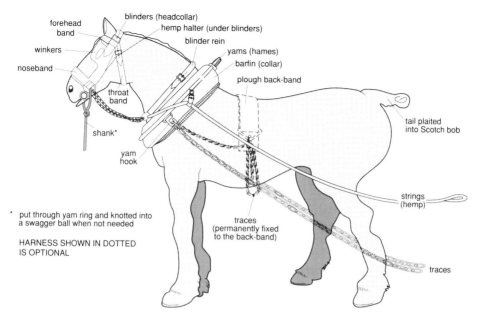

Fig. 4. East Riding plough harness

I mean, if you were just working in the fields would you just leave it or —?

Mr T: Why, clean t'brasses, like – you would keep your brasses clean.

Mr P: You only used to bother just wi' collar – and some didn't even have backband traces, did they. Some just had loose traces.

Their time was not the only thing the lads gave in search of a good turnout: on nearly all farms they also paid for their own brasses, cleaners, and harness decorations. Mr Rispin bought his from the Kilham saddler:

He had bells and all, he had some, you know, as used to have bells on. . . .

I suppose they must have spent a bit of money on their horses, really?

Oh aye, aye. Aye, they did. . . . This Hornby, when he farmed [in Kilham], he always used to buy polish to polish the gearing, like – why dubbin and all such as that, and he would buy 'em their ribbons. You know, they'd wear all sorts o' different colours o' ribbons, tie – when you tied their tails up – he was very good for that. . . . But I've never lived at a spot where they did that.

But you used to buy them yourselves, anyway?

Yes. Oh aye, used to buy 'em yourself.

Each lad had his own set of harness which he guarded jealously. Interference with another lad's was considered a deadly crime, and even more sacrosant was the special set of gears reserved for use with the best waggon on special trips. The

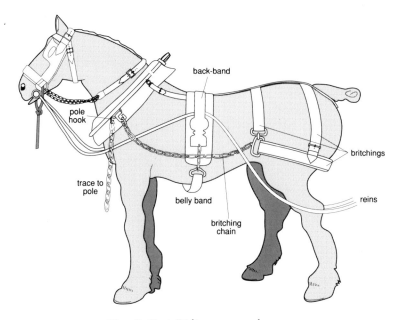

Fig. 5. East Riding waggon harness

waggoner looked after it as well as his own set, and woe betide any lad who borrowed any part of it without express instructions, which would only be forthcoming if the waggoner could not be spared from the job he was on and a substitute had to take the waggon out. When a waggon made a trip off the farm, the farmer's name and address were clearly displayed on the side of it and he expected it to look its best, but during normal work most farmers left the horses' appearance entirely to the lads. Mr Fisher remarked, 'No, as long as they were getting t'work done and that, they never bothered much.'

They only became personally interested when their horses were on display to the public, especially at shows or other village festivals, booning days[1] when a new farmer was given a free day's labour by all his neighbours, or similar occasions. Then the good name of the farm was at stake and lavish decoration was looked for. Yet the lads still got no time off to make their preparations, the farmers relying instead on their concern for their own prestige to make them willing to sit up half the night getting everything ready. Mr Rispin related how he took some Kilham children to the seaside as part of a cavalcade of waggons from every farm in the village:

Oh [they were] decorated up, you know – it was a big occasion was that. Flowers on t'britchbands and all that there, and bows and all. . . . I took 'em one Wednesday, when I come back at night time – well, you set off at six and then it was nine o'clock when you got back at night – used to be a three-hour going to Brid, you know, with a waggon. And when I come back at night,

110

foreman said, 'You haven't to take nowt off that gearing!' I had to go to Driffield next day, just two in t'waggon; he always liked horses and I had to go right the way along t'back street and then right away up t'front street just to show the horses. Aye. And I believe I only wanted a barrel o' beer back with me. That was all I wanted. But it was just to show them off. Aye. But he was like that.

On normal jobs there was often little harness to be decorated and, in any case, 'You didn't want a lot because it was making it heavy for them, you see. Oh, you used to plait their tails, and a bit o' ribbon and a brass or two at front,' said Mr Fisher. Many lads simply concentrated on keeping everything neat and clean, especially boys who had insufficient money to begin buying decorations. The intricate plaiting of the tail with interwoven ribbons of different colours, known as a Scotch bob, was often the only decoration on, for instance, a horse that was ploughing. Even where the routine made it difficult, however, lads would do their best to turn out a good looking team. Mr Tate said:

> I could always tie a horse tail as well as anybody, it didn't matter a bugger who he was, I could tie a tail up on him. I've tied 'em up hundreds of times walking behind them, walking to t'field. We never had time at Wilde's farm to tie 'em up before you went to work.

Their personal pride was also heavily involved with the work they were doing and there was a continuous effort to do every job better than the previous time. This determination to outdo the other lads, and one's own usual standards, was not rooted in any strictly agricultural requirement: it stemmed from the lads' own desire to master their job. It is clear, moreover, that these constant efforts to plough well, or harrow well, were not limited to a minority of interested lads. There was a genuinely widespread concern, reinforced, perhaps, because this also prevented a job becoming boring. Ploughing took up a significant part of a lad's year and after a while one furrow easily became much like another. The implement and the horses needed watching even on the best land, and where they ploughed swing intense concentration was often needed to produce an acceptable result, but it was a repetitive job and concentration suffers with repetition. If each furrow was turned into a test of skill, the work took on some elements of a game.

A lad who had a good relationship with his horses could trust them to drive themselves most of the time while he concentrated on the implement he was using. Mr Rispin and Mr Playforth said:

> Mr P: Why, there were a lot of horses that you needn't have had [strings] on, we'll put it that way – weren't there?
> Mr R: Oh aye – just wi' talking to them. . . .
> Mr P: I mean, often when you were ploughing you used to have your strings on but you never used to use them.

Such an understanding could allow showing off a little in the fields, both to impress the other lads and to create a bit of a diversion, breaking the work up a little. Mr Easterby knew one waggoner who was widely admired because he could guide his horses to pull a waggon between two stooks of corn, without touching either, just by talking while he stood on the shears. At other times control over the horses could be used for a bit of fun, as in the instance Mr Playforth recalled:

> We had one [horse], Boxer . . . and I was [in a field] with Freddy Wright; and John turned in at bottom . . . and he had Boxer. And Freddy just whistled at yon end and these horses stopped at bottom, like, and John said, 'Go on!', and Freddy whistled again and they stopped: and we were right at top end o' t'field and horses at t'bottom. And then Boxer whinnied out, as much as to say, 'Can't you hear him? I can.'

The relationship between lad and horse stopped well short of the point where the horse became a pet, however. It was on the farm to work and the lad was there to make it work. There was little room for sentimentality, hardly more than there was between the bullocky and the cattle he was fattening for slaughter. If a horse was capable of actively co-operating with its driver, unlike a machine, it was also capable of being awkward, lethargic, or even downright vicious. A farm horse weighs around a ton and working with such a large animal contained an element of danger even when it meant no harm. One constant hazard was the tendency of a horse to kick out if it felt at all menaced, and horses often disliked sudden movement too close to them at the rear. They could mistake a lad for another horse and lash out instinctively. Usually the lad was very near and the horse had too little room to make a really effective kick, as Mr Fisher recalled, 'I was real near, you see, and if you're real near – it just . . . catapulted me. But apart from a bruise or two I was all right.' This could not be relied on, though, for he had a friend who was not so lucky:

> It came a thunderstorm and they were all coming up [from the fields], like, but got wet through, and he was walking real near – that was for a bit o' shelter, and I think she thought it was another horse getting too near. And she kicked and hit him in his body, and he died. They got him to hospital, but he died.[2]

These accidents, and worse, had to be accepted as risks inherent in horse-keeping. There was no way of anticipating every action a horse was going to make. Mr Johnson recalled a silly accident that nearly killed him:

> There was some, when they got used to [reversing], it wasn't trouble backing into shed, it was stopping 'em, 'cause, I don't know, they used to like to do it. I had a mare of my own once and I backed into a shed, and then I didn't back it right back but . . . there was something I had to go behind this cart [for]. . . . This mare, after I'd gone back – 'course she didn't do it purposely or anything, but she shoved this cart back and trapped me [against the wall] – well, all I could do, they called her Violet and when you called a horse's name it went on [moved forward], you see, and it was squeezing t'wind out o' me and I just had, I could just shout, 'Violet!', and she went on, you see.

This irreducible minimum of accidents was greatly increased by carelessness, as Mr Masterman confirmed:

> I've been trampled on . . . wi' young uns. Wi' breaking young uns in. Trying to catch them. I had four in a loose box . . . , I was trying to get halters on 'em to break 'em in, start to break 'em in. Well, I was amongst 'em and I had two men holding 'em in the corner, only one of them opened the door and let them out. And they run over to it and on the way they run over me to get out! . . . I just got a bit bruised . . . When the horses saw the door open they all ran for the door. And the feller said, 'I am sorry.' I said, 'Aye, its all right being sorry!' No, I just got trodden on.

Mr Playforth recounted in a joking fashion how 'Jack Bryan . . . , he found he'd put blinders – he put 'em on his wrong horses, so he had to change 'em. He was in a roller. So he takes blinders off, aye, but horses had gone! Smashed roller up!' No-one was hurt, but every runaway was potentially lethal. There was no way of enforcing safe working practices and there was often pressure to work faster, so every now and then some lad's luck ran out. Showing off could be another contributory factor, for standing on the shears of a waggon, as Mr Easterby's friend did, was illegal, because in a tight turn the waggon body swept right over them, but it was a widespread practice. On farm land the traffic regulations which outlawed it could not be enforced, even if anyone had wished to.

A newspaper reported in 1910 that: 'A waggoner employed by Mr Wilden of Sledmere was killed when his horses bolted. Scurr had hold of only the first horse's reins and was not in control of the shaft horse. He was dragged 200 yards and a wheel ran over him.'[3] He had been relying on the lead horse to keep the rest of team in check, and when they all panicked he had insufficient control to halt them. He had probably been driving his horses in this fashion for some time, ignoring the risks because nothing had gone wrong before. Descending hills with a loaded waggon was particularly dangerous, for they had no brakes. A chain through the spokes locked the back wheels and the waggon skidded down, held back by the sheer muscle power of the team. Special iron shoes went underneath the wheels to save them from wearing a flat patch on the tyre. If the team once let too much momentum build up, the weight of the waggon began pushing them downhill and unless they reached the bottom quickly a mad race developed with the horses trying to keep in front of it. If they were outpaced they were thrown off their feet, and some dreadful accidents happened all too often on the steep descents off the Wolds, such as Garrowby Hill on the road from York to Bridlington, near Stamford Bridge.

Anyone who could not ensure that his horses were pulling their weight would be in constant trouble with the waggoner, the foreman, and the farmer. If a horse was shirking or lashing out the lad had to find out why, and resolve the problem as best he could. Most people felt that violence in general was counter-productive, but that there were occasions when, more as a psychological assault than a physical one, it was best to get in first rather than risk serious injury as a horse became more and more unruly. Mr Masterman explained:

You weren't very proud of telling about some of the things you had to do, you know . . . , 'cause they didn't like you ill-treating animals, you know, and if anybody does, they aren't very well liked: well, sometimes you had to be a bit rough. It was no good letting any animal get the boss of you. Else you might as well not be there. 'Cause they'll turn on you if you do.

Mr Baines said:

There's no bad horses born, its just what they've been learnt and letten do. They should be learnt properly and schooled properly and there shouldn't be any cruelty attached to 'em at all. 'Cause its same with a kid. You can bray a kid until he turns round on you. . . . And always have something in your pocket for a horse when you went into field to catch it. And it knew you had summat. You got while you could rustle a bit of paper, or [shake] your handkerchief, and it'd come trotting to you. No, there's no bad horses born; there's no bad – wicked foals, its just where they've been learnt by cruel men and not showing 'em what they had to do, and not making 'em do what they had to do. You've to be stern and firm. And kind. You start braying anything, I don't care what it is, it'll darn well turn away and it'll run away from you. Its only natural that; its fear, i'n't it? I mean, we used to have, well it used to be a pleasure to go in your stable and see your horses all fit and whinnying, and looking round at you as you went in, you know, on a night to feed up. . . . And you knew then that you were kind to them horses and they were looking forward to you going in. They were meeting you with a greeting, wa'n't they?

Some held that a few horses were naturally vicious or difficult, but everyone agreed that a firm kindness was what produced results. Mr Walker held that any horse could be won over by a good handler: 'I think myself you could make a horse, anybody interested.' However, it took courage and a confidence in your own ability to apply this policy and there were many who were so unsure of themselves, or too used to brutal treatment in their own upbringing, that they dared not try to build a partnership with their horses. They assumed that every horse had to be forced to work. Given the percentage of the young male labour force employed as farm servants, it was inevitable that there would always be a number who did not particularly like horses. Further, the inevitability of horsework for most lads probably left many unable to express their dissatisfaction. Their inner tensions ensured that they did not adopt the right attitude to win their horses' trust, over-reacting to anything that seemed to threaten them. Mr Lawler recalled:

Well I had a mare that come to our spot and the feller what brought it said, 'Be careful with this bugger, she'll kick you bloody brains out!'
I says, 'How many times has she done that to you?'
'Oh,' he says, 'I've had to be careful with her.' However, I took her in t'spot and I looked after her, and, do you know, she never made a mistake wi' me. No.

Mr Jarvis commented that the sole result was often to annoy or frighten the horse so that jobs took longer and were not done as well, which encouraged the lad to blame the horse and step up his beatings. Mr Masterman became involved in an incident at a railway station that proved how needlessly violence could originate:

There was a farmer, a neighbouring farmer, and a man, came with a young horse to t'truck – he'd sold it and they were putting it on the train to go away . . . . Well, they took this horse up and when it got to the door into the truck the man went into the truck. When it got up to t'door it wouldn't go, and he pulled at it, and it threw its head up and hit its head on top of the doorframe of this box. Well, it was frightened: it wouldn't go anywhere near the truck then. Well this feller was a bit of a bad-tempered feller, you know, swearing and going on, and he'd got a shooting-stick and he started using his shooting-stick on this horse. Well, the station master was a chapel man and he didn't like it. He went away and left 'em. Well, eventually, he tied this horse to the railings, did this farmer, and he went around into the office. Now, I said to the man that was with – I knew him, . . . I said, 'Well, what do you say if you and me puts this horse in this box, Paddy?' He was an Irishman, Pat Kennedy.

'Well,' he said, 'I wish you would.' 'Cause he knew this feller was getting a bit mad.

'Well,' I said, 'We'll put him in then.' I hung my coat over its head and tied my sleeves under its jaw and, do you know, it walked straight in? Put its head down. 'Cause if you blindfold an animal it always puts its head down. . . . Well, I learnt that in the army.

At times like this, the really skilled horsemen stood out from the rest with their ability to make light of a situation that, in ordinary hands, could become a crisis. It was this blend of experience and ability which allowed them to cope with even the most difficult horses that others could not manage. Even so, some horses remained at least a nuisance as Mr Fisher remembered:

One was very nasty. She would use her back legs and then her teeth as well. When I was away once there was one of the other young chaps thought he would [feed her] – t'foreman, when he used to feed it, he didn't use to go up to her, he used to push the feed through from next door. And this young chap thought he would be clever, you see – he went up . . . , it was all right when he was going up, it was when he was coming away, . . . she just grabbed him in t'middle o' t'back, fetched a piece out of middle of his back just like [an old] penny. It went dark you know – you'd have thought he had a penny stuck on.

Working with such horses was always difficult and it could be dangerous unless a cure was found for their problems. Mr Playforth and Mr Rispin told me:

Mr P: I had four in a reaper . . . one of [them, I've] never seen one kick like her. Rose. First day she kicked and she knocked swingletree end off and it swung round, hit me right in t'middle o' back; I was standing at her back. . . . Next day she jumped astride the pole and lay down. . . . Them what was in

115

poles, they had straps round their collar, you know, and they were carrying t'weight o' t'reaper. And I had to get my knife and cut that strap [to stop it strangling her], and then next day, I had to take her again the following day, and she just reared overend and she . . . knocked first horse draughts off [i.e. the swingletree the lead horse was attached to] and then off! And we went round i' circles, round i' circles . . . , and, however, I eventually got her stopped and that was it, she hadn't to go in a reaper no more. But it was a queer feeling, I know. Freddy Wright once had her gallop away with a horse and cart down here.

Mr R: Aye, aye . . . straight over that dyke into t'hedge. Aye.

Mr P: He pushed a shaft, one o' t'shaft ends right into t'bank, and it went under a tree root. It got in right under t'tree root and he couldn't get out.

Mr R: Oh, it was a rum horse, was that.

Mr Tate had a similar experience while working with drag harrows:

I used to like two helters on her, one like, to horse hames, and one tied back so she couldn't run forward. And I thought, 'Why, she's off nicely, I'll lowse t'second un,' and all of a sudden she turned mad! And she pulled and pulled, you know, while she couldn't get her breath and she rolled over – well I had to cut her band to get her loose – couldn't lowse her. . . . However, she jumped up and ran round t'drag and pulled t'drag over. Just missed . . . nearside . . . animal, just went to one side on it.

In trying to cure a horse of these bad habits, it was important to establish the cause of its behaviour; Mr Masterman said:

You had to find out whether it was temper or nervous. It wasn't always temper. Well, you had to find out and then you knew what to do. . . . You could get them to work if you knew: if it was temper, well maybe a good hiding would do it good, but if it was nervous it made it worse.

Thus, a distinction was drawn between ordinary kickers, which kicked for many reasons, and jibbers or reesty horses that kicked out of bad temper at being harnessed up ready for work. If the horse had simply been allowed too much leeway in the past, the remedy was usually to make its activities as unpleasant as possible for itself, as Mr Baines said:

You get horses that won't pull so you do all sorts of tricks with 'em. Sometimes you get 'em and, same as I've done: I've backed 'em for twenty minutes with a load on and when I've said, 'Come on,' they've been pleased to go forward. . . . You have to use your craft with 'em. . . . I've putten roasted taties under their tail and hit 'em with a shovel. Red hot roasted taties. And then you had to be quick to keep on with 'em! They'd suddenly move. You know, you get – you couldn't do them things today. No. You'd get horse that'd come for you with its mouth, you know. Used get a poker hot, or owt

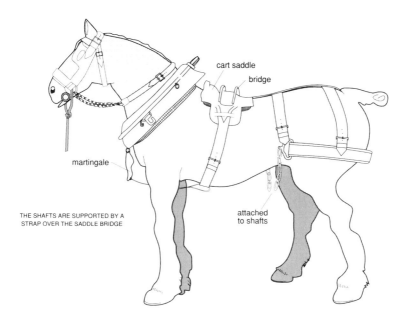

cart saddle

bridge

martingale

THE SHAFTS ARE SUPPORTED BY A
STRAP OVER THE SADDLE BRIDGE

attached
to shafts

Fig. 6. East Riding shaft harness

like that, you know, and just wait while it came. You know, in t'stable, when you went up t'side on it, just carrying your poker at this side. Some horses'd come over to crush you. So what I used to do was, soon as a muck fork were nearly done I used to saw t'tines off it so there was only half o' t'tines left on and they were blunt, and a piece o' shafting, and I used to carry it in front of me, broad way on. If horse came over, it used to lean on fork first, you see. It learnt it – used say, 'Get over!' and as soon as it touched fork it used to know, and it learnt 'em not to do it.

He also described a very common method of curing one member of a team of slacking. The pull of each horse is transmitted to the implement via a system of swingletrees which act as levers arranged to ensure each horse does its fair share of the work. If one horse was slacking it was possible to adjust the swingletrees so that it had to pull harder merely to hold its own. Unfortunately the principles involved were a little complex and many lads actually eased the horse's burden by mistake. Another cure for slacking was a variation on one mentioned by Mr Baines: the horse was made to do something else until it was glad to return to its real job. Mr Tate:

I once was horse raking . . . [a] forty acre [field] and Dick come to me. He said, 'I'll take horse while thoo goes for thy dinner,' and then he said, 'Bring

Billy back;' that was the blood horse. So Billy had to go into t'horse rake: well, [I] gets on, gets yoked and set off. Billy never struck up. He just messed about . . . , and without a word of a lie, I don't know however he did it, but he was the wrong way round in the shafts when he finished! I don't know whether some of the chains had come off. . . . Dick had him and lowsed him out and he said, 'Slip [cart] saddle off,' and he jumped on his back and he went right round hedge-side, right as hard as ever t'horse could gallop. He said, 'Let's have him yoked now.' And Billy went straight away after. He weren't to tell to get on.

A nervous horse could often be persuaded to work by distracting its attention from whatever was worrying it, Mr Baines said:

You get a horse with maigres and that, it starts to throw its head about . . . . They're like somebody in a fit, you know – I've seen people stroke their face and if you didn't stop them they'd . . . go into a fit . . . . And we had one of the nicest grey horses at Barlby Hall I should think anybody'd wish to see, and it had maigres. And I could take it and do anything with it – but I had a cure for it, like, I had a wire rope . . . round under its jaw and when it used to start I used to jerk it, you see, used to get it out of it: used to be worried, more worried about what I was doing than what it were trying to do itself, you see.

Mr Masterman also found this approach effective:

I had [a horse], it would go till about nine o'clock in a morning, ploughing, working – it was when you got to the end of the field where you yoked and you lowsed out to go home; it would stop, and it wouldn't go. And when you wanted it to go it would fly back and knock the draughts all adrift, and you had to go and put 'em together again, and then when you wanted to go again it would do the same thing again, or start to kick. So I used to – I'd a little nut, cycle nut, that wouldn't rust and I used to tie a bit o' string through that and drop it into this horse's ear, and then tie the string round its ear so I could get it out. And do you know, it never used to kick; it would go all day and never kick . . . , its mind was on this nut, do you see.

Sometimes an unrealised physical defect was to blame and then the remedy was to change the gears, or whatever else was causing the trouble. Mr Appleyard had one horse that had an extremely tender mouth and so over-reacted to the bit. He hooked his strings to the bridle ring above the bit, rather than to the bit itself, so tugs on the reins were damped before reaching the mouth. After that there was no trouble. Similarly, humouring a minor obsession frequently caused much less trouble than attempting to cure it. One horse Mr Tate had would not allow anything to be put over its head, so a normal collar could not be got onto it, and without a collar work was impossible. However, open-topped collars were available: they could be opened to go round the neck and then fastened with straps. They were normally only used on horses whose heads were too oddly shaped to allow a collar to be fitted normally, as the broken top made them weak, but it worked in this case, even though the horse remained difficult and bad-tempered. It was only if all such attempts to understand problems failed that a good lad resorted to beatings or other painful remedies like Mr Baines' red hot potato. Mr Fisher recalled:

> Kindness is the best remedy if you can do it. But [one horse], . . . kindness was no good to him. He would kill you if you were kind to him. And trap you, or owt, like. Big stick was best for him. Get him fast and give him a good few sharp strokes with a stick and then he would go like a good lad. 'Cause I tried it at first, like, I tried [kindness] . . . , but it didn't work with him. As I say he would have killed me had I kept at that, like; you know, he would have got me in time. Trampled me and that. So I always used to get him fast and when he did start, you know, have a good stick and one or two sharps on his backside – he was off then. He wouldn't move otherwise. He would stand and come straight up, stand on his back feet or owt, like – come round and look at you and all such as that. Till you give him a few good [strokes] on the behind: he was off. But you had to have him fast or else he'd get away if you hadn't. Always used to have two halters on him, one, you know, to the horse collar and one back to t'draughts . . ., so that he was pulling all the lot with his head if he wanted to get away. And if I had him with hisself in a cart or rully or owt like, . . . I used to have what I called a safety band, used to put it on his front leg through his collar ring, then if he tried to get away I pulled that; it would throw him down. . . . As long as you had that on he never used to try.

Some devices for getting horses to work were widely known, such as fastening straps over a horse's back from shaft to shaft (when it was in a suitable implement), which interfered so heavily with its kicking action that it could do no damage. Others were thought up by the individuals concerned and in many cases the common experiences they all shared led to the constant re-invention of the same device, or related devices embodying the same principle. Mr Fisher described how he invented the safety strap he mentioned before:

> Sometimes you used to clip [their coats] and such as that, and they would get you to hold the front leg up. So they didn't kick, you know, when they were clipping 'em behind and that. . . . If they started knocking . . . about much and you could keep that leg up [they couldn't raise another without falling over]. So I thought, well, if I had a rope on [one leg] and put him on three legs he couldn't go very fast, could he?

To enhance their reputations the lads kept their techniques to themselves as much as possible, though, of course, the fact that many had to be performed in public limited the extent to which secrecy was possible. Very few horses could not be persuaded to work by one method or another, but if one seemed impossible it was sometimes handed over to someone highly skilled to see if they could do anything with it. Mr Fisher had developed a personal technique for really difficult horses:

119

It might just have been my own remedy, like, I don't know [but] . . . if you had one that was bad to do with, get one that nobody could manage: 'Oh, give it to Fisher, he'll make summat on it, give it to Fisher.' And if they were very bad I'd bring it in on a night, not give it a bite to eat, and then stop up with it all night, like for about three nights, and go up granary and . . . get some different things, and you would soon find out which – what they liked best. And then maybe lay it in the rack, you see, or crib, and every now and again just give her a handful of this and do that for a bit, about three nights as a rule, and carry some of that with you in your pocket, and every now and again go up to her, give her a bit, and they'll get to be, they'll turn round and look at you. They would turn round, you know, and look at you, ask for it. It always worked wi' me. . . .

Did people know how you did it or did you keep it to yourself?

Oh no, I kept it quiet. Might have thought I was a fool! Stopping up three nights.

Would they – could anybody use them after that or was it just you?

Oh yes. Some of them. Some they couldn't. Some was a bit, just a bit difficult. In fact I remember one, I'd had it, oh, I should think six or seven months and I thought anybody could take it, and there was another chap thought he would take it; he had it so long and when I looked he was stopped, and instead of going it was turned round looking at him. And then he fetched two more men, one had his helter, pulling, what could be done; another man on the plough behind, you know, steering the plough, and he had a real big stick – by, he was hitting it with this stick. Been today, he would have been for it, wouldn't he? He was doing all he could with this stick. She wouldn't move. All she did – used to jump in the air. She wouldn't go forward. Anyway, he had to unyoke her. But the boss hisself could take her. Oh yes, the farmer hisself, he could take her. No bother.

A horse that was totally unwilling to work was not worth persevering with for long, for it would cause too much disruption and loss of work. Mr Masterman said:

I had one at Thorngumbald, the last farm I worked at [as foreman], he bought it off a horsebreaker; he only gave £10 for it. He ought to have known it was no good for that price. It used to strike at you with its forefoot. I don't know why, but it did. I had a pair o' new trousers on one day and it had just got a set o' new shoes on and it struck at me, ripped my trousers right from here, right through the knee, right down – nail head . . . . It didn't cut me, it tore my trousers and – you get 'em like, but this one, its mother died, and it had been brought up with a bottle, and a man let his children play with it, you know, as a pet. And that's what ruined it. You know, it spoiled it altogether. It never was no good . . . . I sold it one day when t'boss was out. A feller came, he offered me 14 guineas for it. I said, 'Here,' . . . . The boss were glad. He said, 'Oh, I'm not selling it.' 'Well,' I says, 'I will. If I can get a price for it.' And I got 14 guineas for it, so that was four ginueas more than he gave for it. Oh, it was no good, 'cause there was only me could drive it. When I was working wi' tractor or doing other jobs it was running about field. Well when I took it back to work it was bad as ever again. See, nobody else would drive it, they were all frightened of it. One feller was leading hay: I tied it to t'rully, back of t'rully, while we had our dinner, and fed it and this man went with a bucket o' water for it and he had to creep under the rully to get out o' road. It set about him. So it got to be as there was only me would have it.

A farm was better off without such a horse, but unless it had been bought as a bargain, like Mr Masterman's, the farmer would lose heavily for there were only three possible markets. He might find a farmer who looked on anything bought cheaply as a good deal, regardless of its quality or there was the knacker, or, Mr Baines said, certain carters specialised in such horses:

There was a chap in Wakefield . . . . He used to get horses from all over . . . , and he'd buy horses that was no good at all really, you know. You couldn't do anything with them, you couldn't yoke 'em in harrow, you couldn't put 'em in a cart. And you could have 'em for what they called knacker price – at that time o' day, £5 apiece. I'm talking about forty year since. And I was managing a farm for a chap and he used to see this [man], he used to say, 'Well, I've horse yonder, if you like you can have it, if you can make owt on it.' And he used to send me for it. And rummest horses you ever saw in your life, they've done all sorts o' tricks with 'em . . . . They'd put a clinker under its tail and hit it with a shovel to make it go, you know. What they called jibbing horses, wouldn't pull. He's had horses yoked in carts and they've been leading coal and coke, and they've stopped in middle o' Wakefield for no reason – well, could be a reason, but for why we don't know. And they couldn't shift 'em at all. They've had to fetch two more horses to pull 'em. One method he used to do – cruelty, you'd get locked up today if you did it – used to put a chain round that horse's neck and yoke it onto another horse in front of it, and let other horse pull. And I've seen 'em stand with their necks [stretched right out] afore they'd shift, but they generally went in t'finish.

Mr Masterman said that such horses were often extremely good workers if you could stand their tantrums and foibles. He also said that it was the insurance companies who effectively ended the trade by making it known that they would not pay out on a claim for injury to a workman if his horse was known to be violent. Thereafter the carters had to buy more placid horses or risk being sued for large sums. Vicious horses, fortunately, were not common on farms and the average lad could get by without the kind of horsemanship the very best acquired. Even so, the average lad should not be thought of as in any way unskilled. A Leeds horseman told me that, between the wars, it was said that at many establishments in the city, anyone who turned up 'with a turnip under one arm and an East Riding accent' could get a carter's job, if there was one going, in preference to a native of the city.[4]

Given the age of the lads, this is all the more remarkable. It can only be put down to the satisfaction most of them derived from their work, and to the extent to which a good horseman achieved widespread public admiration through the general discussions of everyone's horses, and the work they did. On the other hand, life on the farms was a long way from being the strenuous idyll it would be easy to show it as. The horses often towered over the boys, and they were far stronger than those who had to control them and work them. Lads lived with the constant, if minor, risk of accidental or malicious injury, or even death. The ideal relationship between a lad and his team was a partnership which he dominated, and if this ideal could be realized, as it usually was, he derived far more from his work than most jobs could offer. However, that partnership had to be worked for and maintained. It did not simply happen naturally and its roots were in a world of practical necessity that overrode feelings.

Notes to Chapter Ten

1. See Day, *Horses*, p. 35, for a description of a booning day.
2. See *Y.E. Press*, 10 Nov. 1910, p. 6, for a comparable fatality where a horse killed a lad by kicking him as he opened the stable door.
3. *Mal. Mess.* 3 Feb. 1900, p. 4.
4. Mr Hobson, untaped interview, p. 3.

22　The basic activity of the winter months was ploughing. This photograph shows a metal, wheeled plough posed as if in action. This field has virtually been finished and on this soil the plough is leaving sharply defined furrows, though they lack the heaviness of those on clay soils. While there is little actual decoration of the horses beyond Scotch bobs on their tails, their coats are gleaming and everything is carefully looked after. Taken near the coast, probably around 1900, an interesting touch is the photographer's shadow which can be seen in the foreground.

The wheels on the plough control both the width and the depth of the furrow according to how they are set by the lad. The large wheel runs in the furrow and the horizontal distance between it and the plough coulter, or cutting blade, determines how wide a sod is turned. The vertical distance between its lowest point and that of the small wheel on the unploughed land determines the depth of furrow cut by the plough.

23 A wooden swing plough, viewed from the land side, in use on stubble after harvest in Holderness, c. 1914. Swing ploughs had no wheels and the quality of the work was entirely dependent on the skill and concentration of the ploughman. All ploughs were designed to balance around the body, and the ploughman guided it and kept a constant depth by the leverage of the long handles, hence the name 'swing'.

A three-horse team was required on this soil, as it is a heavy clay. During fallowing, the great clods of turned earth that can be seen were often baked by the sun to brick hardness which could rub a horse's legs raw and put it out of action. Wooden ploughs were preferred to more modern metal ones for this work because the beam would flex rather than bend out of true if it began to dig into the heavy soil.

24 On the Wolds all the ploughs on a farm were usually sent out to work together, one behind another, rather than each taking their own patch as was more common elsewhere. This was known as foxhunting and it could be an impressive sight. Five teams are visible here, and the first four are drawing double-furrow ploughs. Assuming there are no more teams beyond the edge of the photograph, this group is ploughing nine furrows on each run down the field. (Taken near Bridlington, c. 1930.)

25 A three-horse team harrowing with zig-zag harrows at Raisthorpe, *c.* 1900. After the plough has turned over the soil and allowed the frost to crumble it and kill weeds, it is necessary to break up the furrow pattern to create a smooth seed bed. This was relatively easy work for the horses even though a three-horse team is being used. The left-hand horse is tied to its neighbour's trace, not its collar as was normal when working a pair. Note that the lad has fastened his jacket with a piece of chain.

26 A cultivator in use at Thorngumbald in 1927. The spring-mounted tines of this implement dug into the ground and broke it up with a far more positive action than a harrow. Consequently it was very hard to pull and needed a three-horse team. Lads made no attempt to push the work along at a fast pace because of the risk of injury. These implements have become much more common with the use of tractors that can provide the sort of power needed to make the most of them.

27 A Cambridge roller at Manor Farm, Thixendale. This was a special roller designed to grind down the clods of earth that were too heavy for normal harrowing. Each ring on the implement rotated independently and it was much lighter than a conventional roller since it was not intended to compact the soil as much. (Taken late 1890s.)

28 Once the seed bed was prepared, the seed was sown using a drill which cut small grooves and dropped seeds into them at regular intervals. This photograph shows drilling proceeding at Manor Farm, Thixendale. The man in the centre is driving the leading horse with reins, but as the lines of seed had to be perfectly straight, another man guides the horse in the shafts with a pole to keep the drill exactly on course. The third watches the drill coulters and ensures that blockages do not create bare patches where no seed has been sown, a job often undertaken by the foreman. (Taken late 1890s.)

29 This drill, also on Manor Farm, Thixendale, was probably a turnip drill as it has four double coulters, which sowed fertilizer and seed simultaneously. Here the man watching the coulters also has to drive the horses, and Mr Johnson said that farmers increasingly expected this for corn drilling as well. 'You walk, not behind your horses, you walk behind the wheel, . . . because you were supposed to keep a straight mark, you see. Well, you had to keep glancing [at the coulters] to see if your corn was coming down, you see, and while you were doing that you'd maybe put a bend in. Now you hadn't to be larking, that was a particular job and, you know, if you had a spout bunged up from one end of the field to another then you were stuck – oh lord, it was bad work and nobody liked to do that.' (Taken late 1890s.)

30 The heavy roller was used after sowing, when the corn was showing above ground, to compact the soil. It was also known as a 'sleipe' or smooth roller and because of its weight it required a large team which was driven in the same way as in a waggon. The front horse is, however, controlled by strings rather than reins. (Taken on Manor Farm, Thixendale in the late 1890s.)

31 Drinking luance at threshing time at Fotherdale Farm, near Thixendale in the 1920s. Left to right: Ted Paul (drinking), Arthur Brown, Arthur Paul, Geoff Marson (towards the front), an unknown pouring a drink, Jimmy Boyes, Charles Rose who owned the threshing set, George Paul, John Dale, and John Grice, the son of the farmer here, Peter Grice.

32　From time to time during the winter, often when they had bills to pay, farmers broke into the long haul of cultivation to thresh the corn that was stored in their stackyards. Taken at Rillington *c.* 1890, this photograph illustrates beautifully all the aspects of a typical threshing day. The engine is an old-fashioned portable one with double shafts to allow a horse team to pull it from farm to farm. The water cart and two tip carts carrying coal kept it running. Note the large number of men required to pass corn from the stack to the machine, break open the sheaves, feed them in, and then deal with the corn, straw, and chaff that came out. A great many casual workers depended on threshing days for work at this time of year.

33 A horseclad and his horse in front of straw stacks at Manor Farm, Thixendale. Straw was the residue of threshing, but it was not mere waste as it would be on many farms today. Most of it was turned into farmyard manure by the stock and returned to the land, a basic necessity before the modern use of chemical fertilizers became possible. (Taken late 1890s.)

Chapter Eleven

The Foreman and the Horses

The foreman was the head horseman but he has hardly figured in this specialist role so far because we have been looking at the daily routine. His job was to provide the skills that the lads had not had a chance to develop, and to put time in when the lads were fully committed in the fields. Most farms in the East Riding bred from their mares, and foremen came into their own particularly with the breeding and rearing of foals. On the other hand, few farms treated horse breeding as anything more than a minor side-line undertaken to maintain their stock of working horses, so this had to be managed along with other duties. Surplus foals were sold, if possible, into the towns, where the best prices were obtained, and the county was well placed to take advantage of this demand. In 1920, the list of towns using more than 1,500 horses, twenty-six in all, included Hull and six from the West Riding. The group of the next largest users, totalling fifteen towns, included Halifax and Grimsby.[1] Only the best were usually taken for urban work, and while others might be sold to other farms, the income so obtained was a relatively insignificant windfall that mattered little to the long term balance sheet of the farm.

East Riding farms took a very pragmatic view of horse breeding, with no firm commitment to any one breed. The East Anglians were fiercely proud of the Suffolk Punch, and the north-east and Scotland made much of the Clydesdale, but the East Riding farmer was happiest with a mongrel tailored to the requirements of his district.[2] Mr Rispin and Mr Playforth, for instance, when I asked if many horses were pure bred, said:

> Mr P: You didn't get many o' them, did you? . . . Not pure bred, like. No, when we got 'em like, they'd be cross-breds you know. Put an ordinary [mare to a pure-bred stallion]. . . . There weren't many thoroughbreds working . . . . You used to have your entire which was thoroughbred and then use any mare, you see, which you had and such as that. I would think they were better for not being thoroughbred . . . Some of 'em'd have nowt but Clydesdales, didn't they?
>   Mr R: Oh aye, I liked a Clydesdale.
>   Mr P: And others'd have nowt but Shires.
>   Mr R: Why, I did like a [Clydesdale] but they were stronger, were a Shire, weren't they, Bernard? More weight lifting, like. Them Shires, they used to

have overmuch hair on their legs, like, and then in winter time you were mucked, clammed up, didn't you?

Mr P: And then you used to take 'em i' pond to get it off.

Mr R: Aye, to wash it off, do you see? But a Clydesdale very seldom did, like.

You wouldn't need such strong horses on the Wolds, would you? . . .

Mr P: No, you used to get some nice horses, a nice type of horse. . . . When I was at Ruston Parva we had twin sisters, by – talk about them moving! They used to go overfast for me! By gum! . . .

Mr R: Most on 'em in Holderness was Shires, weren't they, Bernard?

Mr P: And they were slower working horses. . . . You used to get a heavier horse which was slower moving, but he could do more, he could pull more, like. But, I mean, if he went at the speed these horses went up here, he wouldn't last a day. . . . They could regulate, well, they seemed – I don't know, it was probably how they were bred, but they seemed as though they could work to a pace which they could keep up all day. . . . They didn't use to more or less flag at end o' t'day, unless you were on a real heavy job, like, and then . . . you used drive 'em accordingly, like. You know, if you found they were . . . sweating very heavy, like, you had to ease off, or otherwise you'd do 'em injury, like, couldn't you? Do 'em harm. . . .

Did most farms breed their own?

Mr P: . . . A lot of them used to have two or three coming in a year, you see, which'd replenish you, you see. We always, like, when I was at Hornsby's here, like, we always used to run about four young 'uns, didn't we? . . . Each year.

Historically, the horse of the East Riding was the Shire, but in the present century more and more Clydesdale influence was felt. After the First World War some Percherons (or Persians as the name was anglicised) came over from France. They were very powerful and docile, and seemed likely to make some impact in British agriculture, but with the spread of mechanization in the inter-war years the chance for a new breed had really passed.

While the Shire was the biggest and strongest horse available, many agreed with Mr Rispin that they preferred the speed and intelligence of the Clydesdale. Many more felt that a combination of the two was better than either, for a horse with the good points of both breeds was a formidable animal. The Shires also suffered at this time in the East Riding, Mr Johnson said, from a widespread deterioration in their feet. A good Shire hoof is blue coloured but, increasingly, horses were born with white, crumbly hooves which made them harder to shoe, more likely to shed shoes, and more likely to take harm as a result. This, and a growing intolerance of the problems associated with the heavy feather at the bottom of the leg, led many farmers to experiment with cross-breeding. Certainly even the pure bred Shires of today are much altered, as Mr Jarvis commented:

The majority you see – they say, 'Look at that beautiful Shire horse!' I say, 'You've never seen a Shire horse in your life, lad, when you talk about that, a

Shire horse,' I say, 'Them's Clydesdales, them isn't Shires. . . .' In a Shire
horse he had as much more bone in his leg as them have.[3]

This is a topic guaranteed to start arguments among heavy-horse enthusiasts, and
the two breed societies still maintain separate stud books, but there is general
agreement that there has been convergence in this century.

Simple genetics prevented the average farm keeping its own stallion, for he would
soon be serving his own daughters. Instead, they were mostly kept by a few
specialists who could maintain the highest standards, and they sent their animals out
to all districts. It was a prestige trade which frequently failed to cover its costs, so
many firms used it as an advertisement for selling horses, their real source of
income. Large estates might keep their own, for here prestige and a sense of duty to
the tenantry fulfilled were recompense in themselves. Lord Middleton of Birdsall,
for instance, kept eighteen Shire stallions on his own farm. Mr Carter described how
they were managed:

> They were farm men that took all these entires round [the farms]. But there
> was two chaps in t'Home Farm yard used to look after them stallions, just
> two. And the others was farm men, you see, and they used to start off about
> April and finish about July. And all them men used to go back onto their
> farms for hay-time, you see. These other [two] chaps used to put them into
> paddocks and just rough 'em off then. They didn't keep them up, you see,
> then. They used to go into paddocks and stop there all winter. . . . Some
> [stallion leaders] used to go away from [Birdsall] and they went in April and
> they didn't use to come back while the end of the season, when they went out
> Scarborough way. And some used to come in just weekends, some come in at
> every night [if they were travelling only to local farms].[4]

Many stallions were brought into the riding by rail for the season. Mr Ashby
remembered that near Beverley before 1914, 'Forshaws of Newark used send a man
round the farms with a stallion. There was one or two more, but he was the main
one.'[5] There were even stallions from Scotland. Mr Orr, who travelled stallions for
Montgomery's of Netherhall and Banks, Kirkcudbright said:

> I think it would be about 1924, . . . [that was] the only year I was as far down
> in England, I was travelling in East Riding o' Yorkshire, wi' a Clydesdale
> horse. . . . I stayed at Huggate on the Wolds at the weekend and I went round
> by Sledmere, Driffield, Beverley – I was round in that . . . district, but there
> were no Clydesdale mares, it was all Shire mares, and they were crossing them
> with the Clydesdale.[6]

At the start of the season stallions paraded in the market towns in front of the
farmers. A few locals with a low-grade stallion or two were also present for those
who were not willing to pay the prices the larger firms charged. Each stallion's route
was advertised in the local press and the stallion leader called in at all the farms he
passed to see if they wanted his horse. Providing the mare became pregnant, the foal

arrived eleven months later. The serving season was arranged so that the foals were born in spring or early summer, most commonly in April and May. When the mare came to term she became temporarily the foreman's responsibility, but until then, Mr Baines said:

> They'd do . . . a day's work on t'side of another . . . till they foaled nearly. It were better for 'em, you see, because they were getting proper exercise. And you also – under your care they were getting proper corn and bran and what have you, . . . which kept 'em healthier. They're far different is a Shire, and a working horse, a Clydesdale, such as them, to a riding horse. You can't ride a – you can't go and trot a horse that's heavy in foal. But you can walk a horse up and down, all day long. . . . Probably work them up to a day before they foal. Sometimes you brought 'em home on a morning, they'd foal in afternoon or t'night. No worse for them. As long as you aren't, you know, slogging 'em to death or owt like that, but they're doing a day's work. Same as the horse at side of 'em.

The time of conception was known precisely, but it was impossible to be absolutely certain when the birth was due, as Mr Johnson explained:

> [They] make a bit of a bag, and then maybe a drop of milk'll come out, and then that dries up and its like a bit o' wax on the end of the teat. Well, some people'll tell you, 'A horse is waxing up, she's going to foal,' well they can wax up ten days beforehand sometimes. And then its all nothing. . . . A cow – you can tell a cow better. But a mare, as soon as ever she's due, you know – you know when she's due when you get it all reckoned up and you keep your eye on her. Now, about a few days before she foals, you'll put her into a loose box for t'night, you see, and you maybe go every now and again, maybe go every couple of hours and have a look, or I've known some – there was one place I knew (I didn't live there) but waggoner they used to put down [a bed] for him and he had to sleep, he used to sleep in front [of the box], but I wouldn't have slept in front for nobody. Well now, you can go and see a mare and she's nothing, you know, she's laid down nice and content then, nothing happening: all right for a couple of hours. You can go at couple of hours' end and t'foal's born, he's on his legs, he's running about! Its a funny thing about a mare – they like to be on their own. And they can hold it for a long while, and you can stay and watch 'em and they won't do anything till you've gone. . . . You put 'em in this box well beforehand because . . . they don't particularly like a strange place, and I know one man, well – I was there – I was only a lad but he was foreman, he had a mare foaling, and he knew she wanted to foal and she wouldn't do anything. And she wouldn't foal in that box. And he opened t'door and she came out in t'fold yard, and she foaled in t'fold yard, like. . . . She'd determined she weren't going to foal in that place, you know.
>   . . . Nine times out of ten a box had half doors, you know; a top door, and you only shut top door when t'was real bad weather. Very bad, cold weather,

you know. And I've looked over, you know, gone outside and just hang my head over t'half door, bottom half, and watched a bit and you knew very well she wanted to foal and she wouldn't do nowt till you'd gone away, you know. No, you know, they're a bit tricky. . . . They can fox you. They can go and go a week over and – it isn't very oft they foal beforehand, unless there's something wrong, a mare. But its very seldom they want any help, a mare. Very seldom. . . .

Say you're a man in charge o' four horses, you can be the waggoner, third lad, whatever you are. Now, when that mare goes into that box, when you get up in a morning you maybe feed what horses you have left, and then go and see that mare. Well, if she's all right you fetch her out into t'stable and feed her as normal. But as soon as she foals you're finished with her, the foreman or master or whatever takes over and, . . . any animal, you know, doesn't want feeding heavy for a few days after, till they settle down and that. Well, you know, they give her bran mashes and such as that and, for a start, first drink they have, they warm the water, you know, take t' chill off. . . . That foreman or master or whatever – that lad had finished with her for most of a week. . . . You generally rested 'em for a week. I've heard some just give 'em three days but I didn't believe in that. . . . Now then, she still stayed in that box with that foal, you know, but the lad she belonged, he fed her again, you see. But she always stopped in that box.[7]

The foal was not speened, or weaned, until harvest time but it was a rare farm that could afford to let a mare stand idle for that long, usually only one where breeding was a main undertaking. It was more usual to send the mare back to work after a week, and though it was possible to take the foal with the mother and let it suckle as it needed milk, most separated them, which caused practical as well as emotional problems for the mare, as Mr Baines went on to say:

We used to milk mares, you know . . . when you came back [from work] your mare'd be flush with milk and on the way home she'd start whinnying because it used to be painful, I should think, to her, and she used to whinny for her foal, you know, and dance about a bit and act the goat a bit, knowing she was going to feed her foal and get shut of her milk, to ease herself. Well you used to get a cloth, . . . get warm water and a cloth and wash her bag for her really well, and then take half her milk away from her into a jug or a basin, or owt like that. We used to drink it, mare's milk. You see, if you took her to her foal, her foal'd get too much. . . . You used to have to put your foal in a box on its own – your hardest job were getting your mare out o' your box and leaving your foal in. 'Cause it'd jump, have a jump at bottom door, you know, so you used to shut both doors and see that they were secure. And then when . . . foal used to hear its mother come into yard it used to create and you had to watch then, 'cause it'd bowl out and jump onto you – you know, go mad to get to its mother. Till they got used to it . . . as they got, you know, two or three weeks old.

After being weaned the foals were removed from any real contact with the horselad and the adult horses, as Mr Johnson described:

There was maybe two or three foals, you know, on that place, but it was best to get 'em a mate [to keep them company if there wasn't], you see, they settled down better. Now them foals, they were all turned together then and put in a box and kept for, oh, a week or ten days till they'd forgotten their mother. You see, and then they could go outside, like, you know, and come in at night for a feed, you know, or such as that, and then of course, in low lying districts they'd maybe stop out all winter, you see; you didn't have no trouble with them, you know – take them some feed, like, twice a day in hard weather, or once a day in [better conditions], but on the Wolds where we were, any foals I had, you turned 'em out at day and they always slept in at night.

I asked Mr Tate and.Mr Playforth if anyone looked after them at this stage in their lives:

Mr T: Well, only to feed 'em, like. They would feed 'em in a trough, you know, in grass . . . anyone would go and feed them in winter.

Mr P: Often beastman, wasn't it? . . . Anybody that was handy, like. . . . Bit o' chaff and a few rolled oats or summat.

Mr T: When I was at Grange, we used to have some young uns – you know, in t'paddock – there was two in t'paddock in that box and two in a cartshed in t'fold yard. And he was a hard feeder was old Philip, you know – t'master. He used to come to Kilham every night, and I know when he went to Kilham I used to go round with another bag. . . . Aye, if it were a wet day I used to feed 'em, I used to say, 'I'll feed young horses.' Yes, I was coming out of the granary with some oats in a bag: he said, 'By God,' he said, 'You've getten a lot in!'

I said, 'Well there's only same as you give them,' I said, 'If you'd like to see 'em ta'en out, like,' I said, 'I can show you how many tins [measures] there is.' But there was twice as many, I think, if he'd counted them!

Breaking was the transition between foal and work horse. It was not a single event, as Mr Johnson pointed out, 'I don't know whether you watch cowboy films on the television but you can see 'em, they make me smile sometimes; they catch a wild horse and then in five minutes they're riding it. Well it must be a different country from this.' Breaking was a long and intermittent process. It can be said to have started more or less at birth, and only ended when a horse knew its job fully, a space of four or five years. Breaking was a name most people felt would be better changed since it suggested that the idea was to bring the horse into abject submission. Mr Baines:

You can't break a horse in with cruelty, nor a dog, nor anything else. You break them in by making them do what you want them to do and what you're telling them to do and rewarding them when they do it. . . . [If] a young horse went all right at work, first time yoked, I used to yoke it an hour, and of course then it were sweating really well. And then I used to bring it home and I'd take it an hour next day. Now if I got one that was just awkward I'd keep it there till I tired it out, then it knew I was boss; I were master and it were mastered.

The aim was to teach a horse that co-operation paid while awkwardness did not. Breaking the horse's spirit did not come into it and a broken-spirited horse would have been much less useful than an independent but co-operative one. There were many bad horse breakers who lacked the skill or the inclination to do the job properly and they did untold harm, storing up a lot of trouble for the people who had to use the horse after them. Good breakers never used any more force than was needed to keep them in control. They each judged situations differently, but their aim was always to show the horse that it could not beat them. Mr Masterman, for instance, believed in bringing the struggle out in the open and having it out once and for all, where others were content not to force an issue:

When I was breaking horses I used to feed 'em well. Some people used to starve 'em, they said they were easier to break in, well, maybe they were, but if a horse had any badness in him, when he gets his strength up and gets going he'll show it. Well I used to feed 'em and that, and I thought, 'If they've any badness they'll show it now.' Instead of after when they got [more powerful]. I only had one that was really, you know, a bit bad to do with but he was all right at finish. You know, I used to like to see 'em fight. . . . I liked to see 'em rear and plunge and – you know, they were breaking theirselves in . . . then. But one that would stand – docile – do anything with it, I used to always be suspicious of it. I thought, 'Well, you'll do summat someday.' And they usually did. They killed or there was summat wrong with them.

The real struggle was psychological rather than physical and he was horrified by reports of a man who claimed to break horses more quickly by harshness:

When I was a youngster there was an American came over here, . . . to teach people how to break horses in. Well I knew some of the young farmers . . . went, and it was £5 for a lesson. He would teach the young farmers his methods. He broke a horse in in a few hours. Supposed to do. But I think eventually they sent him home, they wouldn't allow him to – Galvayne, they called him. Because they used to say then, . . . if they'd a bad horse and he was bad to break in, they would say, 'Well, why don't you Galvayne him?' But what Galvayning was I never knew, I never saw it, but I expect it was very cruel, it was punishment for a horse, like. He did, he maybe did break 'em in. . . . It was a wicked job. But I knew two young farmers went. . . . I understand that when they finished with a horse it was a white un. With lather and sweat. It was punishment. Well that was no good.[8]

Lads might help out at any stage of breaking, just as Mr Tate earlier described helping to feed the foals, but even if a waggoner was considered fit to break a horse, it would have interfered extensively with his normal duties, so it had to be done by the foreman or the farmer, or if neither of them would take it on, there might be an old labourer who had a way with horses. Otherwise, recourse could be had to one of the men described earlier as casual workers: men with enough skill to set themselves to many jobs and amass a better income as a freelance than any labourer could. There were no full time horse breakers because it was seasonal work. If a Kilham farmer wanted such a man around 1914, there was George Allen in Harpham, the next village, or another in Driffield. Since these men depended on past results as a reference for future work they mostly knew their trade. On the other hand, if a foreman or a farmer were bad breakers there was often no-one to stop them ruining young horses year after year. The worst thing about bad breaking was that if a horse was made to work by force, whoever looked after it in future would probably have to continue in the same vein, and he might well be injured by it.

The first stage in breaking was to get the foal used to being handled and led about by men. This was known as swinging and it started very early. Mr Masterman said:

> About a week old I used to start, while their mother was eating, in the crib; while the mother was having her food I used to put halter on; just keep walking round and round. Its no good trying to lead 'em forward, because they won't go. You can't pull 'em. They would sit down and pull; you can't shift 'em. But they don't like their heads pulling round. They don't like their necks twisting. And I used walk round and round. Keep pulling their heads round. Then go the other way. you know, eventually they get to follow you.

The longer it was left the harder the job became because a foal's ability to resist being led develops rapidly. Mr Johnson commented: 'I've had to swing 'em . . . at three years old. By, they were strong and its hard work that: it was three or four men's job.' A good horseman never regarded this job as finished. The foals might not need his attention in the fields, but he visited them all the same so that they got to know him well and never forgot their initial lessons. This went on until they were about two years old, when they had learned to follow a pull on the halter every time without resisting. A well-handled horse achieved this automatically, but a neglected one took more training. This was the point where Mr Masterman used to force a struggle with the horses he was in charge of:

> You put two halters on 'em, and you have a post in a field, a post about a foot square; about three foot out o' ground and on the top o' that you have a bit of iron, a swivel with a ring in. And you put two halters on the horse and there we generally had a thick rope about twenty or thirty foot long. We used to tie that to the halter and then the other end to this ring on top of this post and we used to make the horse gallop round it. And make them try to get away – pull – sometimes they used to sit down and pull. . . . You must have a strong rope: you mustn't let them get away or break it, else, they break it once; they think they can do it again, you see. Otherwise they won't follow where you

lead 'em. . . . And, well, I used to set them off straight across, full gallop, and they thought they were free. When they got to the end of the rope it used to pull them up sudden. But they didn't do that again. You couldn't get them to do it a second time. By, it didn't half used to pull their neck!

The next stage was mouthing and there was no room for mistakes. The horse had to be accustomed to carrying a bit in its mouth, which had to remain tender enough to respond to tugs on the bit or else it could not be driven and Mr Johnson explained:

A breaking bridle is different from an ordinary bit: they have what they call keys on . . . in the middle of the bit: . . . They're in the mouth and they tickle their tongue, and it makes them they're always chewing. Now you do that. You can't mouth a horse, not properly, under three weeks. You turn him round in his stall and you tie him to the pillars [with] what they call pillar reins one at either side. . . .
     We used to put them in in a morning, let them stop till dinner time, take the bits out ('cause they couldn't eat with them) and give them their dinner and put them back in again till, oh, say five, six o'clock, maybe then take 'em out again. Now you did that every day for three weeks. But if it was a tender-mouthed horse, it used to go there [the corner of its mouth became sore] first on iron bits, so you used to take that out – you had to watch for it, take it out, and there were some wooden bits, slightly thicker but, you know, they didn't cut. But if you cut horse's mouth there, you know, wi' chewing, and it skins there [in the corners], now then, eventually that horse is harder, what you call harder-mouthed horse; when it does heal up and get better, it's harder than it would have been naturally.

When Mr Masterman was a foreman at Thorngumbald he broke all the farm's horses. So did the neighbouring farm's foreman who was not a good horse breaker and regularly ruined the horses' mouths, so that, 'if you tied 'em to an empty waggon, they'd pull it about the yard with their head . . . , real heavy-headed. But when I'd finished 'em you could have driven 'em with a bit of knitting wool, they were that, you know, tender-mouthed.' Everything else built on these foundations, as Mr Johnson described:

You put 'em in what you called long reins: they were about five yards long. They were really plough strings. Now plough strings aren't reins . . . , they used to be made locally [by] bandmakers, rope makers, twine makers, and they were made of very good stuff, they were [very thin with loops for handles]. . . . Now when you started a [young] horse, you had what they called breaking strings. They were just a bit thicker and heavier than ordinary. And you went outside, you know, and went to 'em and went into a field; generally you had a bit o' room and 'course you got them used to answering the reins, you see. You pulled left, he went left. It took you a bit, you had to have a lot o' patience.

Wearing harness and getting used to pulling implements came next, as Mr Rispin and Mr Playforth said:

Mr P: You had them to yoke then . . . , and you used to have some rum jobs then, you know, putting them into traces. Then they used to start to kick, probably.

Mr R: Aye, that's right, you had an old horse tied onto him, didn't you, Bernard? And then you yoked him to an old sled or owt –

Mr P: A sleeper or owt o' that . . . , something to hold him back, like, you know. . . . Get their legs over [the traces] and then you used to have to loose traces off to get it from between their legs. . . . Maybe get strings under the traces. . . . Used to pull their tails down – jam 'em tight, you couldn't get it out.

Mr R: The more you pulled, the worse they kicked, like: you had no hold on 'em. . . .

Mr P: Oh, you wanted danger money.

A steady old horse to go alongside a youngster was essential at this time to calm it down, or if that failed the old horse could physically hold it back as they were firmly hitched together. Sometimes one was put on either side of a young horse for better control. In so far as was possible, the harness was made less likely to irritate the young horse, band traces replacing steel ones to prevent them grating along its flanks. After a while they were hitched to real implements, as Mr Johnson explained:

You put 'em in a plough and two of you generally went and you had an old horse at side of 'em, and one man drove the old horse and steered the plough and the other just watched the young one, you know. And then, oh, maybe a few days of that – well, depended on the young horse, how he'd settled down, you know – one man could generally [manage on his own]. . . . but you never worked 'em a full day. And you never put 'em to any hard work, you see. Just in light work and half a day at a time and then you didn't – that was perhaps spring o' t'year, you didn't touch 'em again, you what they called turned them away, put 'em out to grass, and they stopped there till back end, and then you brought them in, but you didn't work them hard then, really. . . . Till they got between three and four and then, you know, they were generally strong enough . . . to go along wi' t'old horses, go on with the other horses.

It only remained to teach them to work in shafts and to back a cart, as Mr Johnson explained:

You put a horse in shafts and he's absolutely lost. He doesn't know what to do, you know – he feels these shafts and he has to steer by the shafts really; push 'em one way and push 'em t'other, or, you know, shove it back, and that's a thing you have to have a lot of patience in. You know, you put horse in shafts and you go down that road, and you want to turn that way, well you sometimes have a job because he thinks that shaft is pushing at him and he shouldn't go that way – you have to learn them to push at the shafts. And same, pushing a thing back, that takes more doing than anything. Getting a horse learned to push a weighted rully. . . . Now there was some used to like it – after they got used to it; you see when you come home on a night with a cart or a waggon or whatever you had, you backed it into a shed. And that was one of the things a young horse took a lot of getting used to – backing into this shed.

In different parts of the country some people drove almost entirely by reins, and some almost entirely by commands, but in the East Riding a mixture of both systems were used. The basic words of command which the horses were taught were 'gee back' for turn right; for turn left it was 'whauve', 'arve', or 'orve', depending on local pronunciation; and 'whoa' or 'whee' meant stop. For starting, a variety of words were used. Sometimes the horse's name was called, but they also responded to 'go on', 'gee up', 'come on', and others. Stopping and starting commands were fairly standard over the whole country, but the turning commands varied with local dialects so, as Mr Johnson commented: 'If a horse went away from where he'd been trained, . . . fifty, sixty miles away, well they had a different word, you see, and he had to be trained over again.'[9]

Horses also had to able to ignore noises and to go in traffic without panic, especially if the farmer wanted to sell a horse into a town. A buyer would be more easily found, at a better price, if it could be guaranteed that the horse would make the transition to the new environment quickly and easily. If the horse was not to be sold it was still a good idea to get it used to these hazards because even a farm horse went into towns or to stations. Threshing days were also extremely noisy, but this could be utilized for training by having a man gradually lead the youngster nearer the traction engine and threshing machine over a period of hours, calming it all the while.[10] During the Second World War Mr Playforth went out with the last horse to be broken on their farm in search of traffic for a similar acclimatisation process. The Wolds were then extensively used by the army for tank training:

What a job I had. I'd been right up Pockthorpe and all round there and I'd never met any traffic, and I had her in strings [walking behind her], so I took her down [Kilham] street – one Tuesday morning; I thought, 'Why, I shall find summat,' and I took her right to t'bottom and I didn't find nowt, came back and turned down that road [to Ruston Parva] and I just got turned in at bottom there again Blacksmith Arms, and a big lorry came behind me; a tank came down in front o' me. And there she was on her back legs: and there was hundreds of soldiers about. And in a couple o' seconds you couldn't see anybody: everybody'd gone and left me. However, I got by and I went right up Driffield road, down [to] Robson's shed and I turned round and came back again and just as I'm coming back, over comes (against Top there) a lorry with a sheet flapping. . . . And she made one dive down that hedge-bottom, why its a big [one] . . . and she jumps right down there, and I had strings here, and she just swung me right into hedge-bottom and trailed me down there. But I hung on.

Even though training was still not complete, the horse would now be given to one of the lads and it would learn by doing henceforth. All the lads would have been eyeing it up for some time, as Mr Rispin and Mr Playforth recounted:

Mr P: You'd get a nice one broke, and it would match up, say, with thirdy pair or summat, and thirdy used to say, 'By, I want that one!' And he'd turn to [the foreman] and he'd say, 'can I have that there, like; can I have it, like?' He was always wanting it because it matched his other ones. . . . Lads, you know, as soon as you'd got him going and they thought, 'Oh, he'll go nicely on side o'mine, like, you know; I'll have that, I'll see foreman.'

Mr R: Aye, you talk about that Bob . . . , he was a grand horse, but when he was a young horse Tom R— lived with me, like, and Tom was scruffling like, and he was real smart, and they came down one morning, getting up like, and Tom says to me, he was off to scruffle and he says, 'Can I take Bob this morning?'

'Why,' I says, 'You can do but I wouldn't be pestered with a young horse like that scruffling – what about —'

'Oh no, he'll be all right!'

And he took him, like. Well, I wouldn't have been pestered with him, like, you know. He had him to learn, like, to keep straight down row, d'you see. He was a good horselad was that.

Thereafter the foreman was finished with the youngster, which would be looked after by a succession of lads occupying varying places in the hierarchy as its powers rose and waned. Mr Fisher said:

We used to call them old when they got ten. But some would live to . . . twenty. But they wouldn't work. Not what we used to call a full day's work. When they got ten and twelve they were no good for a waggoner – we used to say they were no good for a waggoner's horse then. I used like 'em about five or six, just at their best then, five or six.

The length of their lives was largely determined by the individual farmer's policy. An old horse was invaluable for steadying new recruits to the workforce, particularly while they were being broken. There were other times when its knowledge of what was expected of it was worth more than strength vitiated by ignorance. Such horses were ideal for giving to very young lads because they would look after a boy quite as much as he looked after them, doing jobs correctly despite him. They would tolerate his inevitable accidental mistreatment of them where a spritely young horse would not, and no boy of fourteen or so could control anything but a co-operative horse. Some farmers discounted this, preferring to work their horses until, said Mr Walker:

They were absolutely jiggered. Twelve or thirteen year old or maybe summat like that.

And then off to the knackers?

That's it. Finished. Get all the iron out on 'em, steel out on 'em and then, that's it. . . . That's how they used to carry on. 'Course there was lots o' times when one used to die. Or maybe a couple every year.

Whether the farmer worked his horses to death or used them with care, their fate was everywhere the same when they reached the end of their useful life. They were work horses, and no matter how much affection was given to them while they were at work, a horse that could not work went to the knacker for the standard price of a few pounds. A very few might be put out to grass, but they had never been pets so they never really had a chance to engage anyone's sympathy for their incapacity.

While it was working, a horse was the concern of the lad who drove it and he would resent any undue interference. It was the waggoner's job to check that the horse was treated properly, and the foreman limited himself to watching for any signs that the waggoner was not coping, whether through ignorance or weakness. He only became involved with individual horses in exceptional circumstances; usually illness or injury. In times gone by, he had doubtless tried to handle all but the most serious trouble himself with folk-remedies, but by this century he simply sent for the vet unless he was sure it was something simple . If the horse needed a course of treatment or constant attention, then the foreman was heavily involved, not only to ensure that things were done correctly, but also because, as in breaking, he was the only man with a flexible enough schedule to take it on. There were always a few bottles of patent medicine around a stable – various drenches for colic and other ailments, plus the inevitable Elliman's Embrocation – and the foreman supervised their administration. If there was any doubt at all, the vet was called in. A small farmer with no foreman might take more risks because he was dealing with his own property, but a foreman played safe.[11]

The foreman generally remained in the background with regard to the care of the horses, coming forward only at important times. Although some older lads who had a natural flair for horse keeping were as skilled as anyone, most would inevitably not become really good all-round horsemen. The average lad could cope perfectly well with routine horse keeping, and with minor deviations from the routine, but the system of using single lads depended on there being someone else on the farm to supply the experience they lacked. His role had far more influence than its direct effects for if he was a bad horseman his interventions would often be misjudged, and the horses would suffer. More than that, however, he broke the horses in and was responsible for getting them ready to work. If that was badly done, the normal farm routine could only be maintained by force, and that easily developed into cruelty, as we have seen in the last chapter. A boy who began by spending two or three years on a farm where the horses were badly broken would pick up bad habits he might never lose, no matter how co-operative horses on later farms were, which would create friction between him and a good foreman. A good foreman kept an eye on the horses not just out of duty, but because he had broken them and knew them well.

Notes to Chapter Eleven

1. F.M.L. Thompson, 'Horses and Hay in Britain, 1830–1918' in F.M.L. Thompson, ed., *Horses in European Economic History: A Preliminary Canter* (1983), p. 61.

2. See K. Chivers, 'The Supply of Horses in Great Britain in the Nineteenth Century', in Thompson, *Preliminary Canter*, pp. 31–49, especially 38, for a study of the transfer of farm horses to towns nationally, of the emergence of the pedigree stallion, and of the changing attitudes to the purity of the breeds.

3. See K. Chivers, 'Supply of Horses', p. 35.

4. See also Day, *Horses*, pp. 68–9.

5. Mr Ashby, letter to the author.

6. Beamish Museum tape 1976–1/1. See also Mr Johnson, untaped interview 3, p. 6.

7. See also Day, *Horses*, pp. 71–2.

8. The real Sydney Galvayne came to England in 1884 and appeared before Queen Victoria in 1887. He was a remarkably effective horse trainer, and apparently worked so fast that his methods seemed miraculous. In later years, other men professing similar skills and methods, and sometimes using his name, toured the country. They often had no real understanding of horses and were no more than confidence tricksters, and this seems likely to have been the case here. See *Summerhay's Encyclopedia for Horsemen*, ed. R.S. Summerhays (1952, 5th ed. 1970), p. 139, and J.R. Young, *The Schooling of the Western Horse* (1973), pp. 18–19.

9. See also Keegan, *Heavy Horse*, figs 45 and 46.

10. Mr Appleyard, untaped interview 1, p. 2.

11. See Reffold, *Pie for Breakfast*, pp. 47–8.

Chapter Twelve

Food

Farm lads worked hard all year round and generally they did so without complaint. To a large extent the way they felt about a farm depended not on the work they were asked to do, but on how well they were fed while they were doing it. In 1864, Dr Edward Smith reported to the Privy Council on the diet of the working class, and he said that the East Riding farm lads were better fed than any comparable income group he had investigated. They certainly fared much better than their own parents, who had to feed themselves on labourers' wages. The fact that Dr Smith went so far as to call them pampered and spoilt shows how far above the average their diet was then, and there is no reason to believe it deteriorated before 1900. Flora Thompson recalled that Oxfordshire boys hired onto northern farms at this time always returned home full of admiration for the food they had received while away.[1]

Even in the East Riding, which was one of the highest paid counties for agricultural labourers, married men's wages could not be described as generous, and most families struggled to provide adequate food for all their children all year round. As a family's first children grew up, more arrived and the money available was forced to stretch ever further. As they moved into their teens and began work, they required good nourishment if their bodies, still growing, were to cope with the demands being made on them. Nationally, the appalling number of men judged physically unfit to serve in the Boer War confirmed that in all too many cases they did not get it.[2] As a farm servant, however, the East Riding child personally broke out of this vicious system and also left behind a smaller family, easing the strain on the budget.

In theory, town jobs were better paid, but farm lads were proudly conscious of the quality of their diet. Mr Masterman recalled a time when he worked in a warehouse in Hull:

I nearly got clobbered. . . . There was a feller there I was working with for a bit . . . , he was talking to me about bacon one day. 'Well,' I said, 'You've never tasted bacon.' Well I meant he'd never tasted what the farmers used to cure, you know, it used to be good bacon, did that. And, oh, he was mad was this feller. He set about me, I thought – he was a little old man, I daren't hit him. . . . You get bacon maybe two or three years old, it is bacon.

Farms that lived up to lads' expectations were given the accolade of being 'good meat houses'. They provided large quantities of plain, nourishing food rather than great variety or fancy cooking. Most meals centred round beef or bacon, served with vegetables, pies, and frequently bread. There were normally three meals a day: breakfast, dinner, and tea or supper. When the work was heavy, refreshments known as luance were supplied between meals, but otherwise three meals a day were all a lad got. Dinner was usually hot, while breakfast and supper were usually, though not always, cold. Traditionally, breakfast had been a bowl of milk with boiled bacon in it, but in this century most farms served something similar to that described here by Mr Rispin:

> There was a basin o' boiled milk for you – never a cup, never a mug – it was a basin. And a wooden spoon. . . . Foreman would cut a great lump of beef and there would be bread on t'table in a basket and you cut your own bread. . . . There were ever so many different pies and cheesecakes and all such as that.

Meat was almost invariably boiled or roasted, methods of cooking preferred because they did not require constant attention. All meat then was fatty by today's standards, and the meat the farms used was more so than average, as Mr Baines recalled: 'Of course all t'bacon at that time o' day was off old sows that had got past their breeding stage. And they were all fat, you know. Fat as hell. They were three parts fat and a little bit of lean in it.' Since that time, changes in feeding methods, a desire to minimize the fattening period, and a transformation in the expectations of the public have all dramatically altered the sort of meat which is acceptable to butchers and their customers. Boiling fatty meat had the advantage of preserving its bulk. Mr Pridmore recalled:

> Fat bacon, . . . they used to boil a huge lump o' that in the copper where they used to wash their clothes; and they used to get a lump of boiling beef and they used to put that in with it, and we had this boiled beef for dinner and this fat bacon for breakfast and tea.

The bacon was all cured on the farm by traditional methods and its taste was quite different from that of today. Preparation methods made the fat far more palatable than on modern bacon, which may have been a factor in altering public expectations. It was also kept for long periods before being eaten, as Mr Baines described:

> We used to kill us own pigs. 'Course pigs at that time o' day was hung all over, you know, in t'barn, in t'granaries – there'd be hams and shoulders and sides of bacon. Some of 'em got well maggotted, and all, you know. We used to go to fetch 'em in and cut maggots out for 'em to use, but you could smell that bacon at that time, cooking, all over the farm buildings on a morning.

For breakfast and supper there were no vegetables, but the meal was made up with other things. Bread and butter, or some other fat, was common, but by no means universal. Mr Walker, for instance, was never on a farm that served it during the week. Indeed 'narrow-chinned-bread-and-butter townies' was a common remark that showed it was firmly identified with poor eating such as town folk endured.[3] Pastry was more important, and pies were the standard fillers, as Mr Baines recalled:

> All the pies nearly was a double crust – crust on top. Prune pies about two and a half inches thick, curd pies about two and a half or three inches thick – you know, real good stuff. And home made curd. And the first two years I was in farm service we used to get curd made from – make us own curd, and you changed the milk by using epsom salts when your milk's boiling in t'oven. Finest thing there is for . . . making curds. And we used to have many a time for supper a basinful of curds and put some sugar on, you know, stir them up. You never wanted any opening medicine, you know, with curds being made of —, but they did physick you.[4]

The main meal was dinner, served in the middle of the working day when it was needed most and usually hot. Mr Johnson recalled a typical series of dinners thus:

> Monday: broth day, that used to be, you had soup, suet puddings, boiled beef, vegetables. Now then, next day was pie day, what they called pie day: meat pie . . . ; vegetables, meat and that in. And I tell you, after that meat pie, they used to, a lot of 'em, well most of 'em, used to have what they called a treacle cake. . . . It was a cake not a deal thicker than my hand, what they called a sad cake, not a light cake, . . . and they used to slice it in two and put treacle in, then put [it back together]. And that was afters.
>   Now then. Say, Sunday: roast beef, Monday: pot-on, as they called it; soup. Tuesday: pie day, Wednesday: pot on again, Thursday: pie day, and then for some of them that was six days, pot-on and pie day and then roast beef and that, Sunday. But some used to vary it a bit, had a cold dinner on a Saturday, you know, cold beef and that for dinner.

Besides pies there were cooked desserts, as Mr Masterman recalled: 'Maybe a pudding very near as big as [a] pouffe, like, tied up in a cloth. They used to be good. Apple dumplings, maybe. Rhubarb dumpling, spotted dog – currant dumpling you know, and that. And sauce.' Before 1914, for a drink, Mr Rispin said, 'You had milk all t'week through, morning and night, till Sunday night, then they used to gi'e you a drink o' tea . . . That was for five or six year, and then it got to be [tea] every morning.' The changeover was far from universal and Mr Carter, who only began work after the war was over, recalled, 'It was all milk we got, we got milk to our breakfast and milk to our teas.' It was always skimmed and often boiled: all year round on some places, but on others, as Mr Jarvis recalled, in spring, 'When the horses went out, . . . when t'horses slept out in t'fields, we didn't get boiled milk, we got cold . . . , foreman says, "It'll be cold milk, the horses has gone out. From now on."'

On working days, breakfast was normally at about six o'clock (varying with the sunrise), dinner was at twelve noon, and supper was a little after six in the evening. On Sundays breakfast was later so that the lads could lie in longer, and Mrs Rispin and Mr Playforth told me:

Mrs R: We always used to leave 'em a bit of supper on a Sunday night.

Mr P: 'Cause they had their tea at four.

Mrs R: Aye, that's right. . . . Only on a Sunday night – they didn't get it any other night, but always on a Sunday night, and it was only me that started that.

On weekdays, lads had nearly six hours of work to get through between meals. The general opinion was that the food was more substantial than anything available now, which seems likely, but even so, some lads only just made it from one meal to the next. As Mr Fisher said, 'Sometimes you used to feel that edgy you could nearly eat what horses was eating. Honest.'

Only when heavy work was in progress was luance, or allowance, given in mid-morning and mid-afternoon; usually a sandwich, or some pie or cake, and either tea or beer. During the nineteenth century beer had been the rule, but as time went by the custom changed. There were many reasons for this: for instance, Mr Walker said, 'They wouldn't have beer on their farms, wouldn't some o' t'farmers. You know: such as chapellers and that. They were like teetotal.' Some farmers gave a choice to accommodate teetollers among the men, and others gave beer to adults, but excluded the boys, as Mr Masterman explained:

I was only thirteen, like, when I first was hired. They wouldn't let me have beer. I had to have tea or oatmeal, oatmeal water. And there was a brewery at Keyingham then. . . . Well, I used to go there with a cart for a barrel, and inside there was a barrel set up and there was a cow's horn for you to drink out of. Well anybody could go and they could have three or four or five of these horns. But not me. Old Brewer Jackson, he had whiskers right down to his waist, white whiskers; he wouldn't let me come near any. By, it was good beer.

It might be thought that such an attitude towards youngsters would be common place, but this would be a mistake. Mr Harper recalled, 'Womenfolks wouldn't make us young lads no tea. We had to sup beer along wi' old hands. Th'old hands used to be glad, they used to get half of ours, do you see. We couldn't sup like they could. And it was beer i' them days.' A few farmers still brewed on the farm, but most preferred to buy small beer from the many local breweries. Each man usually got a pint, though a few farms allowed three gills, or a pint and a half.[5] Mostly the rations were doled out by the farmer or the hind, but occasionally a barrel was simply placed in the stackyard and the men helped themselves. When everyone was working away from the farmstead, Mr Harper remembered: 'Sometimes I used to have to go and fetch it wi' two milk buckets . . . holding two gallon apiece. So – you know, when you look at it, when you get sixteen or eighteen men, you know, there isn't much left.' Mr Rispin needed four thirty-six gallon barrels for harvest on one occasion, and with such large orders the farmers could keep the price down, at least until the First World War. Thereafter inflation and taxation took their toll. Mr Masterman said:

It was tuppence ha'penny a pint, but after the war it was a tanner, and then it started to go up and up, and farmers, you know, stopped giving it. They'd maybe give you [tea] in t'morning and beer in t'afternoon [or vice versa], whichever you liked – they would ask you.

One farm we was at, there was a feller in the village, he reckoned to be a, you know, the village idiot and they used to all get him to carry chaff. . . . So the farmer said one morning, 'Now,' he said, 'Which will you have, beer in t'morning and tea afternoon or [the other way around]?' So nobody said anything; this John Robinson said, 'Why, I'll have beer in t'morning if you don't mind, master. Well, if it rains after dinner we shan't get any.' If they had beer after morning – [if it was] raining, [and] they didn't thrash in the afternoon, they were going to have . . . tea again the next morning. They wouldn't get any beer. The farmer said, 'Good lad, John, you're more "R" than "F"! (You're more right than fond).'

When and to whom a farmer gave luance were not questions with strictly defined answers. At harvest and hay-time everyone got it, whether they were involved or not. Jobs, such as threshing, lambing, or muck-spreading, were universally agreed to be luance jobs, but usually only for those actively involved. Other jobs were or were not luance jobs entirely according to the temper of the farmer; broadcast sowing, for instance. If the numbers involved were very small some farmers preferred to offer money instead, as Mr Rispin remembered:

Aye, first year I was married, I tell you . . . I stopped for labourer, . . . and . . . [the farmer] had 170 acre of turnips to sow . . . I had to sow all manishment, you know. . . . He said to me, 'It's luance job, isn't it, Tom?'
I said, 'Aye, aye, its a luance job all right.'
'Well,' he said, 'If you were over-greedy, we'll maybe sort it out and bring [the food out to] you, but,' he said, '[if not] I'll give you eightpence a day luance money.'

Eightpence was worth far more than the refreshments, but it saved the farmer even more in disruption of the kitchen routine.

The lads were called in promptly as the food was ready and they were expected to take just as long in eating it as was needed to get the food down; never more than a quarter of an hour. Mr Tate began farming where all the workers were members of the family except him and one other hired man:

Ten minutes, you know; you hadn't to speak. Just shovelling it in as fast as you could, and out. When I was first there I was talking away, you know, and there were only two of us at t'table. . . . [The farmer] said, 'Tell that lad not to talk!' Aye. And he [the other workman] daren't speak. He used to point to the pies [he wanted]!

Mr Baines recounted this version of a very common joke:

Amongst Farm Horses

There were two bricklayers working on a farmhouse building, at top o' t'roof, and they were all going in for their dinner and t'waggoner were striding on first, you know, then t'next man, seconder, then thirder, and what have you, and t'little lad were running to keep up behind 'em; and he tumbled, so one of these chaps on t'roof says, 'Now lad, gerrup!' He were roaring, like; he says 'Gerrup, lad, and get in for thy dinner!' He says, 'Nay mister. I'll be too late, the buggers'll be coming out now!'

The crockery and cutlery were as limited as the time allowed. Everyone agreed that cups, appeared only for a Sunday drink of tea, if they appeared at all. Even mugs were virtually unknown, for basins were the rule, and, said Mr Masterman, they were the ordinary, old fashioned kitchen type which had 'blue rings around. You know. Hold about a pint and a half . . . You'd one plate – one plate for meat and vegetables, and your same plate for puddings . . . . They didn't believe in a lot of washing up.' Equally, in the fields, when luance came out it was one vessel between two, which led to arguments and some strife as both men's shares went in together. Mr Rispin and Mr Tate recalled that one of the pair always took the top half and the other the bottom, and then, 'some of them bottom halfers, they used to get in first; then they supped top [so] they could get at theirs!'

The foreman, where there was one, usually presided at the table, but in a few cases he followed his employer's example and withdrew to eat with his family elsewhere, leaving the waggoner in charge. Whoever was sitting at the head of the table, carved the meat and served it out – sometimes flamboyantly, Mr Masterman recalled:

Slashed right across a lump o' beef . . . , just [held it] on his fork and his knife, and [he'd] sling it onto your plate. And, you know, some o' them fellers was good shots, they could throw it from one end o' table to t'other and always hit your plate. Never missed you know. Just take their knife and sling a great big lump of beef – half a pound maybe, or more. Well, it was cheap then.

All the rest of the food stood on the table for everyone to help themselves, taking anything they liked and as much as they liked, as long as they ate it, a rule that was never relaxed even for someone who had chosen too hastily, as Mr Masterman once did:

We'd been hay-making, went in to tea about nine o'clock at night. And there was a dish of mushrooms on the table. Well I don't like mushrooms. And I thought it was liver, you know. And I got two or three spoonfuls o' this – it was blinking mushrooms. Well I'd to eat 'em. They wouldn't let you leave anything.

Milk was usually put on the table in a big can and a variety of pies was always available. If they were all eaten more could be had, but a lad could not pick and choose, as Mr Rispin told me:

142

Say you started o' that pie, you had to clean that pie up before you could start on another: there was no saying, say this was a jam and this was an apple or owt o' that, if this was a jam you had to clean that up before you [started the apple]. . . . And then – you all cut your own pie, you know. Say if you were here . . . , and say pie was down there and you wanted a bit, you'd say, 'Pie o'er please.' Then they would reach it up for you. But you all cut your own pie. You started in t'middle . . . , but you always left sort of a chunk in a square, didn't you? There was a proper way to [do it] . . . , and last man what got it, he got t'most inside.

On most farms it was thought more important that no-one should go out hungry than that no half-eaten pies should be left on the table, but at a few the rule was that they should only be started if they could be finished. Some farms, indeed, were known as bad meat houses because the food was so sparse or bad. Mr Tate told me that as long as he was fed well a lad would put up with almost anything else: 'If [the farm] was a rough un, some of 'em would stop, you know; aye, if it was a good food spot, you know. That's what they'd to . . . look after.' His brother stayed several years on a farm where the work was so heavy that horses regularly died from it, simply because he liked the food.

Naturally, when they got together lads discussed the farms they were at, and particularly at the hiring fairs everyone wanted to know which farms to avoid. If a farm was widely judged inadequate over a period of years, its reputation became a real factor in the bargaining at the fair. Those lads who were confident of getting a place, that is the skilled ones, would simply refuse to go there, and the rest would be reluctant. However, the evidence on bad meat houses must be sifted very carefully precisely because this was a favourite topic for gossip. There were many lads who judged farms by their personal tastes, not on the generally perceived standard of its meals. Their objection was real enough to them, since they either went hungry or ate something they disliked, but a farm's reputation did not deserve to be blackened if it was doing all that was generally expected of it. Thus, Mr Pridmore would often fetch a basin of water for himself rather than drink milk.

Personal grievances were sometimes reinforced where a lad was forced to eat something he did not like, simply because everyone else did. Most commonly, this occurred with fatty meat. Some lads, like Mr Baines, loved it, but large numbers could not stomach it at all, yet since the foreman served the meat, they could rarely avoid having it on their plate. Mr Masterman said:

I've seen lads, they've cut a great slab of bacon, fat bacon, and they've dipped it in their milk [at breakfast] and they've – oh, by – it used to upset me, that, 'cause I wouldn't eat fat – I couldn't eat fat beef. I used to put it in my jacket pocket when the foreman wasn't watching and give it dog. But they used to find out, they used to see all this grease come through my jacket pocket and ask me, what was I doing? Then they used to realize: 'Oh, I see: you've been bringing fat meat out, has tha?' Old dog used always look for me coming out o' t'house on a morning with this fat meat. I couldn't eat fat meat.

143

Similarly, rhubarb was something one lad delighted in while another was repelled. Mr Baines again liked it, but his description shows why many others did not:

> It used to be that right tall rhubarb: about as thick as your arm. You wanted a slasher to chop it down with. And then they used to wash it, cut it up – they didn't use to string it, you know, didn't use to peel it. And we used to call it stringy pie; we used to be pulling strings out on our mouth.

Elsewhere, preparation was even cruder: 'They just used to . . . nick it to make it bend, leave a great big root on,' said Mr Tate. In this case, of course, there was room for real complaint about the cooking. Mrs Lawler remembered her brother bringing home some short-cake: 'Said they went on t'table a month, them, while he put 'em in his pocket and brought 'em home. He was throwing 'em at the wall and they wouldn't be broken. . . . They were hard and black.' Similarly, even where there was nothing actively wrong with the food itself, Mr Johnson said,

> There was some, . . . broth one day and pie the next. . . . Generally there was plenty of it, you know, but it was no variety. Places I lived at, you know, maybe had two, maybe just two pie days or two pot-on days and the rest, maybe fried beef or such as that for dinner; you know, slices off the roast beef and, you know, fried up. They used to call that resurrection, really; it was old beef warmed up, but still, it made a change.

Given the limited raw materials and the lack of facilities for any form of fancy cooking, such repetition is not surprising, but it could go to absurd lengths: Mr Brambles said, 'One farmer's lad said he had meat and potato pie fourteen times a week. He even had it cold for Sunday morning breakfast.' It might also be due to more than just a lack of imagination as Mr Masterman pointed out:

> There was one farm – I think the foreman was a bit greedy, he wanted to save money quicker, and . . . when we first went it was apples: apples right away till spring, and then rhubarb started. It was rhubarb right away till apples come in again. I know the boss and his wife went up to t'village one night in their pony and trap, so another lad and me said, 'All right, come on!' We got a scythe apiece and went into garden, and we cut all their rhubarb down.
> *Daughter:* You still like it.
> Oh aye, but not like that – for breakfast, dinner and tea.
> *What did he do when he found all the rhubarb?*
> Why, he never – nobody said anything. They never questioned us. Why Frank Thompson . . . and me; he was the lad just above me. I was fifth lad, and he was fourth.

Hinds, unlike other farmworkers, had a genuine, if small, chance of saving up enough to take a farm of their own but even they rarely managed it before late middle age. It was always a temptation to speed up the process by appropriating some of the money they were given to feed the lads. By using as much home-grown food as possible and so buying as little as possible, especially meat, from shops, quite a tidy sum could be added to a year's savings.

There were other cases where the blame for inadequate food cannot be laid entirely at the foreman's door. The hind and the farmer agreed a price to be paid to cover the lads' keep, and while some men were good enough to stand out for a generous allowance, others sought to make up for their deficiencies by undercutting. When jobs were scarce between the wars competition for those that were available might be at the expense of the lads. A good farmer knew what a lad could be kept for and would not expect to pay less, but there were always others who would simply wash their hands of the problem and allow a hind to take on the job on impossible terms. Mr Brambles told me that in the depression his father, a foreman, became unemployed. They went to live in an outlying cottage on a farm and Mr Brambles senior advertised for a place. Plenty of farmers came to the farmhouse to ask after him, but none seemed to bother after that. The family began to wonder what was being said about them, but it turned out that the farmer was giving a glowing reference and it was this that acted against them, for the prospective employers did not want a man who would want to look after the lads too well.

When they skimped on a lad's food, or allowed their hind to skimp, farmers were just as guilty of breach of contract as the lad who ran away. A waggoner's wage, say of £25 to £30, was usually reckoned to be half in cash and half in his keep, so it can be seen how relatively important food was in the wages of a boy who would only receive £5 in cash in the same year. Unfortunately it was very hard, except in the severest cases, for a lad to prove beyond doubt that a farmer was neglecting his customary obligations. This kind of breach of contract was a singularly mean trick to play on any hired man as they were all short of cash. They could not afford to spend any of it in supplementing their diet, as Mr Jarvis once had to, on a farm where not only was the menu as repetitive as that described by Mr Johnson, but the food was poor as well:

When I got up there, there was, oh, ten or twelve lads besides me. . . . Oh, by God, didn't I get tired of it. . . . Every Monday it was cold meat, suet dumpling and [they bought] treacle – 'course we used to buy it at home for to give to t'cattle, you know, to mix with turnips and caff . . . , and we had it on our dumplings. . . . The butcher would come and the hind wife would buy some meat, and it was meat pie. But crust was about that thick and meat – by God, you very nearly had to have opera glasses on to find it. But plenty of potatoes, . . . turnip. And she used to put brussels sprouts in. . . .

And I says to one of the lads about my age, I says, 'Are we carrying on like this day after day? Day after day? Soup, then meat pie she calls it, then next day its something similar. . . . I's thinking about going back home, but,' I says, 'I left last year. . . , I don't like going back home again. Else my dad'll say I don't try to stick it.' So anyway, I stuck it, oh, all year . . . .

And it was odd house, miles from anywhere . . . , and I'll tell you what we used to do and its God's truth, we used to go to a place called Duggleby, four or five of us. It had a shop and we used to buy a box of kippers and we used to buy a loaf of bread, a big lump of cheese: it only cost about sixpence at that time o' day, . . . and we bought some tea – tea was fairly cheap. We didn't buy any meat. And we bought some sugar. We bought them – and we used to fry up on a night. You know, on a blacksmith's fire, blacksmith's shop fire. So we used to have to blow t'bellows, you know, to get fire going. Well then we had to buy a kettle, and we had to buy some tins o' milk (there weren't no bottled milk then), we'd buy some tins o' milk. And then one o' t'lads didn't live that far away, he says, 'I'll bring a spoon or two from home. I'll ask my mother . . .', and that's how we used to have our suppers like.

A hungry lad would not have the stamina or concentration of someone who was well fed, and they would do as little as possible for someone who was mistreating them. By the time any immediate gain has been offset by this loss in productivity; by the reduced calibre of lads willing to be hired once a reputation became known; and, in the foreman's case, by the prospect of the farmer finding fault with him because things were not going well, it is doubtful if running a bad meat house led to any clear profit. It is probably better attributed to the personalities concerned than to any rational assessment of the money involved. Indeed, one of the few things that is completely clear about bad meat houses is the element of perversity that runs through everything to do with the subject.

This is at its most apparent when the lads' attitude towards such farms is considered, for while they were offended, or even outraged, by individual bad meat houses, it is clear that in general the existence of such farms was much appreciated. Where they did not exist they were invented. Everyone I spoke to had heard of many bad places and most were keen to tell stories about the conditions on them, but only a handful had ever lived at even one, out of all the farms they had been on as servants, and the worst stories were always hearsay. This is not to say that really bad places did not exist. They were perhaps never in dire enough straits to be forced into going to a known one, but Harry Reffold had a very bad time when a Lincolnshire man took over as hind on a farm with a good reputation and his wife was unable to cope.[6] These farms were, however, very rare and stories about them spread so widely because the lads delighted in them, just as people delight in scaring themselves with horror stories.

After their horses, food commanded the major part of farm lads' attention, and it is not surprising that they created a group of legends around the subject. The stories were passed around to an extent that went far beyond any practical concern, and we can be sure that they grew in the telling. We certainly need not take seriously Mr Brambles' recollection of lads on one farm saying that the farmer sent them down to Hunmanby station with a waggon and four horses to fetch a waggon load of prunes: it was meant to be an obvious exaggeration of the fact that they were sick of getting prunes to eat. He also remembered another farm where the lads were so convinced that one day's leftovers came back in next day's dinner that 'they say one chap tied a bit of string round a bone and I don't know how many days it was in t'pie and t'stew. Oh, it went on for days and days did this bone.' That might be true, but it is so like a joke that we cannot be sure. The fact is that certain stories became institutionalized because of their aptness, and fact and fancy merge hopelessly.

Mr Baines' story of the little lad missing his dinner by falling over[7] is nothing but a joke, and I was not surprised that it was told to me by several people; but Mr Masterman's story of cutting down the rhubarb was a personal experience, and yet, with different names, it was widely known as well.[8] It is tempting, of course, to say that Mr Masterman had simply appropriated a story as his own experience, but all the evidence is against it. Rather, some situations arose regularly, and led with equal regularity to the same solutions, perhaps inspired by stories already heard. The experiences of a few made good telling, and they were appreciated and spread by others because they were highly appropriate. They added a bit of spice to a life where, in fact, the majority of lads were well fed and well satisfied.

Notes to Chapter Twelve

1. *Sixth Report of the Medical Officer of the Privy Council* (P.P. 1864, XXVIII), pp. 238, 255–6, and J. Burnett, 'Country Diet' in Mingay, ed., *The Victorian Countryside*, vol. II, pp. 558–61, considers Dr Smith's report and its implications. See also Thompson, *Lark Rise*, pp. 193–4.
2. See John Burnett, *Plenty and Want* (1978), particularly chaps 2 and 7, and also his 'Country Diet.' See also A. Armstrong, *Farmworkers: A Social and Economic History, 1770–1980* (1988), pp. 41–2.
3. See I. Megginson, 'To Be a Farmer's Boy in East Yorkshire', *The Dalesman*, (Oct. 1977), 525.
4. See also Reffold, *Pie for Breakfast*. The importance of food, and the role of pies in particular, is a constant theme through this farm lad's autobiography, besides providing its title.
5. R.M. Wilson, 'Agricultural Terms in the East Riding', *Transactions of the Yorkshire Dialect Society* pt. 38, vol. 6 (1937), 21.
6. See Reffold, *Pie for Breakfast*, p. 44.
7. Megginson, 'Farmer's Boy', 525, has a version of the same joke.
8. Revd M.C.F. Morris, *Yorkshire Folk Talk* (1892), p. 211.

Chapter Thirteen

In the Farmhouses

Keeping a group of lads satisfied that the farmer was performing his side of the hiring contract was no small task, and it was one which fell upon either the farmer's wife or the hind's wife. Preparing food was the part of the job the lads noticed most, but the house had also to be kept clean and tidy, the beds had to be made, and the sheets, which were provided by the farmer, had to be washed. The conditions in the farmhouse played a large part in determining the reputation a farm had, though the lads, being young and single, tended to treat hardship as something to be endured and ignored rather than alleviated, as long as the food was good. On small farms the farmer's wife could probably manage with very little assistance, but elsewhere the work was far beyond the capacity of one person to cope with it, however willing they were. Most wives of large farmers preferred to have a hind and his wife take it all on, and even where the farmers continued to meat the men themselves, their wives would see their role in different ways depending upon the size of the establishment. Some played a full part, while others, on the largest farms, restricted themselves to supervising the female farm servants who would do nearly all the work.

The numbers hired varied from farm to farm, and more were needed in farmhouses where farmers still meated the men themselves. Then there would often be a cook, a housemaid, and a kitchen maid. Young girls often started as nurse girls, minding babies and young children[1] and older ones were sometimes dairymaids as well, helping in the house and on the farm. When the hind had the care of the farm servants, his wife had to do as much as possible herself and any maids hired primarily to work for the farmer's family would be in their house, away from the lads. The girls were hired on exactly the same terms as the lads every Martinmas, except that it had become accepted that they could be given notice and sacked.[2] They were lodged separately, as Mr and Mrs Rispin confirmed:

> Mrs R: Up in the attic.
>   Mr R: Aye, oh aye. Aye. Its right. Right – three stories [up] they were, starving [freezing] to death.
>   Mrs R: You used to get washed in the attic on afternoon and get into your black dress and cap – white cap and apron. And when you went next morning to empty the bowl it was frozen. In summer time you couldn't bear to be in, hardly. You know, just the opposite. Mm, I slept in the attic a lot of years.

In terms of non-stop effort the inside servants were worked even harder than the

34 A waggon-load of corn in sacks on its way from Duggleby's farm, South Dalton, to Kiplingcotes station near Market Weighton in 1920. The threshed grain was taken off the farm in great processions of these stately vehicles. A four-horse team was needed for jobs like this since there would be three or four tons to pull. This was the largest team normally used and would have been very difficult to control when travelling at speed. Note the neat loading, done in the East Riding manner, that fits in as much as possible whilst keeping the load secure on the rough road surfaces of the day. A waggon sheet is neatly folded on top in case of bad weather.

The waggon was the basic means of transport for large loads in the rural East Riding and the waggoner's title derives from his association with it. The awe in which young lads held him came from his sole responsibility for the carrying of these heavy sacks.

35 A three-horse team and a pole waggon delivering corn in sacks at Burdale station on the Malton–Driffield line *c*. 1900. The railway was a vital part of the East Riding rural economy since local markets on the scale needed to absorb production did not exist, and waggons were only economical for short hauls. This waggon has had its sideboards removed as it is carrying sacks, and the wide shelves that overhung the wheels to increase carrying capacity can be clearly seen. Like the pole, the practice of the lad riding the nearside horse, using a saddle and stirrups, was unique to the county. With a three-horse team, as here, reins were used to control the front horse.

36 The railways did not just take produce away, they brought in many other things, including coal and cake to feed cattle, that necessitated regular trips to the station. Heavy loads like these were potentially very dangerous on the steep hills of the Wolds and from time to time people were killed when waggons went out of control. This waggon was from Manor Farm, Thixendale and it was photographed in the village during the late 1890s. It was made in Beverley by the Beverley Cart and Waggon Company, the successors of Crosskill's, the famous old East Riding farm implement maker. Note the driver's whip.

37 Sid Smith, the waggoner, returning from Skidby mill to Woodhouse Farm, Cottingham, after delivering 'sacked corn' to the mill for rolling or grinding for the horses. This would be a regular duty which he did not take as seriously as a trip to the station, so apart from a tie and cap which look like his best, he is wearing his ordinary clothes. (Taken in 1934.)

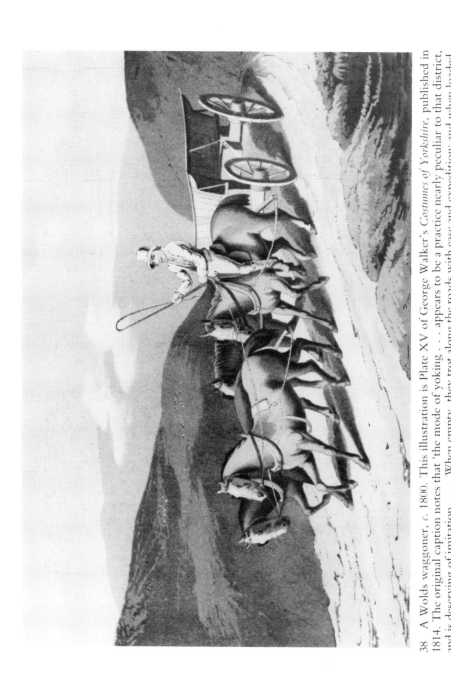

38 A Wolds waggoner, c. 1800. This illustration is Plate XV of George Walker's *Costumes of Yorkshire*, published in 1814. The original caption notes that 'the mode of yoking . . . appears to be a practice nearly peculiar to that district, and is deserving of imitation. . . . When empty, they trot along the roads with ease and expedition; and when loaded, the horses being near their work, and conveniently placed for drawing, labour with much greater ease and effect than when placed at length.' Despite differences of detail, the similarities to photographs from a century later are remarkable.

39 A newly finished waggon outside G.K. Levitt's wheelwright shop at North Newbald in 1904. This one was the property of R.A. Johnson of Rudstone Walk Farm, North Newbald. In most counties waggons had their own distinctive features, and it is worth noting the small front wheels which could lock under the body to give a tight turning circle, the use of varnish on the body rather than paint, and the panelled front. The feature most associated with the East Riding, however, is the draught pole which was used instead of the shafts preferred in every other county. A team of two, three or four horses could be used according to the load to be carried. The boards which raised up the sides and front were removable and only used when it was necessary to keep a load secure.

40 Water is very scarce on the Wolds and in dry times it was often necessary to cart it out to the stock. Mr Easterby is here shown with a water cart on his farm at Brandesburton around 1930. Note that rubber tyres have already replaced the traditional wooden wheels on this home-made vehicle.

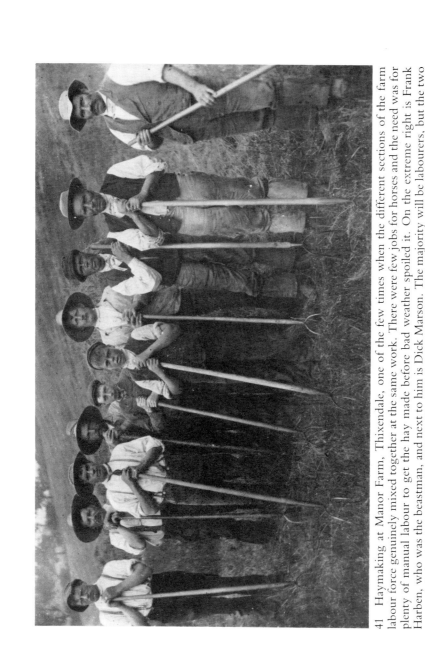

41 Haymaking at Manor Farm, Thixendale, one of the few times when the different sections of the farm labour force genuinely mixed together at the same work. There were few jobs for horses and the need was for plenty of manual labour to get the hay made before bad weather spoiled it. On the extreme right is Frank Harben, who was the beastman, and next to him is Dick Marson. The majority will be labourers, but the two young lads in the centre will certainly be hired lads as will some of the younger men. Where a lot of hay was made, extra hands were hired to live in just for the harvest. (Taken in the late 1890s.)

The mower left the grass in 'swathes' which were turned by hand with wooden rakes while it dried, and then pulled into larger swathes or 'windrows'. Next, it was gathered up into heaps or 'cocks', two of which can be seen behind the group, which protected it until it could be taken back to the farm and put under the cover of a barn or stacked and thatched. The wide-brimmed hats provided shade and kept off the midges. It is entirely typical that no-one has uncovered more than his forearms, for even at work as hot as this could be, undressing any further was regarded as unseemly.

42 As spring turned to summer the emphasis for the lads changed from cultivation to harvesting. Here a team is mowing grass by machine at Kilham in the 1930s. These machines were cheap, simple, and effective and were quickly taken up by farmers. This was not a common sight on the Wolds as, however, so little hay was made, but elsewhere haymaking was a major event in the yearly cycle of farming life. Note the extra bar on the front of the draught pole, hooked securely to the collars, in contrast to the usual loose hitching in a waggon.

43 Reaping corn with a Massey–Harris binder near Driffield, c. 1914. The blade is hidden in the standing corn, but the binding mechanism, which made and tied sheaves automatically, is visible. The sheaves lie scattered in the foreground waiting to be stood up by hand and placed in groups, or stooked, to keep them as dry as possible until they could be carted home. Many farmers were only just acquiring binders in 1914 even in advanced areas like the East Riding, and harvest fields commonly contained several types of reaper, some of which simply cut the corn, and some of which made a sheaf but did not tie it. Because the horses walked to one side of the blade, they would trample down one circuit of the field when they began, so it was usual to cut this circuit by hand with scythes in the traditional manner, thus giving a remarkable combination of harvesting methods.

44 Maintaining a binder in Kilham, *c.* 1930. The binder was the only complex machine commonly used with horses, most implements being very simple with few, if any, moving parts. The binder's levers, gears, and sheaf-tying mechanism required a level of mechanical aptitude never before seen, but that was to become the basis of farm work as tractors came into use. This equipment could also be dangerous, for if the team ran away and pitched the lad riding the horse onto the blade, he would, at the very least, be seriously injured.

45 Mr Pudsey, the Rudston carrier, and a helper loading corn onto a waggon, possibly on his smallholding during the 1920s. Note the way the load is made to overhang the waggon body to get the maximum amount on board. This could only be done safely by systematic and careful placement of the sheaves, so there was no question of simply flinging them on and piling them up.

46 Leading the corn home at High Esk Farm, near Tickton, Beverley in 1927. The finished load towers above the waggon, requiring great care lest it should 'whemmle over' on the way back to the farm. This method of loading sheaf corn was unique to the North and East Ridings. Only two horses were required for this job as the loads were relatively light and the fields were normally dry and firm, enabling the waggons to run easily. This was the only time of year when a lad relinquished care of his own horses, for the need to get the harvest in meant work continued for as long as there was light to see by, and even after, and the horses were used in shifts to keep them fresh. Only a few lads actually drove waggons, so most of them joined the labourers loading in the fields and unloading, or 'teeming', at the farm.

47   East Riding farms had few large barns, so mostly corn was stacked in the stackyard and then thatched, preserving traditional thatching skills despite the lack of thatched houses. This would form the bulk of the farmer's cash income once it was threshed, so no effort was spared to see that the long stacks and round pikes stayed dry whatever the weather. This was achieved by tapering the sides outwards as they rose until they were complete, and then the stacker made a roof shape, which ensured that rain dripped clear rather than ran down into the stack. The ears of the corn always went inside and were laid higher than the butt ends at the outside, so rain would not run in when driven against the walls. The foreman always stacked, and a good waggoner was expected to do so as well. They took great pride in making them look as good as possible, as a visible statement of their abilities. This photograph shows Mr Playforth's uncle in front of a particularly impressive group at Kilham around 1914.

Once the harvest was home, the farming cycle turned full circle and it was time to return to ploughing ready for the next planting.

horselads, though the lads had the heavier jobs to do. Before 1914 many farms would hire a young boy rather than a young girl to work in the house, and it was Mr Harper, who began his career in this way, who gave me the best description of the life they led:

I started work when I was thirteen years of age. . . . I was two year in house as a kitchen boy, do you see, wi' two sisters and a brother. And I used to have to get up at five o'clock at morning, get fire going – and it was an old-fashioned fireside in those days, you know. . . . And there was a reckan bracket 'bout length o' that fireplace [approximately four feet] with all different reckans – small ones, medium and long ones for to fasten brass pans on – or any sort of pans. Well, these brass pans, they were full of milk, one for t'table and the other was for t'calves. And, of course, if a collop of soot tumbled down t'chimney and dropped into one of these brass pans you had to take it off and put it into a bucket for t'calves to suck, and then go and refill it for breakfast – t'men's breakfast. There was ten men, hired in, besides me: I was the eleventh. . . . Milk on a morning, milk at night from Monday morning till Sunday night. . . .

My Monday morning's job was getting all – as soon as ever men got their breakfast I had copper to fill ready for washing, for t'oldest sister to wash. And t'second sister was more my mistress, she used to give me my details what I had to do. Well, I had to help 'em to wash – fetch water out o' t'beck (we had no piped water in them days . . .). 'Course, when they got all t'washing done, I'd wash-house to clean up, wash up, beds to make: both men's beds to make and my employers' bed to make. Every morning as soon as ever we got table sided.

Tuesday: Tuesday morning was baking day. I used to have to go and get two or three loads o' sticks from t'stick hill for my young mistress to bake with. When we got baked I'd all baking pots to wash up and a great big, long table, about six or seven foot long it was, to scrub every morning – every day, sometime, when I'd time to do it. And all pots – dinner pots, breakfast pots, and all t'pots to wash up.

Wednesdays was . . . same wi' t'tables and then I'd kitchen floor to wash. There was fifty-two stone flags i' that kitchen floor, big and little, and they were all to step-stone with this step-stone, all round every edge. And I did that for – that kitchen floor, three times a week [for two years].

And Thursday: Thursday was doing dairies – farm milk dairy and provision dairy. And when I got them done I used to have to go out, clean poultry houses out and we were at it from five o'clock of a morning till seven at night i' those days. . . .

And Friday . . . , I'd all front entrance to do. Their side [of the house] . . . And the fireplace, it was all to black lead. There was no fancy fire sides like there is today. . . . That was Fridays and I used to have to be upstairs, washing all t'bedroom floors out where they slept, and t'same wi' t'men's bedroom: I'd all that to wash out.

Saturday was my worst day o' t'lot because they wouldn't let me get on on a Saturday morning because they were getting fit for to go to Malton market. And I used to have to harness t'galloway up: yoke it up and get them off by one o'clock at Saturday afternoon. And I used to say, 'A merry wind to you!' And my kitchen floor was to do and all, for over Sunday, . . . and I just used to get finished wi' t'kitchen floor and entrance and t'poultry fed for ten minutes to five. I'd a few minutes relax. Then I'd to wait while all t'men come in and got their teas at six o'clock. Then I'd all to wash up again. And that was my routine for two years.

And if we had a party I used to have to wait at table.

So you'd be working even later?

Yes. I'd a bowl in this hand and towel in that for people to dip their fingers in and wipe their hands. And I'd to stand there just like a statue. And my dress when we had parties, was a velvet jacket wi' three silver buttons down there [on the sleeves] and white cuffs, and a white shirt, with a choker (you can call 'em chokers; if you like, them stiff collars) and a pair o' knickerbockers – there was no trousers in them days in gentleman's service – pair of knickerbockers, they were black velvet. Two tassels at either side. And there were pearl buttons down and they fastened at your knee. Black stockings and bright leather shoes with a silver buckle at toe's end. That was my dress when I had to wait on t'table. . . .

Were there many places kept lads in service?

In my young day, round about that way [Scagglethorpe, near Malton], there was more lads in house than what there was maids. 'Cause they could trust you better. For doing things. But when war broke out it knocked it all on the head.

Whether or not the preference for boys actually rested on their greater trustworthiness, we saw earlier that there was certainly a shortage of girls willing to enter farm service. Everything was still accomplished by sheer hard labour and plenty of it, which may help to account for girls' reluctance to work in farm-houses. There were no mechanical aids and the East Riding remained a county where any food that could be made at home, was. Bread was still made on every farm, as Mrs Rispin recalled, 'We used to make eight loaves three times a week. Mondays, Wednesdays, and Fridays.' Bakeries were virtually unknown outside Hull, York, and the resorts in the early years of the century. The market towns had very little use for them, and the villages none at all.[3] There were also all the pies to bake and Mr Tate recalled one farm with thirty men to feed at harvest, including the labourers and the Irishmen, where sixty pies barely lasted through the weekend. Pigs were killed on the farms, and the meat was cured and blood puddings, brawn, etc., were all made on the premises. The dairy supplied the farm as well as the market, and milk, butter, cheese, and curds were all made. All in all, the preparation of food rarely ceased for long, though sometimes it had to be given a lower priority than the cleaning and washing, and this was one reason for having broth days.

Mr Rispin recalled that on one farm his wife cooked for 'sixteen at harvest and two lads, school lads. . . . Aye, had 'em all in. . . . There used to be two tables.

We always had four Irishmen for harvest . . . , there would be twelve on us at one table and t'old Irishmen at another, like. Both had same food, like.' Harvest was by far the worst time in the kitchen because everyone who took part was fed on the farm, not just the horselads. They all required luances of sandwiches and beer or tea twice a day besides their meals, and if much grass was grown, the same pattern was followed at hay-time. Luance jobs added to the workload at other times, and, said Mrs Rispin,

> When they were lambing, you see, [the shepherds] always used to come in for their food . . . and they used to sit up in . . . t'saddle room . . . , and they had a fireplace in and all that. And then we used to – oh, half past nine to ten, take 'em their suppers. Maybe three or four eggs apiece, all such as that. . . . They always came in for a month. You were always at it.[4]

Some of the food had to be bought in, of course. If the hind had taken over meating the men he had to be allowed to deal with the suppliers, usually buying in bulk, Probably the biggest single outlay was on meat, as Mrs Rispin pointed out, saying, 'We used to get two stone at a time . . . , and that's apart from pie meat, like.' Most transactions were conducted on credit, Mr Masterman said:

> Well, my mother used to contract with a grocer – and the butcher. The butcher supplied her each week with so much meat at a certain price. If the beef price went up the butcher lost. If it went down, you lost. And the same with groceries. So much flour, so much sugar, whatever she wanted. Then at six months' end the farmer used to tell the groom to get the trap out and he used to take her to the village, take my mother, and she used to pay her bills. Because she only used to get her wages every six months.

The hind also needed access to some of the farm produce, and Mr Johnson described the system thus:

> [The hind] had a cow, for his own use, you see, and . . . [for] milk for the lads . . . , for their tea and such as that, and then the rest you make butter of. Its his cow, you see, but you have the use of it. You milk it yourself, you see. . . . And then the farmer generally found him potatoes – he'd maybe buy a ton at a time and he'd come up to t'hind and say, 'Well, here's a ton o' taties for you.' And then when they were done, like, the hind would say, 'Well, I'm out o' potatoes,' and he'd buy him some more. So, you know, there was quite a few things apart from money.

The payments in cash and kind that the hind received to cover the lads' keep were entirely separate from his wages. Mr Masterman said that, before 1914: 'If you'd four men you got maybe twenty-six bob or thirty bob, whatever. They weren't all alike. If a man stuck out and he was a good man they'd give him seven and six a week to keep his lads, but some men would go for six shillings.' During the war this rose to fourteen to eighteen shillings,[5] but by the 1930s it was down to twelve shillings per lad from a good farmer, or ten shillings from one not so particular. There was also the matter of the actual accommodation to be provided. Mr Milner had a career of average length, during which he never strayed far from home, and he never lived on a farm where the farmer was an absentee, yet every farm had its own idiosyncracies:

> It was mostly hinds where I meated, excepting Bella: that was my first year off. . . . The hind house was generally somewhere again t'master house, you know. We were two paddocks off at Wharram Percy. Foreman used to have to walk across every night. . . . Cowlam was [attached]. At Heslerton Wold we fed in gaffer's house. They lived front way and we lived back.

On larger farms a separate wing might well have been added to house the lads and keep them separate from the family of the farmer or the hind.

At Manor Farm, Foggathorpe (now demolished) the men's end was clearly distinguishable as a mid-nineteenth century addition to the rear of a farmhouse built in 1743. They would have eaten in the back-kitchen, from which room a back staircase led to the two bedrooms above. The arrangement at Bar Farm, Holme-on-Spalding-Moor, is very similar, with the added back-kitchen containing its own staircase leading to the one bedroom above. In all cases the back kitchen opened onto the yard.

On smaller farms the men's end was less intrusive (often it was not an end at all) but it was just as separate:

Village Farm, Thornton had only one man in the early twentieth century, a general farm labourer who used the back door into the kitchen (which was added to one end of a three bay single range house in the nineteenth century), ate in the kitchen while the family ate in the dining room, and slept in the room above, reached by a fixed ladder. At Bangram Hill Farm, Riccall, one or two men slept in the room above the kitchen, with access by a back stair, and this bedroom was separated from the rest of the upper floor. There are similar houses in Wheldrake where the end room which the men used is not always a later addition. At one the former men's end, consisting of an end room with ladder stair to the room above, had been quite separate on the ground floor from the rest of the house until recently, and had been entered by a door in the gable end.[6]

There was never any attempt to move servants out into bothies as in parts of Scotland,[7] though at Cowlam the lads slept in a room above the stables, which was reached by an outside stair, and they had another room set aside for their use in the evenings. At Duggleby there was a similar arrangement except that they slept over the recreation room. Both farms were very large – indeed, Cowlam, at 1,200 acres, was one of the very largest in the county – and in both cases the lads still ate in the farmhouse.

Wherever it was located, the lads' bedroom usually housed them all together in dormitory-like conditions:

> The servants usually had . . . a ladder leading from the kitchen up which they swarmed in their stocking feet to low and badly ventilated 'chaimers' (as they called them) in the attics. These attics had a pungent smell both of apples and rats. Sometimes, when the mistress was given to being a little 'grand', the hams and chines and sides of bacon were kept up aloft too, so that such 'pictures' did not offend her eyes.[8]

Mr Baines recalled, 'At Barlby Hall there used to be ten of us, all in one bedroom, aye, it were a huge bedroom, like a hall, and they all used to sleep two together.' A single foreman might have a small bedroom to himself since he was of a much higher status than anyone else, but otherwise there was no differentiation. Mr Milner said:

> Why, my first year off I was by myself [on the farm]. I can't ever remember sleeping single at any [other] time: always had double beds.
>   *Not even the waggoner?*
>   No, no. He slept with thirdy.

If there was an odd number of lads the waggoner would claim the single bed, but the only time ordinary lads had any privacy was if the layout of the house prevented them all being put in one room. A farm at which Mr Rispin was hind had two bedrooms for four lads each and a smaller one for two grooms. They were very sparsely furnished as they were only intended for sleeping in. Mr Rispin said:

> Well, I was hired twelve year afore I got married and I never was in a bedroom . . . what was papered. It was clean, mind you, but all whitewashed. And your bedsides – there was no fancy carpets, you just had an old, plain corn sack . . . you used to put down to get your feet on. Mind, it were clean, I aren't saying [it was dirty]. And we all had a box piece . . . , a wooden box.

These boxes were the lads' chest of drawers and suitcase, bedside table, and chair, all in one. Mr Johnson's, which he was still using in the 1970s, was roughly four feet long by one foot six inches wide and two feet deep. Inside were two little drawers attached to one side near the top, thought not all boxes had drawers. They came complete with a lock and key but, said Mr Masterman, in most cases the key quickly vanished and the lock had to be broken. They were solidly made by local joiners, though in later years cheaper, mass–produced tin boxes were sold at lower prices and reduced the market for the traditional design.[9] The wooden boxes were practically indestructible and might well pass down from one member of a family to another. Mr Johnson's remained a clothes box up to his death, while others have become tool boxes, chests, or blanket boxes, and many come up for sale in antique shops. In most bedrooms they were the only furniture apart from the beds, though some had an old table or a few chairs.

As Mr Rispin recalled, in conversation with Mr Playforth, farm servants were not pampered.

Mr R: Maybe people won't believe it but all the years I was there [at one particular farm] I never seed a lamp lit in house – a candle sat on a basin. Aye. To get your meals with. And, like, if you wanted to sit in house there was never a lamp lit i' that kitchen when I was there. No.
   Mr P: And you used to have a stable lamp [an oil lamp enclosed in glass], didn't you [elsewhere]? . . . You used to take them to bed with you.
   Mr R: Aye, waggoner . . . , like, I was waggoner, used take this lamp up.

Inside toilets and bathrooms were, of course, unknown, but the lads were not even supposed to share the use of the outdoor privy on many farms. They were expected to manage in the corner of the foldyard where the privy buckets were emptied.[10] As for washing, Mr Rispin commented, 'I was off twelve year . . . and I never was in a bath. Well, there were none. . . . We kept ourselves clean but, you know, I never was in a bath.' Unless he was near enough to home to use the family tin bath, which was rare, a lad just had a table-top bath. They filled a bowl, stripped off and washed, bit by bit, all over. Hot water was a luxury that was either not available at all or only in very limited quantities. Mr Brambles said:

See, there wasn't running water or anything else like that. You couldn't turn tap on. Used to have . . . old fashioned fireside with a boiler at side . . . , tin tank, hold half a gallon, perhaps: give you that and if there were five or six of you, that's it, that had to do.

If this was not available, water came straight from the pump or water butt, as Mr Baines remembered, 'You used to go on a morning, frosty morning, you know, and t'lad, little lad of all, used to have to go break ice on t'tub; first thing he did was to get water and there was ice floating in it.' Even here the hierarchy was strictly observed, as Mr Rispin and Mr Playforth pointed out:

Mr R: Aye, when I was a waggoner . . . , t'maid would have a tin set, boil a great big tin o' water – I was first to go in and get washed – why, there'd maybe be six wash after me in t'same lot o' water, and it was little lad, maybe left school only a fortnight afore [who came last].
   Mr P: You always had the same towel and by the time it got round to the least lad it was wet through, you know, and they used to pull their shirt out and dry themselves on their shirt and put it back.

During the week even those who needed to shave did not normally bother, preferring to wait until the weekend when they went off the farm. Hair was cut very short, with a fringe, as a rule. Many, probably most, villages had a part-time barber and there were plenty of willing amateurs, including Mr Rispin:

Mr R: I had a pair of old [scissors]. I bought . . . one of these machines, you know, like they have them now. But you went right over t'lot, like. Aye. Oh, you didn't know fancy cuts, like, and . . . oh, I've cutten scores of lads.

Mr P: Poor old George Hall, when he come to – he used to get a 'harvest' cut, they used to cut his topping an' all off! . . . 'I don't want it in my bloody eyes in harvest!'

Mr R: It's true. . . . I used to go right across, oh, I've cut hundreds in my time. . . . Aye, I'll tell you what a lot had it cut with, and I've cutten other lads myself . . . , when you were clipping horses in winter, cart horses (they used to, what you call half clip 'em . . .). One [lad] turning wheel and t'foreman maybe clipping horses: 'Well, which of you wants haircut?' he used to say. Aye, aye.

As for their laundry, there were no facilities on the farm and lads had little time to spare to do it themselves. Strickland said that in the eighteenth century the farm maids had done the washing for nothing,[11] but in living memory, said Mr Milner, 'Always took our washing home. Or otherwise, some woman, living handy would maybe do it for you. What was it they used to charge us? – weren't much, tanner a week, maybe. It all depends on what you had to wash.' On the Wolds, getting washing to a village could entail walking several miles, and even living 'near home' did not always mean being neighbours, as Mr Brambles told me:

Used to set off at Sunday morning to walk – take their washing, bring the clean washing back. I've heard my father say all he could do was walk into the house, pick the bundle up and walk out, just say 'Hello' – that's all they had time for because they had to get back.

Life was certainly not luxurious for farm lads, but it must have compared well with life in the slums of the industrial cities. By their own standards they were being treated fairly, and by most contemporary working-class standards they were not suffering any particular hardship. As Mr Rispin has already made clear, their quarters were neither dirty nor squalid. Few farms offended in this respect and the fact that some of the descriptions leave the impression of a very primitive way of life can be ascribed to the times. This period up to the First World War and, even more so the inter-war years, saw a gulf created between life in the countryside and that in the towns which had probably never existed on such a scale before or since. Greater wealth and better facilities have always led to differences in lifestyle, but this was now compounded by technological factors such as the availability of gas and electricity, the supply of piped water, and the creation of a modern urban infrastructure. A reasonably well-off family in the London of the 1920s had available to it many of the elements associated with late twentieth-century lifestyle, such as electrical appliances and telephones. Farms remained firmly in a previous era and not just in the East Riding, whether those who lived there wanted changes or not. There were doubtless exceptions, but for an ordinary farm dweller of the 1920s, living within the technical and cultural constraints of an undisturbed community, a move into wealthy London society would have seemed like time travel, not just a move up the scale of privilege.[12] Since then, with the spread of rural electrification, water and sanitation schemes, the development of self-contained energy systems such as those running on oil or liquified gas, and the increasing use of motor vehicles and television, the gulf has lessened.

It would have been possible to fill this chapter with stories such as Mr Tate's, remembering Cowlam: 'They used to have to sleep in their stockings, you know, else rats pinched them. . . . They'd to sleep [above] t'stables: horses down there and bedded 'em up there, like. Go upstairs, in their boots, like, and rats used to gnaw all their laces out, they said. Aye.' Such experiences made good stories in later years and have become all the more effective for the general improvement in living conditions that now leaves them even more likely to horrify an audience. They are, however, not typical, and the bulk of the material that makes up the chapter was clearly not contributed with any intention to show how outrageous conditions were by modern standards. Lads were not treated as members of the family, and their quarters were more spartan than their own homes, but that was what they expected. Even in the 1940s and 50s the few lads who remained expected only small improvements, such as the chance to hear the employer's radio playing in another room.[13] As long as they were well fed they were quite prepared to tolerate the conditions. The lads had left their families, and it was the self-contained group they now formed for themselves in the farmhouses to which they looked for support, standards, and approval. However, this group could only function because of the work of the household staff.

Notes to Chapter Thirteen

1. Morris, *British Workman*, p. 57, and on p. 56 he states that hired cooks were unknown in East Riding farmhouses before the nineteenth century.
2. D.N. Pritt, *Law, Class and Society*, I, *Employers, Workers and Trade Unions* (1970), pp. 36–42.
3. Trade directories clearly indicate a lack of bakeries in the early twentieth century. *Kelly's* shows 14 in Bridlington, 6 in Driffield, 5 in Beverley, 3 in Malton/Norton, 2 in Hornsea, Howden, Market Weighton, Pocklington, and Filey, and 1 in Withernsea, Newport (the county's only industrial settlement) and Patrington in 1909. In total they occupy 2 columns for the North and East Ridings combined, including towns and cities, where butchers occupy 12. *Census*, 1911, vol. 10, pt. 2, p. 640 returned only 157 people in the county as engaged in the occupational orders 'bread, biscuit, cake, etc., makers', and 'bakers and confectioners (dealers)'.
4. See also H.L. Day, *My Life with Horses* (Beverley, 1983), pp. 20–4.
5. *Wages and Conditions*, p. 384.
6. V. Neave, 'Living-in in the East Riding', *Vernacular Architecture*, 2 (1971), 18.
7. See Carter, 'Oral History'.
8. Fairfax-Blakeborough, *East Riding*, p. 196.
9. E. Pontefract and M. Hartley, *Yorkshire Tour* (1939), pp. 66–7.
10. Megginson, 'Farmer's Boy', 526.
11. Strickland, *General View*, p. 266. Rev M.C.F. Morris, *Yorkshire Reminiscences* (1922), pp. 310–11, says that this system prevailed in the 'olden times' with no hint of chronology.

12. M. Penn, *The Foolish Virgin* (1952), is an autobiographical account of a young girl moving from a poor foster home in a rural village close to Manchester, to relatives in London who were affluent and abreast of the times. Chap. 1, especially, shows the shock of the difference in lifestyles.

13 I. Megginson, *Mud on my Doorstep: Reminiscences of a Yorkshire Farmwife* (Beverley, 1987), p. 87.

Chapter Fourteen

Leisure

Nowadays it is taken for granted in Britain that, quite apart from holidays, people have several hours of each working day for themselves and that work is usually kept within set and regular hours. Farm servants' contracts allowed no such limitations: a servant was always available for work, in theory at least. Sundays were recognised as days off, but otherwise leisure time only existed when there was no work to be done and this varied with the seasons, virtually disappearing at peak times. The law specifically recognized that a servant's year was not a steady round, which was why the year's wage was paid in one lump sum rather than in equal weekly payments. Before 1914, for most of the year a farm lad had very little free time at all, even by contemporary standards. Labourers on the same farms, for instance, worked about three hours a day less. On the other hand, since a lad had no garden to dig, no house to maintain, no family to see to – in fact he had very little private life at all – he was not seen as being in need of shorter working hours.

There were then six full working days in every week and the lads did not return from the fields until six o'clock in the evening, unless the light failed earlier and made work impossible. After seeing to their horses and having their supper they were then free for the evening in summer, when the horses slept outside, as Mr Masterman confirmed, 'Soon as we'd had our tea we turned horses into t'field. Well, we'd finished with them then. We could go into t'village then.' However, 'Eight o'clock they'd got to go back again in winter-time to feed their horses and be off to bed just turned nine, you see,' Mr Pridmore commented. When the horses slept in the stables, they had to be given a last feed, their beds were shaken up and a check was made to see that everything was in order, a process known as fothering up which took up most of the evening. Mary Simpson's night school for farm servants was very popular in summer, but in winter, the Revd F. Digby Legard wrote, the 'masters don't like to trust them into the village from their farms, which are perhaps a mile or so distant, for fear they should not come back in time for the eight o'clock suppering up which is a perfectly immovable feast apparently, one which never can be infringed upon or altered by half-an-hour on either side.'[1]

Even in summer there was often a curfew, commmonly at nine o'clock before the First World War. Mr Carter started work later when hours were shorter, but even then:

> We had to be in on a night at ten o'clock – had to be into bed at ten o'clock at night or else key was turned. You were locked out. And if you were, . . .

you had to sleep in t'saddleroom. If they wouldn't let you in, that's where you had to sleep. . . . And then, when it got to six o'clock in t'morning, when the others were getting up, used to slip away upstairs and change your clothes.

But some – when I got to Manor Farm, well it never was locked. You could go in any hour you liked – it didn't matter. Just as long as you were up on a morning. But the foreman seen you were up on a morning: he didn't let you lay in bed. When it came to time he would come knocking at door to waken you up, you see.

Sometimes the other lads could let a latecomer in, one way or another, or a lad might be near enough to home to go and sleep there, but otherwise he usually slept in an outhouse. A few hinds imposed the curfew for the lads' good, but mostly it was simply that they had to be about as early as the lads, so they were not inclined to wait up for stragglers. If there was an outside stair, or if an inside stair could be isolated by locking an inner door, leaving the house secure, it was often left open all night.

Despite this total claim to a lad's time from Monday to Saturday, Sunday was a different matter. Mr Johnson said:

You had Sundays off – now that was a funny thing. When I was hired lad, and when I was a farm foreman, and farm labourer . . . , you never did a job on Sunday besides looking after stock – that has to be done, but you never – harvest or any time: if a farmer had come, or a foreman had come, and said, 'Well, I want you to work today,' well, you'd ha' thought, you know, he'd gone barmy or something. Never thought of: they never asked you. And that was when you had work to do with your bare hands, but now, we've got all these tractors, labour-saving implements, and they have to work on a Sunday.[2]

The farmers agreed that they had no right to ask. In the 1860s, when more was demanded of lads, a movement was started to revive Anglican congregations by having farmers send all their servants to church and it met a solid refusal to co-operate. Mary Simpson wrote:

If you expostulate with the farmer, saying, 'You have nothing for the boy to do this Sunday, why do you not send him to the Sunday school and to church?' You will almost invariably receive the same answer – 'They're at work all the week, we can't tie 'em on Sundays.' That is to say, the boy must not be tied for an hour or two on Sunday when it is for his own good. . . . 'We can't force 'em' – 'It don't do to tie 'em' – is thought by too many an admissable plea on the part of the misnamed 'master'.[3]

Lads could stay in bed later and meals were often re-arranged to let them use the day to the full. However, seeing to the horses still restricted them. Mr Tate recalled:

[We] used to get up at seven, Sunday morning. . . . knocked us up at seven. Feed [the horses], well, we didn't hurry like – we [had our] breakfast . . .

159

twenty to eight, but we didn't bother, like. By God, next Sunday morning it
was a bit after six! Had to have 'em done by twenty to eight. . . . And
then . . . you had to be there at eleven – feed 'em while twelve. If you went at
half-past three [for the afternoon feed] you had tea at half-past four, if you
went at four it would happen at five. Used to watch you go, you know. And I
went to Haisthorpe one Sunday and Charlie Prew was thirdy, he fed my
horses at dinner time and I didn't go in while four at night. I said, quarter past
four, 'We'll soon be off for us teas.' We went for our teas and when we came
out they both met us, did master and son. Said, 'Is tha doing thy duty? . . .
thou only went in at four and thou comes for thy tea at half past!'

Mr Masterman was luckier in that in south Holderness the practice, he said, was
that, 'We used to feed our horses and then go into breakfast, but we never used to
feed 'em at dinner time. We used to give 'em hay and used to leave 'em while tea
time.' This was unusual, most lads who wanted a whole day off had to arrange for
someone else to see to the horses, and return the favour another time. As long as this
only happened occasionally, such arrangements were not hard to make and a lad
who visited another farm, as most did, could get his own meals there, as Mr Carter
remembered:

Waggoner would go up to t'foreman and say, 'We've got so-and-so come for
t'day, can he come up for his dinner and tea?'
'Yes, bring him in.'
So they used to bring 'em in for their dinners and teas, then they set 'em off
– have a walk with 'em, wherever they'd come from, and give them a walk
back, half way with 'em.

Perhaps surprisingly, lads did not try to get away from their work in such free
time as they had. While they appreciated the respite from physical labour, they felt
no desire, on the whole, to create a dichotomy between their jobs and the rest of the
lives; Mr Pridmore, for instance, described to me the way they passed their time
when they went into the villages:

These farm lads used to sit on t'wall and they used to talk about what they'd
done during t'day, you know, all been ploughing and drilling or whatever;
used to talk about one another, you know. They were all a jolly sort of lot o'
lads. They all entertained one another in the village, . . . all congregated
together.

In other words, they talked about work. Similarly, lads were in no way ashamed
of their working clothes. Nowadays, most manual workers dress in old clothes
unless they need protective garments or a firm supplies a uniform. The essence of
work clothes now is that they do not matter. In direct contrast, a farm lad's best
clothes, in so far as they had any, were good versions of their working outfit. In part
this sprang from necessity, but this is not the whole story. Before the First World

War the farm lads' dress was highly distinctive and for occasions like hirings could be made to look very smart.

Shirts, socks, and such were usually made at home but outer clothing came from tailors. Most jackets and all trousers were made of corduroy, though some jackets were made of fustian, and a few were of box-cloth, a very expensive felted woollen cloth that was virtually waterproof. On warmer days, the lads appeared in their waistcoats, which were usually double-breasted and sleeved, or in shirt sleeves, though for reasons of decency they never went beyond that, no matter how hot the day.[4] Trousers were bell-bottoms, slit at the bottom, a good pair having pearly buttons above the slit. When they were working the lads used to *tie their caulves up*, or make some slack around the knee by tying a strap below it with the legs hitched up, to stop the tight-fitting pants splitting at the knee during the strain of work. Irishmen used straw bands but the East Riding lads bought special leather straps with buckles attached, known as joskins, hence the town-dwellers' name for farm servants of 'farmers' joskins'. In winter some lads used leggings, either of leather or, occasionally, box-cloth.

Even more revealing was the universally favourite Sunday occupation, described by Mr Masterman:

> We used to go from one farm to another, might be thirty or forty of us all gathered together at one farm, because there was a lot of farms and each farm had five or six single lads; and we used to go to look at their horses, to see who had the fattest; and in harvest time we used to go and see who had the best stacks, you know, and there used to be some stacks – why, people now, if they saw 'em they wouldn't believe. They did look pretty, the stackyards. Sometimes the farmer would come out and he would bring a bucket of beer – they'd great big buckets, you know, all scoured clean, bright: fill that wi' beer, bring half a dozen mugs and basketful of beef sandwiches – stick 'em in the middle of the yard. 'Here you are, lads!' That's how we got our dinners. We could go back to the farm we lived at for our dinner if we'd liked, but farmers used to bring you beer, 'cause it was a shilling a gallon to buy it in a barrel. I never drunk it. They used to buy maybe four or five barrels at once. You know – bob a gallon, why, they used to bring us four or five gallons out – that was nothing to them. But they didn't do that after the war. Got too dear. They used to give you tea, coffee. . . . And a beef sandwich, it was – there was beef in it. There was [a] . . . slab o' beef. Because beef then was cheapest food.

That was in an area of large farms and one where, as stated before, the horses needed no attention at dinner time on Sunday. Where these conditions did not prevail, it was more common for one or two lads to visit a friend on their own, as Mr Brambles said:

> You'd maybe see somebody during the week, 'Have a look over ours on Sunday, just have a look at my hosses, lad, by God, they are fat! They do look well. Just take a walk over, lad.' That was it, . . . away you went and have a

look at so-and-so's horses and see if they were fatter than yours, and if their skins shone more. 'What does tha think to that, lad, now isn't that a beauty?' And then you used to invite them back next week to look at yours.

Mr Baines pointed out: 'Of course people used to talk and they'd say, "By, he can use a pair of horses, yon chap!" you know, and that got back to t'boss and of course everybody was after you then, trying to get you to go for t'waggoner.' Visiting could therefore help a lad's career as well as pass the time. The lads' constant, and usually friendly, rivalry was natural since they all shared a common occupation and, indeed, lived in a world dominated from one horizon to the other by farming. They were fairly isolated even from village gossip, and the younger lads especially were at an age when attention fastens most strongly, even obsessionally, onto hobbies, sports, or some such aspect of life. Emotionally immature, their affections were easily engaged by the horses in their care and the lack of anything else to compete for their interest is evident in the aimless way free time was spent when there was no visiting to be done. There was little chance to ease up and for boredom to set in, but their activities had a definite air of time filling:

I don't really know what we did. We maybe . . . got a heap of straw in t'stables and lay down and have a sleep or something. Anything there was to do. Maybe spend a bit o' time in t'bedrooms, doing odd jobs. Bit o' mending or a bit o' tidying up.

After walking miles at the plough tail over a rough, sticky surface that turned their boots into huge lumps of clay, a lad might well have little energy left, and they were not averse to quiet evenings at such times, telling stories and chatting. A one or two mile walk to the village for the sake of an hour's company, with a walk back afterwards, was not an enticing prospect. Certainly there was very little opportunity to play team games like football or cricket, even on an informal basis, and as to joining teams, Mr Johnson said, 'Wasn't time to play games, you know. We used to play football sometimes, but I could never play – I could kick a ball about but we had to do it in summer-time, no Saturday afternoons, you know.' Mary Simpson wrote to a friend in 1862:

Cricket has just been started at Carnaby, which thins my numbers at the night school. I tell them that if they were tailors and shoemakers I should think cricket very good for them, but as they are at work in the open air all day, I think that to sit still and read and write after their work must be better both for body and mind. Some of the younger ones really over-tire themselves with cricket.[5]

She added a footnote to the letter saying, 'The farm lads came to the same conclusion and most of them gave up cricket.' She had no power to force them to stop, despite her vested interest in keeping her school going in the face of new competition, and it must have been their own decision. That it was a reluctant decision emphasises how large a part circumstance played in keeping the farm lads' way of life from changing towards that of their urban counterparts. The lack of any recreational facilities on the farms reinforces this for the lads' bedrooms were only for sleeping in, and if they wanted to sit down for the evening with a lamp or a fire they had to do it elsewhere. Larger farms frequently provided them with a room, as Mr Masterman said:

> On most of the farms, well, all the farms I was on, they had a place in the building with a fireplace in so you could make a fire, to sit in. They called it t'kip. We used to go into cow-house and pinch milk and boil it, pinch eggs and boil them. If ever farmer's wife found out there was a row.

Round Wharram such rooms had a different name and were less common, as Mr Milner told me:

> A slum was where we sat. 'Twas where we sat at night.
> *Was it attached to the stables?*
> It was at Duggleby. 'Twas in between t'stables and house. And we slept above it. 'Twas like a cottage. We had seats in and we used to get a good fire on. . . . They were the biggest farms as had 'em. At Heslerton Wold, you see, there was no slum there. You had to sit in house-kitchen, where we had our meals.

Such an arrangement kept the lads at arms length from the household. The kitchen had been the place where all evenings were spent, but by the early years of this century very few farmers were still willing to have the lads in the house, and some foremen were following their example. As long as their room had a fire the lads may well have preferred the new situation, however, for it left them entirely unsupervised.

They often spent evenings in the stable for the horses kept it warm. Many an old corn bin will be found to have a fox and geese or merrils board scratched on its lid, a relic of such times.[6] As Mr Milner said, there were plenty of nights when they would 'just sit o'er fire, dark nights. Maybe read, maybe play cards.' They would tell stories, and if a tramp was staying at the farm he might entertain them with news or tales they had not heard before. Mr Appleyard simply enjoyed being near the horses as they settled down for the night. At first, he said, he was surrounded by the noise of their eating and then suddenly, for no apparent reason, there would come a dramatic pause as they all stopped and then started again, in unison. As they grew drowsy they lay down one by one and finally went to sleep. If they felt more lively the stables made a good venue for horseplay:

> After our tea we used to go back into the stable and stay until nine o'clock. They didn't like you to leave stables before nine. . . . They didn't like you to sit in house again t'fire. No, we used to spend our time in the stable – wrestling and boxing, and we used to put two ropes up to the ceiling, and a fork shaft across it, and we were away, trapezing, you know; put a heap of straw underneath so if we fell we didn't hurt ourselves – wrestling and boxing.

We always had boxing gloves. All stables had two pair o' boxing gloves where I was.

Mr Masterman exaggerated about the boxing gloves, but we have already seen that many lads were fond of a fight, whether in fun or in earnest. They were also very keen on music and singing and one lad might entertain the others by singing for them or they might combine with something they all knew. When Mrs Rispin was hired as a servant girl in a farmhouse the maids in the house used to open the windows so they could hear the singing. It was a very rare farm where not one lad had a melodeon or a mouth-organ. Mr Friend played both, getting the tunes from a gramophone, and Mrs Lawler remembered:

> Mrs L: We had about a hundred records. Could beat some o' t'tunes they play now. Like *Tip-Toe Through the Tulips*, and *Bells of St. Mary's*, and a few more like. . . . Oh, I used to like *The Laughing Policeman*.

The village offered much the same range of activities as the farm, but on a larger scale and in different company. Mr Pridmore has already described how they often did no more than sit on a wall and talk of farming, but it was enough of a change to talk to people from another farm, who might see things a different way. The games were also much the same, Mr Brambles said his companions frequently boxed in either a joiner's shop or a stable. In summer, as long as the weather was fine, there was no difficulty in spending the evening outdoors. Moreover, with no fothering up to return for, a lad could spend the occasional night at home, if he lived near enough to get back the next morning in time for work. For a lucky few, the longer evenings also allowed them to go further afield. Carnaby lads in the 1860s, for instance, used to visit Bridlington, a distance of about two miles.[7]

Most villages had a pub, of course, but less use was made of it than might be expected. The majority of farm lads would not be prevented by law from drinking as they would today, for at the turn of the century it was legal for beer to be sold to anyone over thirteen years old, and spirits to anyone over sixteen.[8] Mr Johnson recalled, however: 'I don't know if there was any laws, but they wouldn't have anybody in a pub, I think, under sixteen. . . . They could bring a drink to you outside, might ha' done, but you weren't allowed to go in, really.' In any case, even among the older lads, many only drank occasionally or not at all. Some were teetotal from conviction, some disliked the taste, and some, the vast majority – 'They hadn't money to go into t'pubs with in them days, although beer was only 2d and 3d a pint,' said Mr Pridmore.

This is not to say that no farm servant visited pubs for a pint or two on a regular basis if one was close by, or that no waggoners called in at a pub when they went off the farm on a job, but the cost of regular heavy drinking is amply shown by the cases of those who subbed all year round for this purpose. Even on a waggoner's wage, they could end up with so little to draw at Martinmas that, when they had paid all their bills with shops, they owed the farmer money. Some men went from year to year in this fashion, tied to one farm by debt, but most had more sense. Saturday night was obviously the best time to spend any cash they had, for Sunday gave a whole day for recovering from any excesses. To those at particularly isolated places this could be crucial. Mr Jarvis spoke with feelingly of one of his occasional excursions to see if the world still existed outside Wharram Percy:

We never went anywhere. It was four miles away from anywhere. Pub was miles away – no, you couldn't get a drink. . . . [There was] another lad I'd palled off with, you know, and then there was another bloke. . . . We used to have to walk it from there to Malton. About seven mile into Malton. . . . And if we had any money we used get a drink or two. And there was a German . . . , we used to go there and we used to get a pork . . . sandwich . . . apiece and it used to cost us 4d. And we used to go to a pub over t'way, they called it Cross Keys, and we got a bottle o' beer which cost us 3d. And we carried 'em about half way, then we used to say, 'Well, what about having our suppers?' Then we used to sit down at side o' t'road or on a fence and then we used to have this sandwich and this bottle o' beer. . . .

Of course, Malton, at that time o' day, it wasn't lit up same as it is today. There was only the odd gas light here and there. . . . Used to say, 'Now then, are you going to Malton?' And we couldn't go while about seven o' clock because we had the horses to do. Had to muck the stable up and feed and bed up and such like, so we set off about seven o'clock.

'Are you changing your clothes?'

I said, 'No, I'm not changing mine. I'm just going as I am.'

'Well I am.'

So we all set off across t'fields and walked down to Malton. What we walked down to Malton for, Lord above knows. We just had to go to see somebody. So, anyway, we got to Malton and we used to get a bottle or two of beer and we were same as that fellow from Scotland, 'Malton belongs to me,' when we'd had a bottle or two. . . . Aye, it was weeks before we had another night out like that because money didn't run to it.

A more regular and accessible source of diversion was the chapel, which served as a focal point for more than just worship. For farm servants, indeed, the religious side tended to be only a small part of their reasons for going, as emerged from this discussion with Mr and Mrs Tate and Mr Playforth:

Mr T: A lot of 'em used to go to Harpham [chapel]. . . . They used put an hour in.

Mrs T: Somewhere to go because there wasn't nothing else, was there?

Mr P: They used to enjoy singing, didn't they?

Were many farm lads religious?

Mr P: Well, they weren't religious, were they?

Mr T: Some of them were better than them that's religious, you know . . .

'Cause, you know, a religious man, he puts his religion away with his clothes.

It was generally agreed that the singing was the great attraction for youngsters – a chance to sing in a large group with an accompaniment was much better than anything possible on the farm. Other aspects of the service were not so attractive:

> Mrs T: Louie and me was once at Primitive Chapel and you know that chicken-run [the back row which, in every chapel, was the youngsters' territory] was full o' young lads. So we just turned round – it was right in t'middle of t'sermon and we said weren't there any lights again t'vicarage 'cause we expected two lads coming, you see, and they said, yes, there was, and we both got up and walked out. . . . Well, I daren't do it today.
> Mr T: Well, we used to do it at Harpham if there was a long-winded preacher. Get up and leave him.

The chapel-goers felt no inhibitions about joining in whenever the spirit moved them, so the services were often lively:

> Mr T: David Brown, him that used to be bawling and shouting at other side; singing, you know he was always two lines afront of anybody else,
> Mr P: That Tommy Vickerman and them used to be saying, 'Hallelujah!' didn't they? 'Praise the Lord!'
> Mrs T: 'Amen!'
> Mr T: Tommy Scott used to, didn't he? 'Aaamen!' he used to say.

Chapels were invaluable as meeting places. In parishes as scattered as those in the East Riding there were very few occasions when a substantial number of the inhabitants gathered in one place. Mr Rispin even started courting his wife during a service: 'She was sat in chapel choir and I was in t'balcony and I give her a wink and she winked back and that was it.' This may seem a light-hearted account of the religious life of the community, but this is because the farm servants were not expected to be too serious. The East Riding was one of the strongholds of Primitve Methodism, which appealed particularly to farmworkers, while the better off preferred Wesleyanism, but very few ordinary folk were Anglicans. Methodism laid great stress on the necessity for accepting religion only when truly convinced, and for this it was vital that people should be old enough and mature enough to understand all the ramifications of their acts. Youths were therefore given a lot more latitude than they might have been if they had been Anglicans, but this should not be confused with real irreverence.[9]

Sunday was, inevitably, the day when most of the courting was done, and as we have seen chapel might be a good place to meet someone. Otherwise it had little to offer as a romantic venue. In many cases a lad and his girl friend lived some distance apart, if she remained in his home village, and then all of Sunday was taken up by travel. If they lived close at hand, more frequent courting was possible, but proximity brought its own difficulties. There was a strong current of feeling in the late nineteenth century that no courting should be allowed within a farmhouse. Mary Simpson expressed this perfectly when she wrote to Mary G—, a farm servant she had previously befriended:

> So you have left C— Farm. I have sometimes felt uneasy about you. I met

with a young man who had been working there and told him I knew someone who had gone to live there – not a lad but a girl. When he heard that, he said, 'A girl did you say? Then I pity her. If she's a steady one she won't stay long there.' That was what he said and it made me uneasy, you had a good name for being steady, so I hoped you would still deserve it – but I have heard more since then, not about C— Farm, but about the ways of some other farm houses and what terrible wickedness there too often is.[10]

In her letters, Mary Simpson provides plenty of evidence that only permits the conclusion that she was criticising conduct she misunderstood completely. She quotes enough cases for us to be sure that girls did get pregnant in farm service, and that it was not a particularly rare occurrence. In all of them, though, the couple involved married unless they were prevented by their parents. There was no question of promiscuity. What aroused her was the simple fact of pregnancy, as the following letter to a friend, headed 'Village Morals' in her collected correspondence, shows:

I think you are hardly aware how low the standard is, so low that public opinion, so formidable among the higher classes, is in most cases no deterrent at all from sins against domestic life, to those brought up in cottages. A village mother, whose daughter had married discreditably, said indignantly, when she found it disqualified her from being noticed, 'It isn't as if she'd been a thief – then she never could have held up her head, and nobody would have looked upon her.' She could not be made at all to understand that the comparatively slight offence (as she deemed it) was to be put in the same category with stealing or was to be counted a disgrace. . . . A girl when reproached, answered similarly – 'One would think to hear you talk it was as bad as stealing.'[11]

She took the absence of her rules for an absence of all rules, whereas the situation seems to have been analogous to that found by Peter Laslett in his pioneering work on attitudes in pre-industrial society. He wrote, 'Nothing approaching promiscuity can be inferred from the evidence in either England or France at any time or for any age group, and the whole issue seems particularly inappropriate to the study of life in the traditional world.'[12] The real significance of views like Mary Simpson's was the effect they eventually had on public attitudes rather than their own relevance. We have seen that girls were induced to stop hiring themselves out in the market places, and instead used registries. Certainly, in this century courting was forbidden in many farmhouses, as Mr Johnson said:

You didn't mix much on the farm. In fact, there was some places, say the servant girl started keeping company with one o' t'men on t'farm, one of 'em got t'sack. It was generally the girl – in fact I was guilty o' that myself once. I lived at – well, I was there three years and t'wasn't bad place and the employer didn't mind. Well, we knew that, this woman, mistress o' t'house, she wouldn't allow any courting on t'farm. Anyway, I started taking this girl out and we never came back together or went out together, we met [off the farm]. Well, anyway, she'd been to . . . Beverley market one day and somebody said to her, 'I thought you didn't allow people on your place to court?'

'Oh, I don't.'

'Why, your waggoner and girl is going out together!'

Well, of course, she came back and gave this girl notice, a month's notice. . . . Well, after that, I said to this girl, 'Well, we've tried to, sort of, keep it out of their [way] . . . , we haven't flaunted it in front of 'em,' I says, 'We won't bother; we'll go out o' t'kitchen together, we'll come back in together.'

There were still many farmhouses where courting was permitted, and they seem to have survived the effects of the practice. The maids only had one weekday night off, so the contacts between sexes were, at best, severely limited. After work, lads and girls might join forces to pass the time, however, as Mrs Tate recalled, 'At Pockthorpe we used to go through to play games. Play whist. 'Course they had a daughter and she – we both used to go through to 'em.' Even though there was bound to be some sexual element in the contact on a few farms,[13] the innocence of such evenings provides an interesting contrast to the dark scenarios of Mary Simpson's mind. Indeed, strict control could provoke outrageous conduct in defiance. Mr Tate recalled:

I knew a chap . . . , maid's bedroom was through there, like [separated by a wall] and these lads knocked a hole . . . in the wall so he could get through to her. Yes. That's the truth.

Didn't anybody hear him?

No, I should think the old woman would never go upstairs, you know. . . . It was about a year after, same bedroom, like, I went to see my pal who was in bed, poorly, and I said, 'Is that the one that —?' It was boarden up, like. . . . Aye, wasn't that a rum thing to do?

In many ways the lads' way of life suffered only peripheral changes before it collapsed in the late 1930s, but the way they spent their leisure time is a key indicator of the approach of a modern, consumerist orientation that was quite incompatible with the traditional life of farm servants. Their realization that there were things to do for which money was essential, and which took their attention away from farming, grew throughout this century.

The introduction of the bicycle was a technological innovation that expanded their horizons dramatically, though it came surprisingly late in the day. The modern style of bicycle was perfected during the period 1885–8, but the machines remained highly priced and were aimed exclusively at the middle and upper-class market. The emphasis was on very high quality and individuality rather than mass production, and even the cheaper foreign machines were beyond the pockets of the working-class. Only with the collapse of the fashionable market did the cheap bicycle emerge, and it was a slow process. It was 1908 before a machine could be had for under £6. Prices continued to fall slowly thereafter[14] and, finally, 'Bicycles, well, they got 'em, you know, after the First World War they started to come a little bit, did cycles then, but for years and years there wasn't such a thing as a bicycle,' Mr Carter said. He was not among the oldest men I spoke to but he vividly remembered their coming. Mr Rispin got his first bike in his second year on a farm in 1912. He was then earning £12 a year, which shows why their purchase remained difficult:

> Bernard Stoke at Wold Newton, his father was insurance agent and dealt in bicycles. All our family got a bike. Well, you had to pay £2 down and t'rest at Martinmas. Well my – it was a Farrar . . . , it was a good bike. 5 guineas it was. Well, I had to draw £2 and [the farmer] said, 'Does thy father know?' . . . He wouldn't give it to me till he'd seen my father, my father says, 'Aye, oh yes, let him have £2. I can't lend him £2,' which he couldn't. However, I tell you, this £2 had to come off my £12, well you see, that only left me with £10; well I'd £3 5s to pay for my bicycle, there was my clothes to pay for and my boots. It wasn't leaving a deal.

That Mr Rispin would pay out nearly half his cash wages shows how valuable an acquisition a bicycle was. The lads could get futher afield than ever before, and spend more time wherever they went. Life became much easier for couples courting at a distance: they could spend most of Sunday together. Mr Fisher recalled one lad who regularly made epic journeys of about twenty-six miles in each direction:

> He was hired at Sunk Island and his girl friend was at Beeford, and he used to bike – just at weekends – he used to ride his bike from Sunk Island to see her, and he was coming back one Sunday night. He got to Aldbrough and his bicycle punctured, and he walked from Aldbrough to Sunk Island. When he got to Sunk Island they were just getting up ready for Monday morning.

Bicycles had their limitations, however, for Mr Masterman pointed out that the state of the rural back roads did not suit them:

> We'd no bikes in winter, the roads was too bad. Wherever we went we had to walk. The roads, oh, you wouldn't believe without you'd seen 'em. If you'd got a bike you got stuck through the roads in winter, they were that soft. So, we used to put our bikes away. Give 'em a cleaning and then Vaseline 'em, leave 'em at home in t'spare bedroom, if you had one, till summer, till the roads recovered. When they mended roads in those days, you know, they just put a – where there was water stood they just put a patch of loose stone on and let the traffic run it in. Well, you couldn't go on that with a bike – you'd cut your tyres to pieces. So – you walked.[15]

The First World War was a great agent of change, taking people from what had seemed an inevitable way of life and showing them alternatives. In itself this showed that change was possible, but more than that, it mixed up people from all walks of life and let them compare experiences. Lads were no longer content to lead a self-contained life and farmers recognized that concessions had to be made.

Fothering up rapidly succumbed to give greater freedom in the evenings, for it had always been one of the few aspects of the job that was genuinely and widely unpopular. Most lads deemed it unnecessary as long as someone made a quick check last thing at night. It was really another kind of curfew, and during the inter-war years it was informally abolished on most farms. A Saturday half-holiday was the next goal which all farmworkers were agitating for. This could not be gained informally but the pressure of the National Union of Agricultural Workers, working through the Wages Boards led to slow progress. Mr Rispin remembered the first reductions coming during the war, and Mr Walker said:

> We didn't get Saturday afternoon off till 1921 or 2, maybe more than that, aye, would be. First of all we got an hour off on Saturday. We all started to lowse out at five instead of six, when we first set off, and we kept gradually getting better and better. . . . It was very welcome, like, when we did get it.

The farm servants' way of life began to change as a result, in far more ways than would be thought possible, given that only a few extra hours had been granted. The weekend took on a new dimension: for instance, Mr Milner said, 'We had village [cricket and football] teams and alliances to play for, and cups to play for.' Team sports were no longer the prerogative of the farmers' sons, and this narrowing of social divisions was keenly felt and much appreciated. Similarly, it was now possible to get to see films in the market towns, and this, and other activities, brought the farm servants in direct contact with the main cultural stream of urban life for the first time. They began to compare their lot with that of others and to demand changes, which may or may not have been beneficial, but were inevitable once they began to realise how far behind the general rate of progress they had dropped. They now had the chance to spend as they earned and they saw no reason why they alone should not do so. The previous leisure pattern was a remnant of an older society, geared to a different concept of work that was now struggling to survive. It must be stressed that to talk of the servants' break with this total identification with work is not to criticise them. It was part of a change that had already overtaken most of British society and had little or nothing to do with morality even though it is often couched in such terms. It was simply a product of an industrial society, delayed in the East Riding by its isolation.

Notes to Chapter Fourteen

1. M. Simpson, 'The Life and Training of a Farm Boy', in Revd F.D. Legard, ed., *More About Farm Lads*, (Hull, 1865), 81–2.
2. See Morris, *British Workman*, p. 64.
3. Simpson, 'Training', 81–2.
4. Rex Russell, who worked as a casual labourer on East Riding farms after the Second World War, assured me that when he began to take a few clothes off on a hot day he was told, in no uncertain terms, to stop.
5. Simpson, *Gleanings*, pp. 75–6.
6. Megginson, 'Farmer's Boy', 526.

7. Simpson, *Gleanings*, p. 116.
8. B. Harrison, *Drink and the Victorians* (1971), p. 326.
9. See Revd Woodcock, *Piety Among the Peasantry* (1889), p. 259; Simpson, *Gleanings*, pp. 44 and 49, and Obelkevitch, *Rural Society*, pp. 181, 187, 225 and 231–3.
10. Simpson, *Gleanings*, p. 43.
11. Simpson, *Gleanings*, p. 43.
12. P. Laslett, *World*, chap. 7. The quotation is from p. 130 of the 1st ed. See also Obelkevitch, *Rural Society*, p. 97.
13. See Reffold, *Pie for Breakfast*, pp. 37 and 73–4.
14. See A.E. Harrison, 'The Competitiveness of the British Cycle Industry, 1890–1914', *Econ. Hist. Rev.* 2nd Series, XXII (1969), 287–297.
15. See Reffold, *Pie for Breakfast*, pp. 19 and 77.

Chapter Fifteen

Holidays

A farm servant's holidays were neither periods of relaxation nor of escape from normal surroundings or normal company, such as our own tend to be today. They were fully integrated into communal life so that, even while acting as safety valves that relieved the narrowness of everyday life, they reinforced the solidarity of the farm-servant group, the family, or the village. Our concept of holidays derives from the nature of our industrial society and it bears little relationship to the concepts behind those of farm servants which had clear connections with older, pre-industrial customs. Change had certainly occurred in the nineteenth-century East Riding villages, and it had mostly been negative, but it had destroyed neither the pattern of the holidays nor their spirit. The significant linkages are not always obvious, however, and rarely show up as quaint, folkloristic survivals. Many holidays, and other important events, were dated by the religious calendar, for instance, but in most cases it was simply because it made them easier to remember.[1] Only two of the farm lads' holidays had real religious connotations: Good Friday and Christmas, and these were among the least important.

Good Friday was, in fact, the only holiday given on purely religious grounds, and its observance therefore depended entirely on the individual farmer's feelings about the sanctity of the day, as opposed to his desire to keep the work going on. In some places everyone was at work, while in others like Howden, as described by Mr Baines: 'Good Friday, it were a crime to take horses to work when I was younger.' Mary Simpson wrote: 'Some of the cottagers have remarked that it is 'a queer thing' that the only farmers who did not keep their people at work the whole day were those who had "made no profession,"'[2] that is, the Anglicans rather than their fellow Methodists. Those who farmed on a large scale were more likely to be Anglicans, so, paradoxically, it was employers who were most distant from their men economically, socially, and culturally who gave the holiday. Mr Johnson said:

> On Good Friday we had half a day off, Good Friday afternoon. Well, some of these big Church people they would – odd uns, not a lot, but I know there was some, and they said, 'Well, you can have all day off, Good Friday, if you go to church in t'morning.'

The religious nature of Christmas was really overshadowed by its secular aspects, though to a lesser degree than today, and it was not highly regarded by farm lads. When I asked if they got time off at Christmas Mr and Mrs Rispin replied:

172

Mr R: Oh, Christmas Day, yes, but not Boxing Day. We never got one on Boxing Day. . . . Well, I can tell you what I was doing Boxing Day first year I was off, at Grange, we were quarting some wheat stubble . . . , 1910. . . .

Did you go home for Christmas Day, then?

Mr R: Oh no. You had your horses to do, hadn't you? Christmas Day, just same – and you used to get a good dinner. Oh yes, you always got a good dinner.

Mrs R: Jukes . . . , he always come for his dinner. And all t'labourers, they all come on a Boxing Day. They used to come on a Christmas Day and then they used to come on a Boxing Day.[3]

Mr. Brambles agreed: 'You were tied to be amongst the horses – stopped in t'stable till nine o'clock in a morning and then you were out again at night. It was only like a glorified Sunday.' Since there was nothing special to do, the day just slipped away. The best holidays were those that took them off the farm and produced plenty of entertainment, though of course it had to be made, as no-one could afford to pay for a stay at a holiday resort. The old holidays had to be part of the village community, but by the present century the community, and hence the holidays, were clearly in decay. Where the whole village had once shared, albeit unequally, control of its own existence, nearly all economic and social power now rested in the hands of a few farmers.

With the increased intensity of farming, and the heavy overheads of higher capitalization, these farmers had every economic reason to resent losing more than a minimum number of days to holidays. In any case, the larger the scale of their operations, the less likely their own social life was to be centred in the community, and so they were essentially providing holidays for others rather than themselves. They were not actively hostile to the old ways, for they remained part of the East Riding rural culture and shared many values and ideas with their workmen. Many a farmer would have been more out of place in a group of mill owners than in a group of village labourers, but the social gulf between them and their men made them increasingly observers and patrons of village life rather than participants, weakening their respect for customary holidays. These had been under general attack throughout the early modern period, especially as industrialization spread, and farmers did not need to be villains to cease footing the bill for one event or another, especially if there came a run of difficult years. Some of the old holidays, which had once cemented village society together, were now anachronistic. They were observed mostly for old time's sake and these were the first to go.

Nowhere could a lad take many days off at his own discretion. Mr Johnson said he was entitled to three such a year and as long as the work was not pressing, farmers might grumble but they usually consented. Everyone else was at work so it was easy to get horses seen to by a friend, giving a lad the whole day to himself. Mr Carter agreed:

If you wanted to go to Malton show, or you wanted to go to a wedding or anything like that, you just used to go to t'foreman and say could you have a day off. Oh yes, they'd let you go. It didn't make no difference to your pay, you just got your money you'd bargained for for t'year. They let you have your days off.

The bulk of holidays were fixed to specific days, in contrast, and historically the one that had the most significance for farm servants was, paradoxically, the one they had lost completely: Plough Monday. Throughout the north and East Anglia the first Monday after Twelfth Night had once been a day dedicated to the ploughlad, marking, as Fred Kitchen said, 'the end of the Christmas festivities, when the plough is supposed to start fallowing down for the winter.'[4] It seems to have been completely dead throughout living memory in the East Riding, though Fred Kitchen saw it observed around Doncaster in this century. Traditionally a group of farm lads would take a plough, remove its share, clean it up and decorate it, then drag it round the village in procession, begging for money, food, and drink. They might dress up in outlandish outfits: one lad, for example, who was seen between North and South Cave, was 'in the shape of a man with the horns, head and eyes of a cow.'[5] A mumming play or sword dance might be performed along the route, depending on local tradition. Around Driffield the lads were called the plough-jacks and in other parts of the county they were plough-stots (literally plough-oxen, since they themselves pulled the plough), which testifies to the antiquity of the event.

They were showing themselves off to the village as a distinct group with their collective symbol, the plough. On their particular day they took tribute from the other villagers by right and not as charity. If anyone refused to contribute, if their contribution was judged insufficient, or if there was a collective score to settle, unlucky offenders would find the plough, with the share put back, dragged right across their garden. The village acknowledged the existence of the ploughlads willingly or unwillingly. Such assertiveness was not compatible with a society split firmly into employers and employed, divided irrevocably by the wages that passed from one to the other, and so gradually it ceased. In Goathland in the North Riding, Plough Monday is re-enacted every year,[6] but they have not, of course, revived any of the social structures that made it real. It is bound to lack solidity, capturing only certain aspects, much as still photographs can only record the re-enactment itself in a limited way.

Yet the lads still had a festival dedicated to them in the shape of the hiring fair. Once the business was done and the farmers had left, the servants turned to enjoying themselves. Hirings emphasised their status as hirelings and were essential to the functioning of farms, so they were under no threat, even though the festivities were so enjoyable that they gained the total disapproval of the moralists. The Revd M.C.F. Morris thought things were improving after the First World War but remembered:

St. Martin may be considered as the patron-saint of the East Yorkshire farm-servants; but it is to be feared that they lightly regard his name. . . . As I remember them as a boy, it would be hard to describe a hiring day in one of our East Riding agricultural centres; such scenes of riot and disorder were they. Well do I recollect going through the streets of Pocklington. . . . It was a splendid harvest for the show-keepers, especially if the day was wet, and under that condition of weather the public houses were unfortunately also crammed almost to suffocation. . . . Boys and girls, lads and lasses, men and women were crowded together in the parlours and passages of the inns in a state of wild excitement, uproar and confusion. . . . It was like pandemonium let loose. All this naturally tended to demoralise the young people, and the results can be better imagined than described.[7]

Certainly the fairs were not noted for sobriety. Given their way of life, it should not be surprising that older lads took to the pubs with alacrity at Martinmas. They had a year's confinement in limited company on isolated farms to get out of their system, so, Mr Carter said, 'That's just where it all happened, there. Oh yes, when they got down to Malton and they got their year's wage, you know, and when they got to Martinmas there used to be a lot of fighting and being drunk.' Even Morris admitted that 'it was only to be expected indeed that after a year's work and drudgery there should be some relaxation,'[8] but, living a totally different life, he was utterly incapable of comprehending the strains and tensions a servant had to endure. Such men abhorred the fighting that was so prevalent, a fact confirmed by Mr Walker: 'Oh aye, regular thing was scrapping in Martinmas week. . . . They used to meet, they've had some grievances during the year, d'you see, get some beer into them – well then, outside, and then their jackets off and into scrapping.' It would be pointless to deny that some fought for the sake of it: Mr Walker said of his uncle: 'He never was married . . . He used to fight anything that come up in front of him. Stand up again wall in t'Cheese yard at Driffield and he'd hit anybody. They used to call him 'Banger'. . . . He'd get beat, but he'd beat a few on 'em.' However, there was a reason behind the vast majority of fights, as Mr Masterman explained:

> Say you fell out with another farm lad, well, you didn't fight him then, you'd say, 'All right . . . , I'll meet you at Keyingham Feast.' And then you had a scrap and you had an audience as well. Or if the next one was Patrington – 'All right, Patrington,' or Hedon hirings, Patrington hirings.

Fighting was thereby kept off the farms where its consequences would have been much more socially divisive, as we have seen. Those of all classes who understood farm servants realised this and the police attitude to the day was one of containment rather than rigid control. Mr Harper believed that the Driffield police were told, 'Now then, this is farm lads' day – don't you interfere. Let 'em alone.' They were just there to direct traffic. As long as the lads kept to pub yards and side streets they were left alone for the most part, though Mr Masterman recalled that unofficial action might still be taken:

> There was two at Hedon went down a side lane away from the houses and they were fighting . . . , and [a] constable and [a] sergeant come, and the constable was a man from Driffield, and he watched 'em for a bit and he said, 'Here, take hold o' my cape.' And the sergeant took his cape and he took his tunic off and he went in – he belted both these fellers did t'police constable.
> *Did anybody ever get arrested for fighting?*

Oh no, no. They used to lock 'em up sometimes – if they got a bit too much out o' control they locked 'em up and kept 'em till about eleven o'clock at night, and then turned 'em out and told 'em to go home.

The lack of court proceedings confirm this tolerance. Only a few cases arising out of hirings came before the courts, and there was usually some obvious reason why the defendant had been charged rather than released. Thus, in one case at Beverley, one 'Stephenson participated in three or four fights, and gave the police a lot of trouble. After being detained for some time at the police station, he was allowed to go in charge of friends, but almost directly he got in the street he struck a man in the face.'[9] The man had a previous record and is clearly untypical, while another case, from Selby suggests that the police were wise to stay out of things. A crowd of two to three hundred went to the assistance of Martin Carney, who was drunk and had assaulted a policeman. His brother and a friend enabled him to escape, but eventually all three were seized. As they were taken to the police station, 'the crowd hemmed the police in and badly used them.' Once more the main protagonist, Martin Carney, had a bad record with sixteen previous convictions.[10]

The inescapable point is that the hiring fairs were times when standards were universally relaxed. It was a different sort of licence from that of Plough Monday but it was clearly related, and a lad who was not inclined to participate was not, contrary to Morris's beliefs, dragged in. Mr Carter spoke for many when he said:

Course, that was one class o' people. I know I never had no bother, that way like. It was just a certain gang that used to be on that business. They used to look for it, and they used to get it sometimes. And they used to maybe catch a lot more than what they'd bargained for.

Another point clearly related to an older tradition is the use of the fairs to check the abuse of authority. A lad might hesitate to challenge a waggoner or foreman during the year, but at Martinmas all authority was cancelled, and if a lad was leaving he need not fear retribution. It was even known for boys to set on a particularly unpleasant man as a group, to offset the difference in age and size, a practice known as smallganging. Mr Harper said:

Say you lived on a spot where you had a rough foreman-feller, always kicking lads' backsides. Well, I've heard many a young lad say, 'Ah well, wait while Driffield first hirings! There's many a bloomin' foreman-feller's getten his head broken at Martinmas at Driffield first hirings!'

This periodic removal or inversion of authority, either in fact or as a symbol, was once widespread. There was a wide variety of rituals associated with particular times of year, but they all had the clear intention to hold in check any tendencies towards abuse of power that could not be stopped in other ways.[11] The resemblance to Plough Monday, when lads claimed the respect of the village, is clear, and the value of these established customs was recognised by most of those in contact with the everyday world of the East Riding. It is to be regretted that the reputation of the fairs has been blackened by criticism from people like the Revd Morris and Mary Simpson who, for all their good intentions and superficial desire to identify with local society, were blinded in crucial areas by their class and upbringing. From the heights of their Victorian respectability they looked down at the fairs and saw nothing but chaos, where in truth the fairs were the main force holding chaos at bay for fifty-one weeks of the year. Martinmas had to make up for all those weeks of isolation, and most of the people involved were adolescents, at an age when they were at their most boisterous and restless. If it had become a festival suitable for their praise, it might as well not have existed.

Their attitude to the mixing of the sexes is a clear proof of how unreal their fears were. We have already seen that Mary Simpson managed to remove the girls from the actual hirings, but she was far from happy with the limited nature of that achievement for she felt that any reduction in the contact between the sexes was desirable:

> The people connected with the [fair] shows of various kinds are generally, I am told, among the most depraved of mankind, and take every opportunity to suggesting evil to the young people who gather round to look at them. . . . Any direct influence for good that we have hitherto had had ended with the hours of hiring – some people say has ended where it ought to begin – yet it is something to have been able to keep the poor girls out of otherwise inevitable harm's way.[12]

On the other hand concerning the same period one farm lad wrote:

> Given a fine day the lasses used to enjoy the fun as much as the lads and as they were accustomed in my day to work in the fields with the men at hay, harvest and taty-scratting times one really cannot see how it is any more contrary to the rules of decency and order for them to stand together in the open market.[13]

The fairs were boisterous and, by some standards, language and behaviour were crude, but there is no evidence beyond that of the critics that anything more serious took place. They suited the farm servants and formed the highpoint, or points, of Martinmas week. This gap between contracts took up at least half of their total holidays and it was the only time of the year when nothing, however minimal, tied them to farming and horses. There was no need to be up at four or five in the morning and everyone had some money to spend. It is no wonder that, as Mrs Lawler commented, they were 'always looking for Martinmas Day, 23rd November – have your week's holiday.'

In fact, 'It was supposed to be seven days holiday but we generally used to have a few extra days,' Mr Johnson said. In places it extended up to a fortnight but it was always termed the Martinmas week and extra days off were a favour from the farmer, depending on his nature, local custom, and his need to press on with the work. Generosity was usually tinged with self-interest, for in December there was little to do bar ploughing, and if that was well advanced a farmer might prefer to let his lads eat and sleep at home for a few days longer. Work ceased on Martinmas Day, which was pay day, and once the horses were fed and watered for the last time the farmer handed out the agreed wages, less any subs that had been made over the year. Mr Masterman recalled his first wage thus: 'I thought I was a millionaire! Nine golden sovereigns. And the old farmer gave me ten shillings extra because I hadn't subbed any.' He added that it was a dangerous time for young lads because everyone knew that they had money in their pockets, and sometimes they were robbed on their way home. Mr Masterman was only paid at six o'clock, but most farmers paid out in a morning. Lads often had a long journey home, and they had several things to do before they could start, especially the older lads:

> Those who were not 'stopping on' for another year had already sent their clothes-boxes home, and so with various sized bundles, we set off, but we had to pull up at t'awd shoemakers' and tailors' shops to get 'oor bills sattled.' At both these local tradesmen's decanters containing rum, gin and whisky were handed round accompanied with plum bread and cheese. An old leaden tobacco jar was invariably on the table for those who wanted a fill, and as we left the shops the shoemaker and tailor both wished us good luck. If the village boasted of a fully licensed house, or a jerry shop, a parting call had to be paid there.[14]

During the year it was only the older lads who could have saved enough to pay for boots or clothes without needing credit, and all these bills were cleared at Martinmas. A farm lad was an extreme example, but credit was a traditional part of the way of life in all rural villages because money, over and above that needed for necessities, could only be earned at intervals. Times like harvest offered the certainty of high earnings, so this credit, unlike its urban counterpart, anticipated certain future income and was not necessarily an entry into a hopeless cycle of debt.

Once their affairs were in order everyone set off home, and during the course of the day families were reunited as sons and daughters arrived. Gossip was exchanged and experiences compared during the evening. Mrs Lawler explained, 'It used to be a right time . . . when you all come home. . . . Used to have dances in t'kitchens to old gramophone, didn't we? Everybody used to say, "You come to our house tonight and we'll come to your house tomorrow night."' More traditional households preferred the fiddle and concertina, but doubtless the end result was very similar. Everyone ate well while they were at home, particularly if they had been at a bad meat house. Roast goose was traditionally eaten on the Sunday, a day known as Rive-Kite Sunday, literally Tear-Stomach Sunday.[15] Those without homes were in a difficult position, however, and relied on other people's kindness. If a good friend took them in they would do as well as anyone, or if the farmer let them stay on they would manage, but there were always a few with nowhere to go. Martinmas was a family occasion and some of a servant's pay was quickly spent in recognition of the support the family gave, quite apart from the many things which had to be bought for themselves:

> Mother, who had washed and mended for us all the year was paid for this both in money and in kind. Next day many a village coal heap was augmented

by a good waggon-load, which the lads brought from Driffield station. One day in Martinmas week was always spent at Driffield, the market of the Wolds, possessing wonderfully well-stocked shops. . . . The lasses wanted a fresh rig-out, whilst the lads needed flannel top-shets. 'A pund o' tea was bowt' as a present for mother, whether she had stayed at home or accompanied her family to assist them in their purchases. Then if dad smoked, half-a-pound of tobacco was taken home for him as well as a bottle of Irish whiskey to serve them both as a nightcap through the winter, or in case either was taken badly.[16]

A couple of days would be spent at the hiring fairs, whether a new job was wanted or not. It was also a good time for ploughing matches, such as the one held on Friday 25 November 1906 by the Portington and Eastrington Ploughing Association to serve the area east of Howden.[17] The railways ran excursions, showing that the farm servants were not totally cut off from general social trends: in 1901 trips were advertised from Malton to York and Leeds on the Tuesday, Wednesday, and Saturday; to Pickering, Goathland, Grosmont, and Whitby on Wednesday; and to Scarborough on Saturday.[18] In some places the time was passed more sedately: 'The Martinmas week has passed very quietly in Hotham. The recreation and reading room, which was re-opened on October 17th for the use of farm servants whose homes were not in the village, was kept open during the week.'[19] Sometimes events were also organized for the evening, for instance, at Leven a 'Martinmas social in connection with the Leven Reading Room took place in the Girls' School, and was very well attended,' in 1910, while near Howden it was reported in 1906 that:

Captain H. Liversidge J.P. of Portington Hall, has organised a series of musical entertainments for the farm servants. . . . The entertainments form a musical festival, which will no doubt be very much appreciated by those for whom it has been provided, and it is held in the Council Schoolroom, Eastrington. The first entertainment was given last night, thirty of the best voices from Selby and district contributing to the programme.[20]

Martinmas was a favourite time for marriages as the yearly bond really did tie people to farms.[21] A lad who married while he was hired out still had to live in for the remainder of his contract, unless the farm was in a village and he could get a cottage there. It was only on completing the year that he was free to take a labourer's job and set up a home and family.[22] The marriages themselves livened up the week for everyone else, but for the couple involved it was their last Martinmas holiday: thereafter the lad would work through the festivities. It is interesting to consider this in connection with the view of hiring fairs as places where girls were seduced and made pregnant. We have already noted the likelihood that sexual relations before marriage were rarely undertaken except in anticipation of marriage, and while it may be true that the general air of excitement and freedom may have led couples to go further than they might have otherwise, it is far more likely that most of what went on was really intense courtship. This was the only substantial period of time a courting couple could spend together and the only time a lad had to approach a girl from his native village. Martinmas was a time when a great many things happened which ordinarily did not, for the simple reason that there was no other opportunity for them.

The freest and best of the other holidays were the village feasts which still flourished thoughout Yorkshire. They were usually held at some convenient summer date, like the hiatus between the hay and corn harvests when, with luck, good weather and little work coincided. They were the equivalent of Plough Monday for the whole village acting together for communal benefit. So far, change had not pushed East Riding village society past the point where it could adapt its feast successfully. Friendly society branches were usually the mobilizing agency that preserved the original spirit best, for by taking them up for their own celebrations, they continued to be organized by ordinary people for their own benefit. Although friendly societies were national organizations for mutual insurance against bad times, they were run entirely by their members at branch level. They provided one area of life where a working man could genuinely feel he was influencing events and helping to shape his own destiny. Where the village feast was not also a club feast, as, for instance, at Barmby on the Marsh, a local committee would be formed to organize it, inevitably drawing its members from the ranks of farmers and local worthies. As a result, this sort of feast was less of a communal event as far as the ordinary folk were concerned, and though the outward forms were much the same, the spirit behind it was a little different.

All the major national societies were represented in the East Riding, unlike poorer areas where farmworkers could not afford the subscriptions of the best ones, such as the Oddfellows or Foresters. If a village could not support a branch of its own, one in a neighbouring village or market town, which would have several, would be used,[23] Mr Johnson recalled how the Foresters dominated the feast at Hutton Cranswick in his youth:

Well, [feasts] happened every year, generally in the summer-time – June, July, you know. They were all finished well before the harvest, and you had a day off. . . . Foresters, Ancient Order of Foresters they called theirselves, they had a big building on their own. . . . Now you went to that hall, say about nine o'clock and there was secretary. There was a little window. I can just see him now, on the balcony, and he used to put his head through this window, just a little window, and read all the club members' names out, and, you know, you answered your names . . . A lot of the bigger villages had a band. And they used to engage this band for this feast day and you formed up and marched behind the band to the village church, you came out and marched back, you perhaps went down t'street and up again. You didn't go right round the village.

And then you went for this club dinner, as they called it, you see that was free: to all club members that was free. And you had a big dinner (ours was on the third Wednesday in June, I remember that well). . . . They used to invite a few of the big bugs, you know, and chairman of the council, perhaps the vicar and schoolmaster and such as that. 'Course they made a speech but we weren't that much interested in that, us lads, we used to want to get out because on the village green or in a field . . . there were roundabouts, you know, steam horses we used to call them. Well, there was them coconut shies, Aunt Sallies, and shooting galleries, you know: all these. They used to come for that day. All amusements you could mention. Sweet stalls and all that. Used to go till we had to get our teas: 'course I lived there and went home but them that was away, they got their teas anywhere – pub or home refreshment room – and then we went back to the village green and used to, well, it was open as long as they had customers; when the customers went home, ten or eleven or twelve o'clock, you know, they had to shut up then, but if they had customers they would go on practically half o' t'night.

Some villages had more than one club, like Rillington which held its feast on the last Tuesday in June. William Harrison (born 1869) described it thus:

They marched round the town at night, you know, club feast night; three clubs banging into the drums, they were – used to liven it up. . . . There were the Druids, and the Foresters and the Shepherds; and that was three clubs and they used to have tents set up in the public [house] yards, . . . and they used to have their dinners in there.[24]

The procession was the society's chance to show off the strength of the branch and great pains were taken over it. At Rudston, when the Ancient Order of Shepherds marched every member wore a sash and carried a shepherd's crook. Discipline was strict lest the holiday atmosphere should cause members to let the society down, as Mr and Mrs Rispin recalled:

Mr R: Jack Croft, he was in Nafferton, and in Nafferton if you didn't parade at night you were fined sixpence. And poor old Jack got drunk and he went on parade and they fined him half a crown!
   Mrs R: Because they weren't supposed to drop out to get drink or owt.
   Mr R: No, no. Ben Danby . . . , when he was in club and that, he and my father brothers, when you got to t'Top House [a pub], all management, they used to bring 'em a drink out. And if anybody in t'members would step out – a shilling, they fined 'em a shilling. Well, Ben and my uncle, they were always two, I used to pull all their legs about that. Aye, fined 'em a shilling.

It is significant that the clubs went to church rather than to chapel although most of their members were Methodists. Mr Johnson, a dedicated Primitive Methodist, described their use of the church and the vicar's invitation to the dinner without feeling any need to explain. The church remained the natural religious centre of the village, from which the Methodists were excluded for reasons they felt were social rather than theological. Mary Simpson's writings give plenty of conscious and unconscious evidence that it was the Anglicans who maintained an antagonism rather than the Methodists.[25] On this day when the village celebrated its unity, therefore, it ignored the schism and gathered in the place where villagers had been christened, married, and buried for time out of mind. The feasts, in fact, were often held on the patron saint's day, or had been, where it was convenient. There would be no Anglican opposition because it was rare to see more than a handful of ordinary villagers on a Sunday. Some farmers even made church attendance compulsory: '[At] Middledale – he would always give 'em a day off providing they went to church. Well, they would go to church. He was a church man, you see,' Mr Rispin commented.

Like the hiring fairs, all feasts attracted much larger fun fairs than the business done could warrant because they made useful stopovers. Fairs could only travel slowly between major venues, and if they could take any money on the way they would set up for a day or two.[26] Feasts all had sporting competitions as well: a typical programme at Thorngumbald was described by Mr Masterman: 'There would be racing, running, walking, cycle-racing, jumping, and then there would be trotting matches. Jumping maybe – horse-jumping – some of 'em, not 'em all . . . if the field was big enough they would have jumps set up.' Dances and similar social functions were held and the pubs did a roaring trade all day. There were scores of visitors as this was an occasion for family reunions. Barmby Feast extended over Thursday, Friday, and Saturday, and Mr Pridmore recalled it thus:

My uncle that kept the King's Head, he had a big, long room, you know, full length of the house – 'twas called the big room. They used to hold dances in there. He had two men came with their fiddles – one was a fiddle, the other was a big fiddle [a cello] . . . We had a piano in as well. . . . You used to get quite a crowd at feast-time. Well, my parents, they used to cook a whole ham . . . and that used to go on Saturday and Sunday, with the people we had in. And they used to bake buns and tarts, and all that. Oh, tarts galore – plates and plates. We used to have a long table and seats up each side for people . . . , and we used to provide a tea for all our relations and friends, you see. Tell you, we've cleared a ham . . . , a big ham, you know, not just a small one. . . . It were a real good do – people enjoyed themselves. And we had enough for Saturday, you see. . . . Well, your relatives used to stay. 'Course some of our relatives were a bit comical, rough. One of them used to shout, 'Hey up, hast' gone off to sleep up there? We want to come and stand you up in t'corner so's we can get into bed!'

Within a limited area the East Riding population was very mobile and sisters and brothers often went to live in different villages after marriage. By modern standards the distances involved were not great, but even so contact was easily lost and the feast was a chance for families to re-establish their kinship ties. With an appreciable proportion of the population living on scattered farmsteads, villages as well as families had a tendency to fragment, particularly as youngsters were often hired some distance away, while strangers moved in. The village now reinforced its communal ties in the same way. Among the men fragmentation was furthered by the isolated nature of their work, which kept them in very small groups for most of the year. With its concerted action the feast was a good antidote, as shown by the children's tea that ended festivities at Thorngumbald, described here by Mr Masterman:

On the Monday the schoolchildren would have a tea. After school they would go to the chapel and . . . all the seats would be packed up, and then tables set up and they would have a tea. . . . All the village people – one would give a ham, maybe – and it was all given, all the stuff. It used to be a good tea and all, I'll tell you. Ham sandwiches, and custard. Jellies. Things that we never used to have. And then on the Tuesday night they had what was left. Finish off.

Since the turn of the century the decline in village life has been the subject of constant complaint, and statistics show that there are many fewer shops, pubs, schools, and churches in rural areas today than seventy years ago. Even more important, there are fewer jobs and a much smaller proportion of them are in agriculture. Wages are generally low and yet, given the decayed state of the average village's services, people have to travel long distances to obtain many necessities. Village populations have been in decline and the fortunes of the remaining inhabitants are no longer tied together as they were in the old days, for they work in a variety of industries, often at some distance, and their only common bond is that they live in the same place. This decay in the old farming communities is reflected in the diminishing of the feasts since the Second World War. A particularly hard blow was dealt by the rapid decline of friendly societies which came with the growth of the National Insurance and National Health schemes largely depriving them of any insurance function.

A similar but earlier fate befell the harvest or mell supper, another communal festival. Harvest is, of course, the climax of the arable farming year and in times gone by it meant the difference between good and bad winters, even plenty or starvation. Three or four bad harvests in succession could be disastrous, and until the crop was securely stacked no-one dared predict success, for even the best seeming crop could be spoiled by bad weather at a crucial moment. There are few industries where returns are so uncertain, and so when the last, or mell, sheaf left the field it is no wonder that the village celebrated if all had gone well. In the past most families had some direct stake in the outcome, and suppers then expressed communal satisfaction at a communal achievement. All this had now changed. For individual farmers the harvest meant commercial success or failure but, paradoxically, a generally bad harvest could cause high prices until the world food trade ended any chance of shortage, so it could actually result in higher profits for some. For a labourer, high prices meant dear food. He usually wanted to see his year's work end well with a good harvest in any case and, in the long run, bad results, where they led to poorer farmers, would mean fewer jobs and lower wages.

Not every place [had one]. . . . First place I was at, where I was three year, at Cranswick Common, we always had harvest supper. Not only us who worked on t'farm but so many – postman used to come, some o' t'tradesmen as worked for them. . . . That was only place – they were going out then a bit.

During this century, Mr Johnson recalled, suppers took place purely according to the whim of individual farmers. The farmer was not just rewarding his employees for their work, for the village tradesmen were only indirectly connected with the harvest through the work they did for the farm, and the inclusion of the postman lacks even that justification. In the final analysis, the whole village stood or fell by agriculture and the supper, hopefully, celebrated that they all still stood. They had once been visited by guisers, groups of dancers with blackened faces, dressed 'in all sorts of fantastic costumes.' Occasionally, if they came unannounced, they would be refused entry and a battle might develop, but they were usually welcomed with food and drink and asked to perform, whereupon there would commence 'the clatter of the dancers' boots going double-shuffle and various comical figures set the entertainment going at full swing.'[27]

The independence that marks all these old festivals shows clearly. The villagers, disguised, usually came by mutual arrangement, but they did not always wait to be asked and they were not begging for charity. If they were refused entry the battle that ensued may not have been serious but it symbolized a feeling that the festivities were open to all. With the replacement of mutuality by the rules of individual property, such attitudes become more and more difficult to uphold. The guisers were never seen in the present century. Indeed, in some areas, the whole supper was but a memory: around Barmby, said Mr Pridmore, the farmers 'never gave you anything.' Holderness, however, seems to have preserved the traditions remarkably intact. Mr Masterman remembered:

> After they got all harvest in, in the boss's house they used to have harvest supper. It was generally on a Saturday night so that if the fellers got drunk they'd Sunday to get over it. Well, us kids used to go – all the children went . . . , they used to put us all in the kitchen and a couple o' women to look after us, keep us away from the [adults] – let the fathers, mothers have their supper in peace. . . . They were big kitchens, you know – like barns, some o' them farmhouse kitchens, – flagged floors – and there would be the Englishmen at one side, the labourers, foreman, and all the single lads, all at one side. At the other side there would be Irishmen. Well the Irishmen used to have beef, potatoes, jelly, custard, all on one plate, and . . . when they wanted jelly, they would say, 'Reach for the stuff that dithers about.' There used to be beer – barrels of it, you know. There was men hired to come and keep going back wi' jugs to the beer barrels and fill 'em up, putting them on the table. You know, all you'd got to do was get a jug and fill your mug – not glasses: mugs, pint mugs. Great lumps of beef, you know. Bacon, ham . . . . I know I've had to hold my father up a few times. He'd fallen down. Maybe fall into t'ditch.

Other men testified that in their areas there were farmers who held suppers, but that they never worked for them. The collapse of this tradition had many immediate causes: teetotallers, for instance, would find the drinking offensive, and tea and soft drinks were unlikely to be a successful substitute. Some who gave up one year due to a shortage of money no doubt meant to restart, but never got around to it. Given the underlying tendencies, individual reasons hardly matter, and it is worth noting that those which survived were themselves probably not authentic survivals of a pre-industrial age, but Victorian revivals, if the evidence from Lincolnshire is anything to go by. There, the true harvest festivities were actively suppressed by farmers in the early nineteenth century. Around 1860 the Church of England instituted its harvest festival services, which were extremely popular, and the farmers, now highly prosperous, were reviving harvest suppers as personal celebrations almost entirely lacking in communal elements.

It would thus be wrong to take a simplistic view and say that farmers only ever took away holidays or celebrations. Where a holiday or festivity retained a purpose and offered no threat to their authority, it generally retained their active support. They were even willing to go further to solidify a new type of sense of community where they were patrons rather than participants, for if they could cement together the village on this new basis, challenges to them from below could be short-circuited through deference. Many were, for instance, willing to find a waggon with a team and driver to take village children for a day out in the quiet period before the corn harvest. If it was possible, they went to the sea-side as Mr Rispin remembered Kilham doing: 'I've taken scholars to Brid, you know, all t'schools'd go, oh, about eleven waggons, like, two horses in a waggon, taking all the school children to Brid. Well, it was on a Thursday and [the day before] you'd take all the tacklings off and decorate it.' The children of Burton Fleming – the bairns – also went to Bridlington, while those from Sunk Island went to Withernsea. Otherwise they went to a local event such as the Malton stallion procession which the Birdsall children were taken to see. The lad who drove the waggon got a holiday himself, so, predictably enough, 'It was waggoner-chap that got that job – others didn't get a job like that. Just him,' said Mr Carter. Anywhere that two waggoners went in public with their teams and best waggons, rivalry was inevitable. They earned their time off by spending the previous night slaving over the gears, cleaning and decorating them lavishly, as Mr Rispin said. The prestige of the farm was at stake and in many places a formal competition with a prize was established. One year Mr Masterman won £3 in this way, but when the publican who was donating the money realised that a teetotaller had won he peevishly refused to hand it over until Mr Masterman returned from the day out. Normally he quickly recovered his money in the tap room.

Now this holiday was not an old tradition. Bad as the roads were in the early years of this century, they were still better than they had been. A hundred years earlier most villages could not have sent large numbers on a worthwhile trip, and in any case, before 1870 children began work so young that there would have been very few idle children old enough to take. The day trip was a modern concept and was only possible because of the farmers' generosity. It is clear, moreover, that the concept was expanding and creating new traditions in the waggon judging. If the village societies of, say, 1910, had found a stable equilibrium it is likely that after a time new holidays reflecting the new society would have grown up organically to replace the old ones. There would not have been as many and they would not have carried such strong overtones of independence as the old ones, but they would have been an integral part of an industrialized farming culture. However, change was to intensify, not halt, and so growth was largely prevented by the continued destruction of the old way of life. Not until rural workers came to resemble urban workers much more closely, with their holidays prescribed by state action, would the decline in their days off be halted, but at this point holidays became simply time off.

It is impossible to assess the value of holidays, but lads were at least getting more of them than the average urban worker. Whether this compensated for their lack of regular leisure time is a question they and the urban workers would probably have disagreed over, for we are all products of our upbringing and experience. Certainly, a waggoner working for a generous farmer and getting Christmas Day, Good Friday, three odd days, a day at the village feast, a trip to the sea-side, and a fortnight at Martinmas with money in his pocket, had plenty of chance to enjoy himself by contemporary standards. He got more than just relaxation or enjoyment, however, for the holidays were part of a way of life that was capable of coping institutionally with most eventualities, as long as the participants were prepared to accept the fundamental premise that they should see their work as far more than a job. The work itself offered a high level of satisfaction because it involved a partnership with a team of living animals rather than inanimate machinery, but even so, some stresses were unavoidable. The holidays were geared to relieving those stresses in a way particularly suited to the fact that horselads lived within an intensely structured grouping, sharing most aspects of their life.

Notes to Chapter Fifteen

1. See Obelkevitch, *Rural Society*, pp. 265–71. R.W. Malcolmson, *Popular Recreations in English Society*, 1700–1850 (Cambridge, 1973), esp. chaps 6, 7 and 8, gives an overview of traditional holidays and their relationship to concepts of leisure.
2. Simpson, *Gleanings,* p. 66.
3. See Morris, *British Workman*, p. 54.
4. Kitchen, *Brother*, pp. 64–5. See also Morris, *British Workman*, p. 55.
5. Woodcock, *Piety*, p. 40.
6. F. Dowson, 'Folklore of the Plough Stots', *Trans. Yorks. Dia. Soc.*, pt. 37, V (1936), 28–37.
7. Morris, *Folk Talk*, pp. 206–9.
8. Morris, *Folk Talk*, p. 209.
9. *Bev. Guar.*, 17 Nov. 1900, p. 5.
10. *E. News,* 30 Nov. 1910, p. 5. See *Yorks. Her.*, 30 Nov. 1910, p. 8 for a similar case nearby and on the same day.
11. See Malcolmson, *Recreations*, chap. 5, esp. pp. 76–82.
12. Simpson, *Gleanings*, pp. 125–6.
13. Fairfax-Blakeborough, *East Riding*, p. 48.
14. Fairfax-Blakeborough, *East Riding*, pp. 47–52.
15. *Br. Cal. Customs*, III, p. 161, and Gutch, *Folk Lore,* p. 111.
16. Fairfax-Blakeborough, *East Riding*, pp. 47–52.
17. *Yorks. Her.*, 15 Nov. 1906, p. 3.
18. *Mal. Gaz.*, 23 Nov. 1901, p. 2.
19. *H. News,* 3 Dec. 1910, p. 5.
20. *Yorks. Her.*, 23 Nov. 1906, p. 4.

21. See Obelkevitch, *Rural Society*, p. 136 for a similar link between the May hirings of Lincolnshire and marriages there.
22. Mr. Appleyard, untaped interview.
23. J.F. Wilkinson, *The Friendly Society Movement* (1886), p. 194. *Mal. Mess.*, 13 Jan. 1900, p. 3, gives a report of all the friendly society branches in the vicinity. Day, *Life,* pp. 10–19, reproduces the rules of the Rudston Independent Order of Ancient Shepherds from 1865, when his grandfather was a member. Obelkevitch, *Rural Society*, pp. 84–90, gives an account of Lincolnshire feasts that has many parallels, but also significant variations, particularly in their ability to survive, which was much lower.
24. 'Rillington Feast', narrated by W. Harrison, from M. Bateson, The Dialect of Rillington (unpublished B.A. dissertation, University of Leeds, 1958).
25. Simpson, *Gleanings*, pp. 90 and 147–8. See also Obelkevitch, *Rural Society*, pp. 135, 172–3 and 214–6.
26. D. Dallas, *The Travelling People* (1971), esp. chap. 1, with extra information by G. Dallas from the research for this book.
27. Morris, *Folk Talk*, pp. 212–3.

Chapter Sixteen

The Development of the East Riding Farm Servant System

It is clear that the East Riding farm servant of 1914 was part of a complex system that had, by accident or design, come to encompass far more of life than merely working horses, or minding sheep or cattle. The system had many elements that seemed to hark back to much earlier times. The similarity of George Walker's illustration of a Wolds waggoner with his team and waggon in the first decade of the nineteenth century (plate 38), to the photograph (plate 35) of another delivering corn to a railway station a century later is truly remarkable. Descriptions of the farm labour force from the same periods echo this similarity,[1] and accounts of the introduction of tea drinking and such like seem quite out of place in the present century. However, it was also a system that had continued to evolve in the intervening years to maintain its practicality in the face of the changing needs of the county's agriculture and people. The farm servant of 1914 was far more than a curious survival, though a survival he certainly was.

Very few other counties hired single farm servants on any scale in twentieth-century England,[2] and yet farm servants had provided one third to one half of all agricultural labour in early modern times. Sixty per cent of youths spent time as servants before the nineteenth century. Few adult villagers relied completely on wages for their income then. They might own or rent land, whether it was a farm, a smallholding, or a large garden; they might have access to the common land or the waste for keeping livestock; or they might have some trade or occupation that provided a steady income, like being a blacksmith, or a seasonal one, such as droving or horse breaking. Many were available to do paid work for some, or even much, of the time, and many, probably most, depended on earning wages in this fashion. As long as they had their own concerns to see to, however, they were unwilling to commit themselves completely. The enclosure enthusiasts frequently pointed out that the existence of commons and waste land gave otherwise indigent men sufficient freedom to refuse full-time jobs. Many a pro-enclosure tract included a homily on the benefits to the poor of being compelled to work all day, every day, for someone else.[3]

Many farmers needed reliable help with stock, which had to be attended to at set hours every day, and jobs such as ploughing and sowing, which had to be done when the season was right. Servants provided a pool of reliable, full-time labour for those whose families were insufficient to cope with the demands of their holdings, or whose social status or another occupation prevented them taking part directly themselves.[4] They expanded their households artificially, the better off taking in others' children, whose labour was not needed at home and who could not earn their keep within their natural families. Masters thus assumed quasi-parental rights over, and duties towards, their servants, which placed them in an entirely different position from labourers paid by the day or the piece.[5] Peter Laslett pointed out that this had the effect of an informal income tax, with each household matching its numbers to its means.[6] Servants had to be kept all year round, however, regardless of the amount of work to be done, so where timeliness was less crucial, jobs were better done by outsiders on short contracts. Doubtless some of these outsiders worked frequently for one man and came to look on him as their main source of wages, but they were not tied to one employer and constituted no part of anyone else's household, as a servant did.

Servants gave up their independence in return for security, but this did not mean a permanent renunciation, or their domination as one clearly identifiable group by another. They reclaimed their independence by the simple act of setting up their own households and so leaving service behind, usually on marriage. Their period in service was not a loss to them, but a preparation for adult life, and as such it attracted many small farmers' children, who were not driven by necessity, as well as the poor. Servants received better food than poor parents encumbered by large families could provide, and they could pass their adolescent years without excessive supervision, or the tensions often to be found in the family home, and yet they were not thrown entirely onto their own resources. At first their cash wages barely covered essential needs, but as they got older and their wages grew, an increasing proportion could be saved to form the basis of later independence. Their absence from home, moreover, ensured a better life for the rest of the family, partly because wages went further, but also because the small cottages of the poor simply did not have the space for large numbers of near-adults.[7]

Servants, moreover, tended to marry late and this in itself limited the size of families somewhat. They had no need to marry to get away from the parental home, and the longer they remained servants, the better placed they were when they did marry. In 1900 Arthur Wilson Fox was still able to report from Cumberland, north Lancashire, and Westmorland that

> in these counties there are a great number of small farms worked almost
> entirely by the farmer and his family. Many of these farmers have risen from
> the ranks of farm servants, and there are numerous instances in which they
> have become farmers on a large scale. While in the position of unmarried farm
> servants, they are able to save money if they are careful, as they have little to
> spend it on except clothes. Not infrequently a hired man marries a young
> woman who has also saved money as a farm servant or dairymaid.[8]

Couples without similar opportunities, or without the inclination to make the sacrifices and take the risks associated with taking a farm, could still, as John Tuke reported from North Yorkshire in 1800, 'save in a few years sufficient to enable them to marry, and start as housekeepers, in possession of the necessary requisites of their situation.'[9] Both servant and master had reasons for taking part in the yearly bond, and Ann Kussmaul has traced, with great thoroughness, the hiring of servants right through the early modern period up to the middle of the nineteenth century. The system was already in existence even before this period, and it remained a fundamental component in the agricultural scene. On a national scale she traced a cycle of increasing and decreasing usage from a high point in the mid-fifteenth century, through a trough in the mid-seventeenth, to a renewed peak in the mid-eighteenth. When labour was scarce, farmers hired more servants to ensure they would never be without the labour they needed, whereas a glut of workers had the opposite effect. The cost of feeding servants all year, relative to the cash wages labourers received, was another determining factor, but until the late eighteenth century there never seemed any possibility of farmers deciding to dispense with servants altogether.

From this point on, however, the fortunes of servants in the north and south diverged sharply, and by the mid-nineteenth century servants were a dead or dying breed throughout the south and east, and where they seemed to survive, it was because they had lost most of their protection as servants. This is not to say that before 1750 every county used farm servants as the East Riding did later, or that after 1750 there were only two or three possible variant courses of experience; but the East Riding, almost alone among arable counties, preserved a remarkable continuity with its past in the structuring of its labour force. It is easy to assume that rural societies are alike and unchanging, but even the most stable was not static. The different soils of each area dictated different farming practices, and every county had its own customs and access to different markets. Even individual parishes had their own mix of social factors that all influenced their particular social and economic structure.

Although the East Riding kept its servants, it was subjected to most of the same pressures which wiped them out elsewhere. The typical East Riding farm of, say, 1780 was, by later standards, a small one selling a low proportion of its produce.[10] On the Wolds especially, farmsteads often stood in village centres away from their fields and large areas were left unploughed. The next decades were to see, as elsewhere, enclosure, engrossment of holdings, the creation of many isolated farms, improvements in techniques, and the use of better implements.[11] Why a process of change affecting the whole country should have had such divergent effects requires explanation.

Probably the single most important factor was the general rise in population and the ability of each county to cope with it. Nationally, an increase from nine million in 1801 to eighteen million in 1851 was recorded, while the East Riding, not counting Hull, rose from 80,000 to 136,000 over the same period. Unless there was some equally dramatic increase in the number of jobs available, it is clear that any existing labour shortages would soon become surpluses, and this, as we have seen, always led farmers to consider a reduction in servant numbers. In areas where industry existed extra workers who were coming onto the labour market could be absorbed, but industry was largely, and increasingly, located in the north and in the west midlands. Competition from factories caused one after another of the domestic or cottage industries of rural areas, like chair or lace making, to decline leaving whole counties more dependent on farming than they had been for centuries. Moreover, farming itself was changing, a process symbolized by the spate of enclosures at the end of the eighteenth century and the start of the nineteenth. Commons and waste land were vanishing, while the game laws were used increasingly to exact savage retribution on those who took wild birds or animals to supplement their reduced earnings.

In areas where farmers had to compete for labour, wages followed one course, while they followed another where there was less competition. James Caird was the first to attract wide attention to the fact that a gulf was opening between the two areas. He prepared a map showing a high wage north and a low wage south,[12] and many concluded that pastoral farming, which they assumed to be the rule throughout the north, was somehow capable of paying, and also willing to pay, its workers up to twice as much as the rate recorded in some southern counties, which were assumed to be arable. This was absurd, for both London and the industrial towns of South Wales also maintained high wage zones of some size around themselves, and the correlation between pastoral counties and high wages was very slight as Caird's map, in fact, showed.

Far more revealing was the link between industry, on whatever scale, and wages.[13] A single brickworks or a quarry, or one of the agricultural implement manufacturing concerns which developed as the century wore on, could raise wages over small areas, even in the southern counties. In the East Riding, Marshall's flax rotting and scutching works, near Patrington, caused a general 12 to 15 per cent increase nearby in the 1840s.[14] In a county such as Warwickshire, the north was covered by industrial sprawl and farm wages were the equal of any, but the south was entirely rural, with very low wages and poor conditions of employment. Joseph Arch came from this part of the country and his career and outlook show how typical he was of southern farming, where industry was so slight and the rural hinterland so large that its effects were utterly dissipated.

Matters were made worse because migration both within the south and out of it, which poverty might have been expected to increase, actually slowed down in the early nineteenth century, in contrast to the north.[15] Traditionally, London had been a magnet for people from a wide area, but the rate of immigration into the city slowed markedly. Most southern parishes where there were no artificial restrictions experienced a rapid growth in the labour force with no corresponding increase in jobs, a situation made worse by the end of the French Wars. Heavy recruiting for the armed forces had relieved the pressure for a while, but now all these men were demobilized to seek civilian jobs.[16]

Farmers' incomes had soared during the previous two decades, for not only were there plenty of government contracts for supplying the armed forces, but everything else seemed to work towards high prices. With the growth in population, Britain had ceased to be a regular grain exporter by the 1790s, and had instead become a regular importer.[17] Harvests were generally bad, sometimes for several years together, and the wars interfered with the supply of grain from the continent. The growing towns needed feeding but produced nothing themselves. There were fortunes to be made from corn-growing and the temptation to join in was irresistible. Almost any scheme to grow extra grain was lucrative. Enclosures multiplied to give farmers both the freedom to cash in on the trend as they liked, and also access to previously unploughed commons and waste. Much seeming improvement was made with no thought of the patriotism and scientific progress urged by Arthur Young and his fellows. By ploughing ancient pasture on poor soil, in all too many cases individuals simply used up, in a few years of reckless cropping, resources of fertility which had taken centuries to lay down. This certainly happened on the Yorkshire Wolds.[18]

The return to peace was also accompanied by a return of good harvests, and by a decline in fertility of the marginal enclosures. The artificial nature of the hyperprosperity of war-time was exposed. Farming had been like a hot-house plant sustained in a wholly artificial environment requiring only a minor change in circumstances to cause it to wither. The wilder investments made on borrowed money often ceased to pay, and many farmers had put themselves in the ridiculous position of seeming and feeling straitened under conditions that would have been called auspicious by any of their forebears. The famine prices of wartime had fallen, but they had not collapsed.

This was the most prolonged period of natural agricultural prosperity recorded in this country in modern peace-time. Circumstances now made Britain truly an island in food terms, for grain imports, insignificant in war-time compared to demand,[19] were then prevented by the Corn Laws until natural population growth in the traditional European suppliers had used up all exportable surpluses. Russia, the United States of America, and the British colonies eventually filled the gap, but distance and inadequate technology retarded their entry onto the scene.[20] Only when transcontinental railways opened up the vast wheatgrowing areas inland, and when steamships reduced freight costs, would foreign grain begin to pour in. The meat trade was protected even longer, until the 1890s, when reliable refrigeration methods were discovered.[21] Thereafter, a true world market in food began to establish itself, one so large that farmers in this country could not greatly affect prices, which were much lower than British prices had been in isolation.

In many southern parts the farm servant was an immediate victim of farmers' perception of themselves as sufferers of severe economic difficulties. During the wars the larger farmers had been able to aspire towards gentry status, and all farmers had raised their social expectations along with their incomes. From the seventeenth century there had been a growing tendency for farmers to wish to separate themselves and their families from their servants. This now became a conviction that they could no longer share their houses with rough, uncouth youngsters, and that they could not expect their wives to look after them.[22] The food consumed by farmworkers could be profitably sold on the open market instead. Adopting a higher life style meant committing themselves to a cash economy in a way they never had before, and their expectations were often incompatible with the incomes available after the war. When the flow of cash dwindled they often could not pull their horns in, but must press further on, like someone running downhill who realises that he cannot stop without falling, and so runs ever faster, hoping to keep upright until the ground levels out and he can halt safely. So the pressure to cease

48 Horses in the foldyard. In summer the horses slept outside and were called in, as here, for their breakfast, often with a shout of 'Coo up'. The sight of one of these giants rolling over like a dog helps to explain the affection most lads had for their teams. (Taken in south Holderness, probably in 1909.)

49 Plough harness. This was the simplest 'gearing' used, consisting of the collar, chain traces to pull the plough, and a 'plough back band' to prevent the traces tangling with the horse's hind legs, though some preferred to keep things even simpler by not using the back bands. When not in use, the traces were hooked onto the back band. The horses were driven by plough strings with handles to slip over the wrist, though with a good team they were hardly necessary. Note that there is no decoration on the harness for fieldwork. This photograph was taken at Manor Farm, Thixendale in the 1890s, and shows what is probably barley stubble being ploughed for winter wheat.

50 Waggon harness. This was the most elaborate gearing used in the county, with a special back band to hold up the leather reins, and breechings round the horses' rumps. The breechings are connected via the collar to the front of the pole to allow the horses to push a waggon backwards as well as pull it forwards. This was the only way to brake a waggon, though in descending hills the rear wheels were also locked by chains, and a skid was put under them to save them from wear. The driver is standing on the waggon 'shears', a dangerous practice when it was moving as it went under the waggon body when corners were turned. This waggon, loaded with coal, was photographed in front of Manor Farm, Thixendale in the late 1890s.

51 Shaft harness. Because of the use of draught poles on so many implements, and especially on waggons, this gearing was less used in the East Riding than in most counties. The shafts are held up by a chain over the horse's back, and so it wears a cart saddle with a channel to take the weight. Breechings were essential as in waggon harness, but in this case they were attached to the shafts by the dangling chains. The horse pulled the implement or cart by other chains that ran from the hooks visible near the bottom of the collar to the shafts. Note that in this case the horse has a brass on its forehead and two more below the collar, so it may have been going off the farm. (Taken in the stackyard at Manor Farm, Thixendale, in the late 1890s.)

52 The mothers and children of Burton Fleming ready to set out for a day by the sea at Bridlington *c.* 1900. The team is a beautifully matched and highly decorated pair, and the waggon, made by Sisson's of Beswick, would be the best on the farm.

53 Mr Masterman's father with the Shire stallion Hill Top II in south Holderness in 1904 or 1905. Note the heavy feather around the legs which had a tendency to become greasy and cause problems for horselads.

54   Lord Middleton's prize-winning Percheron stallion Dinam Salut with his groom, Mr W. Barnes, at Birdsall in 1931. It was advertised as 'a compact and powerful horse with good action, sound and very quiet. This horse is broken to harness and has been in regular shaft work since last season'. Like most large estates in the nineteenth and early twentieth centuries, the Birdsall estate prided itself on its stud farm but by the 1930s only one or two stallions were kept. In earlier years, few would have been used for work as this one evidently was.

55   Pure bred farm horses were a rarity in the county, but here on the left is a Shire and on the right, a Clydesdale. The favourite workhorse was a cross and only stallions normally had a pedigree. (Taken near Garton in Holderness around 1920.)

56 A mare suckling her foal in south Holderness in the 1930s.

57 This photograph was variously identified as either a young Shire/Clydesdale cross stallion travelling round the farms with its groom, or as a three-year-old horse in breaking tackle, in which case the handler would probably be a foreman. It is undoubtedly part of the set taken at Manor Farm, Thixendale in the late 1890s and whether or not of a stallion, it does show the harness used to keep young horses under restraint during breaking. The straps from the bit to the girth band kept the horse's head down, which makes it easier to control, but even so the relative size and weight of the horse compared to the man shows why breaking was best done as early as possible.

hiring servants was maintained even though it was an inappropriate response to a deflationary era. None of the money coming into farming was willingly shared with the workforce, creating a yawning gulf in the village community. It did not occur all at once, but on a different scale depending on local conditions, and everywhere it was the largest farmers who set the pace, while small farmers might well have been content to carry on as before.[23]

In the 1870s, when prices also dropped alarmingly, many southern farmers on difficult land went bankrupt and holdings became hard, or impossible, to let locally. New tenants were sought in Scotland, Wales, and in the hill farming districts of the north. By and large, they made the farms pay, but they did so by using their own labour and that of their families, by working long hours, and living frugally.[24] On these marginal farms the aspirations of the farmer to the squirearchy had made the difference between success and failure, and though on better land it might not bring bankruptcy, even there it ate money and so ensured that there was never any readiness to better the lot of the poor. Farmers and farmworkers were becoming separate castes fixed by inheritance,[25] and the intercourse implied in taking servants into farmhouses seemed increasingly offensive and inappropriate.

That there was no longer any need to hire servants can readily be shown. It is true that there usually seemed to be very little actual unemployment among villagers, but this masked a great deal of underemployment. Under the Old Poor Law, parishes accepted responsibility for the survival of their own inhabitants in times of need. Anyone genuinely in need was assisted from a rate levied on the parish where they had a settlement. In the early nineteenth century, as hardship grew it was generally seen as desirable to supplement inadequate family wages, as well as to aid the totally workless. This had two profound effects.

Firstly, as servants gained a settlement in a parish by serving for a year, but were never eligible for a wage supplement, farmers who hired them were therefore entirely responsible for their wages. This also created the possiblity that the servants would have to be relieved by the parish if they failed to find work when their contracts ran out.[26] This was a strong incentive to cease hiring.

Secondly, farmers could easily manipulate the system to their advantage if they hired only labourers. They were eligible for wage support, and it was paid by all ratepayers, not just farmers. If the farmers could go further and clear their own parish of labourers they gained even more, for the burden of relief missed them entirely. Taken together, and reinforced by traditional attitudes, this led to a situation where work was found for everyone most of the time, but at very low wages supplemented by meagre allowances and all were treated as labourers. In a subsistence, or near–subsistence, economy, this approach was sensible since every-one then shared in the work and in its rewards, but in nineteenth-century England it was utterly inappropriate. Only a residual proportion of the rewards was being made available and the workmen were deprived of all bargaining power, since the work of most farms would benefit rather than suffer if one or two men were sacked out of hand.

By the time of the New Poor Law, a sort of equilibrium had been established in labour surplus areas, with this underemployment built into it. The extent of it can be judged at peak times, notably harvest, because in a county that normally had a real job for every worker, extra hands were always needed. In the East Riding, tramps and Irishmen were hired in large numbers even when binders, the ultimate in horse-powered mechanization, were in general use, in this century.[27] Where such men were not needed there must normally be a large surplus of labour, regardless of the numbers actually jobless. As the nineteenth century progressed this was true of increasingly large areas. As late as the 1880s Flora Thompson recalled Irishmen being employed around Banbury in Oxfordshire, but by 1902, none were hired anywhere in the county. Indeed by that date the few who helped out in Hertfordshire and Middlesex were the only ones south of Warwickshire and Northamptonshire, and even Nottinghamshire hired very few.[28]

With plenty of men so much in need of work that the threat to mechanize threshing could cause riots across southern England, no farmer there ran any risks by not having servants living on the farm. It is surely significant that the counties which experienced serious disturbances in the Captain Swing riots, and in the rick burning that accompanied rural discontent, were overwhelmingly those in the south and east where farm servants were no longer hired.[29] Moreover, the institution had lost much of its point for those taking part in it there. The idea of saving for a farm was largely ridiculous with wages so low and with the new style of farming. Even saving on a more modest scale was difficult.

It had also ceased to be attractive as a balanced package of rights and duties because, where it did survive (and in places it was surprisingly tenacious),[30] it was dramatically modified by the farmers. First of all, they increasingly paid board wages, that is, they no longer lodged and fed their servants, but paid them the farmers' valuation of their keep. Theoretically the servant could then contract with anyone willing to provide board and lodging, but even the most generous valuation was at cost price, allowing nothing for the fact that the farmer used home-produced food and boarded servants in his own house for his own reasons, not for direct gain. No outsider would provide lodgings at that rate, and there was often no-one available to do so, for the servant was still a servant, working long hours and therefore needing to be near at hand.[31] In 1869 a farming cyclopedia commented on 'the condition of young men employed as farm servants in one of the southern counties, who, being paid board wages, club together to have their comfortless meal cooked in a neighbouring cottage, with no house to call their home; [they are] left to sleep in an outhouse or a hay loft.' This echoed an address to the Sittingbourne (Kent) Agricultural Association on the dehumanizing lot of the farm servant in that county in 1856,[32] and the experience of Joseph Bailey of Dorset, born in 1839, whose recollections of his days as a thirteen-year-old farm servant were published by the Revd A.H. Baverstock:

> He had 2s a week, with a place to sleep in over the milk house, and he had to keep himself in food and clothes. 'It did keep me in bread, sir, and that were all. For I had to keep a bit for a pair o' trousers and shoe leather.' At fifteen he secured another place at 3s 6d a week and gave his employer notice. 'He told me I were a bad buoy, and said I mid ha' stopped on and had the same money with him.' The lad accordingly stopped on, with the increased wages. But as soon as the farmer was able to find another boy at the lower rate of wages,

young Joseph was told he was not wanted, and he had to go and hunt for another place at the same munificent rate of wages.[33]

To talk of servantry surviving in the south can mislead because it implies that the essential features of the yearly bond were preserved, and mostly they were not. A fascinating survival from east Wiltshire is a completed pre-printed contract form, dated 1893, for a yearly hire, reproduced as figure 7. It carefully and specifically removed all the servant's customary rights. He was available to do any job at any time, as required, and he could be asked to lodge on the farm, and to move from

MEMORANDUM OF AGREEMENT made this *twentieth* day of *September* 1889 between *William Bowle Gauntlett*, hereinafter called the MASTER, of the one part, and *Andrew Couzens for his son Jesse Couzens*, hereafter called the SERVANT, of the other part.

The SERVANT hereby agrees to serve the MASTER from *Old Michaelmas, 1889*, to *Old Michaelmas, 1890*, to the best of his ability, more particularly in the capacity of *Cowman*, but also in any work that may be required of him within his power when not employed in the particular service for which he is hired, and to work and lodge, when required, on any of the farms in the occupation of the MASTER.

The SERVANT further agrees to be always at his work *at all hours and times required by the Master or his Agent, and to milk not less than ten cows at a milking and more if required. To be cleanly, quiet and quick in milking, not to ill-treat the cattle, or to use profane or indecent language.*

In return for the above services the Master agrees to pay the Servant *Seven Shillings per week to Old Lady Day next thence to Old Michaelmas, 1890, Eight Shillings per week* And at the expiration of his term, if he shall have conducted himself to the entire satisfaction of his MASTER during the said term, AND ONLY IN SUCH CASE to give him over and above his wages, *Thirty-five Shillings. It is also agreed that any cow found to be only partially milked the Servant shall submit to be fined a sum not exceeding Two Shillings and Sixpence.*

IT IS ALSO AGREED:- That should the said SERVANT absent himself at any time (by being late in the morning or otherwise) from his work, it shall be lawful for the MASTER, as he may see fit, either to rescind this agreement or to deduct from the weekly wages of the said Servant a sum not exceeding *twopence* for every quarter of an hour he is so absent.

IT IS ALSO HEREBY AGREED:- that should the said SERVANT be prevented by accident, sickness, or any other cause whatever, from attending to his duties, an amount equivalent to the time he is so incapacitated shall be deducted from his wages; and it is further agreed that should there be any negligence or misconduct on the part of the SERVANT, the MASTER shall have full power to set aside this agreement, and the SERVANT shall make good any loss the MASTER may sustain from either of these causes.

In witness thereof the said parties have herewith set their hands:-

Witness to Signatures -	W. B. GAUNTLETT
WILFRID F. GAUNTLETT	ANDREW COUZENS
	JESSE COUZENS

Source : reproduced from The English Land Restoration League Special Report, 1893: *Among the Agricultural Labourers with the Red Vans* (1894), p. 16.

This is a transcription of the original, not a direct reproduction. The originals were printed in books of quarto, tear-out sheets. Sections in italics filled in in handwriting.

Fig. 7. Written hiring contract from Wiltshire, 1889–90

farm to farm. Yet no mention is made of providing food or decent accommodation and all the wages were to be paid in cash. The wages varied from winter to summer, and roughly nine per cent was held by the farmer as a bond for good behaviour. There was to be no payment during sickness, and the servant was fully responsible for any damage he did while on his master's business.[34] Lateness and poor work brought fines and the farmer could sack him at will, but the servant could not give notice.

In a pastoral area like the south west there were not the same peaks of frenetic activity as there were on arable farms. It was no great advantage to a farmer to be able to hire and fire from day to day, and a shepherd who knew his flock and his fields was worth more than one, just as skilled, who did not. It did not suit the men, but they lacked even the power to do as other southerners did and demand to be made proper labourers if they could not be proper servants. Only the rise of trade unionism enabled them to shake off this bastardized remnant of the yearly bond, aptly called 'slavery in east Wiltshire' by the English Land Restoration League. This was the yearly bond Joseph Arch knew best, so it is not surprising that he saw it as 'a great curse to the labourer,' and the yearly contract as 'always too good a security for me.'[35] The courts became policemen ensuring that labourers were subordinated to their employers, rather than mediators in a reasonably equal contest.

In the north, in contrast, there was always enough genuine work available to keep farmers hiring on the old terms. The growth and spread of industry provided the bulk of the jobs that were needed, and it must be remembered that much of it, especially textiles and mining, began by sprawling through a semi-rural country-side. Towns were growing fast as financial and marketing centres, or as locations for certain key processes such as cloth finishing, but the impact of industrialization was not limited to compact, urban zones. As late as the early twentieth century, Fred Kitchen (born in 1890) experienced the effects of the extension of the Yorkshire coalfield into his native Doncaster area. He worked on farms for two years from the age of thirteen, but then went to help build the Hull and Barnsley Railway. After six months he returned to farming, but then spent two years on building-sites from 1910 before becoming a miner. He finally returned to farming for the bulk of his adult years. During all these career changes he had never had to move any great distance.[36]

Industry did not reach into the East Riding, but the effects of industrial growth in the West Riding were carried closer than might be supposed. However, we have seen that in Warwickshire mere proximity did not guarantee that an industrial area would maintain a high level of wages. Here, the crucial point was that though the West Riding towns provided relatively few jobs for East Riding men[37], they offered an ideal market for everything the East Riding could produce, and the county had the scope for a rapid and spectacular increase in production, and hence employment. It did not become a county wedded to agriculture because it had nothing better to turn to but specialized in the industry that suited it best in order to exploit a clear opening in the economy of the region.

The Wolds were the most visible symbol of the increased intensity of production, with the sheepwalks and rabbit warrens of the eighteenth century turned into permanent and highly productive arable through the careful application of scientific rotations. The Vale of York saw most of its sour, barren pasture drained and ploughed, and though Holderness had no scope for such dramatic improvements, drainage steadily increased its arable acreage.[38] Until the eighteenth century, farming in the county was backward, with the evidence of its farmhouses suggesting that a significant group of prosperous farmers did not appear before then.[39] Progress was rapid thereafter and of a type to create jobs rather than destroy them. Both servants and labourers were required in larger numbers, since the miles of new hedges and ditches all needed the latter's attention. For servants, the Wolds was the area most reliant on them, with its new farmsteads isolated from the villages and their pool of labour.[40] East Riding farmers experienced the same desires to improve their status, and to distance themselves socially from the developing rural working-class, as did their counterparts elsewhere. Their need for farm servants, however, led them to seek a way to separate themselves while still maintaining the traditional yearly hire.

The foreman proved to be the key figure in this. In the seventeenth and eighteenth centuries, as far as is known, he was a single man employed as a hireling by a few large farmers like Henry Best of Elmswell, near Driffield. From Best's unique record of his farming practices, we can see that he hired his foreman at Martinmas with his other servants, offering five marks [£3.33] for the year, with two shillings or half a crown, 'to a godspenny if hee bee such an one as can sowe, mowe, stacke pease, goe well with fower horse, and hayth been used to marketting and the like, for nowe of late wee imploy and trust our foreman with the sowinge of all our seede.' The next highest wage paid was fifty shillings or four marks [£2.67], with a similar godspenny, which is a substantial drop. Even though the foreman undertook exceptional duties compared to other servants, he was clearly associated both with working the horses and with yearly hiring[41] so he resembled the twentieth-century waggoner as much as the hind. In the late eighteenth century, where there was insufficient horse work to justify a foreman on a large Wolds farm, the shepherd might be made the senior man.[42]

The hiring of foremen spread in the nineteenth century but farmers overwhelmingly boarded their lads themselves. As late as 1848, a description of the East Riding farm labour force, supported by a detailed study of Hornsea, simply does not mention hinds. William Blades remembered the boarding of lads with hinds as a new system in his youth, in the mid-century, and in 1863 Mary Simpson was discussing as a new idea the possibility of foremen taking on this role.[43] Even during this century, Mr Johnson said:

> Any farm any size that day had a foreman of one sort or another. Sometimes he wasn't a married man . . . ., what they called a single foreman, I mean, he lived with the lads, you see. And they'd separate bedrooms . . . . There was odd places where a farm foreman, he just lived in a cottage on his own, you see, and the lads lived in the farm house – just odd places, but nine times out of ten, you know, if there was a hind, he boarded the lads.

Mr Baines was hired as a single farm foreman in the 1920s but went on to work as a waggoner, by choice, which is a crucial comment on the difference between a single foreman and a hind.[44] Newspaper reports of Thirsk hirings, which served a wide area, regularly quoted separate rates for foremen and hinds, as for instance in 1910 when 'managing hinds' were being offered 24s to 26s per week while 'capable farm foremen' could expect £26 to £30 per year.[45] Hinds' rates were also quoted a year later at Howden, a rare reference from within the East Riding, though foremen's rates were quoted frequently at the turn of the century.[46] The hind's married status decisively divided him from the lads he boarded, but his own position, with its constant availability for work, his residence on the farm, and the requirement for a month's notice join together with his continued involvement in some hirings to show a strong residual affinity with the single farm foreman from whom he seems to have evolved.

The term 'hind' is itself an odd one. It was widely used in the far north of England as a synonym for farm servant,[47] but this usage penetrated into Yorkshire only in those parts of the North Riding which generally followed the practices of their northern neighbours. In the early years of this century it was used for supervisory staff only in the East Riding and south Northumberland.[48] The word may have been borrowed from further north to differentiate the married foreman, and it seems to have been little used in the early nineteenth century. However, in 1802, foremen were boarding lads for their employers on Sunk Island and they were already called hinds. This is the first clear reference to the system that I have seen, and it is interesting that the title was already associated with it.[49] Henry Best referred to his chief servant unequivocally as a foreman,[50] but hinds of a sort appear in the wage assessments of 1593, 1669, and 1679 drawn up by the Justices of the Peace, with rates quoted for two supervisory grades, 'a bailiff of husbandry, called an overman, that is hired to a gentleman or rich yeoman that doth not labour himself but putteth his whole trust to his servants' and 'the chief hind of a husbandman that overseeth his servants.'[51] Neither of these definitions is the equivalent of the twentieth-century hind's job, though both contain important elements of it.

The word is Old English in origin, denoting a member of a family or a household. In the north and in Scotland it became particularly associated with married farm servants who might be above the ordinary farm servants, as a journeyman was above apprentices. It was also used for a bailiff or a steward from 1495. How the word survived in the East Riding to become so welded to this one particular role, which only existed on any scale for a century or less, is unknown. It is also impossible to say if it was influence from further north which associated it with married men who did not normally become farm servants in the East Riding at the time. On the other hand, not all the men Henry Best hired on a yearly contract were single.[52] All that can be said with certainty is that a single farm foreman would normally have stood in a very awkward position with regard to the labourers unless it was clear that his authority extended only to the horselads. That the labourers had not been part of the regular labour force in earlier times is suggested by the wage assessments where their rates are all listed separately as piece rates, and they would normally have worked to the farmers' instructions. There were very few foremen anyway, and they would be men who had never married, widowers who re-entered farm service, or good servants using a few extra years to build up their savings for a farm of their own.

By the increasing employment of foremen, and the use of married rather than single men farmers drew back from direct involvement in farm work. It was a gradual process that had not extended to small farmers when living in ceased and it was accomplished in stages rather than in one leap, with the farmer separating himself from his servants within the farmhouse as the first step. The lads had their own part of the house, meals were eaten separately and there was little social mixing. As the farmer ceased to function as head of the servant household, the foreman naturally took his place and as they built new houses for themselves, it was a natural step to leave the lads in the old one and use it as a tied house to allow a married man to take on the foreman's job.[53] This involved an increasing share of the running of the farm on a day to day basis, including the control of the labourers, so it was important that his standing should be increased. Crucially, the farmer had not tried to escape his responsibilities to the lads, as happened in Cambridgeshire, for instance, where the lads paid the foreman for their keep.[54] The East Riding farmer merely delegated his duties to the hind. If a dispute went to court, it was the farmer who was accused of breach of contract, not the hind. There was no hint of the board wages system, and much of the food continued to be provided by the farm.

Of all the English compromises intended to preserve the hiring of farm servants living on the farm, this seems to have been the only one to take on a life of its own. By 1914, the original system was looked on as an oddity in the East Riding and the hind was taken for granted by the lads. It must be said that in 1911 the Census reveals that less than a third of all farmers had a foreman, but it was only these farms which hired lads in any numbers.[55] Those farmers without foremen were frequently without much labour. There was no difficulty in meeting the demand for hinds, for where the best eighteenth-century servants had looked at least to become small-holders, the waggoner of our own century had few prospects other than working for wages for the rest of his life. The hind's job gave an outlet, albeit a poorer one, for his ambition and management skills. In Scotland there were also areas where hiring practices remained little altered during the nineteenth century, and there seem to be strong parallels in their social stability.[56]

For a few, becoming a hind provided the last remaining chance to save to become a farmer, or to set up an independent existence as a carrier or dealer or some such. It was all most labourers could do to get by, but a foreman could continue to save money even while supporting a family, and now and then a chance arose to take a farm tenancy. However, such chances were infrequent and might not prove worthwhile. Mr Johnson, speaking from experience, said:

> A little farmer, say fifty or sixty acre, well he was at a disadvantage really – he couldn't afford to employ a man and . . . there's lots of jobs one man is at a disadvantage by himself. . . . The fifty acre farm, it was only a – well, they made a poor living a lot of 'em. They'd have been better working for a labourer's wage. But my idea was a farm under about ninety or a hundred acres was no good. . . .
>
> There was this problem and all – a man, say he was a farm lad and then he got married . . . , he had it in his head, which I had, 'Well, I'll have a farm o' my own some day,' but by the time he got money scratched up to take that

farm he was getting on. He was maybe forty or fifty year old, his best days had gone, you see, and he hadn't time to do much, you see. I mean, his time was going and, you know, he was getting so he couldn't work so hard. I was forty year old before I got on my own.

Many ex-foremen also found that while their grasp of farming techniques was sound, they had never had the chance to master the entrepreneurial side of the farmer's role. Many could not adjust to being their own masters. In Mr Tate's experience, most ex-foremen ended up working for others again. Indeed, the odds were stacked against them because they only got their chance when no-one else could be found. They were offered the farms others had spoiled, or they were used to keep tenancies in cultivation during depressions, as happened on a large scale in the 1930s.[57] For the majority, the idea of taking a farm was neither practical nor, on the terms it would be offered, desirable. The hind's position was not really an extension of the ladder of social advancement, keeping it in touch with the farmers' more exalted position. For most it was a platform on top of the ladder that provided a relatively satisfying and economically secure way of spending their mature years.

A sense of purpose was maintained in the servant system, motivating lads to bear with it, and since they were undoubtedly living better in the farmhouses than they would have in their families' cottages, there was no need for farmers to resort to coercion to keep up yearly hiring. The outlook of farm lads undoubtedly moved a few steps towards that of an industrial working-class as their status as permanent wage earners became clear and unarguable in the nineteenth century, but before 1914 it was only a few steps. The vast changes of the next quarter of a century showed how much of the total journey had still to be made.

On their side, the farmers needed the lads. Horses had been used in agriculture for centuries, but up to the eighteenth century oxen provided much of the draught power and men's own labour was used directly on a large scale.[58] The spread of capitalist farming, aiming to produce for sale, not for consumption, needed the extra speed and manoeuvrability of the horse, just as recent developments have only been possible because of the extra power made available by modern tractors. With horses it was possible to improve old implements and devise new ones, and the timeliness their speed made possible was crucial to the new cropping systems and techniques. The ox provided draught power when it was needed, which was mostly during ploughing and harvest, but it remained part of the meat-producing livestock. The horse provided draught power and nothing else[59] while using up the production of at least three acres, which was compensated for by the increased productivity of the remainder. Where it differed crucially from later mechanization was that the horses required a large labour force working long hours to service and work them. The farm servants, supervised by the foreman, were the ideal instrument for meeting these demands.

As the nineteenth century wore on the tide of mechanization did not, as might have been expected, result in the loss of jobs, for in fact, the numbers employed in agriculture increased until the 1850s. Complex machines that saved labour, as well as increasing production, were only seen on any scale in the last quarter of the nineteenth century, and even then they affected mostly casual labourers in counties like the East Riding. There was no threat to the lads, as more horse labour replaced hand labour, in fact more servants were needed, and the proportion of them working amongst the horses rather than the other livestock was greater. Moreover, as holdings increased in size and shrank in numbers, the servants became more concentrated into medium and large groups. Such changes were most obvious on the Wolds where enclosure had dramatic effect, in creating both large new acreages of arable and large new farms, while its existing settlement network was least able to cope.[60]

Cottam and Cowlam were neighbouring townships between Driffield and Malton which show the new system at its most extreme, for neither contained a village settlement. Even Cottam House, at 1,100 acres, was not the largest farm, but the census of 1871 gives a particularly clear picture of its domestic arrangements. Stephen Duggleby, the farmer, lived in a house with his family, served by a governess, three female domestic servants, and three grooms-cum-servants. In the hind house lived John Dunn, aged thirty-six, with his family, and they looked after twelve farm servants, perhaps with the aid of the kitchen maid and the nursemaid who also resided there. The servants were all aged between seventeen and twenty, except for a Norfolk man aged thirty.[61] Here we have a clear break with the traditional role of the farm servant as extra labour on the family farm. Many a small industrial firm employed fewer people.

In Holderness there were far fewer wholly new farms and none of them compared in size with those on the Wolds in size. Because many retained some pasture, they needed fewer horses per acre and fewer farm servants. In 1871, the census returns for Long Riston and Arnold, in the heart of Holderness, list seven farms between 100 and 265 acres. They employed servants in twos, threes, and fours, and only two farms had hinds.[62] It seems natural that the gulf between master and man would widen more slowly than on the Wolds, and less obviously, leaving groups of lads less self-sufficient and less introverted. On Sundays, lads from many farms congregated, whereas on the Wolds individual visiting of friends and relations was the rule. There seems to have been less tension within groups in Holderness as a result of their small size, and there are indications that traditional tales and beliefs survived best here,[63] even in this century, indicating greater continuity between past and present.

In the Vale farms were mostly even smaller, for though large areas of waste were reclaimed, the nineteenth century saw holdings subdivided rather than engrossed. The small family farm remained common and servants were frequently hired in ones and twos. If a boy found a kindly family, no doubt he had a better life than on a large, impersonal farm and he would be closest to the original conception of a farm servant. However, small farmers were no longer subsistence farmers and they were under constant economic pressure. Exploitation of young boys who were isolated and alone was easy, and life could be grim.

In comparing their own lot with that of their fathers and grandfathers, with whom they discussed such matters, the men I talked to felt that the few changes that were apparent were not particularly significant. Compulsory education certainly meant that boys in the twentieth century were less free to do paid work than they had been in the early and mid nineteenth century, but its effects were subtle. William Blades first lived in in 1847, aged eight years, as a general servant, but he was not hired by the year until he was thirteen. Generally, the usual age of first hiring seems to have been around twelve or thirteen, and might have been as late as fourteen, which is actually very similar to the twentieth-century pattern. Ann Kussmaul found this to be true in earlier years as well, and suggested that it was because it was only then that youngsters could literally earn their keep. Before that they lived at home and worked at whatever jobs they could get if they needed to. We have already seen that twentieth-century school children were also expected to fit in a good deal of work, so their lives were less changed than might be expected.[64]

Their treatment on farms probably improved, even though the boys of 1914 were still expected to take chastisement that was very violent by modern standards. Similarly, lads were still required to work very long hours at harvest, and long journeys with waggons might mean a very early start, but in 1800 or 1850 servants were sometimes required to work right round the clock if there was a need, just as their contracts specified. Their diet became a little more varied, but the descriptions of the General Views from a century before were not very different from those of a century later. Crockery replaced wooden utensils on the tables, and sparsely furnished though the twentieth-century men's end was, it was better equipped than in earlier times.[65]

By 1914, bicycles and gramophones were just starting to enter servants' lives, but the impact was slight. Without radios or the cinema, and with newspapers virtually unknown among servants, they remained a part of the traditional culture of the East Riding. They had little contact with a wider national culture or that of any group within it, though they were more ready for that now that schooling had reduced illiteracy and altered their vocabulary (which Mary Simpson had found rendered unintelligible the tracts and reading books she hoped to use in her evening classes).[66] The changes in their way of life reflected, albeit distantly, changes in life throughout the nation, but there was no question of them improving their lot by comparison with any other group. Just enough happened to prevent their way of life becoming intolerably anachronistic, allowing it to hold its own and thus, to those involved, to seem to be unchanging.

Any contemporary would have judged the yearly bond to have adapted itself successfully to cope with the rise of capitalist farming, mechanization, and widespread social change. Even the agricultural depression of the 1870s and onwards, which hit the arable areas hard, had failed to destroy its equilibrium. There seemed no reason why it should not continue adapting itself to provide the young people of the county with jobs and their keep in its unique way. The attack on female hiring had removed women from the hiring fairs, but not from the yearly bond. Farmers were boycotting some of the early hirings, but the genuine nature of the bargaining between master and man remained. Trade unionism had made little impact in the county, for the misery that produced Arch's union and its successors to the south was unknown in the East Riding. There were no specific grievances, like the bondager issue in the north-east, to provide a focus for organization. Farmworkers certainly did not regard their lot as ideal, but the fact that Arch's union made only a minimal impact when it held a series of meetings around the county, and that at a time when it was attracting almost messianic surges of support[67] further south, indicates that there were no grievances East Riding farmworkers felt sufficiently strongly about as a group to set themselves in concerted opposition to their employers.

Notes to Chapter Sixteen

1. Strickland, *General View*, pp. 260–2, for instance, contains little that would have seemed strange in 1914.
2. Armstrong, *Farmworkers*, pp. 20–5. This is the best source of greater detail on the generalized experience of farmworkers. See also A. Kussmaul, *Servants in Husbandry in Early Modern England* (1981), pp. 11–18. This is the basic reference book on servants in the early modern era.
3. See, for instance, Young, *Tour*, vol. I, p. 173, and see also E.P. Thompson, *The Making of the English Working Class* (1963, Penguin 1968), pp. 60–1.
4. See Best, *Farming Book*, Introduction and especially pp. xlvi–xlvii.
5. Snell, *Annals*, pp. 258–9, discusses this question as it relates to apprentices, who were in a very similar position.
6. Laslett, *World*, pp. 64–5 and 79.
7. Strickland, *General View*, p. 261. L.M. Springall, *Labouring Life in a Norfolk Village, 1834-1914* (Woking, 1936), shows what life was like when children could not leave home.
8. *Agricultural Labourers*, p. 14. See also Snell, *Annals*, p. 346, where he lays emphasis on the importance of the girl's savings.
9. J. Tuke, *General View of the Agriculture of the North Riding of Yorkshire* (1800), p. 315.
10. J.R. Mortimer, *A Victorian Boyhood on the Wolds*, ed. J.D. Hicks (Beverley, 1978), pp. 3–13, paints a very similar picture even for the 1820s and 30s.
11. Gleave, 'Settlement', 105–118. See Harris, *Rural Landscape*, chap. 3.
12. Caird, *English Agriculture*, frontispiece, and see also pp. 510–3.
13. See E.H. Hunt, *Regional Wage Variations in England* (1974), esp. chap. 1.
14. Caird, *English Agriculture*, pp. 304–7.
15. See A. Redford, *Labour Migration in England, 1800–1850*, revised and ed., W. Chaloner (Manchester, 1964), pp. 97–117.
16. E.L. Jones, 'The Agricultural Labour Market in England, 1793–1872', *Econ. Hist. Rev.*, 2nd Series, XVII (1964–5), 322–38.
17. B.R. Mitchell and P. Deane, *Abstract of British Historical Statistics* (1962), pp. 94–7.
18. See G.E. Mingay, ed., *The Agricultural State of the Kingdom*, 1816 (Bath, 1970), pp. vii, xiv and 361. See also Leatham, *General View*, pp. 38, 44–5, and 50, and Strickland, *General View*, pp. 89–97 and 106–8.
19. Mingay, *Kingdom*, p. vii.
20. S. Fairlie and P.J. Perry, *British Agriculture, 1875–1914* (1973), p. 20.
21. P.J. Perry, *British Farming in the Great Depression, 1870–1914* (Newton Abbott, 1974), p. 51 onwards and p. xxi.
22. W. Cobbett, *Rural Rides* (1830, Penguin ed. 1967), pp. 226–8 provides a trenchant contemporary view. Obelkevitch, *Rural Society*, p. 97 gives an interestingly different slant by stressing that the farmers were now placing their family ties above their communal responsibilities, part of a general social trend discussed on pp. 23–7.
23. T.E. Kebbel, *The Old and the New English Country Life* (1891), pp. 108–18. See also Mortimer, *Boyhood*, p. 6.
24. Perry, *Farming*, pp. 98–101.
25. See A.W. Ashby, 'The Position and Problem of the Farmworker in England and Wales', *International Labour Review*, 31 (1935), 320. See also Armstrong, *Farmworkers*, p. 148.
26. C. Howard, 'Farming at Scoreby', in his *A General View of the East Riding of Yorkshire* (1835), 19–20, shows the universality of this problem by recounting that a temporary depression exerted similar pressures even in the East Riding.

27. See E.H. Hunt, 'Labour Productivity in English Agriculture, 1850–1914', *Econ. Hist. Rev.*, 2nd Series, XX (1967), 280–292.
28. Thompson, *Lark Rise,* pp. 485–7. See also Redford, *Migration*, pp. 141–9.
29. See E. Hobsbawm and G. Rude, *Captain Swing* (1969), chap. 10, and especially the maps on pp. 199 and 202. Snell, *Annals*, pp. 94–5 and 337, provides new information showing the East Riding with one foot in the north, and the other in the eastern arable area.
30. B. Short, 'The Decline of Living-in Servants in the Transition to Capitalist Farming: a Critique of the Sussex Evidence', *Sussex Archaeological Collections*, CXXII (1984), 147–64, is a detailed account of a strong enclave of continued hiring. Sussex was relatively prosperous due to its coastal resorts, P. Horn, *Rural World*, p. 243.
31. Snell, *Annals*, pp. 258–9, notes that traditional apprenticeship declined in a parallel fashion through 'clubbing out', board wages by another name.
32. J.C. Morton (ed), *A Cyclopedia of Agriculture,* 2 vols (Glasgow, 1856), II, p. 172. Quoted in R. Heath, *The English Peasant* (1884), p. 158.
33. Rev. H. Baverstock, *The English Agricultural Labourer* (1912), p. 34.
34. Morton, *Cyclopedia*, II, p. 395, the master was responsible for the acts of his servants unless stated in the contract.
35. Evidence to the Rich Commission (P.P. 1882, XIV) pp. 127–8, q. 60, 227, and p. 140, q. 60, 564.
36. Kitchen, *Brother*, chaps 7 and 12.
37. Holderness, 'Mobility', 450, shows that there was little piecemeal and cumulative rural migration towards towns in the West Riding in the early nineteenth century. See also Redford, *Migration*, p. 127 and map A.
38. Howard, 'Scoreby', 19–20; Harris, *Rural Landscape*, pp. 100–6; and Allison, *Landscape*, pp. 148–151, pp. 158–9 and 167–76.
39. E. Mercer, *English Vernacular Houses* (1975), p. 103.
40. Sheppard, 'Labour Force', 48–50, describes the variation of the East Riding servant to labourer ratio arising from these factors. Snell, *Annals*, p. 219 sounds a cautionary note on the amount of work created by the enclosure process.
41. Best, *Farming Book*, p. 138.
42. Strickland, *General View*, p. 258, Leatham, *General View*, p. 31.
43. Bedell, *Hornsea*, p. 134, Morris, *British Workman*, pp. 55–6, and Simpson *Gleanings*, pp. 42 and 135–6.
44. See Sheppard, 'Labour Force', p. 48.
45. *Yorks. Her.*, supplement, 12 Nov. 1910. See also 15 Nov. 1910, p. 8, and 22 Nov. 1910, p. 8. 16 Nov. 1910, p. 8, also mentions the hiring of hinds at Bedale.
46. *Yorks. Post*, 25 Nov. 1910, p. 10, and see, for instance, 13 Nov. 1890, p. 3; 21 Nov. 1890, p. 3; 25 Nov. 1890, p. 6; 11 Nov. 1890, p. 5; and 28 Nov. 1890, p. 3.
47. H.M. Neville, *A Corner in the North* (1909), chaps 2 to 8 inclusive, is a good account of the system in the far north, with its distinctive use of servants.
48. *Agricultural Labourers*, p. 16.
49. Holderness Agricultural Society, *Extracts*, p. 78.
50. Best, *Farming Book*, various references in the index, but see especially p. 138.
51. J.E.T. Rogers, *A History of Agriculture and Prices,* 7 vols (Oxford, 1886–1902), VI, pp. 686–9; and R.K. Kelsall, 'Two East Yorkshire Wage Assessments, 1669 and 1679,' *Eng. Hist. Rev.* LII (1937), 283–9, the quotation is p.284.
52. Best, *Farming Book*, p. xxxix.
53. See Haggard, *Rural England*, pp. 367–8, for a description of a hind house and its household in this transitional period.
54. *Agricultural Labourers*, p. 15.

55. *Census, 1911*, vol. 10, pt. 2, (P.P. 1913, LXXIX), p. 645.
56. T.M. Devine, 'Social Stability and Agrarian Change in the Eastern Lowlands of Scotland, 1810–40', *Social History*, III (1978), 331–46.
57. See also *Royal Commission*, p. 2, and S. Bensusan, *Latter Day Rural England* (1928), pp. 82–3.
58. Percentages of horses and oxen varied from place to place and over time: J. Langdon, *Horses, Oxen and Technological Innovation* (1986) provides an overview. For the East Riding, see Strickland, *General View*, pp. 230–1; Leatham, *General View*, p. 35; and Howard, *General View*, pp. 118–9.
59. Tuke, *General View, North Riding*, pp. 278–282, compared oxen to horses and concluded that oxen were more economical. He placed no value on the changes in working methods which actually more than compensated for any direct loss. K. Dexter, The Economic Position of the Horse in British Agriculture (unpub. PhD. Thesis, University of Nottingham, 1953) discusses the matter exhaustively in his introduction and in chap. 1.
60. Sheppard, 'Labour Force', pp. 51–4.
61. Census enumerator's notebook, 1871, Cottam township, PRO, RG 10/4809/18–24.
62. Census enumerator's notebook, 1871, Long Riston and Arnold townships, PRO respectively RG 10/4801/ 48–57v and RG 10/4801/58–59v.
63. A. Wilson, 'When Today Meets Yesterday', *The Dalesman*, 24 (1962), 428–30.
64. Morris, *British Workman*, p. 18, Sheppard, 'Labour Force', 47, and Simpson, *Gleanings*, p. 112. Snell, *Annals*, p. 326, gives a table of ages of some nineteenth-century servants.
65. Strickland, *General View*, pp. 208–9 and 261, Morris, *British Workman*, pp. 32–3, and Mortimer, *Boyhood*, pp. 6–7.
66. Simpson, *Gleanings*, p. 3.
67. D. Foster, 'The East Riding Constabulary in the Nineteenth Century', *Northern History* XXI (1985), 209, records police surveillance of union activity in 1872. F. Ross, *Contributions Towards a History of Driffield* and *the Surounding Wolds* (Driffield, 1878), p. 90, notes that 62 people joined the union at Driffield in 1876. J.P. Dunbabin, 'The Revolt of the Field', *Past and Present*, 26 (1963), 68–97 says that the East Riding was the most northerly county to be involved in the unionism, but cites no evidence that would suggest it was seriously involved. Both he and Obelkevitch, *Rural Society*, p. 62, see mass membership of the union as a crucial test for the death of the old deferential relationships between masters and men, of which farm servants had been part. Dunbabin, 'Agricultural Trades Unionism in the 1870s', *Ag. Hist. Rev.*, 16 (1968), 114–41 discusses the relative militancy and quiessence of various districts.

Chapter Seventeen

The End of the Yearly
Bond in the East Riding

The First World War shook the foundations of the relatively isolated and stable community of the East Riding. It had an immediate impact on the horselads far beyond any other civilian group because large numbers of them were liable to immediate military service through membership of the Waggoners' Reserve, an organization unique to the county. Mr Johnson recalled:

> Sir Mark Sykes got that up, from Sledmere. . . . He was in the midst of all the Wolds waggoners and that, that was used to pole waggons, you see. Well the army uses pole waggons – or did then – and . . . , same as a lot more . . . , they were expecting a war. And he thought it would be a good idea to enlist these chaps because they could go [into action] . . . straight away, no training or anything. And he gave 'em a pound and then you didn't do any more, you hadn't to go for any training or owt o' that [but] if war broke out, you were called up straight away. . . .
>
> *Do you think many of them expected to actually be called up?*
>
> It was just easy money. I know a lot as had a shock, a very big shock, when that – they had to go straight away. They joined the A.S.C., the Army Service Corps, you see; they did no fighting or anything like that, they just drove these waggons.

Sir Mark Sykes believed that, in a European war, the British Army would suffer an immediate and severe transport crisis as it tried to move onto the continent. He persuaded a reluctant War Office to let him create this strange corps, which was unrelated to the Territorial Army and which had no real status until war came, because East Riding waggoners were the only farm horsemen in the country used to driving pole waggons. In the event it proved its worth, for 800 waggoners were formed immediately into the Twentieth Company of the Army Service Corps, and when Sykes visited Amiens in September, 1914, they were already in action. None were killed at the front during the war, but Sir Mark's daughter recalled that the men's families resented the call up deeply at the time.[1]

According to Mr Milner so many signed up that 'there was some farms up here that wasn't left with any men at all when they went. And t'middle of – why, just beginning of harvest . . . Oh, Jim Beal that was at Wharram, he hardly had owt but his labourers left.' There was even talk of recruiting school children to help out during the harvest of 1914. As the months went by, the crisis passed and farms found sufficient labour to survive, coping with continued enlistment and conscription, and even managed to increase production to save imports. The government pledged that agriculture would never again be allowed to wither as it had before the war, and the farmers of the East Riding looked forward to a more certain future. The only doubt was whether the soldiers would wish to share it when they left the army. They had travelled, mixed with others of widely divergent backgrounds, and seen that they were poorly paid compared to the rest of the population. Perhaps they had always known this, but it was one thing to spend a few hours in Hull or Leeds and be the butt of urban jokes as a farmer's joskin, and quite another to spend long periods mixing on equal terms with men from towns and cities in an environment alien to everyone. Mr Johnson said:

> The working man was waking up, you see, that things ought to be altered. And a lot of men came out of the forces, well, they had the idea of not going on to farms . . . , they would go into towns. Well, of course, I had the same idea, and I came back and I found out that there was more men for jobs than there was jobs for men, so I went back onto farms. . . . But things were never quite the same again.

Some men, like Mr Ashby, found jobs in the towns and never returned to the land, but the economic situation forced others, like Mr Johnson back to their native districts. With the government intervening to keep crop prices and wages high, the soldiers' return was made less painful for them than it might have been, and there was plenty of work since the arable acreage nationally was over a quarter as much again as it had been in 1913.[2] The pressure for change appeared to evaporate and by 1920 it must have seemed as if a curtain had been drawn across the war years. With a few more years of relative prosperity, the placid course of gradual evolution might have been restored in the East Riding, but those years did not materialize. In 1920 the government reneged on its promises and abandoned its regulation of agriculture in panic as economic crisis loomed. Farm prices and farmworkers' wages crashed, and while the government was forced to resume intervention on a much smaller scale in 1924,[3] the general state of the economy ensured that during most of the inter-war years, and especially the early 1930s, farming was in a state of seemingly ever-deepening crisis. To farmers it was like a nightmare, as Mr Johnson recalled, for he and his brother had decided to stop working for others in 1931:

> We left Helperthorpe and took a farm in Fridaythorpe . . . . , eighty-seven acre. We took this farm when things was – we thought they were at rock bottom. They weren't. There was a man I've known a long while . . . and he said to me . . . , 'You're all right, things is – they're at the bottom. They can't go any lower,' he said, 'they can't.' And he was wrong, they did.
>   And, you see, your values went down, whatever you had, you see, stock, crops, and whatever you had, what was growing or what it was. Instead of getting to be a little bit more money, you see, growing into money, it got

less. . . . Between 1930 and 1942, say, if you made a living and came and paid your debts, you were lucky; a lot of 'em didn't, you know. A lot of the farms was let for – you know, practically give away, just to keep 'em, you know, in order – tenanted and that. Half a crown an acre. . . . There was a lot I know belonged to Sledmere estate . . . but they sold a lot off . . . , nobody wanted farms really. . . .

For ten year, it was a terrible job. You had to, you know, work all hours God sent to make a living, and men out of work in every village, and . . . we had plenty of work but couldn't employ them. 'Cause you couldn't afford to pay them.

Mr Johnson persevered and survived, but in despair his brother gave up his share. They were particularly vulnerable because they had very little capital and were starting off, but even well-established and previously prosperous farmers went bankrupt or, like the Crabtrees, were driven to expedients.

We were faced with two months with no money coming in whatsoever. We were employing five men and they needed their wages on Friday night. . . . My husband had two beautiful Cleveland bay horses; they were the first to go, and we lived on the proceeds of them and paid our wages for the first month. Then came the second month, and the men were queueing up on Friday night. My husband said to me: 'I can't pay the wages. What are we to do?' We had quite a lot of silver – wedding presents – and a few other priceless possessions. We filled the back of our old Wolseley car and my husband and I went into the nearest market town and, believe me, it was the hardest day's work I've ever done to sell that silver to raise the wages, but we did it and afterwards we went across to the nearest pub and had a good meal and a drink, which we badly needed, and then home to pay our men.[4]

Every East Riding village suffered agonies as the farmers economized on their wage bills. In Burton Fleming, Mr Brambles said, 'I can remember when there was over thirty unemployed here. And this village, it was only half the size it is now [1931: 429 inhabitants]. . . . There was no farm work for them.' Mr and Mrs Rispin clearly remembered the social tensions that were produced in small communities like Kilham:

Mr R: In the 1930s, it's true, I bet you there was fifty men out of work i' Kilham. And there was no dole for them, and them that had saved a bit – they was getting maybe five bob, maybe, what they called parish relief, but, say, now, they had fifty pounds i' bank, you had to spend that before they would give you that. By, it used to be awful, didn't it?
Mrs R: They'd even come up and ask you for a day's [threshing].
Mr R: Oh, they would, I used to feel sorry for them, but you couldn't give 'em all a job at threshing day . . . . And there was [a man] . . . here, Bill had three or four bairns, he was only getting about five bob a week, like. He went to thresh, well, somebody shopped him and said he'd been up here threshing.

Feller come to see us, I said, 'No,' I said I never had [hired him]. . . . And I should think, really, it'd be somebody that'd have a job hisself, like, you know, go and [tell] on him, but I did it for him – you don't reckon to lie, like, but there's three bairns.

The farming districts near old industrial centres were no longer cushioned by that proximity. There was a general collapse in farmworkers' wages, but the experience of individual counties varied widely after 1924. County Durham went from being consistently second in the wages league right to the bottom, as its coal exports vanished and other heavy industries also collapsed. Middlesex, on the other hand, prospered, for the rising new light industries of the south-east competed wages up just as the heavy industries of the north had done in the last century. The entirely rural county of Norfolk was relatively unaffected, showing that it was the level of competition for workers which brought about this realignment. After more than a century of successful evasion, the East Riding was now caught in the grip of a depression deep enough to stress its society beyond the capacity of traditional adaptation. Even if the direct impact of the storm did not fall on the county, it destroyed the supports on which its relative prosperity and stability had depended.

The farm servant system was not automatically threatened, for with farm prices so low and ready cash so hard to find for weekly wages, it made a great deal of sense to continue hiring lads who lived on the farm and ate farm produce. Only a proportion of their wages had to be paid in cash, and most of that at Martinmas. It is also possible that there may have been a comparative shortage of youngsters willing to work on farms, despite high unemployment. W.H. Long records that there was a 41 per cent reduction in those under twenty-one years old in East Riding agriculture between 1921 and 1938,[5] and yet there was no replacement of unmarried by married horsemen. It may be that farmers still needed to tie members of this age group to them to be sure of their services.

Technological advance in itself posed no real threat to the horses, on which the system obviously depended. By the mid 1920s tractors were able to offer a reliable and realistic alternative,[6] but they had to be paid for as did their fuel. Horses could be bred on the farm, with surplus foals sold for cash, and they lived on cereals that could only be sold at ruinous prices. Many of the first privately-owned tractors, indeed, were not good advertisements for mechanization. Most had been bought from wartime Agricultural Executive Committees as they were disbanded, and were in poor condition from heavy use. Many were obsolete when they were bought and gave a false impression of the capabilities of newer machines.[7] It must also be remembered that as far as field work was concerned the inter-war tractors were no more than mechanical horses, albeit very strong ones. They had no hydraulic linkages to their implements, and very few had power take-offs from their engines to drive implements, most of which were simply trailed behind, just as with horses. Tractor farming under British conditions could only make clear savings in the early years if farms completely re-arranged their cropping to rely exclusively on cereals, abandoning mixed farming and livestock.[8]

The actual economics of the tractor as against the horse have been intensively studied elsewhere already[9] and it is clear that the balance steadily shifted. By the

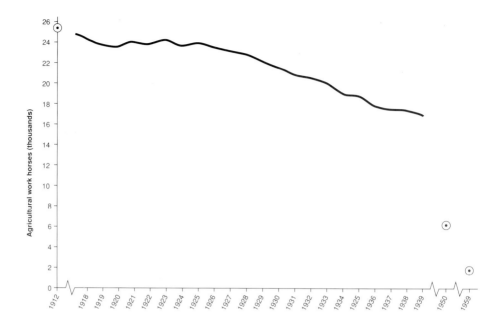

Source : *Agricultural Statistics.* (1912-59)
The numbers used are those for horses which have been broken and therefore exclude young horses and stallions

Fig. 8. The decline in the horse population of the East Riding after 1918

Second World War, mechanization should have advanced far faster if the comparative costs of the two systems were the only significant factors.[10] The fact that the Agricultural Statistics show the number of horses peaking in 1910 and declining thereafter should not be allowed to suggest that horse farming was dying from that date. Methods of counting were changed and it has been stated that the number of work-horses on farms in 1921 had not significantly fallen at all.[11] The war itself required a large number of horses for the armed forces, but the majority of their purchases were from other sources and this had no permanent effect. Tractors, and steam tackle before them, had made only a negligible impact at this time.

From 1921 there was undoubtedly a slow decline in the number of horses, but between 1921 and 1925 there were only about 2,000 tractors at work in England and Wales, compared with 796,000 horses. Most of the tractors would have replaced steam tackle or the barn engines that drove machines such as root cutters rather than horses.[12] When tractors were brought into the fields in the later years of the First World War, it was to supplement the efforts of the horse teams in a ploughing campaign that converted thousands of acres of pasture to growing grain, and the cost was high.[13] That horse numbers began to decline thereafter is a reflection of the hard times starting to afflict agriculture. East Riding farmers certainly remained committed to horses for, even into the 1930s, they used substantially more per hundred acres of crops and grass than the national average.

210

THE MONUMENT SLEDMERE

58 Memorial to the men of the Waggoners' Reserve, erected at Sledmere after the war by the Sykes family.

59 and 60   All trace of distinctive dress has gone from these pictures taken of Mr Masterman's son in the 1930s in south Holderness. Otherwise, however, these two studies of a lad and his horses are timeless and illustrate perfectly the uneasy mixture of change and tradition that epitomised this period.

61 These six farmworkers were photographed on a Hedon farm in 1929. Some were definitely servants, but how many is not known. Compared with earlier photographs their clothing is losing its distinctive character and some would not seem out of place in a factory yard. The leggings on a lad in the front row and the hat and sleeved waistcoat worn by a lad in the rear are the main echoes of the past.

62 These Percheron horses, Badger and Banker, were bought as foals at the Ruswarp horse sales by Jack Oxtoby of Wharram Grange (Massers of Malton, 1940s). They were broken in as two-year-olds by Mr Webb, a professional horsebreaker from Fridaythorpe and they worked at Wharram Grange until they were eight or nine years old, when unfortunately Banker died from a bad attack of colic. Badger was sold to go to work in the York area and so escaped the common fate of slaughter for want of a buyer. This photograph shows, left to right, Jack Oxtoby, daughter Florrie and two of Jack's four sons, Sid and Len. (Taken in the 1940s by Massers of Malton.)

63 The three ages of farm mechanization at work together during the relatively brief overlap in the use of tractors and horses. The man in front is using a fiddle drill, a simple hand-powered device that broadcasts seed without the sower needing to learn the traditional skill of doing it directly with the hands. Behind, a two-horse team harrows the seed in without needing any supervision. Overtaking the horses, perhaps symbolically, is a tractor with a flat roller. Taken in the Vale of York, probably towards Northallerton, in the early 1950s.

By 1939 there were 55,000 tractors at work nationally and the horse population had shrunk to 549,000. Most of the decline took place between 1928 and 1936, with numbers relatively stable thereafter. Since tractors very rarely replaced more than four horses, and often far less, it still seems that at least part of the decline was due to an overall shrinkage in the farmers' power requirement, as would be expected in the depression. Over the same period the number of horses in towns halved and sales of horses off farms were very badly hit, which was a blow to districts like the East Riding where the trade had been a useful side line.[14] In order to save money machinery was not replaced as it aged, and it is fair to say that by the Second World War farming with horses was far from dead, but its grave had been effectively dug. Increased mechanization then became an obvious necessity with the urgent need to save imports by growing more food. However, in the wake of the neglect of the 1930s there was so much work involved in bringing the maximum possible area under cultivation that, in the short term, horses were as essential as tractors. In 1945 there were still 457,000 horses on English and Welsh farms, but, crucially, the population was ageing and young horses were no longer being brought on.[15] It was quite clear that tractors now had a decisive edge, and any role for horses would be a residual one in specialist operations.

Harry Ferguson's use of the power take-off and his addition of the hydraulic linkage to tractors in the 1930s transformed their capabilities.[16] Previously, all machinery that performed operations had to derive power from a land-wheel that rotated as the implement moved over the field. By gears, shafts, and belts this power was transferred to the moving parts of the machine, but it was limited and the self-binder was probably the ultimate in land-wheel driven machinery under British conditions. As the implements were also trailed behind the tractor, the driver had no control over them. This limited their effectiveness and extra labour was often required to mind the implement, but the hydraulic linkage now allowed them to become extensions of the tractor that could be positively controlled from the driving seat. Even threshing machines could be built into a compact combine harvester, revolutionizing harvest methods. The horse-drawn equivalents had required immense teams to pull them and they could only be used on vast fenceless prairies as in Australia and North America. However, at its launch in 1936, farmers literally found Ferguson's improved system too good to be true. Sales were minimal and everyone was looking, unsuccessfully, for the hidden catch. Ferguson found it hard to strike a production deal he was happy with, and it took wartime demand and a collaboration with Henry Ford to bring production and sales to life in 1941. This was the genesis of the modern tractor, which was really a post-war creation.

In 1950 only 289,000 horses remained, and five years later that number had more than halved to 134,000. The East Riding was giving up its horses rapidly and its usage was now below the national average. Costings showed that by the 1950s, a horse team could never be cheaper than a tractor on any job and while tractor numbers stabilized at about 375,000 after 1958, horse numbers continued to decrease. By 1960 a bare 46,000 were recorded, and it was down to 19,000 five years later. Breeding virtually ceased after the war, for no-one wanted young horses. Mr Appleyard, a horse dealer at this time, remembered it as a tragic period for anyone with an affection for horses. He bought, or accepted as gifts, many foals whose owners had no use for them, knowing that the only buyer he would find was the slaughterhouse. He soon gave up the trade.

The heavier horses like Shires suffered most as their main asset had been their sheer pulling power. Only sentiment kept many of the horses which did survive out of the slaughterers' hands and many farmers kept a horse or two for carting and odd jobs long after tractors had taken over the real work of the farm. In pastoral areas the use of horses lasted longer, and small farmers were both less affected by the renewed prosperity of the post war years, and less able to achieve the economies of scale that made tractors attractive. Thus, a survey of Calderdale in West Yorkshire showed that farms there had suffered badly during the war because of their dependence on imported feeds, and by 1944 there was still only one tractor in the vicinity of Halifax.[17] There were still occasional jobs where horses performed well even on arable farms, where little power was needed and there were frequent stops, but once a farm was organized around tractors, any operational economics that could be gained from keeping one or two horses were heavily outweighed by the inconvenience of fitting them into the new style of operations.[18] Mr Rispin recalled, for instance, that at his last farm as a hind:

> The farmer started to keep less horses and [he got] a tractor. Well, tractor on a night, spring o' year, tractor man would be overtiming. Well, that didn't suit them [horse] lads, and it wouldn't have suited me. They were doing over[time], they were doing their horses, but they were getting nothing for it, do you see, and so – a lot of them turned tired like that – they were all, 'Oh well, if he can be riding about on a tractor, [so can I].'

Moreover, while older farmers might be nostalgic for past methods, their sons' desire to be seen to be abreast of the latest technology should not be underestimated. Because the depression had delayed change for so long, the feeling that their farms were considerably behind the times made this pressure all the greater, and once change began, as Mr Rispin has shown, it acquired its own momentum. A family farm might have the flexibility to work a combination of tractors and horses, but the natures of the two were so different that the lifestyle and skills of the specialist horseman had become anachronistic. In the East Riding the fact that the horselads were a highly volatile element in the labour force made it relatively easy for farmers to restructure as they did not need to displace veteran career horsemen.

There was, then, no dramatic change of feeling towards horses in the East Riding in the 1920s and 1930s, and there was plenty of reason to keep hiring farm servants. The farmers' main desire at this time was to save money, and servants' wages dropped like all others. In 1922, for instance, at Hull hirings 'farmers would not hear of continuing last year's terms, and servants were dissatisfied with the wages offered. . . . Foremen obtained £45 and £50 a year, waggoners were content with £25 to £30 and good useful lads obtained from £14 upwards.' In 1918 at Howden, foremen had got £60 and upwards, waggoners £50 to £57, older lads £35 to £45, and boys £20 to £22.[19] Even allowing for variations between hiring centres and the spread of wages in each year, wages had clearly fallen by at least a third.

As we have seen previously, hinds came under pressure to board the lads for less, perhaps 6s per head per week instead of 7s 6d as Mr Brambles recalled it. Mr Baines confirmed that hinds were ending the year in debt, as much as £50 in one case he knew of, because of this belt-tightening. Honest hinds became more reluctant to accept the responsibility of feeding the lads, while lads whose rations were trimmed in line with the reduced allowances were being hit in their most sensitive areas – their stomachs. The trend was far from universal, but on a subject the lads cared about so deeply it was a blow at their acceptance of living-in. More subtly, the general changing of jobs at Martinmas depended upon the standardization of terms of service: once this was reduced, a fear of changing and finding a bad home began to cripple the system disproportionately.

As the inter-war years went by, the lads' continued acceptance of living in as it stood could no longer be taken for granted. The social isolation of the farmhouses was lessening as the economic pressure built up. The radio and the cinema carried a new mass culture even into rural backwaters. Older lads, who had served in the army, did not forget the lessons of the war years, and younger lads learned from them. The new spirit is exemplified by a surge of trade unionism, especially on the large Wolds farms. Nationally, the end of the war brought a huge increase in union membership among farmworkers so that in 1919 the National Agricultural Labourers' and Rural Workers' Union had thirty times as many members as it had had in 1913. This union (which became the National Union of Agricultural Workers in 1920) and the Workers' Union (which was absorbed by the Transport and General Workers' Union in 1924) were both active in the East Riding.[20] Mr Milner recalled that when he was demobilized in 1919 there was already an active union branch at Wharram Percy. Joining the union was more than a gesture, moreover, for there was now a readiness for strikes that had no precedent.

There had already been a dispute over harvest wages in 1918, which was settled by arbitration, and in 1920 men in the Skirlaugh district of Holderness struck over harvest pay. On Tuesday 31 August, 'the organised farm workers of Beeford, North Frodingham, Foston, Gembling, Lissett, Ulrome and Skipsea came out on strike in sympathy.' The Driffield and Bridlington areas remained at work, but beyond Driffield there was more support and the dispute continued for a fortnight.[21] Two years later came the most widespread trouble the East Riding had ever seen. Farmers demanded a massive reduction in labourers' wages and locked out a thousand men. A widespread strike ensued that in some places lasted twelve weeks.[22] In 1926 there was some support for the General Strike, Mr Walker recalled, and those involved made their own demand for a reduction in hours.

Most of these strikes achieved nothing, and that of 1922 was confused from the start, with different groups having different grievances. There was little clear leadership and it was so badly organized that many branches around Driffield, where feeling had been strongest, ceased to exist, including the large Harpham branch, for instance, which was not reformed until 1938. The real significance of the union was that it existed at all and that it had such support. One large farmer, David Holtby of Rudston, actually sold his farm and retired to Cottingham, such was his distress over the new order of things.[23] Others reacted more violently: in the 1920 strike, for instance, 'a Beeford picket visited a certain farm, and the farmer became excited and pointed a revolver at the strikers. He was on horseback and followed the men onto the road.'[24] Similarly, Mr Windass retained a vivid memory from his childhood of visiting his grandfather, who was a large farmer, when news came of pickets nearby. He seized his shotgun and rushed off in his trap in search of them.[25] This is not to say that the strikes were bitter or violent, simply that the farmers were so unused to their authority being challenged that many were caught completely off-balance.

Farm servants' contracts precluded industrial action of any sort in theory, and the hiring fairs were a forum for negotiating where a union could not speak for them. Despite this, where the union was strong, it was strong among the lads as well as the labourers, though there were large areas of the county where the unions were unknown, particularly in the Vale of York, and some people I talked to were unaware of any union activity anywhere in the riding before the Second World War. The reactions to lads who struck varied widely, with some farmers even reaching agreements that lads who would look after and exercise the horses could stay on in the farmhouses and receive their keep. They often occupied their days picketing working farms, which included disturbing the horses to disrupt operations. Elsewhere, they either went home of their own accord or were sent home. Mr Tate said, 'My brothers was home for twelve weeks – best time they had in their life, you know. Had their pay . . . . They'd have strike money . . . , that would pay for my dad's keep, you know. Aye. And they went to all the farm sales there was.' Since Mr Tate's employer had conceded the unions' demands for shorter hours, Mr Tate himself had to continue working. Mr Johnson was a hind whose employer lived off the farm, which placed him in a difficult position:

It wasn't a very big place, we just had two horselads then, . . . we hadn't no labourers, we used to get them when we wanted them and we hadn't any at that time. These two lads said to me the night before . . . , 'Oh, we have to go on strike in the morning.' I said, 'all right,' I didn't say any more. Anyway, next morning I went in as usual, you know, that was before breakfast, in t'stable, and said, 'Why, you want your horses for this job and you'll want your horses for that job.'

'Oh, we're going on strike!' . . . Well . . . [they said] they had to stop on the farm and feed their horses and then they got their lodge. 'Well,' I said, 'I can't give you that. . . . You'll have to be at Speeton' [where the farmer lived] – that was twelve or thirteen miles off – 'and see what they say.' I said, 'I've got no authority to give you that. Just two of you, you know, feeding five horses.' . . . Anyway, they would go. . . .

Well, I was left in a bit of a box, myself. I'd all to do. I used to do all the other stock myself – sheep, pigs, bullocks, and all that, and then on top o' that there's the horses to look after. Well, one, he was a policeman's son . . . and . . . [his father] was going by on his beat, . . . he came to see me. He said, 'Oh well, if I'd known that lad o' mine was coming out on strike,' he said, 'I should have pushed him back but,' he said, 'I was out for t'day. . . . I didn't get back till night and he'd been off all day, and I thought it was a bit late then.' Anyway, I think it went on three weeks . . . and then they wanted to come back. . . . 'You'll have to be at Speeton,' I said, 'You've broken your contract. . . . They may knock your money off for these three weeks you've been off. . . .'

Did any of the farmers make them forfeit their money?

. . . Why, no, I don't think so; they forgot it. . . . They were entitled to really, but – you know, if that farmer had said, 'Well, I don't want you back, you're finished and that's it,' I mean, men hadn't a leg to stand on, you see. Hired lads, it was different from t'weekly men.

This magnanimity may have stemmed from the fact that the strikers had had to give in, and it was fairly general, though Mr Tate did know some who were treated as runaways in 1922 after the strike ended, losing four months' pay: 'They'd worked November while April for nowt.' No farm lad could be sure, when he went on strike, how he would be treated. The yearly bond was pre-industrial in its nature and nothing about it was suited to the spirit of the post-war years. The legal powers behind it rested in the last resort on general consent signified by an agreement to be bound by them, and if farmers had begun using them to keep servants as a group from exercising rights they knew all other workers enjoyed, they would have found difficulty in hiring any servants at all.

Some farmers, during this time of change, did question whether farm servants were worth hiring any longer. One asked Mr Johnson, his foreman, to act as a full-time horse keeper with labourers working the teams. He hoped to gain by having experienced and reliable older men doing the field work, but at the end of the year he reverted to the traditional system. The mood of the times was against innovation in techniques, and many of the expedients nineteenth-century farmers had been able to use to save money at the expense of their employees were no longer possible or acceptable. There was no scope for paying wages out of the poor rates and no possibility of turning the yearly bond into a coercive contract. Farmers saved money by reducing wages, and by reducing the numbers they employed, but there was no financial incentive to end the hiring of servants.

On the lads' side, the main cause for concern was a feeling that they were out of step with the twentieth century. Few had any objections to living in the farmhouses as such, but they were starting to regret the isolation and the lack of any independent social life. This did not happen everywhere at once for change was occurring at such different rates in different places that the social unity of the county fragmented. The impression is that of holding a handful of jigsaw puzzle pieces that will interlock physically, but on which the picture fragments seem to belong to at least four or five different whole pictures. Particularly during the 1920s, there were areas where little changed, and where lads starting work experienced much the same life as men twenty years older had, but elsewhere, change began immediately. Often it was limited to just one or two facets of life at first, but the yearly bond was like an ecological system and change to one facet inevitably resulted in further changes as a renewed balance was sought. In fact, the balance had gone beyond retrieving.

By the 1930s it is really impossible to speak of a single, coherent, county-wide system any longer. There were still places where hiring continued much as it had done before, but even here it was clear to all that the system was under strain. Some hiring fairs had ceased to function except as pleasure fairs, and their business had been lost, rather than redistributed to other centres as it would have been in the past. The servants' way of life was quickly losing its distinctive appearance, as contemporary photographs show. Gone is all trace of a self-consciously different way of dressing and, unless they are depicted with their horses, the lads of the 1930s could be involved in any manual trade.

For any who wanted to lead a life more like their urban counterparts' the most irksome aspect of being hired was having to wait until Martinmas for their pay. They needed regular spending money and they did not want to be constantly begging for subs, but to have it as of right. Mr Milner found some lads at Wharram Percy already drawing weekly pay when he returned from the war in 1919, though in every other respect they remained traditional farm servants. As weekly pay spread it eroded the concept of complete availability for a full year, and lads began to seek greater definitions of the limits to their duties. Hours were reduced so that the standard day in the fields was seven a.m. till five p.m. rather than six till six and, more importantly, they began to talk of treating the time spent with the horses as overtime. This would destroy the yearly bond, where one payment, even if fragmented into weekly instalments, covered all eventualities. Moreover, overtime was relatively meaningless unless lads were paid weekly, so the trend away from yearly pay was reinforced. Mr Brambles recalled:

> I was on a farm, and me and the third lad . . . , I was waggoner . . . , and we were hired weekly. . . . Those other three lads on this farm were paid yearly . . . their wage, it couldn't change until after Martinmas. . . . I went to t'boss and I said, 'What about this overtime?'
>
> 'Oh, I can't pay. I can't pay this overtime pay. . . . Them young lads'll have to do the horses, and you and t'other chap have nothing to do with 'em, like – just start and finish at the same time as the labourers.'

Similar problems caused Mr Rispin to cease hinding when his farm acquired a tractor and the inherently harder work of horse farming was brought home to the lads in a way it was hard to ignore:

> They started to kick . . . , did t'lads, getting up and doing horses afore breakfast, nothing for it. Feed them at dinner – come in for your dinner and then have to go out and feed your horses and nothing for that, and they had to come in, we'll say five [o'clock] to six . . . , you got nothing for it. Well, they started to give over doing that. Well, last year I was there, we only had three lads, like, and ten horses and . . . they kicked . . . , they would do 'em if he would have paid them overtime but he wouldn't pay 'em overtime. Well, that's the reason I left as much as owt, because, you get up for your breakfast on a morning – why, horses hasn't had their breakfast to go to work. . . . I'd never been used to owt o' that: 'I'm packing this in!' . . . .
>
> Now, that lad o' mine . . . , he was hired at [Hornby's] – he was there three year afore he had to go in the army, like, and he got as much for doing horses on that farm as he got in the army all told. Aye, its true. Yes, he was a good

feller was Hornby for paying lads for doing horses. 'Cause he loved horses hisself, like. . . .

No, that used to aggravate me last time I was there, like, you would get up and go for breakfast and lads would come . . . , well, you had to give horses an hour on a morning before they could be taken to work – well, you could have got a lot of work done in the fields. . . . Oh, I didn't blame t'lads, no: I should have done t'same myself.

The inherent inflexibility of yearly pay had been compounded since 1924 by the existence of a legal minimum wage, fixed each year by county wages boards.[26] They actually functioned as the going rates since it took a very good worker to secure more, given the difficult times. Wages were initially fixed in the East Riding for every conceivable position in the hierarchy with, for instance waggoners who carried corn being differentiated from those who did not.[27] Even so, for the average worker, the bargaining at the hiring fairs became less significant.

The other economic function of the hirings, that of bringing masters and servants together to fill all vacant posts efficiently and expeditiously, was also under threat. The use of newspaper advertisements was increasing and the labour exchanges offered another way of finding a job. As we have seen, as long as there was a general changing of places at Martinmas under the yearly bond, these new possibilities had little effect, but after 1918 they began to be considered in a different light, and during the 1930s they made serious inroads. Fairs, after all, can be seen to be an effective way of doing many kinds of business in a society without newspapers or good transport, but now they were dying out in all walks of life. There was a tendency for the hirings to become social affairs where people went to meet friends and enjoy themselves. Everyone I spoke to remembered the hirings as having a real economic function throughout the 1920s, and wage bargaining did not cease overnight because of the Wages Boards, but the rapid collapse of the whole system in the 1930s was only possible because the ground had been prepared.

By the time of the Second World War wages lists were organised entirely according to the age of those hired regardless of their work or job title. A seventeen-year-old carrying corn and doing a waggoner's work found he was likely to be offered the same wage as a contemporary doing far less.[28] The natural level of wages was much lower than was judged socially and politically acceptable, so the natural result was that differentials were severely eroded by the lifting of the lowest wages. The hierarchy could not function effectively under these circumstances, and with the onset of paid holidays, national insurance providing the beginnings of a welfare state, and with far more to bargain about than pay, the hiring system was simply beginning to seem irrelevant. Individuals might lose out, but the complexities of the negotiations over the whole range of conditions of service were now better handled at the Wages Boards. With the hirings therefore declining rapidly in significance, it is not surprising that many lads began to think November was a poor time to take a holiday.

The unionized farm lads seem to have been in the vanguard of these changes, sometimes a decade or more in advance of contemporaries only a few miles away, but it seems clear that the spread of trade unions was more a product of a desire for change than a cause of it. Had the inter-war years been prosperous, with plenty of jobs for which to leave agriculture, it is possible that the hiring system might have adapted itself yet again and survived in an attenuated or modified form. On the other hand, prosperity would have led to much faster mechanization, which would have placed a different strain on the system. As it was, with the depressed state of the economy there was no pressure for creative change from the farmers, and the lads' demands simply led to fragmentation. If some areas seemed to remain untouched, this was not a measure of their immunity but more of their growing remoteness from the reality of the modern economy. When prosperity returned, during and after the war, that reality had to be faced, and they rapidly fell back into step.

It is quite impossible to point to one specific issue and say that that was the key factor in the demise of the system. It was an inner decay that really toppled it, stemming from the growing integration of farming into the national economy, and of all farmworkers into the national society, at a time when all the elasticity had vanished from the industry because of the depression. In many places the war denied the system a lingering death, for the rationing system was the final straw for most hinds. They found it too much trouble to co-ordinate the various coupons and forms needed to supply the lads with the food they expected.[29] In 1946, everyone agreed, hiring through the fairs had ceased and in most places living in was a thing of the past, though Irene Megginson was looking after hired lads for her husband on their farm until 1954. There is probably no way of knowing when the last true farm servant ceased work, for there have certainly been cases since where individuals have lodged in farmhouses out of mutual convenience and with no formal contract. All that can be said is that the system had ceased to be a typical feature of the county's agriculture by the time the Second World War was over.

Notes to Chapter Seventeen

1. Roger Adelson, *Mark Sykes: Portrait of an Amateur* (1975), pp. 167–70 and Morris, *Reminiscences*, pp. 231–4 and *British Workman*, pp. 133–4. *Yorks. Post,* 13 Nov. 1914, p. 10. Antrim, *Rangers*, p. 88.
2. Mitchell and Deane, *Abstract*, pp. 78–9.
3. E. Mejer, *Agricultural Labour in England and Wales,* Part II – *Farmworkers' Earnings 1917–51* (Nottingham, 1951), pp. 9–31, and R. Groves, *Sharpen the Sickle!: the History of the Farmworkers' Union* (1949) pp. 205–11 and MAFF, *A Century of Agricultural Statistics: Great Britain 1866–1966* (1968).
4. Leslie Bailey, *Leslie Bailey's BBC Scrapbook,* vol. 3 (1986), pp. 118–9.
5. W.H. Long, 'Agricultural Labour and its Problems in War Time', *Jnl. Yorks. Ag. Soc.,* 97 (1940), 44.
6. E.J.T. Collins, 'The Farm Horse Economy of England and Wales in the Early Tractor Age, 1900–40', in Thompson, *Preliminary Canter*, 73–4.
7. B.H. Hibbard, *The Effect of the Great War upon Agriculture in the U.S.A. and Great Britain* (New York, 1919), pp. 187 and 190.
8. S.J. Wright, 'The Next Phase in Agricultural Mechanization', *Journal of the Farmers' Club*, pt. 7 (1945), 90.
9. Dexter, *Economic Position*, which also uses the East Riding as a case study and is the source for data from the county in the following section.

10. See N. Jasny, 'Tractors vs. Horses as a Source of Farm Power', *American Economic Review*, 25 (1935), 708–23, a survey of the experience of several countries showing that no one factor was of overriding importance in mechanization everywhere.
11. Collins, 'Economy', 75–8.
12. Claude Culpin, *Farm Mechanization: Costs and Methods* (1950), p. 40, and D.K. Britton and I.F. Keith, 'A Note on the Statistics of Farm Power Supplies in Great Britain', *The Farm Economist*, VII (1950), 163–4. See also Collins, *Sickle to Combine* (1969), pp. 6–9 for a brief discussion of farmers' attitudes to mechanization.
13. T.H. Middleton, *Food Production in War* (Oxford, 1923) pp. 224–8 and 301–2. See also Hibbard, *Effect*, p. 190.
14. A.W. Ashby, *Economic Facts About Tractors*, Farmers Report no. 116, University of Nottingham (Nottingham, 1952), pt. III; Wright, 'Next Phase'; and R.P. Askew, 'The Future Changes in the Number of Horses in England and Wales', *Farm Econ.* II (1936–8), 129–33.
15. W. Carr, A Plea for the Horse and Simple Tackle', *The Journal of the Ministry of Agriculture* (1939), 667–70.
16. C. Fraser, *Harry Ferguson* (1972), pp. 90–8, 106–7 and 135. See also D. Donnelly, *David Brown's: The Story of a Family Business* (1960), pp. 65–8.
17. *Farming in an Industrial Area*, Farmer's Report no. 51, Leeds University (Leeds, 1944), p. 8.
18. W.H. Cashmore, 'The Mechanization of Small and Medium Sized Farms in Great Britain', *The Empire Journal of Experimental Agriculture* (1938), 141. In fact, Dexter, *Economic Position*, p. 209, calculated that even carting with horses was uneconomic on large farms such as those on the Wolds.
19. *Yorks. Post*, 29 Nov. 1922, p. 13; and 2 Dec. 1918, p. 9.
20. Groves, *Sickle*, pp. 174–5, 216 and 245.
21. *Brid. Chron.*, 30 Aug. 1918 and 27 Sept. 1918; *Brid. F. P.*, 3 Sept. 1920; *Brid. Chron.*, 10 Sept. 1920, all in Annals of Brid.
22. Groves, *Sickle*, p. 175.
23. V. Brittain, *Testament of Friendship* (1941), p. 59.
24. *Brid. F.P.*, 3 Sept. 1920, in Annals of Brid.
25. Mr Windass gave this information in conversation with the author.
26. Groves, *Sickle*, pp. 207–9.
27. See, for instance, *Brid. Chron.*, 2 Dec. 1927, in Annals of Brid.; or *Yorks. Post* 28 Nov. 1927, p. 17; Tape 17/2; and see also Ministry of Agriculture and Fisheries, Report of *Proceedings Under the Agricultural Wages (Regulation) Act, 1924 for the Year Ended 30th September 1925* (1926), pp. 44–5 where the formula, 'Rates are also fixed for other classes of workers living in irrespective of age,' is added to the precis of the East Riding and West Riding awards. No other county did this, and the formula appears in each report until that for 1936.
28. Ministry of Agriculture and Fisheries, *Report of Proceedings Under the Agricultural Wages (Regulation) Act, 1924, for the Year Ended 30th September 1936* (1937), pp. 38–9, where it is noted that, 'Fixation of special rates according to the nature of duties was discontinued as from 24th November, 1935.'
29. Megginson, *Doorstep*, pp. 56, 59–60, 72, 86, and 94.

Chapter Eighteen

Conclusion

The unmarried farm servant who lived in with his employer, or his proxy, had ceased to be a figure of any significance in English agriculture after 1945. Men born in the East Riding at the turn of the century, however, had started work as servants on this basis, and none of them could have guessed that the end of the yearly bond was so close. The system seemed set to go on indefinitely, in this county at least. Few farms employed any married horsemen, and those that did were special cases: exceptions that proved the rule. No trend to replace farm servants among the horses with older men ever developed, and the experience of these twentieth-century hired lads is in an unbroken line of descent from the thousands who had worked on the land for centuries before them. It is a unique record in England, for while other counties also continued to use farm servants throughout the nineteenth century, in none was the system universal and self-confident, based on unmarried youths, and associated with a type of farming that required large amounts of hired labour. We have seen that the East Riding lads themselves had a strong sense of continuity with the past.

Conventional historical sources have allowed a certain amount of investigation into the nature of farm servantry as an economic institution, and the plotting of its development over several centuries, but they do not permit much insight into the lives led by farm servants. The level of detail of the lives of actual servants that has been recovered in this investigation is quite beyond anything that could even be hoped for using any other means, and if it is possible to use the insights offered on a wider canvas, it may aid materially in the understanding of events and social systems from periods beyond living memory. Experiences in transferring Western technology to other parts of the contemporary world, and modern studies of the Industrial Revolution, show that development is not a 'black box' problem where technological hardware can be plugged in anywhere at any time. Technology is part of a wider matrix and it simply does not work when operated outside that matrix. Traditional societies are not societies functioning at a low level while they await the arrival of technology. They have reached their own solutions, however bad or perverse they may seem to us, to the problems that confront them, usually through an evolutionary process that leads to great complexity. They must be understood in their own terms.

There is now a high level of interest in studying pre-industrial Europe in order to comprehend the emergence of the matrix which could tolerate and bring to its present state our technological and industrial civilization. We must not, however, see it as simply a precursor with no function but that of ushering in later developments because it did not grow up in that way. Population studies have shown how distinctive the Western European population structure was in its relatively low birth rates. Peter Laslett regarded this form of service (as opposed to the Edwardian type of domestic service) as being 'one of the three characteristics of the western family, along with a high age at marriage and a nuclear family structure' in early modern society.[1] Devices like service and apprenticeship were crucial in postponing adulthood and marriage by positive inducements, and they were part of a concept of society that used the family as a quasi-public institution, woven in on many levels apart from the purely economic. Their crumbling in their traditional form has been seen as an inevitable part of the birth of the modern world.

In the East Riding, however, we have a sizable area where service survived by adapting to change. It was not isolated from change, in fact it was the opportunities opened up by industrialization which gave it the prosperity needed to adapt. The process of adaptation throws light on the wider process of industrialization and on why other areas did not or could not adapt. The motivating forces of the system and the mutual reinforcement it and the wider rural society derived from each other throw light on the role servants played elsewhere in the past. We can only project backwards with great care, but the links with and echoes of the past are so overwhelming that such a projection seems eminently possible and worthwhile, for underlying the divergences between the farming of different counties are many common ideas and themes. Servants were one of the most distinctive features of pre-industrial life and they have too often been treated as a slightly different kind of labourer.

The living-in farm servant functioned as a bridging role for individuals, allowing them to make the transition from true childhood to true adulthood, both socially and economically, while making the most of their capacity to contribute their labour in a way that no other group could. The yearly bond was particularly suited to a society based on households earning a living within a community, rather than one of individuals operating within a capitalist framework. The concept of personal dependence, which underlies the nature of farm servantry, had little meaning once production was organized in large, impersonal units and society was split between employers and employees. The terms of the yearly bond seem firmly rooted in a traditional quasi-parent and child relationship which was taken up by the Statute of Artificers in 1563, but which had existed long before. From then on, a formidable array of legal coercion underpinned the contractual relationship, but the practice must always have been a good deal more flexible than the theory. By the twentieth century, it actually depended on the mutual willingness of farmers and servants to abide by customary rules far more than on recourse to the courts. This intertwining of custom and law is probably typical of much of early modern life, but on the whole it is only where the custom survives down to this century that it can be studied, as dependence on written records of legal formalities gives us an extremely rigid view of the course of events. The development of the bond within a customary, as well as a statutory, framework helps to explain the wide divergence between its versions extant in various counties in modern times.

Only in truly exceptional circumstances could either farmers or farmworkers, and especially the former, be constrained to continue hiring once there was a general desire to abandon it. Mutual respect in a fairly stable society was essential for its long term survival, and this existed in the East Riding, ensuring a stubborn continuity with the past rather than wholesale rebuilding. Especially on the Wolds, indeed, the new isolated farmsteads of the early nineteenth century gave the system a new lease of life. A proportion of the labour force had to be on hand there, in a way that was not necessary in more populated areas. This could have led to such far-reaching internal change that the system of 1914 was simply an isolated special case, but the greatest need of the farmers was for workers to tend and work the horses, for which the traditional farm servant was ideally suited. Changes occurred around the farm servant rather than to them. They themselves became markedly more industrial in their attitudes, and the idea that a farm servant on any but the smallest farms entered his master's family was certainly dead and buried. Even so, the line of descent is so clear that it can be traced with ease, and much survived with little or no alteration.

Certainly, the yearly bond itself remained a reality well past the First World War, though how far it could be amended by alterations like weekly wages and overtime before it was no longer identifiable would be very hard to say. The annual change of jobs and the re-negotiation of contracts certainly persisted throughout, and some lads were still hired in a traditional manner. The horselads were perceived as a special group by themselves and their employers, and the traditional culture attached to the job persisted because it remained relevant to their situation. The cinema was in the town, and radios were overheard from the farmers' or hinds' quarters rather than belonging to the lads. Most of their time continued to be spent in the stables and fields, and the hierarchy still governed their lives.

Ann Kussmaul makes the point that the early modern state used the servant system to delegate social control of a potentially unruly group – adolescent and young unmarried males – to an intensely local level, and that it did so very successfully.[2] The hierarchy perpetuated this by turning it into self control as the groups grew larger and less involved with the farmer. It may have existed in the time of Henry Best, for he normally hired a foreman, three men, and two youths. Mostly they were local and moved after a year. When they remained, their pay usually increased, denoting an increase in status. He refers to a foreman; another who is expected to have many skills and to assist the foreman; a third man who must be 'a good 4-horse man;' a fourth man; a youth; and a boy. The echoes are uncanny, though to set against that we must also say that he paid them four times a year, having agreed a yearly wage at hirings.[3]

It remained, into the twentieth century, an opportunity for growing up that parents and children were keen to take up. Probably the worst that can be said against the system is the agonies some small boys went through, and there was certainly no protection for them built into it. Yet no-one seems to have feared going onto farms, or sending their children there. No-one mentioned such a fear to me and it does not appear in any of the autobiographical works. If this is contrasted with the grudging acceptance of child labour in mills as, at best, a necessary evil, and with the campaigns to find alternatives, it suggests that ordinary people did not see themselves as involved in, and exploited by, a hiring system they disliked but could not avoid. Youths fed well, had decent accommodation by their own standards, and lived in a culture that kept them in order even if no individual did. The hiring fairs may have been noisy and boisterous, and may have offended some, but that these were virtually the only times when the youthful high spirits of farm servants broke out is far more noteworthy than any excesses.

The work itself was usually varied and often interesting. The horses were something the lads could take pride in and fasten their affections on. They were given enough lee-way on most farms to build up a highly entertaining sub-culture based on acquiring extra food for them from under the noses of the farmer, the foreman, the shepherd, and the beastman. If those noses were sometimes tilted so far back that it is obvious the owner was deliberately not looking very hard, it did not spoil the fun. On many farms their group was big enough to keep the lads occupied, especially when young members of the family, extra shepherd lads, and female servants were added in, and in any event, Sunday was a day when isolation could be broken down by visiting neighbours and relations. That they spent most of Sunday talking of farming is further proof that most found their lives satisfying enough.

As they grew older they began to look ahead. For some, a few years on a farm was enough to carry them through to an age when they could seek a town-based job, while others began courting with no real expectations other than spending their married lives as labourers. For the more ambitious, promotion to waggoner, and then foreman or hind, offered the chance to branch out. Some, like Mr Fisher and Mr Johnson, went on to become farmers, while others acquired the capital to set up small businesses that made them at least semi-independent. Going onto a farm at thirteen or fourteen did not mean an irrevocable decision to become a farm labourer had been made. The yearly contracts, the frequent moves they allowed, and above all, the clear barrier to continued work among horses that marriage formed all made lads aware that they did have some choices. This, again, is an echo of the past when adults were not expected to work for others except casually, but to have some means whereby, partially at least, they could support themselves. That such attitudes could survive in a county so dominated by large arable farms is a testament to the start in life the system gave to ordinary young people. It is certainly different from the experience of workers in the arable counties further south, where long years for the same farmer were the aim, jobs being too scarce to risk.

Certainly the hiring system cannot be said to have led to low earnings. East Riding labourers had one of the highest wage rates for any county, and it was generally acknowledged that the older servants lived better than any labourer because they could spend or save most of their cash wage as they liked. Their wages fluctuated from year to year, unlike the labourers', for the annual renegotiation of contracts meant that market forces raised or lowered the going rate every Martinmas. On the other hand, a cut in one year was usually balanced by a gain in another, and inflation could be instantly compensated for, as long as there was no surplus of would-be hirelings. Bargaining was genuine and lads were not afraid to seek more money, or to refuse a job.

This had an important effect on wages generally, for the fact that such a large group were totally immune from being laid off for any reason seems to have strongly influenced attitudes towards the labourers. Most of them were paid up-standing wages:[4] that is, they were never turned away because the weather was bad or work was short. Something was always found for them to do. There were men who were paid daily and taken on according to need, but they were not a numerous group, and most of them were paid this way because they preferred not to be tied. This was in direct contrast to the experience of the south where wage levels were not only far lower, but they were also notional figures, for men were laid off regularly, especially in winter, and then received no pay at all. The old concept that a workman had a right to a living wage in return for honest work[5] had been consciously thrown over. Morton's *Cyclopedia of Agriculture*, published in 1869, and a work much used by practical farmers, contained this passage:

> There is no . . . duty to pay higher wages, because at the existing rates people are very badly off. The wages paid for labour, excepting when kept back by fraud, involve no question of duty at all; they are the simple commercial result arising out of the demand for and the supply of an article of which they are the value.[6]

Morton personally contributed this article in a conscious effort to refute the humanitarian case for paying a living wage. In practice, there was a floor beyond which wages could not fall because social unrest began to threaten, but it was a very low floor indeed. All workers effectively became casual employees, and there seems no reason why this should not have spread to the north, despite its better wages, if it had offered real savings in the wages bill. However, farmers still had to respect their employees in the East Riding. A farmer could survive with a reputation for meanness, but to be thought unfair was something different. As a young boy Harry Reffold was able to enforce the payment of a ten shillings good conduct bonus simply by threatening to shout the news out in Driffield market place if it was withheld, and his employer, a notorious skinflint, gave way immediately.[7] Reputations mattered, and the treatment accorded to employees was an essential element, while hirings were ideal venues for spreading news that would destroy them.

There was no place for hole-and-corner dealing at the fairs and no possibility of playing people off against each other. Both sides, even though composed of individuals acting for themselves, drew great solidarity from the presence of their friends, neighbours, and relatives. For all that has been said and written about hiring fairs, they seem to have served the lads well both socially and economically. They remained the lynch-pin of the system until very near the end, when it was clearly in terminal decline. They were also an epitome of the whole system, with far more functions than they have been credited with in the past. A fair was a subtle combination of a labour exchange, a collective bargaining venue, a release mechanism for social tensions both of a personal nature and those arising from the power structure of the farms, a gathering where family and friendship ties were reinforced after months of isolation, and a chance to purchase all the basic necessities for another year on the farm. If the subtlety was well masked by the proceedings' uproarious nature, its existence should not be denied.

Similarly, the farm servant system had an overriding purpose which we have no difficulty in comprehending: to set to work unmarried youths and men on farms, and to get the maximum effort from them with a minimum amount of effort on the part of the farmer. Too often, traditional systems are not accorded the elementary respect of being allowed to be practical in their context, but must be judged by their quaintness or colourfulness. That this purpose was one shared by early modern employers and up-to-date farmers of the 1920s explains why the system could be maintained. It also had built into it a whole range of other functions, many of them social rather than economic, and when all are taken together, the system is a very alien one for a society where employment has become almost entirely a cash transaction. Just as species adapt totally to their environments, developing specializations suited to every aspect, over the centuries the farm servant was fitted to a particular social and economic framework. That they became extinct is because their ecological niche vanished. Until then, the outward form could adapt itself to changing circumstances because the central core of the system still fulfilled its functions for both employers and employees.

The demise of the East Riding horselads ran parallel to that of their horses, but in a different era, who is to say that we would not have had the rise of a new set of tractor-lads, or some such adaptation? Farm servants died out in the south and east as horse farming was still developing. It was the combination of economic depression and rapid social change that put an end to centuries of history. The assault came on too many fronts and the central logic of the system, that lads were well served by spending their adolescent years as lodgers on farms, no longer seemed appropriate in the mid twentieth century. In passing a final judgement on the system it must be remembered that we are not considering merely an alternative way of employing workers. The most important fact, it seems to me, is that of all the, admittedly scarce, accounts we have of it, very few from the inside are deeply critical. Farmworkers as a whole are known to have resented their exploitation as the victuallers of a society that often grudged them even a living wage and laughed at their rural ways. Groups such as miners were proud of their ability to survive in a hostile work environment and produce coal despite it, but we know they rarely wanted their children to follow them underground. If there had been any widespread revulsion against living in, we would have heard of it. Perhaps the best testimony to its success in the East Riding is the very fact that we have not: that there are so few sources on which the historian can draw. The system simply went its own way on its own terms as long as it was wanted.

Notes to Chapter Eighteen

1. P. Laslett, 'Characteristics of the Western Family Considered over Time', *Journal of Family History*, II (1977), 90.
2. Kussmaul, *Servants*, p. 33.
3. Best, *Farming Book*, pp. xxxvii–xxxviii, 138, and xxxix.
4. See *Second Report*, p. 23, and *Wages and Conditions* II, p. 383.
5. See, for instance, Thompson, *Working Class*, pp. 67–73, on the old 'moral economy' as he terms it.
6. Morton, *Cyclopedia*, II, p. 173.
7. Reffold, *Pie for Breakfast*, p. 57.

Glossary

This glossary has been compiled to assist readers with terms that may be unfamiliar, either because they are in dialect or because they are farming terms. It is in no way complete as a dictionary and words are defined only according to their use in this book. Where a word seems to be explained by its context or there is an aside in the text, it is only included here if it also occurs in another place where its meaning is obscure.

Arles   See fastening penny.
Arve   Instruction to horse, turn left.
Back door lad   Young farm servant doing general duties, mostly fetching and carrying for the housekeeper in the yard and outbuildings.
Back end   Late autumn and winter, the latter end of the year.
Bad meat house   Farm that fed lads well below their expectations.
Bairn   Child.
Balk   Strip of land in a field left unploughed, often as a boundary if deliberate, but here accidentally.
Beastman   Cowman.
Big fiddle   'Cello.
Blinders   Blinkers, and by extension the horse's whole bridle.
Blood horse   A pedigree horse, usually for riding.
Blue stone of vitriol   Copper sulphate.
Booning day   A day when a new tenant farmer was visited by his neighbours, bringing their ploughs, to help him catch up with the ploughing he had inevitably not been able to do.
Box cloth   Heavily felted woollen cloth. Of good quality and very waterproof, so it was used for coats for coachmen, etc., who might spend hours outside in the rain sitting on the box of the coach. Used by some horselads for leggings because it did not fray.
Box lad   A young farm servant employed to see to the loose box(es) where the light horses were kept.
Bray   To hit, beat.
Brid   Bridlington.
Britchings, Breechings   The set of harness straps extending backwards from the cart saddle and down over the horse's flanks, giving it something to push back against when in shafts and ordered to stop.

Glossary

Bullocky Farm servant employed to look after the bullocks fattened up in Wold farm yards over winter. At other seasons he would work among the horses or act as a general stand in, but he had no place in the horselads' hierarchy.

Butter of antimony Antimony trichloride, used as a drug by horselads.

Caff Chaff.

Cart saddle The saddle used to support a chain across a horse's back, usually when it was working in shafts. It consisted of a pad underneath a channel for the chain, which made it impossible to sit on.

Chaff cutter A machine, operated by hand or power, for cutting straw into small pieces which were more attractive and digestible for the animals. It is so named because it cut straw into chaff, not because it cut chaff.

Chaimer Chamber, the bedroom the farm servants slept in.

Chicken run The back row at a chapel where the youngsters gathered.

Choker A high collar worn by Mr Harper as part of his servant's uniform when waiting at table for a wealthy farmer.

Chop The cut straw produced by the chaff cutter [see above].

Collop Lump, large piece.

Come on Instruction to horse, set off.

Crib Manger.

Drag Heavy harrow, almost a cultivator.

Draughts Swingletrees (see later).

Drinkings Refreshment taken during a break from work, or the break itself.

Dress To clean, remove dust and dirt from seeds or grain before sowing or after harvest.

Entire Stallion.

Fastening penny Money given to seal a bargain struck between a farmer and a servant at the hiring fair. Until the twentieth century its acceptance bound a servant completely, but in this century it could be returned until Martinmas to cancel the contract.

Feather The heavy hair traditionally seen below the knee on the legs of a Shire horse.

Fenugreek A leguminous powder used as a drug by horselads.

Fest See fastening penny.

Fifth lad See hierarchy.

Fiver See hierarchy.

Fond Mentally retarded, foolish.

Fother up To fodder up and see to the horses last thing at night, giving a last feed of hay if needed.

Fourther See hierarchy.

Fourther lad See hierarchy.

Fourth lad See hierarchy.

Foxhunting A method of ploughing common on the Wolds where a group follow one another round the field rather than taking individual sections.

Frostmould The friable top soil produced by the action of frost.

Furr A furrow.

Fustian A heavy cotton cloth with a nap, formerly widely used for working-class men's clothing because of its durability.

Galloway A small, sturdy horse, suitable for riding or pulling a trap.

Gearing, Gears Harness.

Gee back Instruction to horse, turn right.

Gee up Instruction to horse, set off.

Gelding A castrated horse. Most colt foals were gelded.

Gill A liquid measure. In Standard English, a quarter of a pint, but a gill of beer is a half a pint in many places from Yorkshire and Lancashire northwards, including the East Riding.

Godspenny See fastening penny.

Goesunder A chamber pot, which goes under the bed.

Go back Of seed, which often reverts to its ancestral types if grown on the same land for years at a time.

Good meat house A farm where lads were well fed.

Go on Instruction to horse, set off.

Gripe To suffer from stomach pains.

Guiser Someone in disguise or fancy dress, in this case a dancer in traditional costume.

Half-clip To clip a horse's coat around its legs and lower body. Done in winter to stop the coat holding sweat after exertion, which can chill the horse and cause illness.

Headland A belt of land at the top and bottom of a field being ploughed which is used for turning the plough round. It cannot therefore be left in neat furrows and must be gone over when the rest of the field is complete.

Heating Of the horse's blood, a condition that made the skin itchy and caused the condition of the horse's coat to deteriorate.

Heck A hay rack in a horse's stall.

Helter Halter, a rope or hemp bridle with a rope or strap attached by which the horse's head can be controlled; sometimes just the rope or strap alone.

Hierarchy This was not a term used on the farms and there were, in fact, two methods of organizing hierarchies, one used in the Vale of York and the other over the rest of the riding. At the head of both, in practice, came the *waggoner* or *wag* but, except in the Vale, he was counted as second man after the foreman. Apart from on small farms he was responsible for keeping the other lads in order, and had special duties such as carrying sacks of corn, a task beyond the youngsters. He physically took the lead whenever the lads worked as a group, and he set the pace of the group. In the Vale the next lad down was the *second waggoner, second lad*, or *seconder* but on the Wolds and in Holderness they passed straight on to *third lad* or *thirdy* and *waggoner* was included in none of the lesser lads' titles. On a small farm he could be an ordinary ploughlad in charge of his own team, but on a large one outside the Vale he was often expected to show more than average skills. A good thirdy welcomed the chance to learn in order to be ready to become a waggoner. The *fourther* or *fourth lad*, was therefore third most senior lad outside the Vale, or fourth most senior within it, where he might be called the *fourth waggoner*. After this came the *fifth lad* or *fiver, sixer* or *sixth lad, seventher* or *seventh lad*, etc. All these were usually just plough lads with no special duties who, outside the Vale, saw to their own horses. Few farms in the Vale employed anyone below a fourth lad and anyone below fiver was likely to be quite young in any part of the riding, though in charge of his own team and expected to do fieldwork with the rest. After all of them were accounted for, a new sequence began with *wag lad* who assisted a waggoner having six horses to care for rather than four. He worked with the rest in the fields and might be of any age, though the smaller the farm, the younger he was likely to be. *thirdy lad* would likewise assist the thirdy but there were far fewer of these, and of *fourthy lads* and so on, and they were more likely to be boys not ready to care for horses on their own.

Hind   A married farm foreman who boarded and fed the farm servants on behalf of the farmer who employed him.

Hiring penny   See fastening penny.

Hirings   The hiring fairs held each Martinmas in all the market towns to let farmers and servants meet and negotiate contracts for the next year.

Hit-and-miss   A design of slatted, unglazed window used in stables where one set of thin, vertical slats could be positioned either in front of the other set of slats, leaving open gaps between, or the gaps, closing them.

Hogg sheep   A young sheep from weaning to its first shearing.

Horselad   A farm servant employed to work among the horses. The vast majority were aged between thirteen and twenty-five years old.

Jerry   A chamber pot.

Jibber   A horse inclined to resist being made to work, often by kicking or biting.

Joskins   Literally, the straps used to tie up trousers beneath the knee to create room for it to bend, but also used as a jocular description of farm servants as the farmer's joskins.

Kip   A room set aside in an outbuilding for the lads to use in the evening.

Lead   To carry goods, to bring back to the farmstead.

Least lad   The smallest boy hired on the farm among the servants, a title used as well as the one describing his place in the hierarchy. He generally got the jobs no-one else wanted.

Loaden   To load a waggon, also to describe something already loaded.

Lowse out   Literally, to loose out, let loose the horses from their implements when it was time to go back to the farm.

Luance   Allowance; food and drink provided by the farmer during periods of heavy work, sometimes to all the staff and sometimes just to those involved in the work. A luance job was therefore a heavy job.

Lunch   A snack; literally, a thick slice of some food.

Make no profession   Not to join a chapel congregation in a formal sense. This might apply to Anglicans or to youngsters not old enough, or committed enough, to be counted as members although they attended, or to adults who did not wish to go beyond attending services, even though they counted themselves as Methodists.

Maigres   Of horses, a condition where the horse could be sent into a convulsive fit.

Malting barley   Barley suitable to be turned into malt for use in brewing and distilling.

Manishment   Manure.

Meat   food, or to feed.

Mell supper   Harvest supper. The mell sheaf was the last sheaf of the harvest.

Mouth   Of horses. To render the horse's mouth tender so as to make it more responsive to the bit, and to accustom it to having a bit in its mouth.

Nurse girl   A young girl hired as a farm servant to mind infants. Often the first job for a girl leaving home.

Orve   See arve.

Persian   Percheron, a breed of heavy horse originating in France and just starting to make an impact in Britain as tractors came in.

Piker   Someone using a pitchfork.

Quart   To plough at ninety degrees to existing furrows, a method used in fallowing.

Reaper   A machine designed for cutting corn rather than grass, but sometimes used for either.

Reckan bracket   A bar over a fire from which reckans, or hooks, can be hung to hold pots during cooking.

Reesty horse   See jibber.

Ridge   A section of a field marked out to be ploughed as one piece. The action of the plough throws earth from the side of the piece to the centre, creating a low ridge. This was often encouraged to create better natural drainage or to guide water into drainage tiles laid under the furrows between ridges.

Rig   Yorkshire pronunciation of ridge, with the same meaning for ploughing. Also used to refer to the ridge of a stack, the topmost layer that sealed up the roof shape above it.

Right   In full possession of one's faculties, as opposed to fond.

Roar   To cry loudly, sob.

Rully   A flat-bed vehicle on four wheels. Similar to a waggon but without any sides. In other areas it is called a rolly or a lorry and the motor lorry is its modern equivalent.

Scotch bob   The decorative plaiting of a horse's tail to keep it clean and out of the traces.

Scruffler   A horse harrow designed for use between rows of crops such as turnips.

Seconder   See hierarchy.

Second lad   See hierarchy.

Second waggoner   See hierarchy.

Seventher   See hierarchy.

Seventh lad   See hierarchy..

Shears   The turntable from which the front wheels of a waggon are suspended to make them steerable. It projects enough in front of the body to be used for standing on, but if the wheels turn it goes under the body, making it a dangerous place to stand.

Shim   A hoe, or to cut glancingly with a hoe.

Side   To remove the cutlery, crockery etc. from a table after a meal.

Sittings   See hirings.

Sixer   See hierarchy.
Sixth lad   See hierarchy.
Skellbase   A partition between stalls in the stables or cow house.
Slasher   A sharp hedging tool for slashing away branches.
Slum   See kip.
Smallganging   The practice of young boys and lads from a farm attacking an older bully as a group, usually at Martinmas, to teach him a lesson.
Spean   Wean.
Srutted   Sprouted, of corn. Corn that has been left so long in a wet season that the grain is germinating while still on the plant.
Stable lamp   An oil lamp of sturdy construction suitable for use in a stable.
Stalled   Overfed to the point of losing all appetite, particularly where the diet has no variety.
Stanning   Literally standing, a stall where one or two horses are tethered with only enough room to stand or lie down but not to walk around.
Starving   Frozen, very cold.
Statties, Stattuses, Statutes, Statute hiring fairs   See hiring fairs.
Step stone   A rubbing stone used to put a decorative white edge to steps or flagstones.
Stick hill   The stored heap of firewood for use in the house.
Strike   Of turnips, see gap.
String horse   That horse in a team wearing the reins and therefore under the direct control of its driver.
Swing   To accustom a horse to being led with a bridle on its head.
Swingletrees   The wooden or metal bars to which a horse is directly attached, by traces, from either side of the collar, so as to allow a steady, centralized pull to be transmitted along a single further chain or hook to an implement. It keeps the traces apart and prevents them chafing the horse. By linking swingletrees to a cobble tree, a larger version, two or more horses can pull a single implement.
Swing plough   A plough without wheels. It balances on the plough body and furrow depth and width are maintained by the leverage the ploughman exerts through the handles.
Table-top bath   Washing oneself all over using a basin of water on a table.
Tacklings   Harness.
Taty scratting   Potato picking.
Teem   To unload.
Thack   To thatch.
Third lad   See hierarchy.
Third waggoner   See hierarchy.
Thirdy   See hierarchy.
Thirdy lad   See hierarchy.
Tommy owt   A worker willing to take on a wide variety of jobs and act as a stand-in wherever he was needed. On the larger farms he would be a farm servant specifically hired for this purpose, but otherwise he might be a labourer who simply liked a change.

Topping   The fringe in a haircut.
Top shets   Literally, top sheets, bedding.
Vent hole   An air hole in a wall.
Wag, Waggoner   See hierarchy.
Wag lad   See hierarchy.
Went on   See go on.
Whauve   See arve.
Whee   See whoa.
Whemmle over   To topple over.
Whoa   Instruction to horses to stop.

Select Bibliography

A. Oral Sources

Twenty-nine tapes were recorded during research, but numbers 1, 2 and 14 contained no material relevant to this book. They have now been deposited at Sheffield University in its Centre for English Cultural Tradition and Language. No complete transcripts exist, but there is an index of subjects covered. As every extract quoted in the book is attributed to a speaker, except where there was a specific request for anonymity, footnote references to the actual taped interviews were felt to be unnecessary. The biographies of the main contributors at the start of the book show which speaker was recorded on which tapes.

Occasionally information was added after the recorder was switched off and some interviews or sections of interviews were not taped, either by request or because of mechanical failure or inappropriate locations. I first talked to Mr Appleyard, for instance, in the cab of a truck he was driving for a living, with a noise level that made recording impossible. There were seven full interviews and six fragments of this type, which were noted as soon as possible after the event, as fully as possible. They have not been used as direct quotations and details of them are also added to the biographies.

B. Manuscript Sources

1. *Primary*

Public Record Office
Census enumerators' notebooks, 1871, for the following townships

Arnold RG10/4801/58–59v
Bellasize RG10/4765/34–41v
Cottam RG10/4809/18–24
Cowlam RG10/4809/24v–25v
Folkton RG10/4814/89–96
Long Riston RG10/4801/48–57v
Newton upon Derwent RG10/4757/89v–95v

Nunburnholme RG10/4759/89–97
South Dalton RG10/4771/14–22v
Thorngumbald RG10/4798/17–25v

2. Secondary

Theses and Dissertations
Bateman, Margaret, 'The Dialect of Rillington' (unpublished B.A. dissertation, Leeds University, Institute of Dialectology, 1958).
Dexter, Keith, 'The Economic Position of the Horse in British Agriculture' (unpublished Ph.D. thesis, University of Nottingham, 1953).

C. Printed Sources

The place of publication is London unless otherwise stated

1. Primary

(i)   Parliamentary Papers
Sixth Report of the Medical Officer of the Privy Council, 1864, XXVIII
Royal Commission on Labour, 1893–4, XXXV.
Report by Mr Wilson Fox on the Wages and Earnings of Agricultural Labourers in the United Kingdom, 1900, LXXXII.
Second Report by Mr Wilson Fox on the Wages, Earnings, and Conditions of Employment of Agricultural Labourers in the United Kingdom, 1905, XCVII.
Report on the Earnings and Hours of Labour of Workpeople in the United Kingdom, V, Agriculture in 1907, 1910, LXXXIV.
Report on the Wages and Conditions of Employment in Agriculture, I, General Report, and II, *Reports of Investigators*, 1919 IX.

(ii)   Agricultural Statistics
Published by the Board of Agriculture and Fisheries until 1918, then by the Ministry of Agriculture and Fisheries till 1952, and thereafter by the Ministry of Agriculture, Fisheries and Food. The volumes from 1912 to 1939, 1950 and 1959 were all consulted for the horse population figures, given in table 3 until 1920 and table 2 thereafter.

(iii)   Newspapers
Beverley Guardian
Eastern Morning News (Hull)
Hull Daily Mail
Hull News

Malton Gazette
Malton Messenger
York Evening Press
Yorkshire Herald
Yorkshire Post

Various clippings from: Annals of Bridlington, Taylor and Matthewman, P.L., (eds.), Bridlington Public Library.

(iv)   Books and Articles – General
The place of publication is London unless otherwise stated.
Best, Henry, *The Farming and Memorandum Books of Henry Best of Elmswell, 1642*, ed. Woodward, Donald, British Academy Records of Social and Economic History, New Series, VIII (1984).
English Land Restoration League, *Special Report, 1893: Among the Agricultural Labourers with the Red Vans* (1894)
Holderness Agricultural Society, *Extracts from the Minutes of the Holderness Agricultural Society, 1795–1850* (Hull, 1883).
Kelsall, R.K., 'Two East Yorkshire Wage Assessments, 1669, 1679', *English Historical Review*, LII (1937), 283–9.
Kelly's Directory of the North and East Ridings of Yorkshire, 1909 (1909).

(v)   Personal Reminiscences
The place of publication is London unless otherwise stated.
Austin-Hyde, F., 'Old Time Martinmas Hirings', *York Times* (Autumn 1962), 26–8.
Day, H.L., *Horses on the Farm* (Beverley, 1981).
Day, H.L., *My Life with Horses* (Beverley, 1983).
Holtby, Winifred, *South Riding* (1936).
Hudleston, N.A., 'Jottings From a Farmer's Notebook', *Transactions of the Yorkshire Dialect Society*, vol. 10, pt. 56 (1956), 23–27.
Hudleston, N.A., 'Notes on Yorkshire Words Relating to Horses', *Transactions of the Yorkshire Dialect Society*, vol. 10, pt. 59 (1959), 20.
Kitchen, Fred, *Brother to the Ox* (1942).
Megginson, Irene, *Mud on my Doorstep* (Beverley, 1987).
Megginson, Irene, 'To Be a Farmer's Boy in East Yorkshire', *Dalesman*, vol. 39 (1977), 524–7.
Morris, Revd M.C.F., *The British Workman Past and Present* (1928)
Mortimer, J.R., *A Wolds Boyhood*, ed. J.D. Hicks (York, 1978).
Reffold, Harry, *Pie for Breakfast* (Beverley, 1984).
Thompson, Flora, *Lark Rise to Candleford* (1939).
Wilson, Ann, 'When Today Meets Yesterday', *Dalesman*, vol. 24 (1962), 428–30.

(vi)   Contemporary Material on Farm Servants
Barugh, William, *Master and Man: A Reply to the Agricultural Labourer as He Really is* (Driffield, 1854).
Eddowes, Revd. J., *The Agricultural Labourer as He Really Is: Or, Village Morals in 1854* (Driffield, 1854).

Eddowes, Revd J., *Martinmas Musings: Or Thoughts about the Hiring Day* (Driffield, 1854).

Morris, Revd F.O., *The Present System of Hiring Farm Servants in the East Riding of Yorkshire with Suggestions for its Improvment* (Driffield, 1854).

Simpson, Mary E., *Gleanings: Being a Sequel to 'Ploughing and Sowing'*, ed. Revd F.D. Legard (1876).

Simpson, Mary E., 'The Life and Training of a Farm Boy', in Revd F.D. Legard, ed., *More About Farm Lads* (1865).

Simpson, Mary E., *Ploughing and Sowing; Or, Annals of an Evening School in a Yorkshire Village, and the Work that Grew out of it*, ed. Revd F.D. Legard (1861).

Simpson, Mary E., *Why Church is Better than Chapel or Meeting: A Word to Those who Like Chapel Best* (1863).

(vii)   Contemporary Material on Local Farming, Pre-1900

Bedell, W., *An Account of Hornsea in Holderness in the East Riding of Yorkshire* (Hull, 1848).

Bell, T., 'The Yorkshire Farm Prize Competition, 1883', *Journal of the Royal Agricultural Society of England*, XIX (1883), 506–80.

Cobbett, William, *Rural Rides* (1830, Penguin, 1967).

Defoe, Daniel, *A Tour through the Whole Island of Great Britain* (1738, Davies, 1927).

Howard, Charles, *A General View of the Agriculture of the East Riding of Yorkshire* (1835).

Leatham, Isaac, *A General View of the Agriculture of the East Riding of Yorkshire* (1794).

Legard, G., 'On the Farming of the East Riding of Yorkshire', *Transactions of the Yorkshire Agricultural Society*, 11 (1848), 69–120.

Legard, G., 'Report on the Mode of Cultivation Pursued upon Neswick Farm, nr. Driffield, the property of John Grimston, Esq., occupied by George Legard, Esq., and Mr T. Wheatley', *Transactions of the Yorkshire Agricultural Society*, 1 (1830), 25–32.

MacVicar, J.Y., 'Report on the Practical Management of a Strong Land Farm', *Transactions of the Yorkshire Agricultural Society*, 12 (1839), 75–91.

Marshall, William, *A Review of the Reports of the Board of Agriculture from the Northern Department* (York, 1808).

Marshall, William, *The Rural Economy of Yorkshire* (1788).

Strickland, H.E., *A General View of the Agriculture of the East Riding of Yorkshire* (York, 1812).

Tuke, John, *A General View of the Agriculture of the North Riding of Yorkshire* (1800).

Young, Arthur, *A Six Months' Tour through the North of England* (1770).

2.   *Secondary*

(i)   Books – General

Allison, Keith J., *The East Riding of Yorkshire Landscape* (1976).

Antrim, Angela, *The Yorkshire Wold Rangers* (Driffield, 1981).

Armstrong, Alan, *Farmworkers: A Social and Economic History, 1770–1980* (1988).

Ashby, A.W., *Economic Facts about Tractors,* University of Nottingham, Farmers' Report no. 116 (Nottingham, 1952).

Best, S.E.J., *East Yorkshire: A Study in Agricultural Geography* (1930).

Burnett, John, *Plenty and Want* (1978).

Caird, James, *English Agriculture in 1850–51* (1852).

Collins, E., *Sickle to Combine* (Reading, 1969).

Craven, M., *A New and Complete History of the Borough of Hedon* (Driffield, 1972).

Culpin, C., *Farm Mechanization: Costs and Methods* (1950).

Dyson, B., ed. *A Guide to Local Studies in East Yorkshire* (Beverley, 1985).

Edwards, P., *The Horse Trade in Tudor and Stuart England* (1988).

Evans, G.E., *Ask the Fellows Who Cut the Hay* (1965).

Evans, G.E., *The Horse in the Furrow* (1967).

Fairfax-Blakeborough, J. *Yorkshire: East Riding* (1951).

Forster, G.C.F., *The East Riding Justices of the Peace in the Seventeenth Century*, East Yorkshire Local History Series no. 30 (York, 1973).

Freeman, C.B., *Mary Simpson of Boynton Vicarage: Teacher of Ploughboys and Critic of Methodism*, East Yorkshire Local History Series no. 28 (York, 1971).

Frow, E., and Frow, R., *A Survey of the Half-Time System in Education* (Manchester, 1970).

Green, F.E., *The History of the English Agricultural Labourer, 1870–1920* (1920).

Groves, Reg, *Sharpen the Sickle!: the History of the Farmworkers' Union* (1949).

Gutch, E., *Examples of Printed Folk-lore Concerning the East Riding of Yorkshire* (1911), County Folk Lore Series, vol. 6.

Haggard, H. Rider, *Rural England* (1902).

Harris, Alan, *The Rural Landscape of the East Riding of Yorkshire, 1700–1850* (1961).

Hasbach, W., *A History of the English Agricultural Labourer* (1908).

Heath, F.G., *British Rural Life and Labour* (1911).

Hibbard, B.H., *The Effects of the Great War upon Agriculture in the U.S.A. and Great Britain* (New York, 1919).

Hobsbawm, Eric, and Rude, George, *Captain Swing* (1969).

Horn, Pamela, *The Rural World*, 1780–1850 (1980).

Hunt, E.H., *Regional Wage Variations in England* (1974).

Jones, Eric L., *The Development of English Agriculture* (1968)

Kebbel, T.E., *The Agricultural Labourer* (1887).

Kebbel, T.E., *The Old and the New English Country Life* (1891).

Keegan, Terry, *The Heavy Horse, its Harness and Harness Decoration* (1973).

Kussmaul, Ann, *Servants in Husbandry in Early Modern England* (1981).

Laslett, Peter, *The World We Have Lost: Further Explored*, 3rd ed. (1983).

Lewis, P. and Jones, P.N., *The Humberside Region* (Newton Abbott, 1970).

Lones, T.E., ed. *British Calendar Customs*, 3 vols. (1936–40).

Long, W.H., *A Survey of the Agriculture of Yorkshire*, Royal Agricultural Society of England County Agricultural Surveys, no. 6 (1969).

McCloskey, Donald M., *Essays on a Mature Economy: Britain after 1840* (1971).

McCutcheon, K., *Yorkshire Fairs and Markets to the End of the Eighteenth Century*, Thoresby Society Publications vol. XXXIX (1940).

Malcolmson, R.W., *Popular Recreations in English Society, 1700–1850* (Cambridge, 1973).

Mejer, E., *Agricultural Labour in England and Wales*, pt. II. *Farm Workers' Earnings 1917–51* (Nottingham, 1951).

Middleton, T.H., *Food Production in War* (Oxford, 1923).

Minchinton, W.E., ed. *Wage Regulation in Pre-Industrial England,* (Newton Abbott, 1972).

Mingay, G.E., *The Victorian Countryside*, 2 vols (1981).

Ministry of Agriculture, Fisheries and Food, *A Century of Agricultural Statistics: Great Britain 1866–1966* (1968).

Morris, Revd M.C.F., *Nunburnholme, its History and Antiquities* (York, 1907).

Morris, Revd M.C.F., *Yorkshire Folk Talk* (1892).

Morris, Revd M.C.F., *Yorkshire Reminiscences* (1922).

Morton, John C., *A Cyclopedia of Agriculture* (1856).

Neave, David, *Notes on the History of the Church and Parish of Holme-on-Spalding Moor, Yorkshire* (n.p., 1970).

Obelkevitch, James, *Religion and Rural Society: South Lindsey, 1825–75* (1976).

Pedley, W.H., *Labour on the Land* (1942).

Perry, P.J., *British Farming in the Great Depression, 1870–1914: An Historical Geography* (Newton Abbott, 1974).

Radford, J.D.D., *A Study of Tractors and Horses*, University of Leeds Farmers' Report no. 130 (Leeds, 1956).

Redford, A., *Labour Migration in England, 1800–1850*, 2nd ed., revised and ed., W. Chaloner (Manchester, 1964).

Ross, F., *Contributions Towards a History of Driffield and the Surrounding Wolds District in the East Riding of the County of York* (Driffield, 1898).

Snell, K.D.M., *Annals of the Labouring Poor* (1985).

Thompson, E.P., *The Making of the English Working Class* (1963).

Thompson, F.M.L., ed. *Horses in European Economic History: A Preliminary Canter* (Reading, 1983).

Ward, J.T., *East Yorkshire Landed Estates in the Nineteenth Century*, East Yorkshire Local History Series no. 23 (York, 1967).

Whetham, E.H., *British Farming, 1938–49* (1952).

Wilkinson, Olga, *The Agricultural Revolution in the East Riding of Yorkshire*, East Yorkshire Local History Series no. 5 (York, 1963).

Woodcock, Revd H., *Piety Among the Peasantry* (1889).

(ii) Articles and Parts of Books – General

Archer, J., '"A Fiendish Outrage:" A Study of Animal Maiming in East Anglia, 1830–70', *Agricultural History Review*, 33 (1985), 147–57.

Arthur, D. and Arthur, T., 'Available for Hire', *Folk Song Review* (Sept. 1972), 6–8.

Askew, R.P., 'The Future Changes in the Number of Horses in England and Wales,' *The Farm Economist*, II (1936–8), 129–33.

Blaug, M., 'The Myth of the Old Poor Law and the Making of the New', *Journal of Economic History*, XXIII (1963), 151–84.

Blaug, M., 'The Poor Law Re-examined,' *Journal of Economic History*, XXIV (1964), 229–45.

Britton, D.K. and Keith, I.F., 'A Note on the Statistics of Farm Power Supplies in Great Britain', *The Farm Economist*, VI (1950), 163–70.

Carr, W.A.C., 'A Plea for the Horse and Simple Tackle', *Journal of the Ministry of Agriculture*, 46 (1939–40), 667–70.

Carter, Ian, 'Oral History and Agrarian History – the North East', *Oral History*, 2, no. 1 (1974), 34–44.

Cashmore, W.H., 'Mechanization of the Small and Medium Sized Farm in Great Britain', *Empire Journal of Experimental Agriculture*, 6 (1938), 141–9.

Churley, P.A., 'The Yorkshire Crop Returns of 1801', *Yorkshire Bulletin of Economic and Social History*, 5, no. 1 (1953), 179–97.

Collins, E.J.T., 'Labour Supply and Demand in European Agriculture, 1800–80', in Jones, E.L. and Woolf, S.J., eds, *Agrarian Change and Economic Development* (1969).

David, P.A., 'The Landscape and the Machine: the Mechanization of the Corn Harvest in Victorian Britain', in McCloskey, D.N., ed., *Essays on a Mature Economy: Britain after 1840* (1971).

Davidson, T., 'The Horseman's Word', *Gwerin*, 1 (1956–7), 67–74.

Davidson, T., 'Plough Rituals in England and Scotland', *Agricultural History Review*, 7 (1959), 27–37.

Devine, T.M., 'Social Stability and Agrarian Change in the Eastern Lowlands of Scotland, 1810–40', *Social History*, III (1978), 331–46.

Dudman, R.A., 'Of Horses and Tractors', *The Farm Economist*, VI (1950), 181–8.

Dudman, R.A., 'Power and Farming', *The Farm Economist*, VII (1952–4), 254–7.

Dunbabin, J.P., 'Agricultural Trades Unionism in the 1870s', *Agricultural History Review*, 16 (1968), 114–41.

Dunbabin, J.P., 'Labourers and Farmers in the Late Nineteenth Century', *Bulletin of the Society for the Study of Labour History*, 11 (1965), 6–9.

Dunbabin, J.P., 'The Revolt of the Field: The Agricultural Labourers' Movement', *Past and Present*, 26 (1963), 68–97.

Duncan, J.F., 'The Recruitment and Retention of Workers in Agriculture', *Journal of the Yorkshire Agricultural Society*, 106 (1955), 41–6.

Fairfax-Blakeborough, J., 'The Internal Economy of Yorkshire Farms Fifty Years Ago', *Journal of the Yorkshire Agricultural Society*, 88 (1931), 76–89.

Fairfax-Blakeborough, J., 'A Note on Equine Terms in Yorkshire', *Transactions of the Yorkshire Dialect Society*, vol. 9, pt. 59 (1959), 21–4.

Fairfax-Blakeborough, J., 'Yorkshire's Language of the Land', *Journal of the Yorkshire Agricultural Society*, 90 (1933), 77–90.

Fairlie, S., 'The Nineteenth Century Corn Laws Reconsidered', *Economic History Review, Second Series*, XVIII (1965), 526–75.

Foster, D., 'The East Riding Constabulary in the Nineteenth Century', *Northern History*, XXI (1985), 193–211.

Gleave, M.B., 'Dispersed and Nucleated Settlement on the Yorkshire Wolds, 1770–1850', *Institute of British Geographers, Transactions and Papers*, 30 (1962), 105–18.

Hirsch, G.P., 'Labour Requirements and Availability in British Agriculture', *The Farm Economist,* IX (1959–60), 518–20.

Holderness, B.A., 'Personal Mobility in Some Rural Parishes of Yorkshire, 1777–1822', *Yorkshire Archaeological Journal,* XLII (1967–70), 444–54.

Hunt, E.H., 'Labour Productivity in English Agriculture, 1850–1914', *Economic History Review, Second Series,* XX (1967) 280–92.

Jasny, N., 'Tractor vs. Horse for Farm Power', *American Eonomic Review,* 25 (1935), 708–23.

Jones, Eric L., 'The Agricultural Labour Market in England, 1793–1872', *Economic History Review, Second Series,* XVII (1964) 322–38.

Jones, R.B., 'Yorkshire Farmers are Buying More Tractors', *The Farm Economist,* III (1939–41), 148–9.

Lee, J.R. and Upfold, S.J., 'Tractor Costs on a Mechanized Farm', *The Farm Economist,* II (1936–8), 190–2.

Long, W.H., 'Agricultural Labour and its Problems in War Time', *Journal of the Yorkshire Agricultural Society,* 97 (1940), 44–7.

Long, W.H., 'The Development of Mechanization in English Farming', *Agricultural History Review,* 11 (1963), 15–26.

Long, W.H., 'Regional Farming in Seventeenth Century Yorkshire', *Agricultural History Review,* 8 (1960), 103–14.

McConville, I., 'Some Aspects of the Human Geography of the East Riding', *Hull University Institute of Education, Studies in Education,* 1 (1951), 32–7.

Minchinton, W.E., 'Agricultural Returns and the Government During the Napoleonic Wars', *Agricultural History Review,* 1 (1953), 29–43.

Nicholls, G., 'On the Condition of the Agricultural Labourer, with Suggestions for its Improvement', *Transactions of the Yorkshire Agricultural Society,* 9 (1846), 68–99.

Plant, S., 'Horse Displacement and Land Liberation Resulting from the Introduction of a Standard Tractor', *The Farm Economist,* VI (1948–51), 301–3.

Sheppard, J., 'The East Yorkshire Agricultural Labour Force in the Mid-Nineteenth Century', *Agricultural History Review,* 9 (1961), 43–54.

Short, B., 'The Decline of Living-in Servants in the Transition to Capitalist Farming, a Critique of the Sussex Evidence', *Sussex Archaeological Collections,* CXXII (1984), 147–64.

Thompson, F.M.L., 'Nineteenth-Century Horse Sense', *Economic History Review, Second Series,* XXIX (1976), 60–81.

Upfold, S.J., 'Horse Labour Costs, 1929–30', *The Farm Economist,* I (1933–5), 8–9.

Waites, B., 'Aspects of Thirteenth and Fourteenth Century Arable Farming on the Yorkshire Wolds', *Yorkshire Archaeological Journal,* XLII (1967–70), 136–42.

Wilson, R.M., 'Agricultural Terms in the East Riding', *Transactions of the Yorkshire Dialect Society,* vol. 6, pt. 37 (1937), 16–30.

Wright, S.J., 'The Next Phase in Agricultural Mechanization', *Journal of the Farmers' Club,* pt. 7 (1945), 90–101.

Index

Appleyard, Mr, 48, 163, 211
Ashby, Mr, 8, 37, 101, 125, 207

Baines, Mr, 21, 23, 26, 36, 37, 45, 48, 50, 51, 57, 59, 60, 61, 67, 77, 87, 89, 98, 99, 102, 103, 114, 116, 118, 121, 126, 127, 128, 138, 139, 141, 143, 144, 153, 154, 162, 172, 197–8
beastman, 16, 18, 23–5, 29, 48, 102, 128, 223
  beastman-lad, 23–5
beer, 140–1, 161, 175–6, 184
Best, Henry, 61, 69, 197, 198, 222
Beverley, 8, 9, 43, 54, 55, 58
bothies, lack of, 152
box lad, 52, 89
Brambles, Mr, 23, 36, 37, 49, 83, 146, 154, 155, 161, 164, 173, 216
Bridlington, 5, 8, 21, 54, 57, 58, 213

Caird, James, 11, 191
Captain Swing, 194
Carter, Mr, 17, 46, 50, 55, 63, 77, 84, 89, 125, 139, 158, 160, 169, 173, 175, 176, 185
Christmas, 172–3
clothes, 57, 71, 150, 160–1, 216
  -boxes, 153
community, 173, 183–6, 192–3, 221
Corn Laws, 192
courts, ch 3 and 80, 176, 196, 215
courting, 167–8, 179–80
custom and tradition, 3, 18, 39–40, 43, 56, 60, 69–70, 146, 172, 174, 176, 178, 184, 188, 201–2, 224–5
  coping with change, 221–2
  decline, 213, 215, 218
  retention of Old Martinmas Day, 56

Driffield, 5, 8, 21, 24, 54, 55, 58, 61, 72, 174, 179, 213

enclosure, 11, 188, 190–1, 192
English Land Restoration League, 195–6

fallow, 10, 17
family relationships and structure, 86, 106, 172, 178–9, 182
farm servantry, nature of, 188–90, 221–2
  and industry, 190–1, 196, 209
  in southern England, 190, 192–6
farm servants, see horselads
farmers, ch 3 and 13, 17, 20–3, 25, 45, 46, 53, 54, 59, 75, 76, 77, 79, 96, 99, 100, 103, 151, 173, 177, 185, 199–200, 201, 207, 208, 212, 215
  boarding servants, 152, end 192, 199
  and the history of servantry, 190, 192–3, 196–7
  agricultural clubs and National Farmers' Union, 56, 67, 68, 71, 104, 106
fastening penny, 30, 33, 61–2, 68–9, 197
Filey, 5
First World War, 51, 61, 206–7
  Waggoners' Reserve, 206–7
  effects of, 155, 158, 160–1, 169, 174, 207
Fisher, Mr, 12, 28, 34, 51, 52, 61, 76, 80, 99, 100, 110, 111, 112, 115, 119, 134, 140, 223
food, ch 12 and 60, 145, 182, 184
  luance, 88, 138, 141, 142, 151
Friend, Mr, 21, 48, 59, 164
friendly societies, 180–1, 183
funfairs, 63, 182

Galvayne, Sydney, 129
Good Friday, 172
Goole, 9, 54
'Great Depression', nineteenth century, 193, 202
  twentieth century, 207–18
groom, 29, 52, 88

Harper, Mr, 23, 24, 61, 63, 140, 149, 175, 176
harvest, 17, 24, 26, 28, 38, 115–6, 193
harvest supper, 183–5
hay making, 25, 28, 38, 142
Hedon, 9, 39, 54, 57, 64
hind, development of, 197–200
hiring fairs, chs 5 and 6 and 41, 50, 55, 143, 174–80, 215–6, 217, 224
runaway hirings, 37
labour exchanges at, 72
girls at, 57, 71, 72–3, 202
tokens to show trade, 59
hoeing, 26
Hornsea, 5, 9, 54
horselads, corn carrying, 50, 90, 101
fighting, 78, 80–1, 84, 93, 175–6
discipline, 74–83, 92–4, 176
half-timers, 88–9, fn95
hierarchy, ch 7 and 46–9, 217
hygiene, 154–5
illness, 34, 48
hours of work, 45, 140, 158–60, 216–7
mobility, 40–3, 53, 55, 121, 182, 217, 222–3
least lad, 52, 76, 84, 91, 154
runaways, 35–8, 75
sleeping quarters, 153, 156
slum, 152, 163
and sport, 162, 170, 182
horses, accidents with, 112–22
breaking, 94, 105, 128–34
breeding, 123–7
command words, 133
drugs, 104–6
feeding, ch 9 and 48, 74–5
foaling, 125–7
fothering up, 158, 164, 170
grooming, 48, 96, 108, 119
harness, 108–11, 117, 130–2
illness, 100, 135
lifespan, 134
and mechanization, 200–1
sale of, 12, 121, 123, 211
stallions, 125
team sizes, 46
Howden, 9, 54, 56, 57, 61, 64
Hull (Kingston-upon-), 5, 6, 9, 54, 56, 57
Hunmanby, 54

industry, East Riding, 6, 9
Irish workers, 27, 150, 150–1, 161, 184, 194

Jarvis, Mr, 25, 35, 41, 58, 114, 124, 139, 145, 165
Johnson, Mr, 16, 21, 22, 25, 28, 30, 43, 46, 47, 55, 56, 57, 74, 77, 79–80, 81, 89, 92, 93, 96, 97, 98, 99, 100, 101, 102, 104, 106, 112, 124, 126, 128, 130, 131, 132, 133, 139, 144, 151, 153, 159, 164, 167, 172, 173, 177, 180, 181, 183, 197, 199, 206, 207, 207–8, 214, 215, 223

labourers, 10, 16–20, 25, 47–8, 75, 141, 150, 158, 179, 193, 198, 199, 223, 223–4
Lawler, Mr and Mrs, 48, 59, 114, 144, 164, 177, 178
Lincolnshire, 1, 6, 20, 26, 55, 146

Malton, 5, 8, 54, 56, 57, 58, 72, 165
Market Weighton, 9, 54, 56, 61, 72
marriage, 18, 189–90, 223
and hirings, 62, 179–80
married horsemen, 17, 215, 220
Masterman, Mr, 24, 28, 41, 90, 92, 113, 113–4, 115, 116, 120, 121, 129, 130, 131, 137, 139, 140, 142, 143, 144, 151, 153, 158, 160, 161, 163, 164, 169, 175, 178, 182–3, 184, 185
Milner, Mr, 12, 24, 34, 47, 76, 77, 81, 84, 102, 104, 152, 153, 163, 170, 216

Patrington, 9, 54
Playforth, Mr, 17, 27, 28, 34, 40, 60, 102, 106, 108, 111, 112, 113, 115, 123, 128, 132, 133, 134, 139, 154, 165, 166
ploughing, 41, 47, 49, 60, 79, 81–3, 90, 111
Plough Monday, 174
Pocklington, 9, 54, 174–5
Poor Law, 193–4
population growth, 190–2, 221
Pridmore, Mr, 17, 40, 52, 60,138, 143, 160, 164, 182, 184
pubs, 164, 165, 182

religion, 14, 79–80, 87, 140, 165–6, 166, 172–3, 181–2, 183, 185
Rispin, Mr and Mrs, 17, 27, 28, 36, 40, 43, 47, 51, 52, 59, 91, 102, 106, 109, 110, 111, 115, 123, 132, 134, 138, 139, 140, 141, 142, 148, 151, 153, 154, 164, 166, 169, 170, 172, 181, 182, 185, 212, 216

Saturday half-holiday, 170
Scarborough, 31, 54, 57, 61, 72
Second World War, 218
Selby, 8, 9, 54, 57
shepherd, 16, 18, 23–5, 29, 47, 151, 197, 223
shepherd-lad, 23–5, 84–5
shops and shopping, 63, 151, 169, 170, 178

Simpson, Mary, 13, 14, 58, 158, 159, 162, 166–7, 177, 181, 197, 202
Smith, Dr E, 137
stables, 74–5, 97, 163–4
stacking corn, 51, 90, 91
Statute of Artificers, 221
Statute of Frauds, 68
Statute of Labourers, 59
steam power, 11, 210
Sunday, 96, 158–62, 165–6, 223

Tate, Mr and Mrs, 23, 24, 34, 36, 43, 48, 59, 89, 90, 92, 93, 99, 108, 111, 116, 117, 128, 141, 142, 143, 144, 156, 159, 165, 166, 168, 200, 214, 215
Thirsk, 55, 56, 59, 72, 198
threshing, 25, 88, 208
tommy owt, 47, 52
tractors, 121, 209–12
trade unions 69–71, 170, 202, 213–5, 217–8
    Arch, Joseph, 66, 69, 191, 196
tramps, 26–7, 163, 194
transport, 52, 55, 62, 150, 156
    bicycles, 168–9

village feasts, 180–3

wages, ch 3 and 1, 17, 22, 24, 26, 61, 103, 137, 169, 178, 188–9, 197, 198, 212, 223
    subs, 22, 164, 178, 216
    keep element, 145, 151–2, 212–3
    holiday pay, 173
    Agricultural Wages Boards, 217
    board wages, 194
    effect of industry on, 191
waggon driving, 50–1, 105, 109–10
Walker, Mr, 28, 79, 87, 114, 134, 138, 140, 170, 175
West Riding of Yorkshire, 1, 20, 37, 50, 86, 174, 196
Withernsea, 5
women, 26, 148
    see also hiring

York, 8, 54, 57, 59, 61, 62, 72
Young, Arthur, 11, 192